The Last Christology of the West

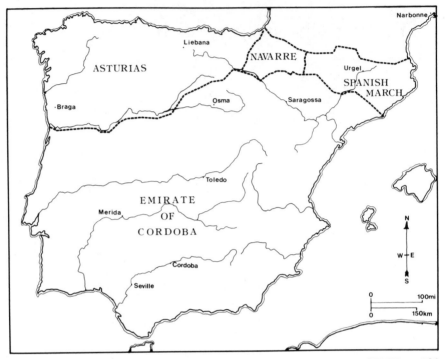

SPAIN, ca. 790

The Last
CHRISTOLOGY
of the West

Adoptionism in Spain and Gaul, 785–820

John C. Cavadini

University of Pennsylvania Press
Philadelphia

University of Pennsylvania Press
MIDDLE AGES SERIES
Edited by
Edward Peters
Henry Charles Lea Professor
of Medieval History
University of Pennsylvania

A listing of the available books
in the series appears at the
back of this volume

Copyright © 1993 by the University of Pennsylvania Press
All rights reserved
Printed in the United States of America

Library of Congress Cataloging-in-Publication Data

Cavadini, John C.
    The last christology of the West : adoptionism in Spain and Gaul,
785–820 / John C. Cavadini.
        p.   cm. — (University of Pennsylvania Press Middle Ages
series)
    Includes bibliographical references and index.
    ISBN 0-8122-3186-4
    1. Adoptionism.   2. Spain—Church history.   3. Jesus Christ—
History of doctrines—Middle Ages, 600–1500.   I. Title.
II. Series: Middle Ages series.
    BT1320.C38   1993
    273'.6'0946—dc20   93-9444
                                                                 CIP

To Nancy

with honorable mention to Julia, Katie,
Peter, Louis, David,
Mary Rose,
and
Eva

Contents

Abbreviations

CCCM	*Corpus Christianorum continuatio medievalis.*
CCSL	*Corpus Christianorum series latina.*
CSCO	*Corpus scriptorum Christianorum orientalium.*
CSEL	*Corpus scriptorum ecclesiasticorum latinorum.*
CSM	*Corpus Scriptorum Muzarabicorum*, 2 vols. Edited by J. Gil. Madrid: Instituto "Antonio de Nebrija," 1973.
DHGE	*Dictionaire d'histoire et de géographie ecclésiastique.*
DTC	*Dictionnaire de Théologie Catholique.*
Flórez	*España Sagrada*, vol. V. Edited by H. Flórez. Madrid: 1750.
Löfstedt	Beatus of Liebana and Heterius of Osma, *Adversus Elipandum Libri II*. Edited by B. Löfstedt. In *CCCM* 59. Turnhout: Brepols, 1984.
MGH	*Monumenta Germaniae historica.*
PG	*Patrologia Graeca.* Edited by J.P. Migne.
PL	*Patrologia Latina.* Edited by J.P. Migne.

Preface

Over the years that this project has taken to complete I have accumulated a manifold indebtedness, both among the many new friends I have met in the course of writing, as well as among the many old friends who have found themselves impressed into service. It was Keith Egan (now of St. Mary's College, but at that time of Marquette University) who first suggested to me that Alcuin was a figure who had not received his fair share of attention. The original recension of this project was my doctoral dissertation at Yale, and in this regard it is to Jaroslav Pelikan that I am indebted for teaching—and then allowing—a flexibility and consistency of vision sufficient to sustain this project from beginning to end. Mary Rose D'Angelo, James Buckley, Kathryn L. Johnson, R. Emmett McLaughlin, and Joseph P. Wawrykow all read the complete manuscript or parts of it at this stage and offered me assistance that was most valuable. Villanova University provided a summer grant which enabled me finally to finish the dissertation.

The process of rewriting and expanding the text took almost as long as the original work. I am especially indebted to those who read the whole of the manuscript at various stages and offered detailed comments, far beyond the call of duty: Celia Chazelle, David Ganz, E. Ann Matter, Thomas F. X. Noble, J. J. O'Donnell, and the two anonymous readers for the University of Pennsylvania Press. In addition, there were many helpful conversations which directly or indirectly bore fruit in these pages. I would like to mention in particular Barbara Agnew, Michel Barnes, Roger Brooks, Margaret Gibson, Anthony Godzieba, John Immerwahr, Stephany Kyriakos, Cyril O'Regan, Bruce Mullin, William Wilson, many students, and three of my colleagues at Notre Dame, Catherine LaCugna, Blake Leyerle, and Jean Porter. Unfortunately, I have not always listened to the advice of my friends, and thus for the errors that remain I have only myself to blame.

My sister, the late Juliane Cavadini McGinnis, provided through her generosity and initiative crucial computer assistance, and David Klawiter, of the Department of Academic Computing at Notre Dame, has given freely of his advice and time. For the earlier stages of this project I am indebted to the assistance of my parents, John and Dorothy Cavadini, and to my uncle, David Cavadini. It is finally my great honor to acknowledge the assistance of my wife Nancy, whose unflagging help with editing and matters of judgment, and whose profound and deeply committed support on so many levels, remains my greatest debt and my deepest inspiration, and it is to her that I dedicate this book.

Introduction

The Muslims made their first landing in Spain in 710.[1] By 712 they had conquered Toledo, Merida, and Saragossa. In the seven-year period following their momentous victory in 711, Arabic occupation extended over almost the whole of the Iberian peninsula, short of the mountainous regions in the north. Thus ended the Visigothic period in Hispanic church history. Thus too began that period known to subsequent generations as the Mozarabic. It was within this period of Spanish ecclesiastical history, indeed almost at its beginning, that the controversy we are about to examine took place.

"Adoptionism" is a word without a fixed historical reference, as there have been several theologies, historically unrelated, which have been given this name. It is associated with a variety of second- and third-century figures including Theodotus the leather merchant and Paul of Samosata, with certain currents in Arian theology,[2] with twelfth-century figures such as Abelard and Gilbert de la Porrée, and more loosely with such fifth-century Antiochene theologians as Theodore of Mopsuestia and Nestorius. The word (sometimes spelled "adoptianism" in this context) is also used to refer to the group of late eighth-century Hispanic theologians who, along with their opponents both Hispanic and Carolingian, will be the subject of this study.

In the last decade of the eighth century, this group of Hispanic theologians were condemned for teaching that Jesus at his baptism was adopted into his position as Son of God. These theologians included the dramatic and irascible personage of Elipandus, archbishop of Toledo from 753 to his death around 805, and his defender Felix, urbane and intellectually accomplished bishop of Urgel in the Pyrenees. Whether or not they were actually teaching the doctrine for which they were condemned will be an issue explored in this study. For now it is sufficient to note that their teaching was indeed condemned, and at no less than three councils called by Charlemagne, in 792 (Ratisbon or Regensburg), 795 (Frankfurt), and 799 (Aachen or Aix). Their dossier of denunciations also included a warning in 785 by Pope Hadrian I against Elipandus's teaching, and a condemnation endorsed by Pope Leo III in Rome in 798, among others.

The common view that the Visigothic Kingdom of Hispania was isolated from the rest of Europe and from the East has been discredited by recent work.[3] Nevertheless, Spain's position in Western Europe was socially and politically unique. There was an extraordinary degree of cultural continuity between Roman Hispania and the Visigothic Kingdom which succeeded it. Settled as a federated people in southwest Gaul in 418 by the Romans, the Visigoths expanded into Spain after King Euric (466–84) declared himself independent of Rome in 475 (the last Western emperor having been deposed in 476). In 507 his son, King Alaric II (484–507), was defeated by Clovis. Thereafter, the Visigoths' power was limited to the Iberian peninsula and the Gallic province of Narbonnensis. The history of Spain proper begins then in 507 with Alaric's successor, his illegitimate son Gesalic.[4] But it is really only with the reign of the great King Leovigild (569–586), the last of the Arian kings, that Visigothic power was definitively established over the whole of the Iberian peninsula, including the kingdom of the Sueves in Galicia, incorporated into the Visigothic Kingdom in 585.

Despite their successful growth and consolidation of power, the Visigoths did not destroy the civilization of the Hispano-Roman majority whom they undertook to rule, but actively patronized and therefore preserved it. They left the Roman governmental structures and legal system intact; it remained applicable to the conquered majority. Conquered and conquerors coexisted in their own separate spheres of legal rights. Decisions on the highest level (e.g., regarding military matters and the disposition of large Roman estates) were made by the king and his circle of Gothic retainers, but for the most part the Visigoths allowed the Hispano-Romans a degree of autonomy unique in the whole of Europe.[5] Even the Catholicism of the Hispano-Romans was tolerated by the Arian Visigothic monarchy.[6] King Reccared's conversion to Catholicism in 589 can be seen as just one more, if rather definitive, step in this curious process of the cultural assimilation of conquerors to the conquered. And once the Kingdom became Catholic, there was decisively less reason for the Roman population to retain any sympathy for last outposts of Byzantine presence in the peninsula, finally removed by 624.[7]

To call Spain isolated is thus to misapprehend and underestimate its uniqueness. Unparalleled among the "barbarian" kingdoms that succeeded Roman power, Spain alone integrated achievements of cultural continuity and unity with the achievement of political unity over such a large amount of territory. One could count the achievement of ecclesiastical unity as well. The metropolitan see of Toledo grew in power and influence until it was able to press for a degree of uniformity greater even than that which Charlemagne achieved.[8] There are no parallels to the succession of Visigothic Councils of Toledo, which enacted both secular and religious pronouncements from the sixth to the end of the seventh centuries, and so served as a focus and integration of secular and religious uniformity throughout the Kingdom. Even in the first century of Muslim power, after an initial eclipse, Toledo was able to regain its place as the center of ecclesiastical influence in Spain.[9] The caliber of intellectual and theological culture engendered by these conditions is evident from a consideration of some of the names, glittering by comparison with any other contemporaneous Western culture, of its prominent figures.[10] Thus one must look at Spain not as an isolated, hermetically sealed cultural environment, but rather as a political unity with a kind of cultural poise or sovereignty, preserving traditions from the past, open to influences from the contemporary world, but also able to resist them as it chose with relative impunity.[11]

This was particularly true in matters theological. The major theological influences inherited by the Visigothic Kingdom were distinctively Western, from the region which in the fourth and fifth centuries had been the theologically most creative in the West—North Africa.[12] The earliest Christianity in Spain may have been of North African origin, and in the Visigothic period there was an especially large influx of African Christians after the Vandal kingdom of North Africa fell to Justinian in 533. This included monks who brought with them what manuscripts they had and settled many new foundations in southern Spain.[13] One could almost say that when North African theology began to fall silent in the seventh century and beyond, it was in Spain that the voice of its traditions continued most clearly to be heard.

Nor did Hispanic Christian intellectual culture cease with the arrival of the Muslims and their conquest of the Visigothic Kingdom in the early second decade of the eighth century,[14] because Muslim rule in Spain allowed, as Visigothic rule had before it, for the continuation of certain indigenous cultural traditions. In particular, the Christians were able to practice their religion relatively freely. The "Mozarabs,"[15] as they came to be known, existed in an environment which ultimately was protective of older ecclesial traditions against the sort of cultural hegemony that Charlemagne's renaissance of learning, among other things, entailed. Late in the century, Charlemagne's power extended to the very borders of Spain, including territories that had once belonged to the Visigothic Kingdom. He was stopped in the West only by the Muslims.

Thus, precisely because the Muslim occupation of Spain served to corroborate and seal its political independence from the rest of Europe, theological positions developed on longstanding foundations of learning could have a certain inviolability, a life apart in the protective environment of Spanish culture. There was a base of power for many such ideas. It may not have guaranteed them a successful hearing in Carolingian quarters, but at least it provided a safe retreat for the people involved in advocating or propagating them outside of Spain. In a way, it was the Muslim domination of Spain which permitted the adoptionism controversy to have the character, in its final phase, of an encounter not simply between two mutually exclusive positions on the adoptive status of Jesus, but really between two cultures, between two different ways of thinking about christology, two different christological worlds.

The controversy began in Spain as an affair solely internal to the Hispanic church. Elipandus claimed that Jesus, considered solely from the point of view of his human nature, was an "adoptive" Son of God. He was rebuked by the abbot of a monastery in the Asturias, Beatus of Liebana. Beatus became the leader of the anti-adoptionist party, which always remained strongest in the areas of Spain outside of Muslim control. Felix expanded the debate by teaching adoptionism in and around his see of Urgel, which at least nominally was Carolingian territory from 789. Charlemagne and his circle of theologians were to be occupied more and more as the decade went on with the problem which Felix posed. By the end of the century a considerable body of non-Hispanic anti-adoptionist literature had been produced by Alcuin, Paulinus of Aquileia, Pope Hadrian I, and others. Their work can be usefully compared to the Hispanic controversial literature. The most striking discovery to come from such a comparison is the observation of a fundamental *dissimilarity* which the Carolingian anti-adoptionist literature exhibits, not only with regard to the work of the Spanish adoptionists but with regard to that of the Spanish anti-adoptionists as well. This means, for example, that the anti-adoptionist position of the Hispanic figure Beatus has less in common with the anti-adoptionism of a Carolingian like Alcuin than it has with the Hispanic adoptionist Elipandus. It is difficult to avoid concluding that by the end of the eighth century the Pyrenees separated two different "schools" of christological reflection, each characteristic of the culture which was its matrix.

This comparison makes it easier to see adoptionism as originating in a context for theological reflection peculiar to Spain at the time, a context that constituted the body of presuppositions informing the arguments on *both* sides of the debate in Spain. Adoptionism thus appears precisely as a variant on or development of that body. This means that adoptionism can no longer be seen simply as a declension from the standard of Christological clarity represented by the formula of Chalcedon. Such a view is in part owing to a certain misconception of the Mozarabic church as somehow compromised by accommodation to Islam. But it is also owing to an oversimplification of the process by which christological doctrine developed. Chalcedon was not immediately or in all places recognized as the only standard of christological clarity, nor was it always regarded as a standard possessed of the same degree of definitiveness which we tend to accord to it. No one on the Spanish side of the controversy cites it even once (something which cannot be attributed to ignorance), and Alcuin himself, despite the length and number of his treatises against the adoptionists, cites it only once. Christology in the West was in a much more fluid state than a simplified view might suppose. Thus an examination of the controversy leads one to conclude that adoptionism was not so much a declension from the Chalcedonian standard as a reflection on, and perhaps even a development of, some other standard. Adoptionism is one of the fruits of the tradition of reflection that the eighth-century Hispanic school of christology represented in *both* its adoptionist and anti-adoptionist forms.

One of the reasons adoptionism has been regarded as a declension from some standard is that it is always judged as though its context were the classical christological controversies which ultimately gave rise to the formula of Chalcedon. Thus the framework for understanding it is construed as one in which the two poles to be avoided are "Nestorianism" and "Eutychianism" (monophysitism),[16] and christological language such as *persona* and *natura* is interpreted as having the tension between these two poles as its sole context. From this point of view adoptionism is found wanting; it is essentially a variant of Nestorianism, and a rather muddled one at that. The problem with such an interpretation is that it does not take seriously the way in which the Hispanic antagonists carried forth their controversy almost without any reference to Eastern disputes. Elipandus never calls Beatus a Eutychian, and Beatus, although he is somewhat more willing to pay his respects to Eastern precedent, never calls Elipandus a Nestorian. They do not perceive each other as deviating from a standard where the poles are defined as Nestorian and Eutychian, but rather as deviations from shared christological premises whose most important links are to earlier Western writers such as Tyconius, Augustine, Leo, and Fulgentius rather than to writers like Cyril of Alexandria, Theodore of Mopsuestia, Nestorius, etc. The eighth-century Hispanic christological school is a variant on or development of *Western* christological traditions.

This is to suggest that although Western christology was invoked, for example, at the Council of Chalcedon to provide a solution to an Eastern christological dispute, Western christology did not thereby cease to have a life of its own apart from this particular usage of it. It is true that Western christological discussion was itself partly formed by the role it played in attempting to bring the controversies of the East to a settlement. Yet it is important to remember that the christology or christologies of the West did not originate or develop solely in terms of the debate about Nestorius or Eutyches, nor need it be true that after it was summoned to mediate in that debate it lost all connection to its original frames of reference and became wholly subsumed by the agenda into which it had been grafted. This should be clear especially to scholars who believe that the Formula of Chalcedon, precisely because it was predicated upon christological principles indigenous to the West, was therefore foreign not only to the solutions but to the very questions of the East.[17] But even scholars who do not share this view should be able to see that this particular use of Western christology to mediate an Eastern debate did not necessarily dissolve its identity or reduce it simply to the terms of the debate it helped to solve, or restrict its agenda henceforth to solely those terms. Presumably in many instances it did not completely lose its connection to the articulation of soteriological and ecclesiological questions more indigenous to Western ecclesial circles. Indeed, the christological reflection characteristic of both Elipandus and Beatus is completely understandable in terms of issues and concerns indigenous to Western literature and to the subsequent reception of that literature in Hispanic conciliar pronouncements, quite apart from any reference to Eastern debates.

Defining a Western christology or christological perspective is problematic, although many standard histories of doctrine refer to such a thing and attempt to articulate what makes the "Western" view Western.[18] But it is important to note that this study is predicated on no particular description or preconception of Western christology. The precise way of articulating what is Western about the Western traditions is not as important for this study as is the negative observation that the Eastern paradigms are not invoked by the Hispanics except in an ancillary way, and that the preponderance of source citations are from Western authors. It is *because* the Hispanic antagonists avoid Eastern vocabulary and precedent and choose predominantly Western writers that we can begin to think about christological developments and agendas which are peculiarly Western. *Because* the Hispanic antagonists evince a frame of reference for their christology which seems to be aware of but not predicated on the terms and questions of the classical Eastern debates, we are reminded that Western christology did not begin at Chalcedon, and that it may not have ended there either.

The following study is organized chronologically. The chapters are designated by the names of those persons who dominated each successive phase of the controversy. Chapter One provides a first view of the period and some of its problems, focusing around a dispute between Elipandus and an obscure figure named Migetius. This minor dispute proved to be a prelude to the much larger mobilization of Spanish theological expertise which the adoptionism controversy proper represented.

Chapter Two considers the teaching of Elipandus himself, the first Hispanic adoptionist, and arrives at an understanding of his position on its own terms, quite apart from the interpretation later given to it by Alcuin and other non-Hispanic theologians. The results refute the hypothesis that Elipandus teaches anything resembling Nestorianism, or that his teaching is fundamentally indebted to such Eastern thinkers as Theodore of Mopsuestia or Diodore of Tarsus. It is argued, rather, that his theology is much better understood as an outgrowth of the theologies of Western figures like Leo and Augustine, and of pronouncements of the Councils of Toledo. From this perspective adoptionism appears as a development not of Eastern influences, whether literary or by direct contact with Nestorians who had come to Spain, but of strands in the thought of Augustine and Leo and of the use already made of their thought in Isidore of Seville and in the Hispanic conciliar literature of the sixth and early seventh centuries.

The third chapter considers in detail the Spanish anti-adoptionist position, represented by Beatus of Liebana. This chapter discovers a fundamental similarity between the soteriology and christology of Beatus and that of Elipandus, and therefore permits us to understand both the anti-adoptionist position and the adoptionist position as variations on a common theme. The fact that such hostile and bitter enemies as Elipandus and Beatus can be said to have a common christology suggests that there is a distinctive tradition of christological reflection of which both are a part. One may refer to this tradition as a christological "school" as long as one avoids overstating the case—at present it is only a convenient shorthand for the contrast between the paradigm shared by both parties to the Hispanic controversy on the one hand, and the paradigms of the non-Hispanic anti-adoptionists on the other.

The fourth chapter shifts to Gaul, and treats the phase of the controversy in which Carolingian anti-adoptionists, and Alcuin in particular, take up the leading role in the refutation of the adoptionists. Felix of Urgel is the major representative of adoptionism in this period. The chapter shows that it is Pope Hadrian I, and following him, Alcuin, who first interpret adoptionism as a form of Nestorianism, and who are therefore first to analyze the adoptionist position in terms of a context foreign to it. It is Alcuin who, working from christological presuppositions fundamentally different from those of the Hispanic school, interprets the whole controversy in terms of his own study of the Council of Ephesus and its condemnation of Nestorius. When Alcuin analyzes the teaching of the adoptionists as though its context were a fifth-century christological controversy of the East, he ends by judging not the teaching of the adoptionists, but a distortion of that teaching based on the assumption that christological language such as "persona" and "natura" has the polarity between Nestorianism and Eutychianism as its sole and definitive context. What is finally condemned as heretical is the rendition of their teaching resulting from Alcuin's attempt to "recontextualize" their language by disengaging it from its native cultural links and reading it in terms of another context altogether. The links between this language and other possible—in this case, Western—contexts recede from view. They become invisible.[19]

Since Alcuin's work has dominated the perception of adoptionism in subsequent centuries including our own, it has made it very difficult for modern scholars to see the proper character of adoptionism as a sophisticated and theologically capable development of Western christological tradition, concerned primarily with neither Eastern questions nor precedent. It is because Alcuin judges the adoptionists negatively against a christological standard defined solely in terms of the polarity between "Nestorianism" and "Eutychianism," that they and their teaching have come to appear as a declension from that standard. Perhaps we in the modern period have been too ready to follow Alcuin's lead in judging adoptionism on the basis of a foreign standard. Part of the problem is that almost without noticing it we uncritically accept only one christological standard, fifth-century and Eastern, as applicable to christologies of every time and provenance. We accept only one christological polarity, fifth-century and Eastern, as a way not only of judging the orthodoxy of christological positions, but of defining the very range of options possible to be judged. Other sorts of christology therefore remain invisible. We see, instead of the positions themselves, various configurations of the only polarity we are prepared to admit, some of which may still look orthodox (like Beatus's position), and some may not (like the adoptionists').

By presenting an analysis of a Western controversy in which this way of looking at christologies cannot be made to yield a satisfactory account of the evidence, this study may contribute to the process of making visible again not only the christology of the adoptionists themselves, but also of a circle of christological issues and reflexes which found their home in Western theological settings quite different from those which generated the Eastern disputes. Perhaps it is time to reexamine not only the christology of the adoptionists but that of the whole Latin tradition, quite apart from its roles in resolving or failing to resolve the controversies of the East. This will be the only way to recover a full understanding of and feeling for what is peculiarly "Western" about Western christology. But as Western contexts and concerns become once again visible in their own right, so will something else of interest to the historian—the astonishing power of the Carolingian theologians, habitually belittled as mere transmitters of tradition when in fact, for better or for worse, they have played a decisive role in forming the tradition, as well as in shaping theologians' conceptions of the "Fathers of the Church" for some eleven hundred years now.

1. Migetius

Any history of the adoptionist controversy must begin with Migetius, although this statement is ironic because he does not belong to the history of adoptionism properly speaking. But this curious figure quarreled with Elipandus in the early 780s, and his quarrel has appeared to many as a prelude to the much larger controversy that followed so closely on its heels. The question of interest here is exactly what sort of prelude it was. Did it serve merely as an essentially extrinsic occasion for the promulgation of a heretical or potentially heretical utterance by Elipandus? Or was this quarrel in itself already a fully explicit christological debate, so that the adoptionist controversy, although different in particulars, could actually be seen as a seamless continuity with the earlier dispute? These represent the extremes of a range of possibilities. It is unfortunate, but we will have to decide the question without the help of any writings from Migetius himself, for they have all been lost.[1] We must rely upon reports from hostile parties, and, preeminently, from Elipandus, three of whose six extant letters represent nearly all the evidence that remains.

In an age and place that we have learned somehow to disregard, Elipandus commanded a lavish, almost startling prose, and he did not shrink from urging it in its fullest force against his opponents:

> We have seen, yes, we have seen, and we have laughed at the silly, fatuous ravings of your heart! We have seen, and we have dismissed your absurd opinion as a thing worthy of laughter![2]

Thus does Elipandus, Archbishop of Toledo and Primate of all Spain,[3] greet Migetius, someone whom he had already known, or known of, and respected, at least up till now (about 782).[4] In the course of his letter Elipandus describes and refutes four errors, three of which represent practical rather than doctrinal concerns. To begin with, he accuses Migetius of an exaggerated insistence upon the holiness of priests. The exact claims of Migetius are difficult to recover from Elipandus's citation of them,[5] but it is clear enough that there is some sort of rigoristic purism perhaps of Donatist inspiration. Some have even seen in these lines indications of some sort of a survival of Donatist theology.[6] While it is impossible to make a precise judgment on this matter, it should be remembered that North African theology had always exerted a decisive influence on the Hispanic literary tradition of Visigothic Spain, and that major Donatist influence, via Tyconius, is clearly documented for at least one other author of this period.[7] It is probably best to say simply that Donatist theology was in the air, so to speak, available for appropriation by any group whose purposes aligned themselves with the rigorism of that ancient North African church.

In the second place, Elipandus reports that Migetius issued pro-scriptions against eating with pagans—meaning, of course, the occupying Muslims—as well as against eating food with any sort of pagan association attaching to it.[8] Elipandus derisively asks Migetius if he thought he was holier than our Lord, who, Son of God though he was, ate together with publicans and sinners.[9] Relations between Christians and Muslims in this period, especially in the upper echelons of society, were relaxed if not positively cordial,[10] and Migetius's views must have struck Elipandus as parochial and intolerant, not to mention impractical. It is interesting to observe that Pope Hadrian I was asked to pronounce on a similar question regarding diet regulations in Mozarabic Spain.[11]

In the third place, Elipandus charged Migetius with a wildly fanatical exaltation of the See of Rome. Migetius is cited as having claimed that the power of God is in Rome alone, where Christ dwells, that the See of Rome is without any stain or blemish, that the verse "You are Peter, and on this Rock I will build my Church" had reference to Rome alone, and that Rome was the New Jerusalem which John had seen descending from heaven.[12] The latter point may indicate a certain apocalyptic or millenarian cast to the hopes which Migetius and his followers had lodged in Rome. Elipandus hastened to point out to Migetius that the memory of Pope Liberius might have served to dampen his enthusiasm had he taken time to reflect on it,[13] that the verse from Matthew applied to the Catholic Church as a whole,[14] that even Gregory had complained about how many scoundrels there were in Rome,[15] that in any church there is a mixture of the elect and the reprobate, the wheat and the tares,[16] and that the new Jerusalem of the Apocalypse is not the Roman Church but rather the knowledge of the faith of the Holy Trinity.[17] Elipandus seems especially sensitive on this point. He probably quite correctly saw in this exaggerated valuation of the Church of Rome an intentional affront to his power and position, especially since Spain in general, and the See of Toledo in particular, had by this time acquired a long tradition of relative independence from the Holy See. Communication between Visigothic Spain and the Popes had been extremely infrequent, sometimes uncomfortable, and even hostile.[18] Migetius had probably elaborated his vision of immaculate Rome precisely because it served to provide an authoritative basis for his (apocalyptic?) vision of purity, one that served well to relativize the claims of the compromised See of Toledo. It is ironic to think that the See upon which Migetius had placed such high hopes not only condemned him within a year or two of this quarrel with Elipandus, but also seems to have misspelled his name in the process.[19]

In another, later letter of Elipandus from perhaps early 785, we learn that Migetius was also faulted for his improper calculation of the date of Easter,[20] and that the sphere of his activities was the southern part of Spain, in Baetica.[21] Around 782 his actions and teachings were the subject of some type of formal condemnation proceeding led by Elipandus, often referred to as the Council of Seville,[22] although, since there is no further notice of this Council anywhere, and since no *acta* survive, there remains a legitimate doubt about whether the condemnation actually took place in a council.[23] Whatever the setting, Elipandus prided himself on the scrupulous vigilance for ecclesiastical orthodoxy for which (in his mind) the condemnation of Migetius and his followers was prime evidence. Despite this condemnation, what we must come to speak of as the Migetian *sect* survived until (or was remembered at least as late as) 862.[24]

In its broadest outlines it seems clear that this sect was ritually and ethically rigorist in nature, advocated resistance of Muslim cultural influence and a lifestyle of thoroughgoing separation from the Muslims, and maintained a posture at least indifferent, but more likely hostile, to the established structures of the Church, probably because it viewed the hierarchy's standards of association with the Muslims as a species of unacceptable compromise. A more exact specification of the context and intention of this sect depends upon how the evidence is interpreted. One recent interpretation finds in the quarrel between Elipandus and Migetius a confrontation between two parties of differing opinions regarding the propriety and desirability of collaboration, political and otherwise, with the Muslims, with Elipandus representing the so-called "party of collaboration," and Migetius representing a "radicalist" party opposed to the policies of the *status quo*.[25] Other opinions regard him as a reformer preaching against what he regarded as undue accommodation to Muslim influence[26] or, even more simply, as a fanatic.[27] It seems clear, at any rate, that the sect represented some type of opposition or reform platform vis-à-vis the prevailing ecclesiastical attitude regarding relations with the Muslims, and that it had taken on a rigorist, sectarian, perhaps even apocalyptic mentality, something easily absorbed from North African sectarian literature.[28]

However one decides these issues, it is also clear that the general set of alignments represented by this little sect attracted the attentions of other, less than disinterested, outside parties. This is revealed in an intriguing three letter segment of Pope Hadrian I's correspondence, written between 785 and 791, the third and final letter of which contains not only a reference to Migetius, but also the earliest reference of any source outside of Spain to adoptionism.[29] In the first letter Hadrian is answering the letter[30] of a certain Egila, who had been consecrated bishop by Wilcharius, "archbishop of Gaul,"[31] and sent to preach in Spain. This action had been accomplished with the permission of the Pope.[32] Hadrian comments on reports of Egila concerning customs that seem questionable and concerning disputes in progress.[33]

The second letter is addressed to Egila as well. We learn that it is really just a cover letter, that Egila had supposedly not received the first letter, and that, interestingly enough, Charlemagne had requested that the Pope send Egila a copy of the first letter transcribed from the papal registry.[34] Some few further points are added.[35]

The third and most interesting letter is addressed not to Egila but to "all the orthodox bishops living throughout the whole of Spain." Apart from the new material on the adoptionism of Elipandus,[36] once again this is essentially the same letter as the first one sent to Egila, with one further and rather startling difference: the Pope is alarmed to have discovered that Egila "is not preaching rightly, and is attempting to teach beyond Catholic discipline, following the errors of his teacher, a certain Mingentius."[37] The Pope is embarrassed; after all, Egila was sent to Spain with the papal blessing. Hadrian explains that it was Wilcharius's idea, that Wilcharius had, in addition, assured the Pope that Egila had passed all the requisite catechetical examinations.[38] Hadrian himself seems reluctant to be completely convinced that the reports about Egila are true.[39] Unfortunately, it is more than likely that they were true. In 839 we find a council at Cordoba condemning a sect called the Casiani, whose founding bishop was called Agila, and who had characteristics which are in agreement with what we already know about the Migetian sect.[40] Whatever else the term "Casiani" may refer to, Elipandus in the Letter to the Bishops of France uses this term as a name for Migetius's sect.[41] Given the geographical proximity involved, it is likely that there is a reference to the same sect in both instances.

This brief account of Egila's career in Spain leaves many questions unanswered, particularly what exactly Charlemagne's interests in this sect were and how he found out about it.[42] Was Elipandus's other Hispanic opponent, Beatus of Liebana, involved?[43] Aside from Egila, who kept the Pope informed and how accurate was his information? This question is especially interesting when it comes to the information in the third letter regarding Elipandus's adoptionism. Despite the pope's embarrassment at the outcome, it would have been natural for him, too, to have an interest in a project that could potentially enhance papal influence in a region which had long held itself rather aloof from it. What is clear, at any rate, is that a synergy of various interests, both Spanish and foreign, had converged upon this sect. And while this is historically very interesting, it makes it rather difficult to determine who or what this sect was in itself, if anything, quite apart from all of these interests. Just as one could study the complicated array of political interests which had at one time or another converged upon the Arians without ever understanding the Arians themselves, so in this case, even after reviewing the scholarship which has devoted its attentions to these interests, we are still left wondering exactly who Migetius and his followers were before any of the political considerations. As in the case of the Arians, one must, after all, study their doctrine to find out.

The study of the politicization of Migetius's sect has in fact proceeded without any close study of Migetius's doctrine, and in some cases it has even been dismissed as irrelevant. Among the most recent treatments, some[44] explicitly rule it out of consideration; others assign it a secondary place.[45] It is, in fact, very difficult to find any serious modern consideration of the doctrinal dimension of this controversy. The issue is almost always decided in advance because the doctrinal system of Migetius as stated by Elipandus has seemed so totally absurd to most commentators that they neglect to take it seriously and therefore fail to treat it in any detail. Either Elipandus has misunderstood the issues, or he has deliberately exaggerated or even fabricated the doctrinal charge against Migetius in an attempt to discredit him, or else Migetius himself was mad.[46] However, the seeming absurdity of a teaching is not in itself a reason to doubt its authenticity, and, in any case, it is difficult to understand why historians have been perfectly willing to accept Elipandus's reports about every other aspect of Migetius's deviance while at the same time rejecting this one.

In fact, if the text is interpreted in a straightforward manner, it is clear that for Elipandus Migetius's gravest and most shocking error was doctrinal, and involved some claim about the relation between the divine *personae* of the Trinity on the one hand and the three historical personages David, Jesus, and Paul on the other. Elipandus spends more time in the detailed refutation of this error than in the entire discussion of the other three charges. This is the error "in principio schedulae tuae fetidissimae";[47] it is the error that pridefully bucks itself against the "rule of the catholic faith";[48] it is the error which is understood when, in the insulting introductory sections, Elipandus speaks of the "absurdities" of Migetius (since it is the only error mentioned in particular in these sections).[49] Elipandus goes on to take considerable, precise care to refute Migetius's error, point by point, proof text by proof text. Even if we did not know that he possessed the text of Migetius, we could probably have guessed that he was working from and responding to a text, perhaps paragraph by paragraph, and that therefore we could expect a reasonable degree of accuracy in the reproduction of Migetius's position. Further, Elipandus's refutation uses certain technical terms such as the word *persona* so often and so technically that the impression given is that it is precisely Migetius's use of this term that Elipandus is describing and responding to and not, rather, to some sort of claim about the Trinity in general. It seems very clear, if nothing else, that the text of Migetius made certain claims about the *personae* of Father, Son, and Holy Spirit, and those of David, Jesus, and Paul.

In particular, Elipandus charges Migetius with making the claim that "there are three corporeal persons in divinity," namely, David, Jesus, and Paul, corresponding to Father, Son, and Holy Spirit respectively.[50] It must certainly be admitted that in itself, taken baldly, this does sound absurd. Without looking much more closely than this, those historians who have in fact considered the doctrinal dimension of the controversy at all seriously have tried to make sense of these claims by positing some system, with or without historical precedent, which these claims of Elipandus are imperfectly reflecting. Loosely, the thought of Migetius is characterized as Sabellian.[51] Such a reading is based, in part, upon a questionable reconstruction of the manuscript evidence.[52] Actually, Elipandus elsewhere explicitly remarks that Migetius's heresy is a novelty, not comparable to any other heretical system.[53]

More recently, J. F. Rivera Recio has been able to give this description more content by pointing to a Trinitarian aberration some thirty years earlier in the same locale, and by offering a rationale for this and other collapses of Trinitarian orthodoxy in Mozarabic Spain, including Migetius.[54] Rivera Recio suggests that the rigid monotheism of the Muslims as well as that of the Jews (who tended, with every justification, to see the Muslims as their liberators due to the harsh treatment of the Jews under the Visigothic kings) furnished a strongly anti-trinitarian background, under pressure from which the doctrine of the Trinity was compromised in various ways, including among them the system of Migetius and that of the earlier unnamed Sabellian. This is an interesting suggestion, but there is very little evidence to demonstrate its truth, and it is based on a hypothetical assumption about what sort of doctrinal compromises on the part of the Christians would make Christianity seem more compatible with Islam in the eyes of the Muslims. In fact, other contemporary documents seem to indicate that such compromises were of little interest or consequence to the Muslims,[55] and we would not, in any event, have expected a concession of any sort from the rigorist Migetius. Whether one agrees or not, however, at least this study has the merit of taking the textual evidence regarding the doctrinal deviations of Migetius seriously.[56]

Other scholars have characterized Migetius as representing a revival or survival of Priscillianism. Priscillianism does in fact seem to have survived in isolated pockets for centuries past its latest formal condemnation,[57] and Migetius's Trinitarian doctrine could be construed in such a way that the characteristically Priscillian denial of the existence of the Son before the Incarnation could be recognized.[58] Hadrian, indeed, in his letter to Egila, is reminded of Priscillianism[59] by certain abuses which Egila has mentioned. But he is speaking so generally, and is so ill-informed regarding details, that it is difficult to conclude anything more than that Hadrian has used the name of the handiest, most notorious Hispanic heretic to label the abuses he has discussed. At any rate, the reference to Priscillian is withdrawn at the corresponding place in the later letter.[60]

E. Amann, on the other hand, disregards as embellishment provided by Elipandus the claims made regarding the Father and the Holy Spirit. He thus reduces the controversy to one involving the Son only—reduces it, that is, to one that is totally christological in character. Migetius has, he argues, simply been insisting upon a very strong, perhaps ill put, but finally orthodox, use of the theory of *communicatio idiomatum*, something which had to have been, after all, insultingly repugnant to Elipandus's adoptionistic christological sensibilities.[61] Although of all the modern treatments this analysis by Amann has paid the closest attention to the text of the doctrinal problem, it still seems unsatisfactory. It is too easy to assume that Migetius's position is simply the obverse of that of Elipandus. And, furthermore, the opposition thus construed is one which is preconceived as a sort of classical Eastern christological controversy writ small, as it were. Still further, by simply claiming that the Trinitarian dimension of the doctrine is fabricated,[62] and thus that the dispute was essentially christological, this interpretation assumes a strong, direct continuity with the later controversy. This is an interesting assumption, but it must be recognized that it is only an assumption, and one which remains undemonstrated.[63]

Keeping in mind that Elipandus is probably working from the text of Migetius, we can look at Elipandus's claims more closely. According to Elipandus, Migetius says that there are *tres personas corporeas in divinitate*:[64]

1. a. "quod Patris persona specialiter David esse"—"The *persona* of the Father in particular is David";
   b. "ut Dei Patris persona David esse credatur"—"The *persona* of God the Father is believed to be David";
   c. "ipse est David persona Dei Patris"—"David is himself the *persona* of God the Father."[65]

2. a. "persona Filii Dei asseris quod ea sit secunda in Trinitate persona, quae assumpta est de Virgine"—"Regarding the *persona* of the Son of God, you assert that the *persona* which is the second one in the Trinity is that which was assumed from the virgin";
   b. "de Filii namque persona quod dicis, eo quod ea sit secunda in Trinitate persona quae facta est ex semine David secundum carnem, et non ea quae genita est a Patre"—"What you say regarding the *persona* of the Son is this, namely that the *persona* which is the second in the Trinity is that *persona* which was *made from the seed of David, according to the flesh* [Rom. 1:3], and not that which was begotten by the Father";
   c. "Personam vero Filii non eam esse quam tu asseris Patri et Spiritui sancto aequalem esse, quae facta est ex semine David secundum carnem in novissimo tempore; sed eam quae genita est a Deo Patre, sine initio temporis, quae ante assumptionem carnis dixit per Prophetam"—"But the *persona* of the Son is not

that which you assert to be equal to the Father and the Holy Spirit, namely, one *made from the seed of David according to the flesh* in these recent times—rather it is that [*persona*] which was begotten by God the Father, without any beginning in time, which spoke through the prophet before its assumption of flesh";

    d. "Post assumptionem vero carnis, non eam quam tu asseris, secundum carnem, de qua ipse dicit: *Pater major me est*, sed eam de qua ipse dicit: *Ego et Pater unum sumus*, et iterum: *Ego in Patre, et Pater in me est*."—"[The *persona* of the Son] is not, after the assumption of flesh, the one which you say it is, 'according to the flesh, of which he himself says, *The Father is greater than I* [Jn. 14:28],' but rather that of which he himself says, *I and the Father are one* [Jn. 10:30], and likewise, *I am in the Father and the Father is in me* [Jn. 14:10]."[66]

3. a. "De tertia vero persona Spiritus sancti quod dicis, eo quod Paulus sit"—"Concerning the third *persona*, the Holy Spirit, you say that he is Paul";

    b. "Si Paulus est, ut asseris, persona Spiritus sancti, quae a Patre Filioque precedit"—"If Paul, as you assert, is the *persona* of the Holy Spirit which proceeds from the Father and the Son";

    c. " . . . dicis quia Paulus personam distinguit in se manere Spiritus sancti"—"You say that Paul distinguishes in himself the *persona* of the Holy Spirit abiding there";

    d. "Spiritus sancti quoque personam non Pauli credimus esse, cui datum est ut aliquando de malo efficeretur bonus, sed eum qui [*eam que*, Gil] sine immutatione sui naturaliter semper est bonus"—"We do not believe that the *persona* of the Holy Spirit is also Paul's."[67]

The controversy proceeds on a consistently technical basis. Migetius does not claim, for instance, that David *is* the Father, but that David is the *persona* of the Father, that is, that David's person is the person of the Father.[68] An identical claim is made in the case of each of the three *personae* of the Trinity. Migetius has established no differentiation between the Incarnation of the Word on the one hand, and the way in which the *personae* of David and Paul are the *personae* of Father and Spirit respectively. This, in fact, seems to be his most egregious error.[69] Nevertheless, it seems that

Migetius, when speaking about the second Person of the Trinity, had taken special care not to be misunderstood. After all, the christological reflection and debate of the last three centuries had established a rather complex context for any discussion of this *persona*, especially in connection with the earthly figure, Jesus. Therefore, Migetius is careful to specify that he is talking about the "persona quae *assumpta est* de Virgine," without even mentioning the name of Jesus, since this name would not necessarily serve to identify precisely the subject in question, because of the complexity of the christological question.[70] One cannot fail to note, however, that from the point of view of any orthodox christological tradition in the West since Augustine, it could never be appropriate to speak of a "persona assumpta" in Jesus, or, for that matter, even a "persona quae facta est" in him.[71] Thus it is with every justification that Elipandus points out to Migetius that the second *persona* of the Trinity, is not, "quod ut dicis . . . , ea . . . quae facta est ex semine David secundum carnem," but rather "ea quae genita est a Patre" (2b), and that if Migetius were correct, the Son of God would have had his origin from his mother only, and not "de Patre genitus sine initio." And, later (2c, paraphrased):

> The person of the Son is not that which you posit as the equal of the Father and the Holy Spirit, one which was made from the seed of David in very recent time, but is rather that which was begotten of God the Father without any beginning in time.

The passage just cited, along with others like it, has become the *locus classicus* for pointing to Elipandus's incipient adoptionism.[72] But there is no mention of adoption here or anywhere else in this letter. Instead, the standard interpretation of this and other similar passages is predicated on scholars's all too common assimilation of Elipandus's adoptionism to Nestorianism.[73] It may or may not be true that from a logical point of view adoptionism as taught by Elipandus leads directly or necessarily to a two-person christology that goes by the name of Nestorianism—and Alcuin did not fail to press this case time and time again. But this does not mean that in its own inherent shape and character, *historically* speaking, Elipandus's teaching was Nestorian. In fact, Elipandus insisted time and time again that there is only one *persona* in Jesus,[74] never spoke in any other text of a "persona assumpta," and, perhaps more importantly, was never even accused, by any of his various opponents, of so speaking. Nor does he ever speak elsewhere of "ea persona" on the one hand and "ea" or "alia" on the other. It is difficult to avoid the conclusion that it is Migetius who spoke of this *persona assumpta*, not Elipandus, and that Elipandus is simply reproducing his turn of speech, following the text he has before him. He carefully points this out ("asseris," "dicis," 2nd person singular). The same is true for the other passages cited above where there is a distinction implied between two proposed *personae*. This is not a position which Elipandus holds or even blunders into, but rather a correction of the position of Migetius.[75] To paraphrase, "The second person of the Trinity is not this *persona assumpta*, as *you* say" (a qualifier included in *every instance* of Elipandus's supposed Nestorianism—see citations 2a–d above),[76] "but rather is one who is coeternal and consubstantial with the Father." Elipandus is *defending* the one-person christology which he elsewhere so consistently upholds. His polemical taunt that the Son of God would, if Migetius's position were correct, have had his origin from his Mother only, makes no sense at all unless Elipandus is thought to have been working from the perspective of a one-person hypothesis.

Elipandus does not expand on the christological issue at great length, only just enough, as in the other two cases of Father and Son respectively, to identify sufficiently the eternal *persona* of the Trinity as non-created and non-corporeal. In fact, he spends less time considering the *persona* of the Son than he does considering either of the other two individual cases. It does not seem, therefore, that this dispute was, at its very beginning, a quarrel over christology. At issue was, rather, a system which was essentially Trinitarian, which asserted that "there are three corporeal *personae* in divinity," or, to paraphrase, that there are three created *personae*, three *personae* belonging to corporeal beings—David, Jesus, and Paul—in divinity, three *personae*, that is, who were *assumed* there. Just as the *persona* of the Word can be said to be united to a created *persona* which it assumed into personal union and thus identity, so too is the case with the Father and the Holy Spirit, respectively. This is, very roughly, the system of Migetius, three instances of the personal appearance of God in history, one for each *persona* of the Trinity, achieved, just as in the case of the Word, through union with an assumed *persona*.

This system may seem bizarre from our point of view, but it is not absurd, and it fits very nicely into what Elipandus claims about Migetius's charisma. Elipandus accuses Migetius of presenting himself as "similar to Christ," electing twelve apostles, speaking to a bystander the words of Christ to the good thief, "Amen, Amen, I say to you, this day you shall be with me in Paradise" (Lk. 23:43), and proclaiming that he was about to die and then rise again on the third day. Migetius understands himself, perhaps, to be a prophet, proclaiming the true words of Christ, preaching

the destruction of Elipandus's compromised regime and his own vindi-
cation by resurrection. Such a charismatic view of himself would be congru-
ent with the teaching that God had manifested himself directly three times,
in the *personae* of David, Jesus, and Paul. Migetius may see himself as
somewhere or somehow in this line of charism, maybe the last in the line.

The principal absurdity alleged of Migetius, namely, that God could
be in any way corporeal (i.e., that he perished, or had flesh and bones,
etc.), is thus removed, not by removing the allegations against him, but
by explaining them as a function of a christological paradigm that is extended to Father and Holy Spirit as well as to the Son. It is to be observed
that none of these allegations are problematic in Elipandus's discussions
of Migetius's claims regarding the Son. He hardly brings them up. It is
only in the two cases of the Father and the Holy Spirit that they sound
absurd, and we can see the hand of Elipandus ruthlessly forcing upon
Migetius what would in fact be the absurd-sounding, if not actually absurd, consequences of his system.

But in the case of the Son, where the liturgy and tradition of the
Church had long accustomed the ear to hearing about the Word's incarnation or assumption of a human nature, his self-emptying, his suffering
and his death, in a word, the idea of *communicatio idiomatum*, there would
be nothing absurd-sounding at all. Here the *reductio ad absurdum* would
have to take a different tack, and we thus find Elipandus alleging that
according to the system of Migetius the Son would have his origin from
Mary (and by extension, David) only. Thus it is possible, while discarding
none of the evidence, to accommodate those historians who, not trusting
Elipandus, feel that he manufactured the "absurd" charges against Migetius. We can see both the position of Migetius, as reflected in the substantially correct charges of Elipandus, as well as its polemical reduction to
absurdity by Elipandus.

Although this is conjecture and not conclusion, it is not unreasonable
to suppose that Elipandus, in his more formally promulgated refutation
and condemnation of Migetius, was more careful to correct the christological implications of Migetius's system, using language more christologically precise. He may have pointed out that contrary to the way Migetius
has construed matters, there is no assumption of a *persona* by the Word,
nor is there any *persona* to be assumed. Furthermore, that which is assumed becomes thereby the *adoptive* Son of God, and is not in and of itself
the natural Son of God, as would have to be inferred, contrariwise, from
Migetius's theory that *David's persona* was assumed by the Father.[77]

While this must remain a conjecture, we do possess a writing, cited in a work of the anti-adoptionist Beatus of Liebana, which is certainly one of the very earliest surviving fragments of adoptionist exposition, from a very early point in the controversy, one which in fact may well be a fragment from Elipandus's formal refutation of Migetius.[78] The contents of this fragment are not inconsistent with such a conjecture.[79] It corresponds with what we might expect of a riposte to Migetius's system. It is concerned, as was Migetius, primarily with Trinitarian, not christological, doctrine. Over three-quarters of it is devoted exclusively to the Trinitarian issue,[80] reflecting the balance of the doctrinal section of the earlier Letter to Migetius, and reminding one especially of the section in the Letter where Elipandus gives his summary of orthodox teaching on the Trinity (*PL* 96:864.A13–B6). The issue is the exact identity of the *personae* of the Trinity. The christology enters as a secondary element, necessary to clarify this main issue, with regard to the Son.[81] If it is in fact true that this earliest adoptionist fragment is a reply to Migetius, this would mean that Elipandus's adoptionism *begins as a defense of a one-person christology*. We will examine this fragment more thoroughly in the succeeding chapter, but whether or not we are entitled to make the connection suggested between the two controversies, it should be clear at least that in his letter to Migetius, Elipandus is defending a one-person christology, and that if anyone involved must be characterized as Nestorian it is *Migetius*, not Elipandus.

It might be worthwhile speculating for one further moment on this point. We might say that Migetius has a Nestorian way of thinking, so that even when erring on the Trinitarian question, it is in a Nestorian way. Were they actually Nestorians, or a renegade Nestorian sect? It is not unthinkable that there were Nestorians in Spain at the time, having come from the East with the Muslims. There were also Eastern Christians (whether Nestorian or not) with Latin names.[82] And Migetius's enthusiasm for the See of Rome can be seen more as an act of defiance against Toledo than any true allegiance, a function, perhaps, of his alliance with Egila. In the *acta* of the Council of Cordoba of 839, the sect is, interestingly enough, described as having come from "overseas." Also, the "Cassianist" spirituality of the Migetians, if understood as having some true affinity with Semipelagianism, would not be without some element of congruity to Nestorian spirituality (certainly Nestorius himself had warmly received the Pelagians when they came to him in Constantinople).

Then there is the curious expression *magistro Salibaniorum*, which Elipandus applies to Migetius. Scholars have not been able to come up with a satisfying explanation of the word *Salibaniorum*, and therefore have always assimilated it to *Sabellianorum* without any textual justification. But what if Elipandus is repeating a phrase which he heard someone else using to describe Migetius's followers or people in some way like them? Perhaps the *Muslims* had a name for them, derived from the Arabic root *slb*, a name which Elipandus has repeated in a Latinized (and very likely inexact) version.[83] The word *salib* could, on the one hand, signify "rigid," or "severe." This would certainly have applied to the Migetian sect. The Arabs may have referred to them, somewhat insultingly, as the "rigid ones" or the "hardheads." However, the word also carries the more general meaning of "cross," and, as an adjective applying to a group, *salibiyuna*, refers to "those of the Cross," that is, to Christians in general. This is the more likely meaning for the word. It would be curious if the Arabs had applied it to Migetius and his sect only, for it would apply equally well to Elipandus and the rest of the Visigothic church—unless it is a name the sect carried with it from areas under Muslim control in the East, not the least of which was Persia with its large population of Nestorian Christians. Those Nestorians who came along with the waves of Arab migration to Spain may have been referred to by the Muslims as simply "the Christians." If Migetius's followers were among them, Elipandus is using the name to identify them as such and to insult Migetius, their "teacher." One may not be convinced, but it would be interesting to study the question further.

2. Elipandus

Elipandus is perhaps one of the more interesting figures in the history of doctrine, if rather obscurely remembered. Had his teaching not become controversial, he would have remained nothing more to us than a name in the Catalogue of Toledo,[1] and the author of a letter against Migetius. And although the literature associated with the adoptionist controversy provides us with evidence more tantalizing than sufficient about the way he thought, it still leaves us in the dark, by and large, regarding the biographical detail of his life. We can establish his birthdate with relative certainty at about 716,[2] and we know that he was as inveterate an adoptionist as ever in 800,[3] so that his death must be placed after, but not very long after, that date. He was archbishop of Toledo from about 754.[4] It has been argued, on the basis of vague allusions in the hostile work of Beatus of Liebana, that he was from his earliest years a monk,[5] that he became master of the monastic school which may have included lay students in its instruction,[6] that he was well read in Scripture but even better acquainted with secular—i.e., Arabic—science and philosophy, perhaps, in Beatus's opinion, better than he ought to have been.[7] Everything else we know about the life of Elipandus is coincident with our knowledge of the role he played in the controversy which must be ultimately attributed to him.[8]

Beyond the letter to Migetius, we have at our disposal five further letters and perhaps a fragment of a creed upon which to base a reconstruction of Elipandus's teachings:

    a. "Symbolus Fidei Elipandianae," given by Beatus at *Adv.Elip.* 1.40–41.[9]

    b. Letter to the abbot Fidelis, included, probably in full, by Beatus at *Adv.Elip.* 1.43–44.[10]

    c. Letter to the Bishops of Frankland. Date: 792 or 793.

    d. Letter to Charlemagne. Date: 792 or 793.[11]

    e. Letter to Alcuin. Date: mid-798.[12]

    f. Letter to Felix of Urgel. This is actually two short letters, sent at the same time. Date: 798.[13]

Only two of these documents are actually datable to the early, exclusively Hispanic stage of the controversy which we wish to illuminate here. The others are all later than the Council of Regensburg in 792, the point marking the transition to the later phase of the dispute. This is not, however, a great handicap to us because Elipandus himself, secure in his see thanks to the Moorish power, was never obliged to enter in a substantive way into the give and take of the controversy as it transpired outside of Spain. He was content to sputter apodictically from afar, as provoked or as the occasion required, and finally could offer only a minimal amount of help to Felix of Urgel, the person who actually became the standard bearer of the adoptionist position outside of Spain. Elipandus, even late into the controversy, never incorporated into his teachings the rather sophisticated refinements introduced by Felix. He remains very much a peninsular figure throughout, whose thought continues to be conditioned by the parameters and exigencies of the earliest, formative phase of the controversy. We can therefore, with caution enough to view the earlier documents as more trustworthy evidence than the later, use all of the material authentically attributable to Elipandus as evidence for helping us to gauge the doctrinal character of the earlier phase of the controversy.

Beware the "Beatian heresy"!

The Letter to Fidelis, as it has been preserved for us, is primarily a stream of fulmination against Beatus. The purpose of the letter seems to be to solicit and enlist the aid of Fidelis in a campaign against the critics of Elipandus, who lay by and large to the North, in the area free of Moorish control.[14] Elipandus enclosed with his letter a copy not preserved by Beatus of a letter sent to him by the bishop Ascaricus,[15] who had made a point of formally asking Elipandus what he should be teaching. Elipandus finds this an exemplary demonstration of loyalty and cannot resist pointing it out to Fidelis as an example of the proper posture which should be exhibited toward his person and his see.[16] He contrasts this to the attitude of Beatus, the "precursor of Antichrist," and that of Beatus's disciple, the bishop Heterius, whom, however, he is inclined to excuse on the grounds of his youth,[17] and their adherents, the followers of Antichrist.[18] All these are upstarts who do not want to ask what is right, but to teach it, acting with callous disregard for, and in fact contrary to, Elipandus.[19]

> For never has it been heard that the Libanese instructed the Toledans. It is known to the people of the entire world that from the very beginning of the

["its?"] faith, this see has been luminous with holy teachings, and that nothing schismatic whatsoever has gone forth from it.[20]

It was precisely to avoid such an ignominy that Elipandus and his "brother bishops" in Seville passed judgment on the heresy of Migetius.[21] Elipandus has not wished to bring this particular, present matter to the attention of his brothers, not, that is, until it has been cut off at the root in the region whence it came forth.

> Nevertheless, if the thing is conducted lukewarmly and you fail to correct the situation, then I will bring this back to the attention of my brothers, and it will be a disgrace in the extreme for you if they do find cause for rebuke. . . . I pray that, inflamed by zeal for the faith, you will have a motivation heated enough to drive out the above mentioned error from your midst—so that, just as through your servants [ourselves] the Lord rooted out the Migetian heresy from the boundaries of Baetica, so he might through you thoroughly eradicate the Beatian heresy from the confines of Asturia.[22]

He wonders, further, if Fidelis, when he does meet with the precursor of Antichrist, would inquire of him where, and how, and when, there was born in him the lying spirit of false prophecy which has been speaking in him, and then report back to him, Elipandus, anxiously awaiting the response.[23]

This letter provides us with a picture of a bitter controversy well underway but still at an early stage. Perhaps it is still confined to the north of Spain. If this letter is at all exemplary, Elipandus seems to have taken the tactic of urging his authority as metropolitan upon pastors, bishops, and abbots such as Fidelis, to pressure them into rejecting Beatus's position and teaching the adoptionistic line,[24] which seems to have emanated from Toledo itself.[25] Although it is threatened, there has been no gathering of bishops in synod or council to pass judgment on the anti-adoptionist "heretics." Therefore the first line of the letter (or of the fragment of it which is preserved for us) cannot be the formal anathema of a synod but rather a threat or decree of persecution:

> He who fails to confess that Jesus Christ is adoptive in his humanity, but in no way adoptive in his divinity, both is a heretic, and shall be banished.[26]

There must have been some literary vehicle for the campaign against Beatus, but it cannot have been very extensive. In neither of his letters[27] to the Spanish bishops does Pope Hadrian single out any particular tract of Elipandus for condemnation, nor do the *acta* of any of the anti-adoptionist councils mention any work from this early period, nor does Alcuin. Beatus mentions "ipsum libellum adversum nos et fidem nostram" and that it was read aloud publicly through all Asturia.[28] But the context seems to indicate that he is simply referring to the Letter to Fidelis,[29] while not once in the entirety of the enormous work against Elipandus does he cite any passage from Elipandus which could not have come either from the text of the Letter to Fidelis as we have it, or from the "Symbolum fidei Elipandianae" which he also reproduces. Before Beatus's tract in late 785 or early 786, the controversy was not a particularly literary one, and, we may suspect, not a particularly sophisticated one, at least in terms of the elaboration of a systematic adoptionist christology. Not until Felix was there any such thing, if even then. It may be that the position, at least as a consciously held and articulated teaching, was rather recent. At any rate, there does not seem to be any direct evidence for the interesting but perhaps extreme opinion which indicates a long period of formation under the influence of Antiochene and Islamic thought which finally issued in fundamental concessions to the Muslims.[30]

The "Symbolus fidei Elipandianae"

We may regard the "Symbolus fidei Elipandianae" as the oldest extant exposition of the teachings of the Spanish adoptionists. It is cited by Beatus, so it is earlier than the end of 785. Beatus very clearly distinguishes it from the Letter to Fidelis, and it carries no hint of any controversy surrounding the use of the term *adoptio*—no anathemata, no mention of Beatus or Heterius or any other gainsayer of the adoptionist position, no hesitation or apologetic regarding the use of the term. This "Symbolus" cannot represent the pronouncement of a pro-adoptionistic synod or council because we know from the Letter to Fidelis that there has not been any such council.[31] Since Elipandus nowhere lists or makes reference to any other council held under his presidency apart from the Council of Seville—and, in the letter to Fidelis, where he is intent upon demonstrating the zeal of his see for the true faith, we would have expected this—it is not without warrant, as suggested above, to see in this "Symbolus" a portion of the proceedings of that council.

In fact, as already noted at the end of the previous chapter, the content fits perfectly with what we should expect of a riposte to the doctrinal teachings of Migetius, despite the interference of Beatus, who has edited and abbreviated the "Symbolus," tailoring it to his own anti-adoptionist concerns.[32] Neither adoptionism nor even christology in general appear to be the primary issue in this "Symbolus." It seems, rather, to be a formal clarification of Trinitarian belief, a sort of amplification of the little summary of faith given in the letter to Migetius itself.[33] Over 75 percent of the text is devoted solely to the Trinity, replete with analogies and explanations which have a true heuristic function and which would, at least in the detail they are presented here, have no purpose unless the Church's teaching on the Trinity had become problematic. What christology there is comes in as a secondary element, meant, as much as the analogies and other explanations are meant, to clarify the primary Trinitarian issue, much as Augustine's christology is often subservient to anti-Arian, that is, Trinitarian, concerns.[34] Who are the *personae* of the Trinity? They are a Trinity in one nature and essence of deity,[35] who differ as a stone, the heat in the stone, and the cold still left in the stone differ,[36] or as many souls differ who are, despite their being many, made one by the love of God[37] or as a man and his wife differ, although they are one flesh.[38] The Father precedes the Son not in the order of time (as Migetius's theory would imply), but in origin, just as the stone precedes the heat that is in it when we picture the whole in our minds.[39] The Word, that is, the unique Son,[40] is one, despite his many appellations such as *splendor gloriae, et figura substantia ejus.*[41] And,

> It is he [sc., *Verbum Dei*] who, having emptied himself of his divinity ["deitate exinanita"], was made human, was circumcised, baptized, scourged, crucified, died, was buried, as a slave, a prisoner, an alien, a leper, despised, and, what is worse, made lower not only than the angels but even than humanity, said to have become a worm . . . *I am a worm, and no man* [Ps.22:6].[42]

Still, this is he whose glory, according to his divinity, stupefies the heavens and causes the earth to tremble mightily.[43]

Against Migetius, and in clarification of his own position, Elipandus has pointed out very certainly that the *persona* of the Son, even throughout all of the indignities associated with the earthly figure of Jesus, is that of the Word of God, already described as equal and co-eternal with the Father, and not any separately existing "corporeal" or "assumed" *persona* independent of the Word. Scholars of the adoptionist controversy, convinced that Elipandus was a neo-Nestorian, have consistently failed to notice that this passage represents a ringing affirmation of the continuity of subject throughout the Incarnation,[44] which is understood as a process or series of stages: the subject remains the *persona* of the Word of God, both before and after the point at which he was "made human." This is all the more significant given the early, non-controversial (christologically speaking) character of this document. It is too early for Elipandus to be attempting to cover his tracks.

The "Symbolus," as cited by Beatus, continues:

> Et qui dicit *gloriam meam alteri non dabo*, homo interior ["inter nos?" "inferior?"] in una eademque Dei et hominis persona agglomeratus, atque carnis vestimento indutus. Quia non per illum qui natus est de Virgine visibilia condidit, sed per illum qui non est adoptione, sed genere; neque gratia, sed natura.[45]

This may be paraphrased as follows: "And since he [sc., God] *will not give his glory to any other*, the man who is among us is [not another but rather] one and the same *persona*, of God and of man, *because* it was not through him who was born of the virgin—i.e., the separate 'illum' which Migetius had posited by virtue of having spoken of a 'persona assumpta'—that all things visible were made, but rather through him who exists not by adoption or grace but by generation and by nature, as has already been defined in the Trinitarian section above." Those who would see in the passage "Quia non per illum . . . sed per illum . . ." a frank declaration of Nestorianism or at least a Nestorian slip, fail to observe that the entirety of the passage which has gone before this line is a careful and clear defense of a one-person christology, and that this sentence is connected to it by a "quia" which makes it equally clear that this sentence too is part and parcel of the defense. Elipandus is not affirming the existence of two subjects in Christ, but denying such a theory, as put forward by Migetius.[46] The phrase "non . . . adoptione" is reminiscent of a similar and very distinctive phrase used in the symbol of the Eleventh Council of Toledo for a similar purpose, that is, to identify and define the Son of God in his eternal *persona*,[47] in contradistinction to the claims of the earlier heretic-adoptionist Bonosus.[48] Bonosus and his heresy are known to both Elipandus and Beatus.[49] The use of the negative in the phrase "non adoptione" comes from this earlier way of speaking about the eternal Word, ingrained in Spanish tradition, and does not imply that there is another separate subject or *illum* who is, by contrast, "adoptione."

The "Symbolus" goes on:

> Et per istum [*istud*, Löfstedt] Dei simul et hominis filium, adoptivum humanitate, et nequaquam adoptivum divinitate, mundum redemit. ["And

through him who was son both of God and of man, adoptive in his humanity but in no way adoptive in his divinity [God] redeemed the world."][50]

While Beatus the polemicist tries to show that Elipandus has divided Jesus by distinguishing in him a subject through whom the world was created and one through whom the world was redeemed,[51] there is no such intention here. The reference here is to the Word made human or made flesh. Redemption is accomplished by the *Word made human*, not by the Word before the Incarnation (as was, contrariwise, the case with creation). Redemption is accomplished through "istum Dei simul et hominis filium," he who is at once Son of God and Son of Man, this particular Son, at once of God and of Man. There is one subject here. The phrases *adoptivum* and *nequaquam adoptivum* are clearly referred to the *natures*, and mean nothing more than if in his divine nature he is truly and eternally the Son of God, *non adoptione*, then in his human nature, as a man, he is truly and naturally son of a human being, and, against Migetius, only *adoptively* the Son of *God*.

The precedent for this type of thinking is in the Creed of Toledo XI:[52]

"Hic [Christus] tamen per hoc quod de Deo Patre sine initio prodiit, natus tantum, neque factus neque praedestinatus accipitur; per hoc tamen, quod de Maria virgine natus est, et natus et factus et praedestinatus esse credendus est."

Thus the same subject can, according to this model creed, be both predestined and not predestined. This is not far from the adoptionist position, as I have interpreted it. Madóz gives Augustine, *In John. Ev.* 105.8 as the ultimate source for this article in the creed, but note that in the Augustine text there is no personal subject who is predestined, only an "illud." The creed of Toledo XI represents something of a development over the Augustinian passage, and it is in this same spirit that Elipandus teaches his adoptionism, as a further development of this line of reflection.[53]

The few lines which constitute the remainder of the "Symbolus" deal briefly with the soteriology attaching to the christology just exposited. He, "that one who is at once Son of God and Son of Man," is "God among the gods,"[54] and, even as one who eats and drinks, he remains known to the one (i.e., any follower) from whom he wished to conceal none of the mysteries of his working.[55] The Word is revealed in and because of his humanity, *as* he eats and drinks.

Because, if all the saints are *conformed* (1 John 3:2) to this Son of God according to grace, then clearly together with the Adoptive One they are adoptive

ones, with the Advocate they are advocates, with Christ they are christs, with
he who is little they are little ones, and with the Servant they too are
servants.[56]

In other words, if our salvation is to be "conformed" to Christ, following
Paul, then we must have a Christ to whom we are conformable, a "Christ"
with whom we may be "christs." We cannot be conformed to the divine
nature of the Son, but we can be conformed to him according to grace,
insofar as he is *adoptive*. "For we believe that in the resurrection we shall
be *like* him (1 John 3:2), not in his divinity but in the flesh of his humanity,
namely, that which he received from the Virgin in the assumption of
flesh.[57] This is almost poignantly put. How are we to accept the promise
implied in 1 John 3:2 if it refers to the Son of God in his divinity? We must
despair of salvation, of ever becoming "like him," unless the passage from
1 John refers to a humanity like our own, bodily, and supported by grace.

Letter to Frankland

The main themes of the early adoptionist teaching are laid out in the
"Symbolus fidei," but it is difficult to appreciate their precise significance
as well as their interrelation unless we study Elipandus's later attempts to
expound his own beliefs. Since there is centuries's worth of precedent
against allowing Elipandus to speak for himself, this study must be accomplished in some detail. Most important among the four documents
remaining to be discussed is the Letter to the Bishops of Frankland, Elipandus's manifesto as it were, and we can begin with that. The other documents, two of which are very short and practically devoid of doctrinal
content (Letters to Felix and to Charlemagne) and the third of which is
doctrinal but late (the Letter to Alcuin), will be drawn into the discussion
as needed.

   The Letter to the Bishops of Frankland begins, after an appropriate insult[58] to Beatus, with the following creed-like account of the Incarnation:

> We confess and we believe in God the Son of God, born without beginning
> of the Father before all ages, co-eternal and consimilar and consubstantial not
> by adoption but by generation, and not by grace but by nature. To this the
> same Son testifies [when he says] *I and the Father are one* [Jn. 10:30], along
> with the rest of the passages which the same one, truly God and truly human,
> spoke for us concerning his divinity. But, toward the end of time, for the

salvation of the human race, appearing to the public view out of the hidden and ineffable [bosom] of the Father—the invisible assuming a visible body from the Virgin—he came forth, ineffably, through the inviolably virgin members of his mother. We confess according to the tradition of the Fathers, and believe, that he was made of a woman, under the law, Son of God not by generation but by adoption, and not by nature, but by grace, as the same Lord testifies, saying, *The Father is greater than I* [Jn. 14:28].[59]

The subject of this continuous stream depicting the Incarnation as a process is *God, the Son of God*,[60] and he remains the subject throughout. He is the subject of all the metaphoric participles of movement, "egrediens," "non recedens," "petens," as well as of the participles "apparens" and "adsumens," and the verb "enixus est." He it is, the invisible, who without leaving the substance of the Father came to this lower world, assumed a visible body, and was born. He it is, who, once he was "made of a woman, made under the law," received a birth which was not by nature from the Father *but by adoption and grace*. He has become, in this sense, adoptive. Observe that *there is no new subject introduced here*. The predicate "by adoption" does not apply to an independently or priorly extant man with a private subject or *persona* all his own, but to the Word *as a man*, to the Word after the Incarnation, but to the Word nonetheless. It is in this connection most important to notice that Elipandus never uses the verb *adopto* in the way in which he used the verb *assumo* in the passage just cited, that is, as an active verb or participle with a direct object. The Word "assumes" flesh or a body or a human nature or even—something which is a commonplace in Western christology—a "human being."[61] But he is never said to have "adopted" anything, as though this were merely a more radical way of saying "assumed."[62] Nor, for that matter, is anyone ever said to adopt anyone or anything. Observe the following examples of usage, typical of Elipandus: God, the Son of God, *assumes* a visible body (present active participle with direct object), but is made under the law and thereby exists *by adoption* (ablative);[63] he becomes "primogenitus" *by assuming* a true man from the virgin (gerund with direct object), thereby becoming "primogenitus" *in adoption and grace* (ablative with preposition): as "Unigenitus" he is *without adoption*.[64] As "primogenitus" he is possessed of the fullness of anointing and as such is *adoptivus* (adjective).[65] *By assuming flesh*[66] (gerund with direct object), the "Unigenitus" has, in these last days at the end of time, become "primogenitus," by grace and *by adoption*[67] (ablative). Note the adjectival uses of the word,[68] and notice too the interesting usage in Elipandus's letter to Charlemagne, "iste nefandus presbyter et pseudopropheta asseverat Dei filium in forma servi deitate exinanita nequaquam ex utero virginis *adsumsisse adobtionem.*"[69] The Son takes up or assumes *adoption*, not an adopted one (i.e., "adoptatum" or "hominem adoptatum"). He himself takes up adoption. Finally, in Elipandus's letter to Alcuin, note the type of coordination exhibited between the usage of the verb *suscipio* and that of the stem *adopt–*: " . . . tu negas Dei Filium de stirpe Abraham . . . *carnem* non *suscepisse*, ut esset *adoptivus* filius?"[70] i.e., the Son of God takes up flesh (active with direct object) so that (or with the result that) he might be (or is) an adoptive son (adjective).[71]

There is never, finally, a point at which the Father (e.g.) is said to have "adopted" the Son or a human nature or a man, etc. The point is much more subtle, namely, that *by assuming* flesh or a body, etc., the *Word*, the "Only-begotten" with regard to nature, becomes the "First-born" in adoption and grace:

> We believe in and confess that God the Son of God, Light from Light, true God from true God, the Only-begotten of the Father without adoption, became First-born at the end of time by assuming a true man from the Virgin in the adoption proper to the flesh, and thus is in nature Only-begotten, and in adoption and grace First-born.[72]

That the eternal Son could come to exist or have a birth "by adoption" is less surprising than it may at first seem. The Word's birth "by adoption" is a function of a voluntary lowliness, the result of the "self-emptying" described at Phil. 2:7. Elipandus's adoptionism can be thought of as an exegetical elaboration of this self-emptying, and usefully located within the context of older Latin traditions of reflection on Phil. 2:7.[73] For Elipandus, the self-emptying is not complete—or salvific—until it reaches the point of adoptive sonship.[74] It is the Son of God himself, who by emptying himself, takes up adoption. Therefore, Beatus errs because

> he asserts that the Son of God, in the form of a slave, emptied of his Godhead [*deitate exinanita*], never assumed adoption from the womb of the Virgin.[75]

The phrase "in forma servi deitate exinanita" is a clear reference to Phil. 2:6–11. Even as early as the "Symbolus fidei" the middle term between the pre-existence of the Word and his being made an adoptive man was his self-emptying.[76] Now we may consider the further evidence of the Letter to the Bishops of Frankland:

> Why is there any hesitation to say that the Son of God, according to the form of a slave, emptied of his Godhead, corporeal and visible and palpable, is

adoptive?[77] Beatus the Unspeakable is unhappy if anyone says that Christ, according to the form of a slave, is adoptive, even though John the Apostle and Evangelist is not afraid to call the Son of God, emptied of his Godhead, an "advocate" (that is, adopted), and in the form of a slave, "full of grace" [Jn. 1:14].[78]

The phrase *deitate exinanita* assures the continuity of subject by recalling the narrative of self-emptying from Phil. 2:6–7 and its development in the creed-like introductory section of the Letter to the Bishops of Frankland, where it was clear that the lower stage,[79] whatever its character (including "adoptive"), was something reached by a subject continuous with that pre-existing in the "form of God."[80]

In this context, it is not an absurdity but merely part of the paradoxical character of the Incarnation that the Word can in some sense become "adoptive." Using a passage from Augustine's *Enchiridion*, where Augustine, with reference to Phil. 2:6, speaks in the same type of paradoxical language, Elipandus develops his thinking as a kind of gloss on the Augustinian text:

> For although he was the unique Son of God not by grace but by nature, he was made a Son of Man so that [*ut*] he might be "full of grace," he himself, the one Christ . . . who *although he was in the form of God, did not think it robbery to be* what he was by nature, that is, *equal to God*.[81]

Strictly speaking it is logically impossible for the Word of God to be full of grace, but it is precisely the point of this christology, derivable, as it is, from Phil. 2:6–7, that the eternal Son was made human *so that* he could become the subject of grace, so that he could, with Elipandus, become a son by grace as well as by nature. Echoing this passage from Augustine, Elipandus will ask Alcuin,

> Do you deny that the Son of God took up flesh from the line of Abraham *so that* he might become an adoptive son?[82]

Further, in the Letter to the Bishops of Frankland, Elipandus cites this passage from the *Enchiridion* twice, taking care to gloss it so that it is clear in precisely what context the language of adoption is being used.[83] There is no question of an independently existent man who was at some point, either after his sufferings or before, adopted as the Son of God. It is rather the eternal Son who, by emptying himself of the form of God (= his *deitas*), makes it possible for himself, as a man, to become "full of grace," which for Elipandus means "adoptive." Elipandus's adoptionism is a creative but genuine development of a purely Western tradition of reflection upon and exegesis of Phil. 2:6–11.

This tradition includes Leo. Almost half of Elipandus's later letter to Alcuin is cited word for word from the Letter of Pope Leo I to the Emperor Leo I.[84] The portion of the letter cited includes a full quotation of Phil. 2:6–11 and an exegesis which is especially interesting because of the way it interprets the "exaltation" of verse 9. Leo is trying to explain how the subject of Phil. 2:6–11 can have received any exaltation, and for Leo, that subject is the Word. Leo answers that the exaltation applies to the *forma servi*, but that, just as the Lord of Glory can be said to have been crucified (1 Cor. 2:8), so also it can be said that he was exalted.[85] It is along these same lines that I am claiming that Elipandus would call the Lord of Glory *adoptive*. From this perspective, Elipandus's adoptionism can be seen as a particular use of the Leonine casting of the *communicatio idiomatum*.[86]

Further, the eternal Son's self-emptying of the *forma Dei* of Phil. 2:6–7 specifically represents a self-emptying of his *deitas*. Insofar as he is made human he exists "deitate exinanita." For Elipandus this means an emptying which refers not only to the nature of deity itself, but also to whatever relational features are defined or conditioned by participation in deity. If the Son's relation to the Father can be characterized as "Light from Light, true God from true God,"[87] this is a characterization of a unique relation, but it is defined in terms of substance or nature. Elipandus's claim is that the Son's self-emptying means that this same unique relation is shorn of any such definition and becomes exhibited in another nature. But it is the same relation. There is no new *persona* defined when it becomes manifested in another nature. "In natura,"[88] that is, in the divine nature, as "Light from Light," the Son is "Unigenitus," but by taking up a true human being from the Virgin he becomes with regard to the Father "Primogenitus,"[89] still uniquely related, but "in adoption and grace," as appropriate to the human nature. His status as Unigenitus is not impeached or removed; rather, the self-emptying of the Word has permitted this unique relation to be exhibited in the terms which respect the limitations of another nature. That is why this self-emptying is salvific. It is the same *persona* who is at once Unigenitus by nature and Primogenitus by adoption. Since the unique relation defining that *persona* remains undisturbed, that same *persona* retains its identity even in the assumption of a wholly different nature. From this point of view Elipandus's christology may be seen not only as a continuation and development of patristic christological reflection on Phil. 2:6–11, but also, coordinately, as a continuation and development of the two-nature, one-person christology of such Western figures as Augustine and Leo.[90]

Elipandus's soteriology may also be viewed as a development of certain Western themes and sources, and in this case it is Hispanic ones in particular that come to mind. We have already observed how in the "Symbolus" a soteriology of "likeness" and "conformation" is developed from 1 John 3:2. In the Letter to the Bishops of Frankland, Elipandus cites this verse in full and then goes on to discuss the idea of "likeness" and "conformation," developing it in terms of his "Primogenitus" christology. Citing Rom. 8:29,[91] the source of the vocabulary of the "primogenitus" terminology, as well as its connection to that of "conformation," Elipandus explains what it means to become "like" the Son of God. It does not mean that we become similar to divinity or to his divine nature, but that we become his "brothers."[92] By taking up adoption he has become the First-born[93] and has deigned to have brothers and sisters. Elipandus develops his thinking as an interpretation of passages from his Hispanic forebear Isidore. One passage in particular, from the *Etymologia*, receives particular attention:

> He is called "Only-begotten" according to the excellence of divinity, because he is without brothers, but is called "First-born" on account of the taking up of the man, in which through the adoption of grace he deigned to have brothers in relation to whom he would be the "First-born."[94]

And it is insofar as we "participate" in the adoption by grace that we become "brothers" to the First-born and *in this way* "conformed" to him.[95]

Thus we are like him not simply by nature but by *relation*. For Elipandus a similarity in nature is not enough to be salvific; rather, the similarity in nature makes possible *a relation* which is salvific. The Word's "taking up of a human" is that *in which* through the adoption of grace ("susceptionem hominis in qua per adobtionem") he deigned to have brothers. Insofar as the Word deigned to have a birth "by adoption," he deigned to become our brother, and thus to make us, *like him*, children of God. As already noted, this does not compromise his uniqueness as Primogenitus. Elipandus is careful to secure this uniqueness by following Augustine's time-honored exegesis of John 3:34.[96] To the saints the grace of anointing with the Holy Spirit has been given only "ad mesuram,"[97] that is, "by measure," whereas only to the Son of God, the First-born, has it been given fully,[98] maximally,[99] without measure. It is fair to say that for

Elipandus, the Word's assuming of a nature which is consubstantial with ours is not in itself salvific but permits a relation to him which is.

Observe that Elipandus's soteriological scheme leaves behind the most prominent theme in Augustine's and Leo's soteriology, which is the emphasis on the Savior as *Mediator* between God and man (1 Tim. 2:5). This theme is present in the writings of Elipandus only in long citations where it has no particular prominence.[100] It is accepted but not emphasized or developed. The preferred term for the Savior, as we have seen, is "First-born." This follows a tradition which is Hispanic, and even more particularly, Isidoran. Note in this connection article 56 of the creed of Toledo XI:

> For he who before the ages was called "Only-begotten" was made "First-born" temporally: "Only-begotten on account of the substance of Godhead; "First-born" on account of the nature of the assumed flesh.[101]

The "qui" ("he who") refers to the eternal *persona* of the Son. Observe how he can be both *unigenitus* and *primogenitus*, without any lapse in the continuity of subject, because of his assumption of the flesh. This is the sort of thinking to which Elipandus's adoptionism must be compared, not Nestorianism, and it is important to observe not only that sources for this passage in Toledo XI are in Isidore,[102] but that through Isidore, it is ultimately Augustine who is speaking.[103] Elipandus's teaching is the term of a process of Hispanic reflection on a theme in older Western (here Augustinian) sources. It is, one could say, an interpretation or a reading of those sources, and in that sense a development of their teaching.

Further, it is not necessary to look much beyond certain elements in the Hispanic (now "Mozarabic") liturgical tradition, to find the origin of the vocabulary of "adoption" and to explain the tenacity with which Elipandus clung to this vocabulary, especially since the liturgy would be a point of distinction between Christian and Muslim, and a mark of the resurgence of Toledo. Elipandus cites the liturgy frequently.[104] This does not mean, however, that Elipandus used the word in the same sense that the liturgy used it, or that we can even be sure what the liturgical usage originally meant.[105]

For our purposes, it is enough to try to understand how he read those texts which he cites, that is, to recreate their context in *his* thought, or, to put it another way, to observe the way in which this traditional liturgical language of "adoption" provides a perspective from which Elipandus reads earlier christological sources like Augustine, Leo, and Isidore. Thus, although the liturgy speaks of the passion of the "adoptive man," for example,[106] this does not mean that Elipandus thought of this man as someone "adopted" by the Word, by the Father, or by anyone else. We have already noticed that he himself never speaks this way, and there is no evidence that he read such liturgical texts this way either. His understanding of these texts is finally available to us only in the way in which he uses their distinctive terminology on his own or in his treatment of themes in other, earlier texts which do not use this vocabulary. We could say that Elipandus uses liturgical language that is familiar to him as the home base for a very striking and creative reading of familiar themes in Western christological sources, and that, in a complementary way, his reading of these sources becomes an interpretation of the liturgical language he started with.

Was Elipandus "Nestorian"?

Having paid careful attention to the teaching of Elipandus on its own terms, it is time to turn to the centuries-old assessment of Elipandus's teaching as a species of Nestorianism. This allegation has taken two distinct forms, one theological and one historical. Theologically, it is charged that Elipandus's teaching amounts to the heresy that there were two persons in Christ. This heresy is called Nestorianism because it has been associated somewhat unfairly with Nestorius, Patriarch of Constantinople 428–431, ever since he was condemned at the Councils of Ephesus in 431 and Chalcedon in 451. The charge that Elipandus is teaching Nestorianism dates back to Pope Hadrian's Letter to the Hispanic bishops of 785.[107] As recently reformulated, the argument runs as follows: Elipandus proposes two mutually exclusive sorts of sonship in Christ, adoptive and natural, and therefore, despite his insistence on the unity of Christ's person, he in effect posits two different sons and hence two persons in Christ—Nestorianism.[108] This argument will be studied more carefully in the discussion of Alcuin and Felix below. It suffices to note here that arguments like this ultimately analyze Elipandus's adoptionism on premises other than his own. Elipandus's notion of *persona* is perhaps not the same as that assumed by the argument. It may even be a critique or rejection of its Augustinian premises.[109] The standard view of adoptionism assumes that the premises of the debate, such as the meaning of *persona*, are givens, and thus goes on to judge Elipandus's christology as though it were an articulation of these givens (e.g., that "sonship" is simply the name of a relation between two *personae*, with no reference to substance). From this point of view Elipandus's christology will always seem self-contradictory, or even deceitful.

While these theological issues will occupy our attention more fully below, the characterization of Elipandus's teaching as logically a form of Nestorianism has led some scholars in recent decades to argue also that historically speaking Elipandus was in fact influenced by the beliefs of Nestorian Christians with whom he had come into contact. These scholars note what they feel to be certain emphases and themes uncharacteristic of what one might expect to find in a late Western author, and character-istic instead of the Nestorians's Antiochene sort of christology, with its emphasis on the distinction between Jesus and the Word of God. It is theorized that Elipandus may actually have known Nestorian Christians himself, or been influenced by their writings, or by the writings of the prominent Antiochene theologians whom they revered such as Theodore of Mopsuestia.

However, the theory of formative Nestorian influence on Elipandus is supported by virtually no historical evidence. It may be reasonable to posit the presence of Nestorians in some parts of late eighth-century Moz-arabic Spain,[110] but it is beyond our powers at present to decide how they were regarded by or assimilated into the general Christian populace. And the presence of a Nestorian population, even if amply documented, is not in itself evidence for Nestorian influence on Mozarabic christology. Nor is it precisely clear what "Nestorian" might describe in this case, since Nes-torian teaching was probably not homogeneous over time, or even, per-haps, over geographical area.[111]

Also, the *motive* for Elipandus's Nestorianizing is alleged to be de-sire for some form of accommodation to the Muslims, either as part of an outright collaborationist movement [112] or as the concession of an overly generous apologetic moment.[113] The major difficulty with this theory is that there are no concessions to Islam, major or minor, dis-cernible in the texts of Elipandus. On the primary sticking point between the two religions—the oneness of God—there is absolutely no discussion or even hint of problematic or compromise. Elipandus is thoroughly and (in the letter to Migetius) even militantly orthodox on the Trinity. That the Trinity was in fact a contemporary issue of debate between Christian and Muslim is shown by the AD 781 *Apology of Timothy I*, which is a record of conversations on two separate days between Timothy I (Nestorian patriarch 780–823) and the Caliph Mahdi.[114] At one point[115] the Patriarch notes,

> And our King said to me: "Do you believe in Father, Son, and Holy Spirit?"—And I answered: "I worship them and believe in them."—Then our King said: "You, therefore, believe in three Gods?"

The next five pages[116] are an exposition of the Trinitarian doctrine in an attempt to explain how it does not represent a belief in three gods, all to no avail, since the argument is renewed and even intensified on the second day, with the King insisting that "Neither three nor two can possibly be said of God,"[117] and that "The number three denotes plurality, and since there cannot be plurality in Godhead, this number three has no room at all in Godhead."[118] This discussion, continuing for more than twenty pages,[119] takes up the greater part of the second day, with the King holding his own all through it, never conceding the point. Nor does Timothy, despite his involvement in an apologetic on this highest level, give any ground.

Further, were it even granted that Elipandus was an open and professed Nestorian, it would still have to be remarked that even the Nestorian christology was distasteful to the Islamic view. For example, in the *Apology of Timothy*, the King cannot bring himself to assent to the Nestorian christology of the patriarch. The discussion on the first day begins with the question raised by the King: "'What, then, do you say that Christ is?'"[120] His consubstantiality with the Godhead is offensive to the King, since it implies plurality in the Godhead. Nor can the King accept the Nestorian christology because, as he keeps on reminding the patriarch, it implies that Christ is two. At one point the King, critiquing the position of Timothy, says,

> There are, therefore, two distinct beings: if one is eternal and God from God as you said, and the other temporal, the latter is therefore a pure man from Mary.[121]

The King continues on with his objections until, without being convinced of his error on the charge of duality, he changes his line of attack to focus on the consubstantiality of the Son. He asks, "How can the spirit [namely, the Father] who has no genital organs beget?"[122] On the second day the topic of christology is again taken up. The King and Timothy both agree that the Monophysite slogan that "God suffered and died in the flesh" is incorrect.[123] But, after Timothy's explanation of his own position that "the

Son and Jesus Christ died in the flesh,"[124] the king, although conceding that Timothy believes "more rightly" than the Monophysites ("'[for] who dares to assert that God dies?'"), flatly refuses any further concession: "'In what, however, you say concerning one Word and Son of God, all of you are wrong.'"[125] And this is the last word. The two depart cordially, but without any agreement or concession from either side. Timothy had even pointed out that in the Koran Christ is the Word and the Spirit of God, but even this fails to suffice as a basis for the apologetic to succeed in convincing either side of even the partial validity of the other position. It must be concluded that at least from this contemporary Muslim perspective that there is no clear advantage associated in Muslim eyes with the advocacy of a christology which is Nestorian.[126]

But the actual christology of Elipandus was not Nestorian. It is true that Elipandus's insistent defense of a one-person christology does not necessarily disqualify him as a Nestorian since the Nestorians also taught a "one-person" christology. But in a fully developed Nestorian system of "two-natures, two-hypostases, one-prosopon," the word "prosopon" means something very different from the Latin word *persona* in general and Elipandus's use of it in particular.[127] For Elipandus, the *persona* of the Son is understood clearly to be that of the Word, the second Person of the Trinity, and any notion of some sort of prosopic union between the Word and an assumed, created *persona* or *prosopon* is roundly and specifically ruled out as in the letter against Migetius. The Nestorian *prosopon*, on the other hand, was a locus for the predicate son and for the unitive worship and honor which they gave to the "son," but little else.[128]

Finally, Elipandus's depiction of the Incarnation as a process in which the subject—the consubstantial *persona* of the Word—remains constant throughout, is a far more unitive scheme than even Theodore of Mopsuestia could assent to.[129] Especially since in Elipandus it is given as an interpretation of Phil. 2:6−11 fully in keeping with Western precedent, it is not likely to have come from Theodore, Nestorius, or any of the other Antiochenes, who paid relatively little attention to this passage or interpreted it very differently. For example, Timothy I, Nestorian patriarch and contemporary of Elipandus, shows very little interest in Phil. 2:6−11. He does not cite it even once in the *Apology*, and only four or five times in his *Letters*. The *Nestorian Collection* evinces equally little concern for these verses from Philippians. Verses 6−7 are cited occasionally, but the citation is always partial—the word "exinanivit" fails to appear even once. Further, where the passage is actually treated, it is exegeted in such a way as to separate out two subjects, one according to the form of God—"he who takes"—and one according to the form of the servant—"he who is taken":

> Think within yourselves that which also Jesus Christ [thought] who, though he was in the form of God, assumed 'the form of a servant.' [Note the omission of "emptied himself."] For whom else would he be calling 'the form of God' but Christ in his godhead, and whom else again would he be naming 'the form of a servant' but Christ in his manhood? And the former, he said, took, while the latter was taken. Therefore it is not possible to confuse the properties of the natures, for it is impossible that he who took should be he who was taken or that he who was taken should be the taker. For that God the Word should be revealed in the man whom he took . . . this we do maintain.[130]

The "exaltation" and bestowal of the name above all other names in verses 8–9, is predicated of a human nature which is an independent subject unto itself.[131] This very divisive way of interpreting Phil. 2:6–11 is as old as the Antiochene tradition itself, where it first finds expression in Diodore of Tarsus.[132] Theodore, in his infrequent citations of the passage, formats the distinction between the "form of God" and the "form of the servant" with his other, customarily divisive, metaphors (e.g., the temple which was assumed vs. the One who indwelt it).[133]

Finally, it is instructive to compare the Nestorian Creed of 612 to Elipandus's "Symbolus Fidei," both of which either cite or allude to Phil. 2:7. Elipandus's "Symbolus" focuses upon the moment of the self-emptying of the Word, and comes up with an exposition of the Incarnation in which the subjectivity of the Word is maintained throughout. The Word is made a man (not "in the likeness" of a man), is crucified, and dies. For the Creed of 612, read by contemporaries of Elipandus as attested to by its inclusion in a collection of texts drawn up at that period, the narrative of the Incarnation runs differently:

> . . . for our salvation, the son of God, God the Word . . . came into the world . . . . And because created natures were not able to behold the glorious nature of his godhead, in an extraordinary manner out of the nature of the house of Adam did he fashion for him a holy temple, a perfect man, from the blessed virgin Mary . . . ; and he put him on and united him with himself, so that henceforth we know as one prosopon our Lord, Jesus Christ, the Son of God . . .[134]

The *prosopon* which is the basis for the "conjunction of the union" (line 24) exists as a result of the union ("henceforth"), *after* the union, which itself is clearly a joining of two subjects, as explained in the exegesis of Phil. 2:6–7 that follows (cited above).

The word *adoptio* itself is used differently by Elipandus on the one hand, and the Nestorians or Antiochenes on the other: for Elipandus it provides a predicate of the Word himself; for the Antiochenes, in the rare instances of its use, it is a predicate of an independently (at least in theory) existent man who may, in addition, have been spoken of as having been "adopted" at a particular point in his career, something which Elipandus would never have permitted.[135] Finally, the assertion that the Word was born and suffered could not have been anything but abhorrent to the Nestorians, while, in addition, the question of Theotokos does not even arise for Elipandus. It is impossible, in sum, to continue to believe either that Elipandus was a Nestorian,[136] or that he was decisively influenced by Nestorians or by Theodore of Mopsuestia.[137]

If this is not the correct solution to the puzzle of the context for Elipandus's adoptionism, the only solution warranted by the evidence is much simpler. Elipandus himself conveniently provides us with a list:

> We make our confession according to the doctrines of the venerable Fathers Hilary, Ambrose, Augustine, Jerome, Fulgentius, Isidore, Eugenius, Ildefonsus, Julian, and others who are catholic and orthodox.[138]

This list, with the addition of Leo and Gregory upon whom Elipandus also drew heavily, reproduces almost exactly the roster of major sources for the Creeds of Toledo.[139] Elipandus's actual practice is in agreement with his list: almost every citation he makes is from one of these Western authors.[140] There is no warrant for looking outside of this circle of tradition for the context of Elipandus's adoptionism, since every element of it makes sense from within this circle.

Some scholars note with disapproval that Elipandus does not mention Nestorius in the list of heretics he anathematizes for the Bishops of Frankland.[141] To them this lapse adds to the evidence that Elipandus was a Nestorian sympathizer. Yet a different construction may be put upon this evidence, for after all Elipandus does not mention Eutyches in the list either, nor does he charge Beatus or Heterius (that wild ass)[142] with being a Eutychian, or a follower of Eutyches, or acephalite, or any other term recalling the monophysitism of the fifth century or its descendants. In fact, Elipandus, who is never at a loss for an appropriate name for Beatus, never insults or critiques him by calling him a Eutychian, even though he charges Beatus with not taking the flesh of Christ seriously.[143] This cannot be explained by ignorance of Eutyches or of his position.[144] The point is, rather, that the Eastern controversies of the fifth century and later are the wrong context for the interpretation of Elipandus's theology. Elipandus does not list Nestorius or Eutyches in his anathemata because he is simply not interested. He does not think in terms of the polarity Nestorius-Eutyches or in the christological categories, largely Eastern and fifth century, which define it. His thinking is a development of themes that are found in Latin authors without any reference to Eastern positions or Eastern figures.

It is thus especially noteworthy that he prefers to compare Beatus's error to that of Faustus the Manichaean,[145] explicitly using a citation from Augustine to make his point, instead of invoking the Council of Chalcedon and its condemnation of Eutyches, despite Elipandus's continuing and insistent defense of what became its formula, "one-person, two-natures." This cannot, once again, be attributed to ignorance.[146] Rather, Elipandus does not recognize the formula as specifically and exclusively as *Chalcedon*'s: it is a common element in major Western sources, still available for reflection and development. And, although Elipandus cites Leo heavily, the vast majority of the Leonine material comes not from the famous Tome to Flavian, but from the Letter to Leo I, Emperor.[147] It is also significant that neither Leo nor Gregory is included among those in his list of "venerable Fathers." Elipandus has pretty much the same list of "Fathers" as Leo himself has, if the Greeks are excluded from Leo's list.[148] It is as though Elipandus still considers himself a part of the current of christological reflection which includes, but which was not closed by, Leo. Christology is still an area of doctrine open to development. What we call Elipandus's adoptionism is not a new christology invented from whole cloth, but a highly original attempt at explaining older christological thinking found in traditional Western sources. From Elipandus's point of view, if it is orthodox to say with Augustine that the Son of God, the Word, became "predestined" and "full of grace," and if it is orthodox to say with Leo that the self-emptied Word was "exalted," then it is perfectly orthodox, and even necessary, to say that the self-emptied Word became "adoptive."[149]

3. Beatus

If Elipandus seemed elusive as an historical figure, his outspoken contemporary critic, Beatus of Liebana, has left us with an even fainter shadow. We know for certain only that he was a monk,[1] probably an abbot[2] and a priest as well,[3] in the northwestern region of Spain called the Asturias,[4] one of the areas never controlled by the Muslims. The little *Vita*[5] found in a Martyrology of Astorga places his death at 19 February 798, and portrays him as a counselor of the Queen Adosinda,[6] wife of King Silo of Leon. As Beatus mentions her himself,[7] we can well believe this, and imagine therefore that he was a personage of considerable esteem and influence in northern Spain, even outside of the monastery, and even after the death of King Silo in 783. Beatus counted the young bishop Heterius of Osma among his disciples,[8] and evidence already reviewed suggests that he had been able to rally a considerable body of supporters to his side in his dispute with the Archbishop. It is interesting to speculate here: was Beatus attempting to set up Heterius, a person over whom he had complete influence, as a rival bishop to Elipandus, not necessarily as a rival bishop of Toledo, but as a bishop in a new see, one in the "free" regions, which would be a rival to Toledo? Although one may not agree with the depiction of Elipandus's teaching as an accommodation to Islam, it is possible that Beatus is trying to paint Elipandus as an accommodationist, and has singled out his use of the word "adoption" in order to make the point that the bishop of Toledo was a heretic compromised in his theology. Beatus says that the Church in Asturia was divided—presumably between a party loyal to Elipandus and one dissatisfied. In setting up Heterius as a rival, perhaps with Adosinda's patronage, Beatus would be giving a certain legitimation and direction to the party unhappy with the awkward circumstance of belonging to a see in what was, in effect, a hostile country. It is significant that the only section of the *Adversus Elipandum* that is given in Heterius's own voice is a recitation of the "Ephesine" (actually the Nicene) Creed, as though from some sort of public ceremony meant to demonstrate that Heterius, unlike Elipandus, was of unquestioned orthodoxy.[9]

Such as it is, this must for the present remain our portrait of this obscure but charismatic and politically canny figure from the mountains of Asturia, apart from whatever impressions about his character may be made to emerge from his writings themselves. To these writings we must now turn.

Compared to what remains of the literary output of Migetius and of Elipandus, there survives of Beatus's works a sizeable theological corpus consisting of two major works. The first is the long *Commentary on the Apocalypse*,[10] completed in 776 but revised twice by 786.[11] There is hardly an original paragraph in the whole work,[12] but it does show us a scholar well acquainted with Western Patristic scholarship on the subject, and is a valuable source for recovery of the lost *Commentary* on the Apocalypse by Tyconius, on which Beatus has relied heavily.[13] In addition, there is a tradition of manuscript illumination associated with the text of this *Commentary* which has made the MSS of this text valuable to the art historian and even more valuable for the theologian than they would have been unadorned.[14] The second work, the "Letter" against Elipandus, is actually a full length treatise (130 columns in Migne) divided into two books and written about 785.[15] The bishop Heterius is given in the salutation as a co-author but the extent of his contribution is unclear and perhaps rather minimal.[16] The work has an unmistakably eschatological cast. There are many borrowings from Beatus's own *Commentary on the Apocalypse*, as well as from a wide variety of other, almost exclusively Western[17] authors. Some of these citations are probably from works now lost. Certainly there is some reliance on Tyconius. Note the following, for example:

> There are heretics called Circumcellions, who for the love of martyrdom kill themselves. Such also are those readers [of Scripture] who seek to completely strip the soul from the body of the letter.[18]

The sections surrounding this passage[19] have as a topic the interpretation of Scripture in its various senses. The juxtaposition of a reference to the Circumcellions, a name with mostly local, fourth-century African significance, with a rather sophisticated theory of the interpretation of Scripture, cannot fail to lead the mind to Tyconius or some other writer of the same background.[20] Also, the preoccupation with the mystery of who exactly is in the Church, with special concern for the status of heretics, has a strong savor of Donatist provenance.[21] Note too the long section, probably a citation, on how to tell a Catholic from a heretic, even though both are within the same Church.[22]

However, despite what is probably a greater frequency of recourse to citation than we are probably aware of, there is no question that this work shows Beatus as a capable thinker in his own right, the master of an excellent and chaste prose, a scholar able not only to cite earlier authorities but also to appropriate their thought and to use it in a context different from its original one. It is a handsome work, single-minded in intention throughout. It is unfortunate, therefore, that scholars of this century have paid it relatively little attention, and in some cases have actually derided it as stylistically difficult to follow, labyrinthine, and digressive, and theologically docetic, monophysitic, inept, and, ultimately, unfair to Elipandus.[23] The truth is that it has been lying unexamined, theologically speaking, for so long that its theological significance has been forgotten and its fairness to Elipandus as well as its relation to the issue have come to be judged solely on the basis of a few slogans and catch-words taken wholly out of context. At this point, the question to be asked is not how germane the arguments are to the issue, but rather what precisely *was* the issue, theologically speaking? Only a close reading of the text of Beatus can help to answer this question.[24]

Common Ground

In the first place there is an astonishing amount of common ground between Beatus and Elipandus which is never pointed out. Above all, they share a common admiration for the doctors of the Spanish church, especially Isidore. They make frequent appeal to the texts of these writers, and exhibit prominently certain themes distinctive to late patristic Hispanic theology.[25] They both seem to have the same scant regard for Rome and for Roman prerogative. Beatus never invokes the authority of Rome.[26] In his interpretation of the passage "Tu es Petrus," he refuses to restrict the charge even to Peter, much less to the Roman church or its bishop. Elipandus had observed that this charge applies to the whole church; Beatus too will remark that the promise "Upon this rock I will build my church" applies not only to Peter, but to all who have received the name "petrus" from the true Rock who is Christ, just as Peter himself did.[27] Third, like Elipandus, Beatus never cites Chalcedon as an authority,[28] and other reminiscence of the fifth century christological controversies is all but suppressed. Elipandus did not find it natural to call Beatus a monophysite or a Eutychian; Beatus, even in the one place where he does mention Nestorius, does not go on to brand Elipandus as Nestorian.[29] Rather, he consistently compares Elipandus either to the Manichees, who were long the butt of antique Western polemic, or to the Jews, in keeping with the unfortunate and extreme anti-Semitism of the Visigoths in Hispania.[30]

Normally it is not remarkable that the parties on either side of a controversy should have much in common, and thus in some ways it is begging the question to point out the common ground. But where, as in this case, the two parties have been portrayed as so distantly separated in christology as the Nestorians and the monophysites were, it is appropriate to show that in christology they were not that distant, or, even better, that the separation between them was aligned differently than that between Nestorian and monophysite. It is not otiose to point out that they are closer together relative to these poles than previously imagined, because this means that the issue between them is different than previously imagined.

In fact, relative to the poles of Nestorianism and monophysitism, Beatus's christology is almost an exact match to Elipandus's. Beatus's christology follows the model, prevalent in the West since Tertullian, of two natures or substances and one person. The Word made flesh is one Christ Jesus, one person, God and man, just as our body and our soul together make one human being:

> We are taught that Jesus Christ, the Son of God, the God-Man, was born of the virgin, just as the soul is born with the body. Not because there is one substance formed out of or from both of these, but because one person is in both.[31]

Beatus explicitly rejects any theory involving only "one substance." Later he notes:

> The Son alone was made human, not in unity of nature, but in unity of person: Light, begotten of the Father without beginning, assumed our nature. . . . One nature is of the flesh. One substance belongs both to Christ and to us, just as one substance belongs both to Christ and the Father. With the Father, he is both full and complete God, and, with us, fully and completely human. Christ is one person of two natures, God and human, because *The Word was made flesh, and dwelt among us.*[32]

Quoting from a pseudo-Augustinian treatise, he affirms that there remain two substances in the Lord Jesus Christ, God and human, our maker and our Redeemer, even though there is without any doubt one person.[33] The Unigenitus, who is God by nature—so that[34] he might become a true (sc., human) priest in the very person of his divinity—did not receive the person of a human being, but rather the nature. He received into his very own Person a truly real servile nature, or (in the language of Phil. 2:7) the "form of a slave." Thus,

> although in him the nature of divinity was one thing, and the servile nature another, yet there was in the one and same Christ that *persona* of divinity, now the very *persona* of the assumed humanity as well.[35]

Nothing could be clearer than this. The unique Son, the Word, invisible according to his own nature, took up our visible nature, so that, according to the nature of the body, he might be seen.[36] Keeping with strong Hispanic precedent,[37] the fundamental christological structure is sometimes expressed in terms of one person and *three* substances, counting flesh and soul as two separate substances in addition to divinity:

> The Son alone was made human, that is, rational soul and flesh. And because of this, the Word, the soul, and the flesh are indeed three substances, but Christ is one, the Son is unique, the one Jesus Christ our Lord, Only-begotten Son of God the Father . . . one person of three substances, one Christ . . . Behold the Mediator![38]

The same three-fold structure is evident in the following passage on the unity of Christ:

> Behold the whole Christ, Word, soul, and flesh! . . . If you subtract one substance from the three substances of Christ, that is, by saying that it does not belong to Christ, you thereby deny the whole Christ . . .[39]

The usual caveats are given: that the divinity was not changed into humanity,[40] that the Word remains eternally one with the Father,[41] and that divinity remains impassible while the human nature suffers,[42] although, because of the unity of person, one can use such expressions as the "blood of God" and the "crucifixion of the Lord of Glory" with impunity.

Like Elipandus and the later Western tradition as a whole and unlike any monophysite, Beatus refers easily and spontaneously to the human nature that was assumed as a *homo*: the "human being taken up by the Word" (*homo susceptus* or *homo assumptus*).[43] Sometimes Beatus's use of these expressions seems to assign to the *homo* a virtual independence, and this results in christological phraseology which seems at times even more divisive than that which Elipandus is prepared to use. Explaining Jn. 3:13, one of the passages habitually used to illustrate the "exchange of properties" (*communicatio idiomatum*) between the two natures of Christ and hence their unity, Beatus speaks of the *homo* and the *Word* almost as two discrete and separate entities whose unity is merely declared, not explained.[44] Again, after citing a pseudo-Augustinian exegesis of Ps. 67:24, where the foot which is dipped in blood is referred to the human nature of Christ, Beatus goes on to explain that it is the *homo assumptus* that actually suffers, not God. God endures the passion under the affect of a "co-sufferer."[45] This skates perilously close to the establishment of two subjects in Christ. So, too, does the following passage, which seems to separate the "one who takes up" from the "one who is taken up and in whom he dwells":

> Jesus, who was crucified under Pontius Pilate and buried, is himself the Son of God, the Only-begotten Son of God, of two natures, not two [sons]. This very one who is the Only-begotten Son of God is also the *first-born among many brethren* [Rom. 8:29]." And, although the designations "Only-begotten" and "First-born" belong to different natures, yet on account of his *susceptor* (God Only-begotten), the man himself is called "Only-begotten," since the Only-begotten is in him.[46]

Beatus sometimes verges on adoptionism itself, broadly speaking. Consider the following observations on Psalm 44:8 = Heb. 1:9:

> You have heard what he said, *You loved justice*, and on the contrary, *hated iniquity*. Hear what he received for these virtues: *Therefore, God, your God, has anointed you with the oil of gladness above your fellows*. This is said to Christ: "Jesus Christ, you have been anointed, so that you might anoint others by the unguent which fell down into the beard, into the beard of Aaron" [Ps. 132:2]. The unguent in the head descended to the beard, that is, from the true God to the man he deigned to assume. From the man he assumed it fell down into the hem of his garment, which we are.[47]

How similar this is to Elipandus's exegesis of the same verses![48] Beatus's language also more or less faithfully mirrors the divisive language of Jeronme, his authority for this exegesis of Ps. 132:2.[49] There are other passages beyond those cited here in which the exegesis of Beatus seems almost adoptionistic and is very reminiscent of Elipandus's exegesis.[50]

Despite Beatus's tendency to use or to cite language which is weighted towards the divisive end of the range of christological vocabulary, he still operates well within the limits imposed by the general Western formulaic, "one person, two natures," where the *persona* of the Word is the locus of unity, subjectivity, and continuity with the time before the

Incarnation.[51] Beatus demonstrates his profound appreciation of this unity with two remarkable heuristic devices. One amplifies the common body and soul analogy: the *persona* is the locus of union of these two natures because it is always a *persona* to which a proper name corresponds. For example, we say *Peter* is in heaven even though only his soul is actually there.[52] The general rule is "Agit persona quaeque substantia totum una persona," that is, "Whatever any one of the substances belonging to a *persona* does, that the *persona* does as a whole."[53] The *persona* is defined here in terms of *act* and not in terms of the properties or limitations of any nature it may possess. The *persona* is the *agent*, and as such serves perfectly as the locus of a proper name, that is, of the unity and subjectivity of any nature belonging to it.

The second heuristic model Beatus presents is that of a book. The joining of the "externals" of the book—the lettering, the cover, pages, and binding—with its "internals,"—its *meaning*—provides Beatus with an analogy of two very different substances which are, nevertheless, joined in a unity which is anything but artificial. Just so are the two natures in Christ joined: there is an inseparable union of entities which remain distinct, even in their union. They are not mixed.[54]

To summarize:

1. Beatus is not a monophysite.
2. His christology is in many respects similar to that of Elipandus.[55] In fact, apart from the use of the word *adoptivus*, they have a *common* christology, a variant of the one-person, two-nature *homo assumptus* christology long familiar in the West.
3. One need look no further than such Western writers as Augustine, Ambrose, and Leo, together with their seventh and eighth century Hispanic interpreters (especially Isidore, Julian of Toledo, and the Creeds of the Councils of Toledo), to find the sources from which this christology was developed. It is entirely explicable from within these Western contexts.

These three points suggest two others, which can be regarded as theses for further discussion:

4. The issue at stake in the Hispanic adoptionist controversy is the interpretation of this common christology.
5. More specifically, the question centers wholly around the *human*

being who was *assumed*: is he *adoptivus* or not? It is *not* a question of the mode of his connection to divinity, since, on both accounts, his person is that of the Word.

The demonstration of these points will occupy the rest of this chapter. First it will be necessary to integrate the christology of Beatus back into the wider context of his thought as a whole.

Caput et Corpus, Una Persona

The most striking and characteristic feature of Beatus's theology is the virtual equivalence of what we today distinguish as christology and ecclesiology. What contemporary theologians see as two related but ultimately distinct spheres of inquiry are not really distinguishable for Beatus. In his thinking they are two dimensions or movements of a single reflection upon the identity and significance of Jesus.

If this conflation of ecclesiology with christology is one of the most striking and characteristic features of Beatus's theology, it proves also to be its most elegant and moving feature as well. It is very Pauline. If the author of Colossians refers to the Church as Christ's body, and to himself as completing in his own flesh what is lacking in the sufferings of Christ (Col. 1:24), Beatus develops this thinking into the claim, curious at first, that the Church is not only one Body with Christ, but also one *persona* with him. He thus presses the technical term *persona* from christology, to our sensibilities its more traditional locus, into service in ecclesiology.[56]

This notion of the "personal" identity of Christ with the Church undergoes a transition from the earlier work of Beatus to his later work. Its original context is the unequivocal apocalyptic dualism of the source(s) of the *Commentary on the Apocalypse*, where it is often repeated that "there are two parties in the world, the people of God and the people of the devil."[57] We cannot help but be reminded of Augustine, but it is more likely that this eschatological dualism comes from Tyconius, to whom Augustine himself probably owes more than we had at one time suspected.[58] These two "parties" are also called two "cities," one of the devil, and one of God,[59] whose "kings" are the devil and Christ, respectively.[60] Most often, the two opposing groups are referred to as "bodies," with Christ at the head of one and the devil at the head of the other.

As Christ and the Church are one Head with members, so evil human beings are also one body with the devil, their Head.[61]

The children of the devil are those who worship idols,[62] or *appear* to worship Christ while their deeds belie their worship.[63]

An apocalyptic starkness colors all. One must decide between the body of the devil and the body of Christ, continually fighting as they are each against the other.[64] One must be on guard especially against the wiles and deceit of those who seem to be preaching Christ but are actually members of the devil. One is constituted as a member of either body by "imitating" its head.[65] For the members of the body of the devil, this means refusal to worship Christ,[66] including not only those who are not baptized, but also those within the church who are evil, especially bishops and priests who live "carnally."[67] But for the body of Christ, this "imitation" consists mostly of remaining faithful *during persecution*, of enduring and submitting to suffering as Christ did.[68] The body of Christ is constituted by solidarity with him in suffering:

> "Jerusalem," in Latin, is rendered "vision of peace"; but the church cannot have peace here, because it is struggling in persecution. . . . This Jerusalem is under the foot of the woman who stones the prophets and kills those sent to her. In this Jerusalem the Lamb is daily immolated. He is crucified through his members, and he, who suffers daily, cannot have peace in this world.[69]

The Church recapitulates the passion of Christ.[70] It is in this context of the stark apocalyptic call to identity with either the devil's purposes or with Christ's that we must read the following passage:

> Moreover, just as the very Redeemer of the world is one person with the congregation of the good—for he himself is the Head of the Body and we the Body of this Head—so also the Ancient Enemy is one person with the whole collection of the reprobate, because he is for them the preeminence of iniquity and thus a sort of head for them.[71]

This is the only time the word *persona* is used in this clearly non-technical, non-christological fashion, so that it cannot be imagined that either Beatus or any of the sources underlying the *Commentary* meant to mark anything more than the radical solidarity of those committed to either side of the grand apocalyptic rivalry.

In the *Adversus Elipandum* the eschatological context for this peculiar use of the word *persona* is retained. The second book bears the title, "On Christ and his Body, which is the Church, And On the Devil and his Body,

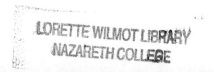

which is Antichrist." We go on to read that evil people constitute the body of the devil, who is their head, and that, similarly, "Christ and the Church is [sic] Head and Body, *one person.*"[72]

> For just as . . . those who cling to the evils which come from the devil (that is, heresy, pride, puffing-up, etc.) become with the devil one person, head and body, so, on the contrary, do those who cling to the qualities (that is, humility, patience, obedience, etc.) with which Christ came into the world.

This "clinging to" or "observation" of the "qualities" of Christ joins head and body, thus constituting the Church, the one Christ.[73] That the primary locus of this unity is in suffering is still evident, although the suffering is no longer restricted primarily to persecution. Every servant of God who has the right faith and loves every person as the self, drinks the cup of Christ. This cup is one, and insofar as we drink it, Christ drinks it, for Head and Body are one person.[74] Beatus responds to the sarcasm and name-calling of Elipandus by informing him that his insults are actually injuries to Christ:

> They are not ours, but rather his, whom we adore . . . And yet, although they are his injuries, they are ours as well, because Head and Body are one person.[75]

It is clear that this consistent use of the expression *una persona* to refer to the unity of Christ and his Church has developed far beyond the desultory and inconsequential usage in the *Commentary*, where it served merely as a marker setting off the cosmic opposition between the camp of the devil and that of Christ. Here, in the *Adversus Elipandum*, the word *persona* is used so profusely in its technical, christological sense that it is impossible not to hear these claims about Christ and the Church being one *persona* without hearing overtones of the technical usage, even if Beatus had not taken care to make such reference explicit. He has, however, taken this care, and with the most startling results. Christ in his humanity has the same substance constitutive of humanity that the rest of us have, but because he is Lord and Redeemer of the Church, having redeemed it with his blood, He is one substance[76] with it in a special way, as a man is one substance with his own body.[77] Christ possesses the substance of the Church as *his own*; it becomes his *personal* possession; it is joined *to his person*:

> The unhappy [heretic] is not aware that Christ is one, God and human being, and is the Head of his Church, in which, as a human being, he is. And God

is the Head of Christ, that is, the whole of the divine nature is the Head of the human being whom the Son alone took up. The Son, as a human being, is the Head of the Church which is joined to this Head. Thus there comes into being the whole Christ, Head and body, one person.[78]

This does not mean that the flesh or humanity of Christ is not truly human, but that precisely because the Word assumed a true human nature, including real human flesh, the Church can be permitted to be "personally" joined to him as well. It is because we can be joined to him humanity to humanity, flesh to flesh, that we can also be permitted to belong to the Word personally as well:

> The Word was made flesh (Jn. 1:14), but it was not changed into flesh, just as the soul of human beings is not changed into flesh. And since the Word dwells in the flesh of Christ, it [sc., the Word] dwells in our nature, because that very flesh is ours. To this flesh is joined the Church, and there [thus] comes into being the whole Christ, one person, Head and Body.[79]

The humanity of Jesus serves as a sort of middle term which, because we are in fact able to join ourselves to it, enables us in some sense to share in the personal unity which it has with the Word. The point is that we do not have union with God in the abstract, but rather as members of the Body of Christ, as united to a human being, that is, to Jesus.

Certainly this is far from monophysitism. In fact, it is reminiscent of Elipandus, for whom it is the human being Jesus who plays such a crucial soteriological role as the "primogenitus." Beatus prefers the term "mediator" for Christ, a term little used by Elipandus but a favorite one of Augustine (ultimately from 1 Tim. 2:5). Christ is the "mediator" precisely because in his role as head of the Church he appropriates us to his person,[80] and thus to God, since his persona is that of the eternal Son. The point is that union with this particular human being is union with God, something which for us, of course, cannot be natural or substantial,[81] but must be "personal." He mediates to us, his substance and his members, nothing less than unity with the persona of the Son, the Word of God:

> Only the Son was made a human being, that is, rational soul and flesh. Because of this there are indeed three substances—the Word, the soul, and the flesh—but there is one Christ who is the unique Son, our one Lord Jesus Christ, Only-begotten of God the Father, who was born of the Holy Spirit and the Virgin Mary and who was crucified under Pontius Pilate. He truly and without any falsehood has God as his Father naturally, from whom he has his deity, so that he is, thus, true God, and there is no other God beside him

[Ex. 20:3]. Equally truly and without falsehood he has for his mother Mary, naturally. And there is no other human being beside him [i.e., no separate *homo* who was or could have been adopted into sonship]. Together with the whole Church, which he redeemed with his own blood, he is the one Christ, one *persona* of three substances. This *persona* is not the Father's nor the Holy Spirit's, but, as we have said, the Son's. Behold the Mediator![82] [The heretics] fail to confess that there is *no other God beside* him, and that together with the whole Church he is one human being, and that it is not the case that the Church is one *persona*, and Christ the human being another *persona*, and the Word another *persona* (so that there would be three *personae*, the Word, the human being, and the Church, just as the Father, the Son, and the Holy Spirit are three *personae*).[83]

This is a very strong claim, but it is also by now a very familiar one, for this notion of the Church's "personal" union with the Word is Beatus's analysis of adoptive sonship, of the sonship which we have through grace. Our "personal" union with the Son of God means our "adoption" into the same sonship which he has eternally with the Father. Our "personal" union with the Word means that we are adopted into a new relation with the Father, into the same relation which the Word possesses, except that we possess it adoptively, by grace. This can be demonstrated and further clarified through an examination of Beatus's exegesis of Phil. 2:6–11, the same passage which was earlier so crucial to a proper understanding of Elipandus's christology.

Regula Ecclesiae

Beatus uses the crucial verse Phil. 2:7 to illustrate his discussion of the notion of *persona* at *Adversus Elipandus* 1.60, where he takes pains to explain as precisely as possible the mystery of Christ's inner structure or constitution. Just as, he begins, a human being, such as Peter, is one *persona* of ("ex") two substances and has the name "Peter," so too Christ is one *persona* only of ("ex") *three* substances (or two natures), and has the name "Christ."[84] It is of no consequence that *only* Peter's body died, or that *only* his soul now reigns in heaven with Christ—it is still properly said that *Peter* died or *Peter* reigns. There are not two Peters, only one.[85] Such is the case, too, when we come to consider the three substances of Christ. One is eternal, equal to the Father, invisible, immortal, impassible, immutable, and without place; but the other two, the rational soul and the body, are temporal and "of" or "from ours" ("de nostro").[86] In virtue of what he has "from ours," the Son who is God, eternal, impassible, and immortal, can and did actually become human, suffer, and die.[87] The Word, the soul, and the flesh are not three Christs, but one Christ the Son of God—even though the flesh which alone lay dead in the tomb was Christ the Son of God, and the soul which descended to hell was Christ the Son of God, and the Word who remained always equal to the Father was Christ the Son of God. These three are one Christ, just as in the example of Peter, his flesh and soul were one Peter.[88] The point is, "Agit persona quaeque substantia totum una persona,"—a "person" does what each of its natures does as a whole and as one person.[89] Although actions take place in a nature, the *persona* is properly speaking the only agent or subject of these actions, and as such is the locus for their unity.

Thus, it is "natural"—it pertains to a *nature*—that the Son is equal to the Father, is everywhere as the Father is, is invisible, impassible, eternal, etc., as the Father is. It is also "natural"—it pertains to a *nature*—that the Son came into the world, was made "a little less than the angels" (Ps. 8:5 [LXX], Heb. 2:7), was localized, and suffered. These predicates, Beatus emphasizes, belong *only* to the Son,[90] not to the Father or the Holy Spirit, but only to the second *persona* of the Trinity. The reason: only the Son has "emptied" himself (Phil. 2:7) by acquiring another nature which represents for him the possibility of suffering and death:

> I say that only the Son dies because only the Son empties himself. His emptying is his coming. His coming is his humanity, a humanity which is soul and body, that is, a full and complete human being.[91]

Note that the emptying itself is not assigned to a nature,[92] because this act in and of itself *does not pertain to a nature*. It belongs only to the *persona*, the Son, who emptied himself, that is, who welcomed another, lower, nature as his own. His emptying himself (in language which is thoroughly reminiscent of Elipandus and his use of Leo)[93] *is* his coming, *is* his humanity (does not "belong" or "pertain" to it), *is* the *homo* full and complete. This human being *is* the self-emptying of the Son of God, the self-emptying of the second *persona* of the Trinity, set before all to see. There is and can be no human being like this human being, for he is constituted, defined, as and by the act of self-emptying of the divine *persona*, the Son.

Paradoxically—and here we must locate the genius of Beatus's exposition of this late Hispanic christology—the Son is constituted as fully and perfectly human *because* he is at the same time fully and completely God.

That is, because this man *is* the self-emptying of God, he must be totally and fully human, otherwise there would be no true self-emptying. He must at the same time be God, who alone can achieve such a perfect self-emptying:

> The man is himself God, the Son of God. And the Son alone, who with the Father and the Holy Spirit is the one God, is a man. He is not one man with the Father and the Holy Spirit, but he is one man with the whole Church, because Christ is, Head and Body, one person.[94]

With this last sentence Beatus has joined together his discussion of the word *persona*, his reflection on Phil. 2:7, and his idea that the church is "one person" with Christ. This means that for the Head of the Church, who shares our nature, all the actions of that nature, including death itself, are acts of the self-emptying or humility of God, and that for those joined to him in that nature it is possible for their actions, which take place in the shared nature, to be equally or at least participatively the self-emptying of God, to be, that is, the act or *work* of God and in this way be saved (remember that it is as the Church's Redeemer that Jesus is head of the Church). The *persona* is preeminently the locus of act ("Agit persona . . .") and the formation of the church is God's act which brings us into *personal* union with God through our Head, the Mediator.[95] Our natures remain ours but become the locus of God's act or work. We are defined ever more closely by active, that is, personal, unity with God through Christ.

One could say that the self-emptying of the Word is the charter or constitution of the Church, an act with which the Church is suffused and thereby defined. The Church is the continuation in our natures of this act of the *persona* of the Word. Thus the self-emptying or humility of the Word is sometimes referred to as a *rule* which forms the church.[96] It is distinguished from the rule which the devil instituted for his members when he grasped at something which was not his, namely the form of God (Phil. 2:6), by saying "I shall be like the Most High" (Is. 14:14).[97] The rule which forms the body of the devil is pride, that *superbia* or *tumor cordis* which elevates the self in a perverse attempt to imitate the stature of God.[98] In contradistinction to this illegitimate will to omnipotence, Christ, lowering himself rather than others, empties himself and forms his Church by infusing through it this act of humility:

> Accordingly, our Lord Jesus Christ, *although he was in the form of God, did not deem equality with God something to be grasped at, but emptied himself, accepting*

the form of a servant, and was made in the likeness of human beings and found in fashion as a man [Phil. 2:6–7]. So that he might proffer us an example of humility and love, he lowered not others, but himself. For, although he was according to the excellence of his divinity the Only-begotten, without brethren, for us he was made the First-born, according to his taking up of a human being, in which [taking up] he deigned, through the adoption of grace, to *have* brethren to whom he could bear the relation of "First-born."[99] He himself, through the prophet, says of these brethren, *Behold, how good and how merry it is for brothers to dwell in unity!* [Ps. 132:1] . . . This rule, which the Church now holds, descends from the Head himself (whose Body is the Church), . . . *just,* as the Psalmist says, *like the oil which descends from the head down to the beard of Aaron* (Ps. 132:2).[100]

The self-emptying of Phil. 2:6–7 forms not only Christ, but also the Church which is his Body. Since this self-emptying belongs first and foremost to the *persona* of the Word and to neither one of his natures in and of themselves, its presence within us, within *our* natures, means that his *persona* has taken us up as well, although through Christ our head. The saving work of Christ is *to make the Church*, to form a humanity united through him, the Mediator, to the *persona* of the Word, and thus children of the Father as he is, only adoptive ones through grace. It is thus that he is the *primogenitus*. He is the primogenitus *because* he is the Mediator. By enabling us to participate in his self-emptying, in his lowliness and humility—in a word, in his *servantship*—he mediates to us his sonship as well.[101]

Beatus versus Elipandus

We are now prepared to turn to the substance of the controversy proper and to isolate its issue. Addressing Elipandus, Beatus says,

> . . . You say to me, "What I [Elipandus] am saying, I am saying with reference only to the human being [and not, to the divine nature]." And I too—what I now say, *I* say with reference only to the human being. [102]

This puts the focus of the controversy in a nutshell. The controversy is focused squarely on the *human being* which the christology common to both Beatus and Elipandus posits as the self-emptying of the Word.

It can scarcely be sufficiently emphasized how much autonomy and independence this *homo* had for these late Hispanic thinkers who have presented a christology in which the very perfection of the identity of Jesus with God guarantees his perfect and complete autonomy as a man. The point is that since the human being *is* the self-emptying of the Word, he must be a human being perfect and complete, otherwise the self-emptying of the Word would not be perfect and complete. It is the paradoxical independence of the human thus constituted that caused the controversy. It is a controversy about how to describe this human being.

In a remarkable passage, Beatus expands on a passage from Cassian [103] to demonstrate how truly complete the autonomy of the man Jesus was. The humility of God, that is, his being human, was so perfect that even the devil, who *knew* that this human was the Son of God, could not resist tempting him:

> The devil said, "We know that you are the Son of God. . . ." [Mt. 4:3]. The ancient Enemy thus did know that God his conqueror had come into the world as the Redeemer of the human race. Yet when he first saw that he could suffer . . . everything which he had believed concerning his divinity came into doubt under the elation of his pride . . . When he caught sight of a human being, he doubted that it was God. Whence the temptation, "*If* you are the Son of God, command these stones to become loaves of bread [Mt. 4:4]. Because, when the devil saw that he was passible, he did not believe that he was born God, but only that he was kept in custody by God's grace. How great the lowliness of the Son of God! [104]

The devil began to wonder whether Jesus was really God, or whether he was merely a human being kept safe in the custody of God's grace and thus essentially similar to the rest of us. For Beatus, this is exactly the mistake of Elipandus. The Son of God's humility is so true and so perfect that it is easy to mistake it for something already familiar to us, and thus to misinterpret the self-emptying of the Word, to carry it too far. And so, citing Elipandus's *Symbolum*, and prefixing the citation (as does Elipandus himself) [105] with a reference to Phil. 2:7, Beatus joins the issue:

> [Paul] in his letters never dared to say, as you do, that on account of the emptying of divinity, "Both we are adoptive ones and he is adoptive; both we are christs and he is the Christ; both we are little ones and he is the Little One" and the rest of the filth which you have dared to utter about our Lord Jesus Christ, including "he is a servant among servants." [106]

Beatus is claiming that Elipandus has not interpreted this crucial passage correctly, and that he must abuse the passage from Phillipians in order to draw his conclusions. Beatus seems continually to be citing and rebutting this slogan, "Et nos adoptivi et ille adoptivus, et nos Christi . . . [etc.]," as though he cannot get over the affront it offers his sensibilities.

The opening chapters of his work are a retort to this offending passage. Attention is focused from the start upon the human being Jesus. The argument is introduced by a citation of Ambrose's *Commentary on Luke*, at the point where he discusses Peter's denial of Jesus. Ambrose points out that Peter's denial is a denial of a *man*: Peter himself says, "I do not know the man!"[107] Instead of saying "I do not know the God," or "I do not know the Son of God," Peter says "I do not know the *man*," yet when he denies this man, he is denying his previous confession that this man was "the Christ, the Son of the living God" (Mt. 16:16).

Beatus remarks that after Peter's confession, Jesus told Peter that "flesh and blood" had not revealed the truth to him, but rather his Father in heaven. Had "flesh and blood," the "human being whom God assumed,"[108] revealed anything in and of themselves, it would essentially have been what the devil concluded from looking at the man Jesus:

> He to whom "flesh and blood" had revealed anything would have had to say, "You are adoptive according to your humanity, and Son of the living God according to your divinity."[109]

Beatus mocks Elipandus here by citing his words as though they were a parody of Peter's confession. But he is careful to center the discussion around the human being Jesus, demonstrating that he has understood Elipandus and that they are talking about the same entity, the "son of the virgin":

> Does someone presume to dissolve the Gospel? Or to believe one part of it and not another? . . . God himself has declared it, the Son has proved it, the earth, quaking, testifies, the waters obey, the elements surrender, stones are split, the sun darkened, and does the heretic, rational as he is supposed to be, pretend that the son of the Virgin is not the Son of God?[110]

Who is the Son of God if not the man whom the Virgin bore? If he were not, the angel could not have announced to Mary, "You shall call his name Jesus, and he shall be called great and the Son of the Most High " (Lk. 1: 31–32), but rather, "He shall be called Jesus, adoptive Son of the Most High as regards his humanity, although absolutely not adoptive as regards his divinity."[111] Beatus, lest he be outdone in the rhetoric of insult, derisively places Elipandus's own words on the lips of the angel.

How, then, do Beatus and Heterius identify the anti-adoptionist position? The anti-adoptionist party believes, not that Jesus as a man is an adoptive son of God, but that on the contrary he is the proper and true son of God.[112] Beatus says that he and Heterius and their followers believe that "ex utraque natura," that is, from the point of view of *either* nature, Jesus Christ is the "unique" and "proper" Son of God the Father. His stature as the "proper" Son of God means, as Beatus explains, that he himself, the one who suffered under Pontius Pilate (i.e., the man identified by the Creed) is true God and is adored and worshiped as such.[113] Therefore, he is not just "one god among gods," or "one lord among lords," or a "christ among christs."[114] He is not just one saint among and fundamentally indistinguishable from all the other saints. He is, rather, the "God of gods" and "Lord of lords."[115] The saints, it is true, are called "christs" and "lords" and "gods," but none of them are called, in one phrase, "Jesus Christ our God."[116] None of them are called, "Christ, the wisdom of God and the power of God" (1 Cor. 1:24);[117] none of them died for the world, only he. None of them by their *own* will were born, or grew up, nor could any at their own will, "put down their lives or take them up again."[118] This is omnipotence, and it belongs not to any god, but to God.[119]

But if for Beatus Christ is not simply one "god among gods," or "lord among lords," he is not simply "one servant among servants" either. Jesus's uniqueness as a human being is not limited to his "lordship," but extends as well to his lowliness, to his character as a "servant," as described in Phil. 2:7. His servantship itself is not the same as ours. Elipandus had claimed on the basis of Phil. 2:7 that the Word, having emptied himself, became a "servant along with the rest of those who serve,"[120] and that his sonship, insofar as it was manifest in the "form of the servant," was adoptive. As a servant or human being, the Word is the adoptive son of God *deitate exinanita*. For Elipandus, Phil. 2:7 means that the Word accepted a human nature and that his sonship is preserved in that nature, although rendered in terms appropriate to that nature. One who is truly a human being cannot be, insofar as he is a human being, the Son of God by nature ("naturaliter"). We can suppose Beatus concurs with this, since he never disputes it. But Beatus will argue that he nevertheless is "truly and properly" the Son of God even in his humanity, even in the form of a servant, even insofar as he is human. The argument at this point hinges on the interpretation of the servantship of Christ in Phil. 2:7. From Beatus's point of view, Elipandus has failed to observe certain distinctions crucial to a proper understanding of the servantship of Jesus. His analysis is wanting.

Beatus offers a contrasting analysis, reminding us that Christ is called the servant of the Father because "he emptied himself, . . . because he accepted the form of a servant, being made in the likeness of humans, and found in fashion as a man."[121] But he becomes the servant *of the Father only*. He himself said, "I have not come to do my own will, but the will of him who sent me, the Father."[122] He is not a servant to God without qualification: he said he had come to do the will of the "Father," not the will of "God."[123] He is not then a servant of God simply because he is a creature of God. The relation to God implied in the term "servant" is not simply for Jesus a function of the creature-Creator relation. If he were a servant to God simply in virtue of his creatureship as we are, it would for him, paradoxically enough, impugn the character of his humanity as real and full because it would imply that he had not really emptied himself, that in some way he had become, as man, servant to *himself*[124]—to himself, that is, *as God*, leaving the self-emptying as nothing more than a charade or else the acquisition of a special privilege in virtue of which he would conversely be Lord or even God of himself:

> For although he calls God his very own Father, since he is by very nature God and is of the essence of the Father, we must still not forget that while remaining God he was also made a human being who existed under God ["sub Deo"], according to the customary law of human nature. How then could he himself be God or Lord of himself?[125]

How could he claim to be really a human being, "sub Deo," if this were, in his case, only a front for the truth, namely, that he is really "under" *himself* in a way that we can never be? How can he thus claim to have really emptied himself, and really become a servant, that is, really become "sub Deo?"

> Therefore he is the servant of the Father only—not servant to himself or his own servant, nor Lord to himself or his own Lord—just as he is son of the Father only, not his own son or son to himself, as he in fact is actually greater or less than himself.[126]

He is not a servant in the same way that his natures are related to each other as "greater than" or "less than." He is not as a creature a servant to himself as Creator, as we are servants simply in virtue of our creatureship. Rather, he is a servant in the same way that he is a son, to the Father alone. The *persona* that is the Word is Son to the *persona* that is the Father. The servantship of the Word is the relation of the *persona* of the Word in his self-emptying to the *persona* of the Father. But it is still the same *persona* that is related to the Father, still the same Son, "true and proper." His self-emptying or servantship does not make him a different kind of Son, an adoptive son. The one who is the servant *is* the one who is the Son, "true and proper." Otherwise there would be nothing remarkable about this servantship. Otherwise, there would be nothing worth noticing about the Christian religion in general.[127]

Thus Jesus has a *perfection* of servantship which we do not have, and can never have on our own. Such is the meaning, Beatus reminds Elipandus, of the rest of the passage from Philippians. His self-emptying is so great that, paradoxically, it represents, and actually is, his lordship of all of us:

> In quo servuus Patri, dominus caeli et terrae, id est angelorum et hominum, Paulo apostolo attestante, qui ait: *Humiliavit semet ipsum usque ad mortem, mortem autem crucis. Propter quod et Deus Pater illum exaltavit et donavit illi nomen, quod est super omne nomen, ut in nomine Ihesu,* Filii virginis Mariae, *omne genu flectatur caelestium et terrestrium et infernorum, et omnis lingua confiteatur, quia Ihesus in gloria est Dei Patris.*[128]

Jesus ("the son of the virgin Mary"—note how carefully Beatus has inserted this phrase into the citation from Philippians) has the perfection of servantship, and therefore represents humanity in its perfection, in its fulfillment. He is not to be conformed or thought to be similar to us, rather, he is the *paradigm*, and we are to be made similar to him, to be, in fact, incorporated into him. He is the new Adam, whose very lowliness, whose very emptiness, is more real than our own, is more perfect, "so that, in his very lowliness, which in figures is preached to us [comparing him to a servant, or a lamb, etc.], no one is similar to him."[129] In short, he did not empty himself to become similar to us, but so that we might become similar to him, so that we, as members of his Body, might come to share in the personal union which this servant has with the Word, and thus, as adoptive children, share in the sonship which belongs to Jesus "properly and truly."[130]

We should appreciate our position fully. It is not without poignancy. For, if Jesus is the paradigm, if it is into his sonship that we are to be incorporated, it is, paradoxically, into his humility that we must be initiated. If we are lords, it is only as *he* is a Lord, in his consummate lowliness and renunciation. His nobility as the true Son of God is present to us, is revealed to us, as a perfect renunciation, and it is that in which we must participate if we are to be "lord" as he is:

> It is from *him* that [believers] are called "lords"—from *him* that they are called "christs."[131] He was made *servant* [Phil. 2:7] of the Father so that he

might *liberate* us from a multitude of "lords," that is, from the multitude of idols, and that we might have as Lord only him who was made for us a servant, that we might be free through him who alone is "free among the dead" and who leads us to this nobility as well. There is no doubt that the highest nobility [i.e., the truest sonship] is present where there is the *servitude* of Christ to prove its presence. He became impoverished for us, so that we by his poverty might be made rich. . . . And what is his poverty, but his humanity? And what are our riches, but his humanity? [132]

For Beatus, Elipandus seems to miss the almost dreadful paradox that our exaltation must be patterned after something which is, in the first instance, a humiliation, a lowering. Christ is not a lord as we are lords; rather, we must possess lordship as he does, in union with his perfect servantship. The roots of this theology in the apocalyptic theology of suffering are still discernible.

Thus it is ultimately not difficult to see why Beatus objects to the christological scheme of Elipandus. For Beatus, it precludes the very saving work which the Christ as Redeemer came to perform. It precludes the building of a church which is joined to him as the paradigm and indeed the locus of salvation. The Head must be in some way different from the Body, and it cannot be simply a matter of degree. For Beatus, the Redeemer is the one who *mediates* sonship, who is the middle term between ourselves and the Father. We are lords *through* his lordship. This is ably expressed in Beatus's exegesis of Ps. 67:17, "Why do you look with envy, O many-peaked mountains, at the Mountain which God desired for his abode, yea, where the Lord will dwell forever":

As [Christ] is called a Mountain, so they [the saints] are called mountains. But why, therefore, should they look *with envy*? Certainly not because God does not dwell in these mountains. He surely does dwell there. But God dwells in these "mountains" *through* that Mountain. In him alone does *all the fullness of divinity dwell bodily.* . . . Our Lord Jesus Christ is the Mountain of mountains, and not just one mountain among the many. [133]

There is no question of a *degree* of difference here. There is rather the relation of paradigm to paradigmed, of a mediation of form, so to speak. As the Head, Jesus is "above" the Body, [134] and thereby identifies and defines it. In another image Beatus uses, Jesus suffuses the church with light, the origin of which is himself:

Christ is the Sun . . . . Just as the sun makes the twelve hours in a day—not the other way around—so also Christ makes and chooses his twelve Apostles. They neither made nor chose him . . . . And thus those who are chosen are adoptive sons—not the one who chooses! Still, the one who chose and the ones who were chosen are one day and one light. . . . This is the one day, that is, Christ and the Church, one persona.[135]

Jesus mediates light to us and makes us the "day" of which he is the "sun." He mediates to us the self-emptying of the Word, that perfection of humility which irradiates the church and forms it as the body of the Word.[136] Joined to himself as body to head, we have communion with his very *persona*, because we have been made to feel, in our own flesh, the self-emptying of the Word. This is how we have been initiated or adopted into the relation which that *persona* has with the Father, namely, sonship.

Beatus's critique of Elipandus is that between us on the one hand and Elipandus's adoptive *primogenitus* on the other, there is no saving difference. We seem to end up, together with the man Jesus, as a relatively random array of "christs," "lords," "adoptive sons," "little ones," and "servants," with no order, no form, no Head except one who is firstborn in the degree to which he participates in grace, perhaps, but who is essentially similar to all of us. As Beatus sees it, the Jesus of Elipandus has no mediatorial role and is therefore negligible. The whole salvific scheme is burst asunder, because union with the *primogenitus* of Elipandus's scheme is a matter of indifference, not of salvation:

> The heretic [Elipandus] separates the Word from the flesh, and preaches God separately and the man separately. He separates Head from Body, and preaches the Head separately and the Body separately. And he, unhappy one, is unaware that the one Christ is God and a human being, and as a human he is the Head of his Church. And the *head of Christ is God*, that is, the whole Divinity is the head of the human being whom the Son alone assumed. The Son as a human being is the head of his Church, which is joined to [himself as] Head, thus making the whole Christ, Head and Body, one person.[137]

Again,

> [The heretic] fails to confess both that the human being Christ is the Son of God and one God with the Father—that *there is no other God beside him*—and that with the whole Church he is one human being, and there is not one *persona* "the Church," and another *persona* "the human being Christ," and another *persona*, "the Word of God."[138]

As was the case with their christology, the soteriologies of Beatus and Elipandus are fundamentally similar. One could even refer to their common soteriology, one based upon likeness or similarity to the human being Jesus, and upon some sort of association or assimilation to this human being as leader of a new body of adopted children of God, as their first-born (Elipandus), in the grace of whose adoption we are called to participate, or as Head of the Body, the Church (Beatus), incorporation into whom grants us an adoptive share in the sonship which he has truly and properly. Beatus, working out of this common soteriological tradition, with its intense focus upon the *homo* Jesus as the locus of salvation, is claiming that Elipandus's christology destroys what he and Elipandus both value in a soteriological scheme because it breaks the scheme apart just at its point of genius, that the human being *is* fully a human being *because* he is also fully God, and for that reason can mediate to us the same fullness of humanity, sonship to God, that he has, although for us it is received, it is adoptive. Elipandus places in jeopardy the unique servantship of Christ, replacing it with the merely natural subservience of the creature to the Creator, thus removing from us the opportunity for transforming *our* servantship into sonship, for being able to use or *redeem* our servantship by its incorporation into his servantship, and *thus* into sonship.

One may raise at this point the question of the fairness of Beatus to Elipandus. Elipandus, as we have seen, accused Beatus not only of being a drunkard, but of preaching a Christ who was not truly human, who, in fact, had no true flesh. Beatus in turn seems at least to have implied that Elipandus taught that Jesus was adopted at the moment of his baptism.[139] Exaggerations aside, however, it seems evident that there was a clearly defined dispute, remarkable for its inner coherence and for the accuracy of the give and take. The dispute was squarely focused upon the *homo* Jesus, the one who was assumed, and the status of his sonship insofar as he was a true human.

One could comment that Beatus fails to appreciate Elipandus's insistence that the man Jesus is the Word of God, although as a man he, the very Word, must be an adoptive son of God if the self-emptying of the Word is to be complete. Although Elipandus avoids the term "mediator," Jesus does mediate to us a sonship which is that of the Word and no one else's. He *is* the Word, and he has become like us so that we may become the Word's brothers and sisters. But his sonship, if it is not adoptive, is not the sort of sonship that a human being can have and thus there is no point in his attempting to mediate it to us. But Beatus has not misunderstood. He simply does not agree. Beatus insists that if the Word has become an adoptive son, the self-emptying has gone too far, to the point where the Word has made himself so much like us that all he can mediate to us is ourselves.

For Beatus, Elipandus's christology is at bottom nothing more than an ideology of pride, pride in the Augustinian sense as the attempt to exalt oneself above God. Beatus presents his analysis of this fundamental error of Elipandus by pointing out that in teaching that Jesus is "an adoptive one among adoptive ones, . . . and a servant among servants," Elipandus has reduced Christ to the level of Elipandus himself. To be sure, he is archbishop of Toledo; nevertheless he is a human being like any other, in need of redemption:

> Too much does he, the primate of Spain, prove himself to be elated with pride, teaching that he himself is, "together with Christ, a christ" . . . . In his madness . . . he makes no distinction between himself and the man who is the Son of God. . . . O blindness! O ignorance of the truth! O too much elation and damnable presumption of self! By believing thus, [Elipandus and followers] are those who prefer themselves to God.[140]

In company with the rest of the heretics, Elipandus "has imagined, under the name of Christ, a sort of Christ which, at the devil's bidding, he has suggested *to himself*."[141] "Who are those believers who are saved," Beatus asks?—"Those," he answers, "who believe that he is the true Son of God and true God, that he alone is to be adored, he whom the Jews took, and crucified, and killed."[142] Not to believe this is not a prudent rejection of monophysitism, but rather the ultimate reluctance of a human being, the refusal to acknowledge God as God is, as God has chosen to be and to act, and to assume, rather, ourselves as standards of perfection, without necessity of any paradigm for reformation. We put ourselves in the place of God and assume that God—and, Beatus adds, his Christ as well—is like us. Beatus rounds out his critique of Elipandus with this brilliant transferral, to the sphere of christological reflection, of the theology of pride which is familiar to any reader of Augustine's *City of God*.

Summary

The picture of the adoptionism controversy which has arisen from the texts considered to this point is one which is far richer and certainly more significant than that presented by ubiquitous scholarly descriptions of that "mischievous opinion classified as Nestorianism"[143] and its refutation, itself not above suspicion and at any rate clumsy. The controversy indeed has had very little significance in the customary view, apart from the testimony it offers to the supposedly shameless condition of Christian teaching in a country occupied by Islam and politically divided. Perhaps it presented an occasion for the sharpening of Alcuin's theological skills,[144] but in itself it was altogether quite negligible.

The picture that has emerged here is quite different. It is a picture of a culture theologically alive and coherent, intelligent, and in reflective dialogue with earlier Western traditions. The controversy does not appear as a sign of cultural decadence, but rather as part of an ongoing life of reflection within the faith of ecclesial circles. One could even talk about a development of teaching or doctrine, one which is especially interesting because it is not the rehearsal of agendas deriving from Eastern conciliar literature, but rather reflection on christology in a wholly native context, with organic links to soteriological and ecclesiological issues as inherited and developed from such writers as Tyconius, Augustine, Gregory, and Leo, and, more proximately, from Isidore and the Toledan councils. The christological discussion is only intelligible within the context of this particular Hispanic theological culture, and in turn, of the Western writers whose theology formed the roots of that culture. The controversy is *not* intelligible if it is assumed to be simply a replay of the controversy over Nestorius and, later, Eutyches, or if its parameters and paradigms are assumed to be the same.

This means that these sources evince a christology in which the poles of orthodoxy are not in the first place Nestorianism and Eutychianism, but rather certain soteriological and ecclesiological concerns as these have been developed from sources that are exclusively Western. The christology is entirely at home in this context of these concerns, and is a development of them, and the evidence does not warrant a search for any other context. This becomes even clearer as one turns to the next phase of the controversy, dominated by the Carolingians, because the adoptionist strand of late Hispanic christology was judged and evaluated in Gaul apart from the context of concerns of which it was a development.

Even a document as early as the first letter of Hadrian to the bishops of Spain, perhaps contemporaneous with Beatus's rebuttal of Elipandus, cannot fail to impress us as hailing from a wholly different, non-Hispanic air, a set of concerns and conceptions foreign to the ones familiar from the Hispanic documents. As soon as the controversy spilled over into the Carolingian controlled Spanish March, the original parameters, concerns, and issues all become lost. The original terms of discussion are forgotten or discarded. The terms begin to be set instead by theologians acting on behalf of Charlemagne, especially Alcuin. With the triumph of Alcuin over the native Spanish theologians, the original concerns of the controversy were lost not only for a moment but for good, and any memory of the possibility of a native, home-grown Western christology either before or after the Hispanic developments was permanently lost as well. From one point of view, the suppression and extinction of adoptionism was the suppression of a peculiarly Western line of christological reflection and development. From another point of view, it was the beginning of a new theological momentum, one which ultimately transcended the narrow concerns of Charlemagne for order within his world.

4. Felix and Alcuin

It is not likely that the controversy in Spain ceased after the initial exchange between Elipandus and Beatus. That exchange was anything but irenic, and the evidence points to a controversy of significant magnitude,[1] one which continued into the very last years of the eighth century. As late as 798, we find Elipandus reporting to Felix with evident satisfaction the latest literary coup of a sympathizer named Milita (otherwise unknown), as well as the success which he had enjoyed employing Milita's writings against "that false prophet, Unbeatus the Horrible."[2] A little later we learn from Elipandus of some other consultations internal to the circle of the adoptionist party.[3] But there are no lengthy literary remains after Beatus's *Adversus Elipandum*, and, after these last two reports from Elipandus, there is silence. There is no other news about events on the Spanish side of the Pyrenees. Instead, attention becomes increasingly focused on the territory northeast of the Pyrenees, territory under Carolingian control.

The mechanism of the spread of adoptionism into Charlemagne's Spanish March is not known, but there can be little doubt that Elipandus's scheming was ultimately responsible. Perhaps he felt that support from an area not under Muslim control could act as a counterweight to the insubordination of Heterius and Beatus, especially if such support could come from a bishop. Support from a bishop in an area not under Muslim control would be even better, for it could tend to offset the Astrurian party's claim that Elipandus's episcopacy was compromised by his allegiance to the Moors. There would be no better place to seek for such support than in Charlemagne's Spanish March, which had once been part of the pre-Muslim Visigothic kingdom of Hispania, and which had therefore once been under the ecclesiastical jurisdiction of Toledo. It is probably with such thoughts in mind that Elipandus first wrote to Felix, bishop of Urgel: "What," Elipandus wrote, "did Felix think of the human nature in Christ?"[4] Nor could Elipandus have chosen a bishop with credentials better than Felix's. After all, Felix had already distinguished himself by writing a famous apology against the Muslims (now lost).[5]

Felix, for his part, may have hoped that stronger links to Toledo would augment his prestige in Urgel. Urgel had only fallen to Charlemagne in 789, and along with the rest of the Spanish March it jealously preserved a large measure of self-rule. Adherence to a Toledan theology could tend to mark out the autonomy of the Christians in the March from the rest of the Carolingian church,[6] against the ambitions of Carolingian reform (e.g., monastic reconstruction). Alcuin depicts a heresy which was dramatically successful in taking root across a broad social spectrum,[7] but nothing is really known about the eastward spread of the adoptionist teaching. There is no evidence of any massive missionary effort. As late as 788 Felix had been able to sign his name to a regional synodal document without drawing even a hint of protest.[8] But by 792 Felix was on his way to Rome to make a formal recantation of his heresy, having been condemned by a council at Regensburg[9] convened by Charlemagne expressly for this purpose. The most likely explanation of what seems to be a virtually instantaneous spread of adoptionism is the attraction of a theology conspicuously Hispanic, and in particular Toledan, in provenance. And not only did adoptionism spread quickly, but support for it in the March and other border areas was deep. To eliminate it, Charlemagne was required to orchestrate at least two more councils in order to effect the removal of Felix, and when that was accomplished in 799, he had to commission a systematic preaching campaign to the areas most loyal to adoptionism.

This campaign was supported by a massive literary effort on the part of Alcuin and others,[10] and the picture of Felix which we have inherited comes almost entirely from the literature produced for this campaign. Felix therefore has no surviving independent voice in this controversy. All of his writings were suppressed and now exist only as extracts and paraphrases in the hostile treatises of his opponents. One must therefore be careful to remember that the Felix we meet in the evidence is very much the Felix which the Carolingians wanted us to meet, Felix as the Carolingians saw him. It is impossible to overemphasize the caution necessary when dealing with an historical figure such as Felix whose identity is virtually coincident with his role in a controversy which he lost. It is easy to forget that the controversy in its Carolingian phase transpired on the border, as it were, between two cultures, one of them highly ambitious, and that therefore it is a priori completely inadequate to treat Alcuin's critique of Felix as though it were both an accurate report of Felix's position and a definitive evaluation and refutation of it as well.[11] One may legitimately worry that such treatments of Felix are really only expositions of the Carolingian view of Felix, not of Felix himself. Unfortunately, Alcuin's analyses of Felix's teaching are virtually never questioned, only repeated, summarized, or extended, despite strong warning signs that they are not completely trustworthy.[12] This is not to imply there was any intention on the part of Alcuin to distort or misrepresent the position of the adoptionists. But it cannot be forgotten that they each come from different cultural milieux and thus do not share the same fund of text, tradition, and predilection. The likelihood of misperception in such a situation is high, and it is only further increased by the stake the Carolingians had in defending their identification of Felix as an outsider.

From Hadrian to Alcuin: A Tradition of Interpretation

In order to more accurately gauge the character of Felix's teaching, it will be necessary first to try to isolate and identify as precisely as possible the interface between the two competing circles of thought, Hispanic and non-Hispanic, which came into conflict. As though teasing apart two strands of reflection, one has to ask where is the dividing line between Felix's own thought on the one hand, and other perceptions and analyses of that thought on the other. Like the ancients, the writers of the early Middle Ages did not use quotation marks, and the gradation between a direct quote, a paraphrase, an analysis, an accusation, and a deliberate lie is often hard to calibrate, and therefore in cases where a particular work is preserved only as citations in another work, it is sometimes difficult to separate the thought which is the subject of commentary or refutation from the *perception* or analysis of that thought by the commentator.

Non-Hispanic perception of the adoptionists begins before either Alcuin or Felix, with Pope Hadrian's critique of Elipandus. This consisted of two letters, already introduced above,[13] addressed to the bishops of Spain, one roughly contemporaneous with Beatus's *Adversus Elipandum* (785), and the other dating from the year or two before the Council of Frankfurt (ca. 793). In the first letter, Hadrian appears to know nothing about the adoptionist position, except that two prelates of Spain, Elipandus and Ascaricus, were "not ashamed to confess that the Son of God is adoptive."[14] This is the "doleful news which has come to us from your region,"[15] probably secondhand, and almost certainly unaccompanied by any written statement or treatise by the parties accused. By whatever agency the doleful news reached Hadrian, he can hardly be faulted for being alarmed, or for issuing a rejoinder from the perspective of a conciliar tradition which the papacy had played a large role in forming. With the condemnations of Ephesus in mind, Hadrian labels the position as Nestorian. This is his *perception* of the Spanish teaching:

> No one, name whatever heresiarch you will, has ever dared to bark such a blasphemy—unless it was that perfidious Nestorius, who confessed that the Son of God was merely and only a human being ["purum hominem"].[16]

Hadrian's perception of the adoptionist position may be further assessed from the charges inherent in the citations he advances against it. The first is from pseudo-Athanasius:

> If anyone says . . . that the Son of God is one individual, and that he who was born a human being from Mary is another individual, adopted by grace, to the point that there are [thus posited] two sons, one who is of God and thus Son by nature, and one who is a human being of Mary and thus son by grace, . . . such a one the Catholic and Apostolic Church anathematizes . . .[17]

The second is from Gregory of Nazianzus:

> If anyone introduces two sons, one who, being "of" God therefore has God as his Father, and a second, who was born of a mother and is not one and the same as the first: may such a one be cut off from that adoption promised to those who believe rightly! There are two natures, God and human being . . . , but not two sons or two gods . . . .[18]

Adoptionism is thus, to put it simply, Nestorianism, that is, the confession that Christ was merely and only a human being ("purus homo"), and that therefore there are two sons of God, one who is related by nature to his Father, and another who is related by adoption. The other citations adduced by Hadrian all emphasize the true dynamic of adoption as Hadrian sees it—that it pertains to *us*, not to Christ, and that He as Only-begotten concedes to *us* the privilege of adoption.[19]

The second letter of Hadrian to the bishops of Spain is different from the first in that it was written with the text of Elipandus at hand. The Pope remarks that he has read the letter Elipandus sent to the bishops of France.[20] His perception of Elipandus's position remains almost unchanged from his first impression, despite his closer acquaintance with Elipandus's defence. But Hadrian's summary of Elipandus's position is not as crude as the first one:

[Elipandus discusses] the adoption of Jesus Christ the Son of God according
to the flesh . . . . [He and his followers] confess that He is an adoptive Son,
not the proper Son, as though He had at one time been completely unrelated
["alienus"] to the Father, or as though, through the assumption of the flesh,
he had been made into someone unrelated to Him . . . . [21]

For Hadrian, this again amounts to teaching that Jesus is *purus homo*, since
he repeats in this letter his citation of the passage from the *De incarnatione*
of "Athanasius," in effect charging Elipandus with teaching that "the Son
of God is one individual, and the human being born of Mary is another."
He also repeats the citation from Nazianzus in fact accusing Elipandus of
teaching "two sons."[22] In other words, even though Hadrian does not
explicitly repeat the charge of Nestorianism, all the elements which in
his earlier letter had seemed to him constitutive of that judgment are repeated here.

Yet he did not actually repeat it explicitly, and the last line of the
passage cited above, accusing Elipandus of turning the Son into someone
unrelated to the Father, could be construed as evidence that Hadrian had
understood and consciously rejected Elipandus's true position. It is in
fact a legitimate critique of Elipandus's position: in making the eternal
Son adoptive, does Elipandus unwarrantedly alienate him from the Father?[23] It seems best to conclude that Hadrian did understand the position of Elipandus, but that from his perspective Elipandus's position still
amounted to Nestorianism because, on Hadrian's analysis, it doesn't matter whether the man Jesus was adopted into sonship or whether the eternal
Son was alienated from true sonship—in either case one ends up with two
sons, one of them merely a human. His perception of the teaching of
Elipandus has remained unchanged, although his analysis has become
more nuanced. His discussion of his own final charge against Elipandus is
helpful in understanding why he felt so committed to it:

You have absolutely fearlessly hissed through that venomous throat of yours
what it is shameful to say, namely that our Liberator is a *slave*! . . . How is it,
hateful whiners, disparagers of God, that you were not afraid to call the very
one who freed you from service to the devil a *slave*?[24]

Hadrian is as incensed at this predication of *slavery* or *servantship* as he was
with the designation of Jesus as adoptive, if not in fact more incensed. He
spends more time discussing this in his own words than he does discussing
any other single aspect of the adoptionist teaching. His point seems to be
that if the eternal Son is alienated from the Father to the point where he

too becomes a slave, it is difficult to imagine how the term "Liberator" would have more than a hollow ring.

Accordingly, Hadrian will not admit any proper usage for the word *servus* with reference to Jesus, insisting that the prophetic use of it was mystical and figurative.[25] To Hadrian the word suggests bondage to sin, a usage far from Elipandus's intentions.[26] Now that the person figuratively referred to in the prophets (e.g., Ps. 115:16; 85:16; Is. 44:2; etc.) as God's "servant" has been revealed in truth to be His Son, it is no longer appropriate to use the word "servant." None of the evangelists or Apostles have done so. Instead, they call him "Lord," and "Savior."[27] Paul in particular, "that trumpet resounding unto all the world," always calls him Lord and teaches all tongues to do the same.[28] Ironically, Hadrian alludes to verses from the very chapter in which Jesus's servantship figures most prominently for Paul, and for Elipandus, following him: Philippians 2. But Hadrian almost ignores verses 6–7, thus ignoring as well that element which in Elipandus's christology served as a safeguard against any duality in sonship or personhood in Christ, namely, the "self-emptying" of verse 7.[29] Hadrian asserts simply that Paul universally calls him Lord, and from that observation goes on to rule out the propriety of any use of *servus* at all.

Hadrian does not seem to be aware of or committed to a tradition of interpretation which seizes upon the self-emptying of Phil. 2:7 as a theme programmatic for christological reflection. Hadrian therefore is unaware of any context that could have kept Elipandus's christology from being a two son christology with two separate subjects, namely the Son of God and the *homo purus*, the Son of Mary. Or, better, Hadrian suspects that to read this chapter from Philippians with too much of an emphasis on the self-emptying of the Word is to open oneself to Nestorianism. In other words, he judges both the christology *and* its proper context from the perspective of Catholic writers from the East and from conciliar decisions about the controversy over Nestorius. For him, christological terms and phrasings derive their absolute values from that context alone, and thus he sees the adoptionist teaching as a species of Nestorianism. One could say that his principled commitment to this context for christological meaning makes other contexts for christological discussion precisely *as* independent spheres of meaning invisible to him. But this means that christologies with constitutive linkings to other traditions and literatures are at a disadvantage because they are not allowed to speak on their own terms.

It seems fair to say we have here located the earliest evidence of an interface between Spanish adoptionism and the non-Hispanic interpretation of adoptionism. In this case there was very little difficulty finding it because both sides of the controversy are available for independent inspection. The difficulty that would be involved if we had possessed only the testimony of Hadrian is evident. It is very unlikely that one could recover the spirit and intent of the original teaching of Elipandus from Hadrian's presentation of it, precisely because Hadrian does not present us with a report of Elipandus's position as much as with a *perception* of it, a perception, furthermore, which is partly formed out of a decision to endorse one paradigm or context for assessing christological meaning over all others.

We may suspect that the Pope's letter, written sometime shortly before the Council of Frankfurt, had an influence on the Council's perception of the adoptionist position.[30] Three documents from the Council were devoted to answering the adoptionists, the Letter of the Bishops of Frankland to the Bishops of Spain, probably written by Alcuin;[31] the *Liber sacrosyllabus* of the Bishops of Italy, written by Paulinus of Aquileia and later revised by him;[32] and the letter of Charmagne to Elipandus.[33] Charlemagne's letter, immensely interesting for other reasons,[34] avoids the technicalities of the doctrinal dispute. Both of the other documents, however, evince a perspective which is completely in continuity with Hadrian's.

The Frankish bishops rebuke Elipandus because he condemns every major heretic but Nestorius in his letter.[35] They ask,

> Did not the holy universal church refute and even condemn your heresy long ago, in Nestorius? . . .—a heresy about which holy Cyril wrote to the priest Eulogius, "Nestorius therefore in his expositions represents himself as saying 'one Son and one Lord,' but he refers the sonship only to the Word of God." And, a little farther on, "For by saying that God the Word is called Christ because He is 'coupled' to Christ, how is this not openly to say that there are two Christs—if Christ is conjoined to Christ, as one individual to another?" For it seems that what Nestorius called "copulation," you call "adoption." What is adoption but that coupling which is a product of love, by which adoption a father joins to himself a son who was not actually his son?[36]

Speaking for the Frankish bishops, Alcuin follows and even develops Hadrian's lead. He perceives the adoptionists to be teaching that God adopted and joined to himself a man who had an independent existence and person apart from that joining, and who thus exists even in his union with God as one individual related to another individual. "Indeed," he comments, "what other meaning could 'adoptive' have except that Jesus Christ is not the proper Son of God, nor, as son of the Virgin, born to

Him, but is rather some servant who was 'adopted' into sonship, as you say?"[37] For Alcuin and the Frankish bishops, this is the only meaning imaginable for the word "adoption"; they concur with the initial perception of Hadrian, and their analysis is an attempt to defend and expand his critique.

In the passage cited above, the adoption of the man is again represented as the elevation of an independent subject from some form of slavery: it was "some slave" ("nescio ex quo servo") who was adopted. Elipandus never makes this claim, but it is clear that the Frankish bishops share Hadrian's horror at referring to Jesus as a "servus." The word "slave" indicates the bondage to sin out of which *we* need to be adopted.[38] The prophets may have called Christ a servant or a slave, but developing Hadrian's original point, this refers not to a "condition of servitude," but to "the obedience of that humility by which he became obedient to the Father even *unto death*."[39] This remark about the "obedience" of Phil. 2:8 is not an attempt to interpret the self-emptying of verse 7 which is not even mentioned; it is tantamount only to the assertion that the will of the Son is that of the Father.

Most importantly, the self-emptying of the *Word* to the point of becoming himself a servant or slave is not mentioned, even though the bishops have noticed Elipandus's use of it.[40] But to them, it seems to make no sense to say that God could empty himself to the point of becoming a slave, and they even chide Elipandus, certain that even he could not possibly be saying *that*:

> If therefore he who is born of the virgin is true God, how could he be adoptive, or be a slave? For certainly you do not dare to confess that God is a servant, or is adoptive![41]

This, however, is precisely what Elipandus *is* saying. But where Elipandus can see the paradox of the Word's becoming "full of grace," the Carolingian bishops and their court theologian see only a disjunction between Word and servant, between the Word and a grace-filled human being whom the Word adopted from slavery. They cannot see how anyone could claim both that the human being Jesus is truly God from the moment of conception, and that he is, at the same time and as a human being, the adoptive son of God:

> If therefore the Son of God was from the very point of conception true God, when was there a time that the human being had been without God, so that he could have been adopted into being God's Son?[42]

Because they are not working out of the same tradition, because they do not feel it as second nature to think in terms of the self-emptying of the Word Himself into servantship, they are blind to what Elipandus is saying. They assert, in effect, that he cannot possibly be saying it. They think of adoption as having for its only possible subject a mere human being ("purus homo"), a human being "sine Deo," and thus they perceive Nestorianism where in fact there is none. A similar analysis could be made for the letter of the Italian bishops as well.[43]

It seems clear that we have observed the development of a tradition of interpretation or perception of a foreign way of thinking, and that this tradition was becoming impervious to change, even when confronted with the adoptionists's own explanations. By 794 (Council of Frankfurt) this way of perceiving the adoptionist teaching would have been almost ten years old, since the time of Hadrian's first letter in 785. It was not a tradition which was completely fixed. Even the Frankish bishops's reply to the Spanish bishops has an element of puzzlement about it, as though Alcuin cannot seem to reconcile himself to what appear to be violently contradictory positions in the adoptionist teaching, namely that Jesus in his humanity could be adoptive without thereby constituting a sonship separate from that of the Word. He seems to keep wondering whether or not Elipandus can really be saying what he is saying, a wonder which never quite, however, shades into a confession of confusion or ignorance.[44] But part of the reason the analysis of adoptionism as Nestorianism appeals to Alcuin is that it gave him a precedent for his confusion: he learned from the passages he quoted from Cyril's letter to Eulogius that Nestorius himself did not openly teach two Christs, professing himself to believe in only "one Son and one Lord," but that his habitual way of explaining the christological union could not be reconciled to this claim and in fact belied it. Elipandus, Alcuin concludes, is inconsistent, just as Nestorius had been. Hadrian's original analysis was correct despite adoptionist claims to the contrary.

It can be fairly said, then, that as attention moved away from Elipandus and became directed more and more at Felix, a precedent of interpretation sufficient to govern conclusively the approach taken to Felix had already evolved. There would be an inclination or a kind of pressure to read Felix not as though he were teaching that the Word himself became adoptive by his own self-emptying, but that a given human being, one like any other human being, was at some point in his life assumed out of slavery to sin into a moral union with the Word, and that this assumption constituted an *adoption* into sonship. There will be pressure to perceive Felix's teaching as a thinly disguised Nestorianism redivivus, that is, not to notice the links which the adoptionist christology had to soteriological and ecclesiological themes in its native culture, and, following Hadrian, to recontextualize the controversy into parameters and paradigms of judgment taken from the East. The tendency will be to see the whole controversy over adoptionism as almost a reproduction in miniature of the classical Eastern controversy between Cyril and Nestorius, the evidence for which was available in the *acta* of the Councils and in such writings as the *De incarnatione Domini* of Cassian, the letters of Leo I, etc. We must be very careful when considering the Carolingian treatment of Felix not to accept too uncritically what may be a brilliant but in the last analysis wrongly placed attempt to make sense of his position by appeal to the ancient Eastern debates as a paradigm.

Felix

It is almost easier to reconstruct Felix's temperament than his teaching. The evidence contains tantalizing glimpses of his personality. Alcuin seems always to have admired his character,[45] and, oddly, to have liked him. Even after a decade of polemic and the removal of Felix to a perpetual, if hardly inelegant, imprisonment, the two seem to part on good terms.[46] Their debates were not rancorous, but remained relatively polite, civilized, and substantive. In part this is due to the temperament of Alcuin, who managed to be consistently polite even to Elipandus. But certainly it is due as well to the urbanity of Felix in manner and in person, something evident not only in his ability to win people over to his point of view,[47] but also in the refined and unpretentious quality of his prose.

Another aspect of his character, which has proven more problematic, at least to modern scholars, was his alleged habit of alternatively abjuring and relapsing into heresy. After Felix was condemned at Regensburg he formally recanted, once at the council and a second time in Rome before Hadrian himself and before the tombs of the Apostles.[48] Perhaps because such a solemn process seemed sufficient guarantee of his intentions, he was not deposed from his see, although we cannot be certain of this simply from the silence of the sources. In any event, whether he "escaped"[49] from Carolingian custody, or was allowed to go free, he seems to have reinstated himself in the see of Urgel at some point,[50] resumed his alliance with Elipandus, and also resumed teaching adoptionism, though it is not at all clear how quickly he resumed teaching. True, the Council of Frankfurt, principally famous for its condemnation of the iconodulism of Nicaea II, condemned him in 794 along with Elipandus. However, apart from the condemnation itself (and even here he is coupled with Elipandus and receives no separate attention),[51] he is mentioned only once in all of the mass of literature that emanated from the Council of Frankfurt, while Elipandus's name is consistently brought up. Most if not all of the Council's agenda was occupied not with the refutation of Felix's teaching but of Elipandus's teaching, as that was known directly to the members of the Council from Elipandus's letters. No document of Felix is ever mentioned, nor is there even any particular teaching associated uniquely with him. He is condemned by association with Elipandus and adoptionism, and perhaps only to reaffirm the earlier condemnation of his teaching or to adduce that condemnation as a precedent for condemnation of Elipandus. Felix is not deposed by this Council, and is called "Felix Orgellitanae" even in his condemnation.

Therefore, the suggestion that he resumed teaching adoptionism almost immediately upon his release, although almost universally accepted, cannot be conclusively defended from the evidence. Instead, the earliest sure evidence that anyone had perceived Felix to be teaching adoptionism again is three years later, in a letter Alcuin sent to him in late 797 or early 798.[52] It is clear that Alcuin was not well informed even then on the particularities of Felix's teaching, and this in itself is further evidence that Felix's teaching was not well known outside of his immediate range of influence. There is really no charge in the letter other than the use of the unsanctioned word "adoption,"[53] nor is there anything much more substantive in the meager descriptions of Felix's teaching given in Alcuin's *Liber Alcuini Contra Haeresim Felicis*, or *Libellus*, written shortly after his letter to Felix of 797–798.[54]

Felix's next move was his response to this letter. Alcuin had received this response by mid-798.[55] It was actually a short treatise in which Felix not only answered Alcuin's criticisms, but also gave what would appear to have been a systematic explanation of his own position, supported by passages both from Scripture and the holy doctors. It is the surprise and shock that this treatise occasions in Alcuin that actually seems to precipitate the flurry of anti-adoptionist activity in 798 and 799. Alcuin discovers to his horror that Felix is introducing a "new" and worse twist to his teaching, the assertion that Jesus Christ is in his humanity not only the adoptive Son of God but, insofar as he is a human being, "God" in name only, "nuncupatively."[56] Alcuin's shocked reaction is echoed later in 798 by

Pope Leo III, who convened a synod at Rome to condemn Felix's new teaching.[57] Meanwhile, Alcuin sent to Urgel three of his friends (Leidrad, bishop of Lyons; Nebridius, bishop of Narbonne; and Benedict of Aniane) to persuade Felix to come to Aix to argue his position in a face-to-face debate.[58] They were to promise him safe-conduct. Alcuin prepared for the debate by beginning his compilation of extracts for the treatise which was to become the *Adversus Felicem Urgellitanum Episcopum Libri VII*, or the *Seven Books Against Felix of Urgel*, completed only after the conclusion of the debate.[59] To this period also belongs the second anti-adoptionist treatise of Paulinus of Aquileia, his elegant and accomplished *Three Books Against Felix*, from which Alcuin may have drawn some of the arguments and citations used in his later works.[60]

Felix did accept the invitation to debate despite the obvious dangers. He and Alcuin argued for a week—Felix, it seems, with brilliance and style enough to have almost convinced many there who seem in the heat of the moment to have forgotten which side they were supposed to be on.[61] He was however ultimately defeated, professing himself to have been convinced by the argumentation of Alcuin and not by any force, and he issued thereupon a formal recantation of his teaching and confession of orthodoxy.[62] This time he was deposed,[63] and was consigned to the custody of Leidrad for the remainder of his life.[64]

Leidrad's custody was not harsh. Whether he was confined to the limits of the archiepiscopal palace grounds, or simply to the city of Lyons itself, he seems to have had no limits placed on his ability to associate with people, and at some point his conversations merged into full-scale clarification and teaching. Agobard of Lyons, Leidrad's *chorepiscopus* until he became his successor two years before the death of Felix in 818, is our chief source of information. While still *chorepiscopus*, he overheard some of the conversation in Felix's salon, and he felt obliged to rebuke Felix.[65] After Felix's death in 818, Agobard found among his possessions a pamphlet set out in question and answer form. He found the teaching of this pamphlet so alarming that he decided to burn it, but at the same time to publish a refutation of it which preserved a judicious quantity of extracts, such as would be sufficient to refute it.[66] Many scholars have seized upon this final relapse as confirmation of their conviction that Felix's character was fundamentally flawed, that his resolve for reform was so impossibly evanescent as to have been non-existent. And thus, while many are willing to make excuses for Elipandus,[67] no one, in the last analysis, has anything very kind to say about Felix.[68]

The evidence may, however, be susceptible to a different interpretation, especially given the cultural gap separating Alcuin from Felix. At very least the evidence clearly indicates that Felix's thought *developed*. A first phase occurs between 792 (Regensburg) and 797 (Felix's response to Alcuin's *Ep.* 23), and a second between Felix's condemnation in 799 and his death in 818. It is not unreasonable to suppose, if one is willing momentarily to suspend allegiance to the Carolingian portrait of Felix, that his condemnation at Regensburg and his own recantation before the Pope began for him a process of re-thinking and clarification of thought, a process of revising his teaching in such a way that it would be clear that he was not uttering heresy, even (from Felix's perspective) to an amateur theologian like Alcuin.

It is not possible to mark the stages of the first phase progress of thought or to say precisely when it came to term. Felix did keep a very low profile in the years just after Regensburg. It is just possible, though, that the new element in Felix's teaching, definitely formulated by early 798 in response to Alcuin's letter (*Ep.* 23), was Felix's attempt to explain his teaching in such a way that it could be understood better by his accusers. Certainly he took the time to respond in a very thorough fashion to Alcuin's letter. And he did have the confidence to appear before Charlemagne himself, whose subject he was, a confidence most likely inspired by the conviction that he could now demonstrate the orthodoxy of his teaching. After he failed, he issued a confession of faith.[69] Convinced, however, of the orthodoxy of his way of thinking, he initiated yet another course of rethinking the teaching in an effort to present it in a way that would not be offensive. As reported even by Agobard, his last set of teachings contains no mention of "adoption" or of "nuncupation," words forbidden by the Council of Aix. Some may see in this a cynical attempt to obey the letter of the law but not its spirit. But this is a judgment which is not clear a priori; it is an interpretation of the evidence which needs to be defended as much as any other. A closer reading of the texts shows that a sympathetic view of Felix is at least as likely.[70]

Alcuin and Felix, Part I

We have already seen that Alcuin did not stop thinking about adoptionism when the Council of Frankfurt ended, and that in 797 he had written to Felix (*Ep.* 23). What did Alcuin hope to accomplish by writing at this time? He appears to have taken up the problem of adoptionism immediately after his installation as the Abbot of St. Martin of Tours in 796,[71] assembling an experimental portfolio of material from the treatises of the "holy fathers"[72] more extensive than the one used in the Letter to the bishops of Spain, and in the winter of 797–798 he decided to reopen the question with Felix by sending him *Ep.* 23. It is important to recall that, so far as we can tell, it is still only Elipandus's writings which Alcuin has read up to this point, and that therefore Alcuin's polemical work against Felix, up to and including the *Libellus*, is actually based on Elipandus's articulation of the adoptionist position. With good reason: since Elipandus had written in the name of the "Hispanic prelates" as a body, Alcuin assumes this to be Felix's position as well.

Alcuin's letter to Felix is noteworthy for its conciliatory tone, and its confidence that the dispute can be resolved since there was relatively little dividing the two parties. Alcuin's patristic research seems to have engendered an optimism that the preponderance of the Catholic tradition lay in his favor, that he had therefore analyzed the Spanish bishops's teaching correctly, and that this should be enough to convince such a theologian as Felix. Felix was a morally upright and intelligent man who had somehow strayed into the ultimately self-contradictory mixture of truth and heresy which, for Alcuin, adoptionism always was. Alcuin probably felt that his presentation of the results of his reading of the fathers would be enough to tip the balance in favor of the truth. Surely Felix would see that it is "only by this name of adoption" that he was separated from the opinion of the fathers.[73] Alcuin does not mean that this is a dispute simply over terminology, but rather that, given the force of their common commitment to tradition, of the "many things in [Felix's] writings which are just and true,"[74] why should Felix "*want* to place the name 'adoptive' onto Jesus,"[75] why, that is, should he not see that according to the fathers, to do so is inconsistent with the shared premises "just and true?"

In deference to his own conciliatory tone, Alcuin does not condemn Felix as a Nestorian here, or even classify his teaching as such. But his assessment to that effect is still operative, as shown by his citation of Cyril of Alexandria's letter to the monks "against Nestorius,"[76] as well as by his citation of Gregory the Great's warning against thinking of the Redeemer as "merely and only a human being" ("purus homo"). For anti-adoptionist polemic from Pope Hadrian on, this was the telltale sign of Nestorianism. Alcuin cites a number of traditional passages which distinguish the proper use of "adoptive" as a predicate applicable to *us*, who have been redeemed, but not as a predicate applicable to the one who did the redeeming.[77] He concludes that to call the Redeemer an adoptive son is to render him a "purus homo" like ourselves, with the result that he is no longer the true Son of God, but rather—and this is a new accusation resulting from Alcuin's most recent reflection—a "false god."[78]

Alcuin published his research, the grounds for his optimism, in the *Libellus*. If the letter he had sent to Felix was polite enough to omit the explicit equation of adoptionism with Nestorianism, this little book is forthright enough:

> Behold! A certain part of the world has been infected with the poison of heretical depravity, asserting that Jesus Christ is not a true Son to God the Father, nor a proper Son, but an adoptive son . . . . The Nestorian heresy has fled clandestinely from the East—where it was condemned by the synodal authority of the 200 fathers—to the West. The result is that just as the visible sun ebbs from our eyes in the West, so now it is there too that the sun of justice begins to retreat from the hearts of the faithful. Nestorius impiously denied that the most Blessed Virgin Mary was the genetrix of God, claiming that she was only the bearer of a human being; similarly, these people, deceived by the same depravity, deny that she is truly the bearer of the Son of God, claiming rather that she is the genetrix only of his adoptive son. . . .[79]

This is a square and confident charge of Nestorianism.[80] Alcuin here appears so securely confident of his analysis of the adoptionist position as a species of Nestorianism that he mocks the very idea that it could be anything essentially new or indigenous to the West.[81] It is really only an Eastern heresy which has escaped to the West.

In none of the later anti-adoptionist writings of Alcuin is it clearer than in this little dossier[82] of christological authorities how close is the relation between the rapidly solidifying tradition of perception of adoptionism which Alcuin inherits and the analysis of adoptionism which he develops, initially summarized in the citation given just above. Plainly, the analysis is not based on Elipandus's teaching itself, on its own terms, and at this point it is still only Elipandus's work which Alcuin has seen. Elipandus is barely cited, and then in only the vaguest possible way. The analysis depends instead upon Hadrian's original *perception* of Elipandus. The analysis amounts simply to an articulation, elaboration, and defense of that perception.

Alcuin carefully exhibits his continuity with the early perspective of Hadrian by including among his citations the very passages from Gregory of Nazianzus and "Athanasius" which Hadrian had cited in both his letters, where they served to advance the claim that the adoptionists taught "two sons," one of whom was only "a human being adopted by grace as we are."[83] Other passages which Hadrian had included in his letters are included here as well, especially those concerned with distinguishing between us as adoptive children of God and Jesus as the Only-begotten Son.[84] Alcuin also selects a passage from Gregory the Great's *Moralia in Iob*, which he uses to repeat Hadrian's charge that the adoptionists are teaching that Jesus was a *homo purus*.[85] Alcuin also recycles some of the citations he included in the Letter of the Frankish bishops, and adds to these not only an ampler supply of Western authorities,[86] but also a large supply of citations taken directly from the *acta* of the Council of Ephesus and from other writings directed against Nestorius.[87]

Alcuin develops his analysis of the adoptionists's teaching on the basis of all of these texts. He reveals what he believes is its fundamental flaw:

> It seems that the cause of the heresy in the mind of those erring is that they hold Christ to be adoptive because they think that *to assume* and *to adopt* are one and the same thing . . . and they think that *grace* and *adoption* are identical as well . . . .[88]

To put it more succinctly, they mistake the grace of assumption for the grace of adoption.[89] Alcuin very persuasively points out that not all examples of grace are examples of adoption: David, for example, had any number of proper, non-adoptive sons, but only one, Solomon, was by David's grace and favor allowed to inherit the kingdom.[90] Or, there could be a case in which a single father has several sons, all adopted except one, and yet the grace of inheritance may nevertheless rest upon him, the natural son.[91] In the case of ourselves our adoption as children of God comes by grace only *after* we are made as human beings; in our case, therefore, the work of grace is called adoption. Grace, for us, *is* adoption. But in the case of Jesus, who was not first conceived and then adopted into sonship through grace, but rather had the grace of *being conceived* as both true God and true human, or as the true and unique Son of God, it is more appropriate to speak of the grace of "taking up" or of "assumption."[92]

These are brilliant analytic comments, a theological achievement. Alcuin speaks here with authority, with the voice of hard won insight, persuasive in its internal consistency. But admiration for Alcuin's extraordinarily clear thinking can easily lead one into assuming that his comments are in fact an analysis of what Elipandus was actually teaching instead of an analysis of what Alcuin *perceived* Elipandus to be teaching. All of Alcuin's comments presuppose a paradigm in which there is a *homo* who is the subject of some sort of grace of elevation. Whether the elevation is

described as assumption or adoption is really secondary to the fundamental paradigm in which a human being is elevated by grace to sonship.
Alcuin *assumes* that this is also Elipandus's frame of reference, and thus he
renders Elipandus's teaching as though it too were a theology of the elevation of a human being to sonship. Since Elipandus talks about Jesus as
adoptive, Alcuin concludes that he must be teaching that an independent
"homo purus" like ourselves named Jesus was at some point in his life
adopted by grace into sonship. There is no doubt that this is Alcuin's
version of adoptionism. Perceiving himself to be contradicting the adoptionist position, he says that it is *not* the case that Jesus "was conceived or
born and *then* received, through grace, an adoption which resulted in his
being Son of God."[93] But even his articulation of the non-adoptionist
alternative hinges upon a *homo* who receives the grace of being "assumed"
into union with the Word. Thus even here the subject of the grace is a
human being who, if not actually another subject separate from the Word,
nevertheless *virtually* constitutes one, separable at least in thought and for
the purposes of argumentation.

There is in Alcuin's report and analysis of Elipandus no hint at all of
what we have proposed as Elipandus's true position, namely that by the
self-emptying of the Word, by his assuming of a human nature, he—the
Word himself—becomes "full of grace" or "adoptively a son." For Elipandus there is no question of a man who was adopted into sonship. That is
a caricature of his position. But for Alcuin the only alternative to this
analysis of adoptionism yields an absurdity, a logical disjunction, namely,
that one and the same person be both an adoptive as well as a natural son:

> With a blindness that is shameful they affirm that in his divinity [Christ] is
> the proper Son of God the Father, but in his humanity is the adoptive son of
> the same God the Father. But if this were the case, there would be two sons,
> because as we have already said there is no way that there can be only one
> person common to a proper son and to one who is adoptive, for one of them
> is a true Son, and the other not a true Son.[94]

Notice how (after the *nequaquam*) Alcuin virtually repeats Elipandus's position, *but as an absurdity which no one could reasonably hold*. Someone could
hold, and still be rational, the position that there were two sons, one elevated by adoption to sonship and one naturally the Son. The only problem
with this is that it is heresy. But the alternative, that one *persona* is somehow both proper and adoptive, is for Alcuin not even rational. It would
involve, almost, the belief that God himself became adoptive,[95] a statement

which is for Alcuin a manifest absurdity—but one which is actually, although very obliquely stated, the position of Elipandus. The paradox which Elipandus taught is thus transposed by Alcuin into the key of logical contradiction. Alcuin cannot *see* the actual position of Elipandus because for him it amounts to nonsense to which no one could possibly adhere. Elipandus's view is for all practical purposes invisible to him.

The reason Alcuin cannot help but perceive Elipandus's position as an absurdity is that, like Pope Hadrian before him, he is working out of a christological paradigm in which there is no significant reliance on the self-emptying of Phil. 2:6 as the fundamental parameter for reflection. This is not to say that Alcuin was not aware of Phil. 2:6–7.[96] But it appears in his text only when one of the passages he cites from the fathers contains it, and even then it is never singled out for comment, nor does Alcuin ever make the attempt to integrate it into his own analyses except insofar as the *forma dei* and *forma servi* language helps to establish the fact that in the Incarnate Word there were two natures, for which these Pauline phrases provide a convenient, biblically grounded shorthand.[97] Alcuin thus has no framework with which to construct a perspective on adoptionism different from Hadrian's. He has no reason not to follow the precedent of interpretation set by Hadrian. A consideration of the next phase of the controversy will serve to corroborate these suggestions.

Alcuin and Felix, Part II: The *Seven Books Against Felix*

It is especially important to remember that Alcuin's first work against Felix is in essence a set of arguments directed against adoptionism as taught by *Elipandus*. The *Libellus* was addressed to Felix in the hope of convincing him as Charlemagne's subject to be reconciled to the orthodoxy of the realm, but it operated on the premise that the teaching of Felix was essentially similar to that of Elipandus. No other reading of the evidence is warranted because most of it indicates that Alcuin's firsthand acquaintance with adoptionism to this point came from Elipandus's Letter to the Bishops of Frankland. There is no citation of even the simplest passage from Felix, whose position is instead represented in general terms corresponding to a standardized perception of adoptionism. Up to this point, therefore, we have been able to locate with some precision the interface or gap between the two conflicting cultural traditions because we had independent attestations to either side. We could compare Alcuin's treatment of adoptionism to Elipandus's version of his own teaching. But as we move on to a study of Alcuin's refutation of *Felix*'s position, the interface between the two traditions will become much more difficult to locate precisely because we will have no way of independently evaluating Alcuin's use of Felix. We do not have the text of Felix to look at independent of Alcuin's treatment of it, except, of course, as Felix's text had chanced to be preserved by another of his enemies.

We must therefore at this point change the way we have been working. We must at this point *make an assumption* about the location of the interface between Alcuin and Felix. For the purposes of argument let us assume that the interface is to be located at exactly the same place it was between Alcuin and *Elipandus*, such that the teaching of Felix is continuous in intent and in spirit with that of Elipandus, without excluding the possibility that he had put into place certain refinements or adjustments. It is not unreasonable to make this assumption. The correspondence which survives between Elipandus and Felix shows that Elipandus had warm regard for Felix and felt confident discussing items of strategy with him, though they were engaged in a common endeavor.[98] Also, given Alcuin's failure to perceive the true intent of Elipandus's teaching both in his earlier refutation of it and in his later attempt, it is appropriate to be suspicious of his treatment of Felix. If we are to begin by assuming anything, it really ought to be that Alcuin does not give us an accurate picture of Felix's teaching. And finally, this assumption has never been tested. All of the standard treatments of adoptionism accept Alcuin's account of Felix without question, and without noticing that this too is an assumption which no one ever stops to justify as an appropriate starting point. By adopting a new starting point, we may be able to make progress beyond the impasse of stereotypes which has come to govern commentary on this controversy.[99]

When Alcuin read Felix's response to his conciliatory letter of late 797, he was shocked and even somewhat chagrined at the new and obviously much worse error of preaching that Jesus in his humanity is only "Deus nuncupativus." This discovery was probably so alarming to Alcuin because it destroyed his confidence that he could make Felix see how small a distance separated Felix's position from his own. There would be no easy reconciliation. As we have already noted, after Leo III condemned the new teaching at his synod in Rome, the strategy of Alcuin and Charlemagne was to invite Felix to a face to face public debate, which occurred at Aix in 799. The *Seven Books Against Felix* were completed shortly after this debate on the basis of research undertaken in preparation for the debate, incorporating some of its give and take but for the most part following and refuting point by point the letter or pamphlet of Felix which had started all the trouble in the first place.[100]

In the *Seven Books Against Felix*, Alcuin's fundamental perception of adoptionist teaching remains absolutely unchanged from the earlier polemical works, except that it is further solidified and more perfectly assured. Amid a veritable shower of citations from Scripture and from earlier authorities,[101] the judgment of adoptionism as a form of Nestorianism is reissued full strength.[102] Alcuin is more convinced than ever that adoptionism is reducible to Nestorianism because of Felix's new teaching that Jesus was "true God" insofar as he had the divine nature but "Deus nuncupativus" insofar as he was human. For Alcuin, to call Jesus in his humanity "Deus nuncupativus" and to distinguish this from his status as "true God" according to his divine nature amounted almost to a flat declaration of Nestorianism in which the two natures of Christ were made to correspond to two separate *personae*, one who was "God" and one who was "not God." How can one *persona* be both "God" and "not God"? To Alcuin this is a logical disjunction.

Alcuin remonstrates with Felix: he cannot see any rhyme or reason, any coherence, in Felix's teaching.[103] He praises Felix for what appears on the one hand to be a perfectly orthodox confession that "the same one who is Son of God is also Son of Man," that there is a "singularity of person" in Christ,[104] that "He is the true and proper Son of God, and true God, who was . . . born twice, namely, once without flesh, of His Father without mother, and once of a mother but without a father," and that "He is true God whose birth, in either case, is ineffable."[105] Alcuin cannot understand how Felix can produce such a chain of perfectly orthodox professions, wholly untrammeled by error, yet still go on to defend virulently heretical premises wholly opposed to the former. Could it be some sort of trick? Or could Felix, like the demons in the Gospel, be so overwhelmed with awe at the mystery of Christ that at times he just cannot suppress a terrified, if momentary, confession of the truth?[106] Alcuin sees nothing in Felix's position but self-contradiction:

> "True" and "not true" can in no way be one; thus "true Son" and "not true Son" may not both refer to one son; nor can "true God" and "God nuncupative" be one God, because the truth of divinity is one thing, and the bare honorary title of divinity (as in Moses and the other saints) another. But there is no way that both predicates can be in one *persona*, because the nobility of truth is one thing, and the generosity which grants honor quite another.[107]

Since it is nonsense, then, to say that one *persona* is both "true Son" and "not true Son," or "true God" and "not true God," Alcuin concludes that Felix must, if he is to avoid nonsense, admit that his adoptionism is tantamount to Nestorianism, i.e., to a teaching which implies the existence of two *personae* in Christ.[108] No one can teach adoptionism and maintain with consistency that "there is a singularity of *persona* in Christ," and thus part of the appeal of analyzing adoptionism as a form of Nestorianism was that it seemed to make sense out of nonsense. But, as Alcuin had already indicated in the Letter from the Bishops of Frankland, it supplied a parallel to an ancient system of thought which seemed to offer a precedent for the adoptionists's blindness. Alcuin knows that Nestorius did not believe himself to be teaching "two persons" in Christ, but that, given his presuppositions and language, he actually was. Felix, like Nestorius, does not explicitly teach "two persons," and in fact tries to avoid it but to no avail.[109] He makes exactly the same mistakes that Nestorius made.

Alcuin's argument is extremely persuasive. The principle mark of its persuasive power is that it has been not only admired but endorsed by the theological mainstream since the ninth century and in fact formed the theological mainstream. No one has ever thought to ask whether Felix's teaching was *in fact* merely a logical disjunction. No one has ever thought to ask whether there might exist any legitimate way to speak of one *persona* as both "true Son" and "not true Son," or both "true God" and "not true God." Is there any legitimate manner of speaking in this way? It may have been precisely the agenda of Felix to explore the implications of such a way of speaking, and, indeed, to suggest not only that it was a legitimate way of speaking, but a necessary way. Too often it is assumed that Felix simply blundered into logical incoherence almost without noticing it; but he may have been trying to make a critical observation, perhaps a very fundamental observation on the meaning and function of such an important theological term as "persona."

It is clear at any rate that Alcuin did not perceive anything but logical disjunction in Felix's position, and the analysis above of Hadrian's and Alcuin's early anti-adoptionist work made it clear, too, that neither have or use the same frame of reference for christology as the Hispanic theologians. This was discovered principally through a study of their use of Phil. 2:6–11. By focussing attention on Alcuin's use of this passage in the *Seven Books Against Felix*, perhaps it will be possible to specify further the frame of reference from which Alcuin reads and perceives the reflection of Felix.

In the first place, when Alcuin uses Phil. 2:6–11 in the *Seven Books*,

whether citing it on his own or as part of a patristic excerpt, he cites verse
7 relatively infrequently. When he does cite it, he almost always omits the
exinanitio of vs. 7, preferring instead to comment on the language of "taking up" or "receiving." More frequently, he chooses to omit comment on
this verse completely, selecting instead a verse from the last part of the
hymn, the part referring to the *exaltation* of Christ. Indeed, for Alcuin the
topic of the hymn is not a self-emptying at all but rather the exaltation of
a human nature or a "homo," a particular human being. Alcuin does not,
by and large, read the hymn from the vantage point of the pre-existent
Word, but rather from the vantage point of a human nature or "homo"
that is exalted.

For example, Alcuin cites a short exegetical comment on Phil. 2:8–9
from Augustine:

> Augustine bears genuine witness to the Son of God made human and truly
> *exalted*, according to Apostolic voice, *above every name in the heavens or on the
> earth*. He says, "What he himself as Son of God, God born of God, had
> already possessed, was given to Him as a human being, according to whom
> [*secundum quem*] he was made *obedient even to death on a cross*." If, therefore,
> something was given to him in the dispensation of the flesh which he had
> already had in the nature of his divinity, it remains that he himself, born of
> the virgin, should be believed and confessed to be the true Son of God.[110]

The exaltation described in Philippians is a *giving of sonship* to someone,
clearly, to a human being. Alcuin cites Augustine not because Augustine
denies the propriety of speaking of the exaltation of a human being, but
because Augustine helps him make the point that this human being is
given something he already had, and that thus his exaltation is not an
adoption. But the focus of attention remains on the exaltation; the issue,
for Alcuin, is what to call it. Alcuin uses the passage from Augustine as
the basis of a reduction of Felix's teaching to a logical disjunction:

> For who is unaware that as regards a given father the *persona* of an adoptive
> son is one *persona* and that of a proper son is another? For no father, even
> according to human custom, can adopt his own proper son to himself, as
> though he were unrelated: nor could he make someone whom he had
> adopted into a proper son, since the fact that someone else has sired him has
> already precluded blood relation.[111]

Since it is logically impossible for anyone to have adopted someone
who is already his own son, the only rational alternative is that he has
adopted someone else's son. Thus despite his disclaimers, Felix must be

teaching that the Father has adopted into sonship someone who was not originally his own son but instead a "purus homo." But this, of course, is Nestorianism.[112]

It is most important to observe the connection between Alcuin's reduction of Felix's teaching to a logical disjunction and his use of Augustine's exegesis of Phil. 2:8–9. However the exaltation of Phil. 2:8–9 is described, as an "adoption" or otherwise, for Alcuin the focus of Augustine's passage is on a human being or nature who is exalted. Since Alcuin reads Phil. 2 from the perspective of the exaltation of a human being into sonship, he does not see that there could be another perspective in which the adoption in question is not perceived as the exaltation of a human being or of anything else, but as an *emptying* of someone who was not already a human being. Not only for Elipandus but indeed for the anti-adoptionist Beatus, Phil. 2:6–11 was to be understood from the perspective of the eternal Word whose Sonship, insofar as it existed in a human being, was a grand act of self-emptying belonging to the Word. The question dividing Elipandus and Beatus was whether or not such an *emptying* could properly be called an adoption, or could properly be said to result in an adoptive status for the Word as a human. Alcuin, however, views the passage from the point of view of the human who is being exalted or elevated, and for him it is a question of the correct description of *this* event. But once the question is put this way, there are in fact only two alternatives, namely Nestorianism (there is one Son who is naturally the Son, and another who was adopted to sonship), or nonsense (the same son is both naturally the son and adopted into sonship). Alcuin does not see in the hymn from Philippians the event which the adoptionists are trying to describe, and therefore he does not understand the christology that results from the attempt.[113]

This is even clearer in the one instance where Alcuin himself cites Phil. 2:7 outside of a patristic excerpt. This is important because Alcuin's own exposition of this verse should help to determine the frame of reference in which he uses the vocabulary of the verse elsewhere—for example, each time the phrases *forma Dei* and *forma servi* are used. It is especially important to fix precisely the frame of reference for the phrase *forma servi* because it was the adoptionist claim that Jesus was in some sense truly a *servus* that had so aroused the anxiety of Alcuin and of Hadrian before him.

After citing Phil. 2:7 with a small explanation, Alcuin selects a passage from Augustine to help establish his own interpretation of it:

Christ's double nativity gives to the one Christ a double nature. The same one who is God begotten of His Father, this same God, is a human being [born] from his mother. The Apostle, accordingly, calls these two natures which he possesses from either parent two *forms*, saying of him, *Who, although he was in the form of God, did not deem equality with God something to be grasped at, but emptied himself, taking the form of a slave.* You see that in the one person of Christ, a mystery of *two forms*, of two natures, is contained . . . . Of these two *forms* the blessed Augustine also, in the first book of his exposition on the Holy Trinity, says, "*He emptied himself, taking the form of a slave.* And he did not receive the *form of the slave* in such a way that he lost the *form of God* in which he was equal to the Father, but rather the *form of the slave* was received in such a way that the *form of God* was not lost, with the result that the very same one was son of the Virgin who was also Son of the Father." And, a little later on, " . . . Therefore, the *form of God* took the *form of a slave*, each one being God, each one being human [*utrumque Deus, utrumque homo*], but each one God on account of the God who takes up, while each one human on account of the human being who was taken up."[114]

In the first place, apart from the actual citation of the verse (preceding the passage just given), there is no mention of the emptying of Phil. 2:7. Further, in the most generous concession Alcuin will give to the subjectivity or the vantage point of the Word, the action taking place here is not his self-emptying, but rather that of his *taking* or *receiving* of something into his possession, namely, the *forma servi*. The language of emptying has been totally replaced by the language of acquiring, or, even better, interpreted by it.[115] There are insistent accompanying reminders that the Word in this transaction does not "lose" anything. What is acquired is a "forma servi," a phrase which thus becomes just another way of describing the human nature or "homo" that was "taken" or "received." The Word does not become a servant; in fact, it is difficult to see how he becomes anything at all: his becoming human is depicted as his acquisition of another nature, and if he is human it is on account of the "human being" who was thereby "taken" or acquired, not on account of the "God who did the taking."[116] One cannot fail to notice that this is very divisive language, language so divisive that if Felix had uttered it Alcuin might have attacked him for it.[117] There is a virtual division of subjects here. In Augustine's description it remains virtual, but it nevertheless serves to separate any taint of "servanthood" or "slavery" from the Word—it is siphoned off, so to speak, onto the "acceptus"; it finds its locus there, it finds, one is tempted to say, its *subject* there. Nothing really "happens" to the Word; such an eventuality is carefully guarded against.[118]

Since for Alcuin the "forma servi" is simply another way of referring to the human nature or "homo" that the Word took up, it is offensive for him to think of Christ as a "servant" or a "slave." Unlike Elipandus and Beatus, Alcuin does not understand the term as a description of the *end* result of the self-emptying of the Word, but rather as a description of the *beginning* point of a process whereby a human being was taken up into unity with the Word. Therefore, Alcuin sees the adoptionists's assertion that Jesus is a "servus" as a claim that this human being was "adopted" from the status of servant to the status of son. Alcuin wants to argue that this *homo* cannot have been a "slave" or in any way "servile" precisely because that would imply that the exaltation described in Phil. 2:9–10 was an *adoption*—an adoption from the status of bondage to sin to the status of sonship to God—and that Jesus would therefore share this dynamic with the rest of us sinful human beings. How then would he be able to save us, since he would himself have been in need of salvation? This is Alcuin's anxious query,[119] and he is in perfect continuity with even the first letter of Hadrian on this issue.[120] He again reaffirms Hadrian's point that although the prophets did speak of Christ as a "servant," this was done figuratively, by way of foreshadowing,[121] and that when we speak of servantship or slavery, properly speaking the reference is to slavery to *sin*. Alcuin will go on to point out, therefore, that when Paul speaks of the *forma servi* he is careful to make it clear that this designation does not refer to any "slavery" on the part of the human nature, but rather refers to the perfect obedience of the human being who obeyed even unto death on a cross.[122]

Alcuin takes up the issue again at the beginning of Book VI, responding to a challenge offered by Felix. Felix had asked, "What could be born of a 'handmaiden' [Lk. 1:48] except a *servus*?"[123] Alcuin wonders whether Felix has forgotten that like does not always come from like:

> Where is your intelligence? You fail to consider the many genera of animals that are created from the earth, and the diversity of fishes produced by the waters! How is it that living creatures can be created from the insensate, that is, from the nature of earth or water? Or how can trees be born of dust, and of the trees, flowers and fruits?[124]

Alcuin does not deny that the blessed Virgin is called a "handmaid," but Felix ought to yield to the omnipotence of God, who should be able to create anything he wishes out of a "handmaid."[125]

Alcuin stops to admire a passage from Cassiodorus, who applies Ps. 87:5, *He was found free among the dead*, to Christ. He contrasts this to Felix's ungrateful calumny in calling Christ a "servus conditionalis,"[126] a servant by condition or state. This, he says, is an "insult" to the benevolent subjection, i.e., the obedience, which Christ embraced to set the human race free. Far differently, Alcuin recalls, does Gregory feel about this liberation:

> Jesus, the Mediator between God and human beings, had mercy on human beings in the form of a human being, which he assumed. By this mercy, for the redemption of humanity, He says to the Father, "Free him, that he not descend into corruption." [Job 33:24]. . . . It is his to speak, to show humanity the "Free him" by assuming a free nature belonging to a human being.[127]

Alcuin has selected a passage from Gregory that echoes the language of Phil. 2:7, *formam servi accipiens*, but the word *servi* has been omitted in favor of *hominis*, and the word *accipiens* replaced by the more active *sumpsit*. Alcuin has Gregory explain that this means the "assuming" (a still stronger word than "sumpsit") of "a free nature belonging to a human being." Alcuin uses this passage to *identify the subject* of his dispute with Felix about servantship. It is not the self-emptied Word but the "human nature" which was assumed.

Alcuin's point is that this *homo*, this human being, this virtual subject, was not a slave or servant, did not owe death as a debt for sin, and could therefore embrace "even death on a Cross" voluntarily. As a consequence of his obedience, he would be "exalted" and given the "name above every other name."[128] Alcuin cites the exaltation part of the hymn *verbatim* and complete (verse 8.b–11), and rounds it off with an interpretation that ensures that no part of this hymn, either the "taking" of the *forma servi* or the exaltation of the *forma* thus taken, could be interpreted as the "adoption" of a servant or a slave into sonship. This, clearly, is his perception of what Felix is teaching.

All the remaining uses of Phil. 2:6–11 in the *Seven Books Against Felix* conform to the model of interpretation just given. Where verse 7 is cited, the emptying language is almost entirely neglected, while the language of "receiving" or "taking" the form of the slave is emphasized. The "obedience" of verse 8 is seen as the obedience of the *forma servi*, where this phrase refers to a virtual subject, the *homo assumptus*.[129] This results, oddly enough, in a christology which is more divisive than the christology of the adoptionists, and which sees the adoptionist christology as an extremist version of itself, a version in which a virtual distinction is made into an actual distinction. There is an almost exclusive concentration on the Word's "picking up" of another nature, his acquisition of something additional which he unites to his *persona*, an "assumption" which must not be understood as an *adoption* of a human nature into sonship. The human nature, the *homo*, is left co-existing with the Word as a virtual, if not actual, second subject in a unity which is forcefully described,[130] but which, after all, is never really explained. Perhaps the closest Alcuin comes to an explanation is his curious teaching that the *persona* of the *homo assumptus* "perished" in the assumption,[131] making way for the one *persona* of the Word. In this teaching we see the clearest articulation of the status of the *homo assumptus* as a *virtual* subject, a human being who was almost a subject in his own right, but lost his subjectivity in deference to the assumption by the Word.

Apart from this teaching, if we want an explanation of the unity of person, we must content ourselves with Alcuin's rather flat citation of the laconic Mt. 19:6: "What God has joined, let no man put asunder."[132] In other passages, Alcuin states the unity of Christ more expansively, but hardly explains any farther. At one point, he defends himself against Felix's charge, reminiscent of Elipandus's charge against Beatus, that he confuses the two natures, or teaches only one nature:

> We do not confess two natures in the one person of Christ that are, as you charge, with Eutyches,[133] confused, but rather with the Catholic Church we confess and believe that [the two natures] are so ineffably conjoined that—while their properties remain in their integrity—the divine is imparted to the human, and the human to the divine. There is in this holy and wonderful conjunction not the conversion of deity [into something else], but the exaltation of the humanity: that is, God is not changed into a human, but a human was glorified in God. Nor did the divine nature lose that which it had been, that is, God, but rather human nature began to be what it had not been, and thus, as we have said often and will always say, Christ is, of two natures wonderfully and ineffably united, wholly and truly the one Son of God.[134]

This description of the unity of Christ reflects the model of understanding which had governed Alcuin's reading of Phil. 2, in terms of an exaltation of a human nature. We are given an admirable and insistent description of the unity, but there is no explanation or elaboration of it. It remains "ineffable." Alcuin reminds Felix that he ought not to try to scrutinize the ineffable mystery of divine benevolence with human rationalizing, especially since he is not even able to discern how it is that his own soul was, in his mother's womb, inserted into the primordial globule of his physical frame.[135]

> For God the Son, without your help, did what he willed to do: for he knew, by the wisdom of God, how to pour himself into a human nature without any diminution of himself, and to become, in ineffable unity, a son of man in time, he who, before all times, was the Son of God through whom time was made.[136]

One could have imagined, perhaps, a reference to the "emptying" of Phil. 2:7 here. Instead there is the customary insistence of the absolute lack of diminution, and the continuity of subject is affirmed, if at all, with the rather awkward metaphor of "pouring in" or infusion, not too unlike the Nestorian metaphor of "indwelling," a metaphor which Alcuin is in other places at pains to refute as implying a divided subjectivity in Christ.[137] It could equally well, given the preceding comparison to the generation of body and soul, seem almost Apollinarian. The point is that the metaphor is obscure, and the reason it is obscure is that Alcuin has no clear understanding or articulation of the unity the metaphor is meant to illustrate.

Alcuin's descriptions of the process of the Incarnation, so to speak, concentrate almost exclusively on the relation between the *natures*. He pays virtually no attention to the persona *except* as a locus of unity, and even then barely, and without explanation or identification. Sometimes the *persona* is not even mentioned, as in many of the passages cited above.[138] Other passages seem to mention the one *persona* in Christ only because it is the opposite of the Nestorian hypothesis of two persons, and thus serves to distinguish the orthodox from the heretical.[139] Of course, the formula *una persona* is used in many of the citations Alcuin gives,[140] but Alcuin rarely extrapolates from these instances of usage or goes on to develop them. Where he does comment, it is very terse. For example,

> There can exist in one *persona* the passible and the impassible, the mortal and the immortal, just as a human being is immortal in soul and mortal in flesh: thus also is Christ impassible in divinity and passible in flesh, and yet, one and the same, as a whole, is God and man: Christ is one in the *forma Dei*, and Christ is one in the *forma servi*, and the one Christ equal to the Father is the one Christ "less" than the Father. The same one who is God is a man, one Son of God the Father wholly and properly, and also as a whole the proper son of the Virgin his mother.[141]

Alcuin states admirably the way in which the *persona* is the meeting place for the coexistence of direct opposites, but apart from the fleeting reference to the co-existence of body and soul, which really only begs the question, there is no explanation of how or why a *persona* might be a fit place for such co-existence.

We may observe, as well, that Alcuin continues his discussion[142] by citing a passage from Pope Leo I to the Emperor Leo I, where the process of the Incarnation is explained as an *exaltation* of the *forma servi* to unity with the deity in the one *persona* of the Son. The irony is that *Elipandus* had cited this very passage to Alcuin in his fiery letter of retort, but Alcuin has produced here a much abbreviated version in which all mention of or allusion to the self-emptying of verse 7 is left out, while verse 9, the exaltation and giving of the name, is cited explicitly. The result is that the *persona* mentioned appears only as an odd sort of receptacle for the two natures it unites, the one it originally possessed and the one now "exalted" to its possession. Once again, there is little attempt to explain this unity, and the failure to interpret Phil. 2:6–11 in the light of the self-emptying of verse 7 makes it difficult to conceive of the personal unity of Christ in any sense other than that of a vaguely defined metaphysical locus which "acquires" another nature. The failure to balance the "accipiens" of verse 7 with the "semetipsum exinanivit" has led, in this case, to an inability to speak very fully or meaningfully about the "persona" of the orthodox formula.[143] One cannot help but be reminded here of Augustine's famous declaration (in the *De trinitate*) that the concept of "persona," when applied to God, is essentially empty, and feel that it has somehow come to term in Alcuin's discussion of adoptionism.[144]

This contrasts strongly with the Hispanic theologians, for precisely what characterized their thinking was a developing notion of the term *persona*, an infusion of the term with some significance of its own, centered around a particular way of reading Phil. 2:6–11. Beatus had pointed out explicitly what was true both of his own way of thinking and implicitly of Elipandus's, namely, that in the self-emptying described in Phil. 2:7 we have an instance of an act which belongs truly and properly to neither of the natures of Christ but solely to the *persona* of the Word, a *persona* which becomes thereby defined not only by its relation to the Father as in Augustine,[145] but by its status as a specific *agency*. This is not to say that the whole Trinity does not work the Incarnation, as Beatus and Elipandus both are careful to point out, but it does mean that only the *persona* of the Word "emptied *himself*," and that this act therefore in some sense serves both to define this *persona* and to provide the basis for continuity in the subject who is Christ. All of the actions of Christ, from the point of view of either of his natures, are moments in this one definitive act of the *persona* of the Word. Elipandus and, presumably, Felix, go farther than Beatus is willing to go, teaching that the self-emptying of the Word means that he becomes in his human nature an adoptive son. But this does not involve a division in the *persona* of the Word because its identity is not exhausted by its relation to the *persona* of the Father, as it is in Augustine's scheme. Its identity is not merely *coincident* with that relation. For the adoptionists, the Word is always a "son," and always uniquely so, but, depending upon the nature you are considering, "proper" or "adoptive."

Whether or not such a scheme is acceptable—and the christology common to both adoptionist and Hispanic anti-adoptionist does not stand or fall on the acceptability of this particular variant—*Alcuin's* critique of adoptionism does not even begin to graze it because he is not operating with a concept of *persona* that is developed sufficiently to enable him to perceive the issue. He argues ably against a position in which a human nature, full and complete, is adopted into the status of Son of God and for that reason becomes God's adoptive Son. Alcuin points out convincingly that this would lead to a doctrine of two sons, because it implies that the human nature possessed a *persona* which could be initiated into a new relation with the *persona* of the Father. Insofar as *personae* are identified or defined solely by their relation to other *personae*, the same *persona* could not both be adoptive and not adoptive. But if the *persona* could be perceived as something at least partially independent of its relations, then there is no reason why one *persona* could not have more than one relation to another *persona*, and a continual self-emptying could arguably generate the paradoxical situation in which the prerogatives associated with one relation are continually being renounced, "not grasped at," in the acceptance of the humility associated with another relation. The act of self-emptying unites the two, but both must continue to *be* if the act is to have any meaning. Self-emptying is a reflexive action which is necessarily paradoxical: the self must be retained even in its emptying.

Alcuin, with characteristic persistence, does ultimately penetrate to one of the true sticking points between the two traditions of reflection, as opposed to the false one of Nestorianism. For the adoptionists, sonship is a function not only of *relation* but also of *substance*. One cannot be properly speaking a son unless one is born of one's parents's substance. That is why both Elipandus and Felix insist that those who say that Jesus in his human nature was *properly speaking* the Son of God are in danger of teaching that his human nature was a sham. Alcuin notes, by way of refutation, that

> The thorns of your entire infidelity spring up, I am convinced, from this one root, that in your opinion it seems impossible to be a proper son in any way other than being born as a whole from the nature of one's parents.[146]

Again,

> You, full of your physical way of thinking, do not imagine that the power of God can have a proper Son unless something is undergone like that which the substance of the flesh suffers when it gives birth to flesh.[147]

Alcuin is pointing out the truth: the adoptionists do believe that sonship involves more than simply personal relation. They notice that when the Son is called "God of God and Light of Light,"[148] sonship is being described in terms that presuppose or demonstrate a continuity of substance, and that, it would seem, the same criteria should be applied when christology is the issue as when relations within the Trinity are the issue.

What Alcuin does not see, however, is that the adoptionists have developed a conception of *persona* commensurate with their understanding of sonship. Alcuin can appeal only to the omnipotence of a God who can "have" or even (the ultimate in oxymoron) "make" for himself a proper Son out of any nature he pleases.[149] Because there is a relatively impoverished notion of *persona* involved here, Alcuin cannot explain the unity which results from the taking up of another nature into sonship except by appealing to the sheer ability of God to *make* himself whatever he wants to make. But the adoptionists can go on to explain that the agency of this human being, the agent that is this human being, is the *persona* of the Word himself, and that thus he is the Son of God, even if not, in this created nature, properly the Son. It is still the same individual subject, continuous with the Word who, in his divine nature, is the natural son. It is just that He has, for our salvation, emptied himself of even that prerogative. The accomplishment of the adoptionists is that they have come up with an understanding of *persona* which accommodates our common sense understanding of sonship as a continuity of substance. This understanding is not only that of common sense, but the one which underlies, even in Augustine, any Trinitarian theology that derives from a creed which talks about "God from God, Light from Light." It is not, perhaps, a coincidence that the whole controversy began with Elipandus's refutation of a Trinitarian heretic. One could argue that the adoptionism of late eighth century Spain in part represented an attempt to coordinate or correlate more precisely the Trinitarian usage of the term *persona* with the christological usage of the term.[150]

Conclusion: What is New and What is Old?

For Alcuin, the struggle against adoptionism was the struggle of an ecumenical and traditional way of thinking against a dangerous parochial innovation.[1] Alcuin constantly emphasizes the lack of precedent for the teaching of those whom he derisively calls the "new doctors," reminding Felix that the adoptionist vocabulary formed no part of the the preaching of the Apostles, and cannot be found in the Gospels or in the letters of the Apostles, in the holy fathers and doctors, in the Apostles's Creed, or in that of the Council of Nicaea. He rebukes Felix for introducing a "new sect,"[2] and points out that no other church in the world, least of all the Roman church, teaches adoptionist doctrine.

For Alcuin, tradition was important because it guaranteed that contemporaries would have the same access to Jesus as did those who actually lived in Jesus' time. Alcuin remarks that it is only by walking through the estates of the Fathers that we will now arrive at the banks of the River Jordan.[3] He opens his last major treatise against the adoptionists by claiming that his work will have the same intention as that of the Fourth Gospel, namely to give the reader the opportunity to come to have faith that the human being Jesus was the Son of God.[4] But this evangelical, almost kerygmatic impulse will be carried out by appealing to the authority of Scriptures and the truth of the Catholic faith, that is, through tradition. Alcuin's reliance on tradition is thus not simply an exaggerated reverence for the authority of age, but rather an affection for works that will grant to a contemporary sure access to the same options for faith available to persons in the Apostolic age.

This is a very appealing and confident view of tradition. Nevertheless, in its very confidence that a distance in time can be bridged there is also an awareness of that distance,[5] and at least the shadow of the anxiety that it needs bridging, in the face of threats from novelties that would tend to obscure access to the past. By contrast, the Hispanic theologians, and the adoptionists in particular, do not evince precisely this same awareness of the past and of their relation to it. They certainly cite the Fathers, but there is less sense that they are doing so in order to bridge a distance in time. There is less sense of an awareness of a distance in time between the Apostolic age and the present, at least where that distance would be in some sense problematic. Elipandus, Beatus, and Felix (as far as we can tell) never talk about entering "the vast meadows of the Fathers" in order to "cull flowers," or of inspecting the "stores of the Fathers" for herbs to make a healing confection.[6] Their use of older texts is rarely if ever accompanied by such methodological reflection. It arises more spontaneously, more naturally than this, and so there is less a sense of being in a time different from that of the Fathers, of being at a vantage point where the works of the Fathers can all be viewed as a discrete whole, as "fields" or "stores," a set of resources from the past. Instead, there is more a sense of existential continuity with the past, a confidence that one's own ecclesial and theological tradition is connected to it rather than separated from it. There is, for example, Elipandus's indignant retort to Beatus that the See of Toledo had never been known to err from the very beginning of its faith, and also the way in which his list of patristic authorities is virtually the same as Leo's, the Greek writers excepted. There is no conscious project of recovery or preservation; there is the feeling rather of organic connection to a past that has been seamlessly inherited.[7]

This is not to say that adoptionism itself was an "old" way of thinking, or that Beatus's anti-adoptionist christology as such had any special claim to antiquity either, but rather and quite simply that they were organically linked to the Western and specifically Hispanic ecclesial culture in which they found themselves. These christologies developed out of and in the midst of reflection on ecclesiology, the liturgy, soteriology, etc., where the parameters and paradigms for such reflection came almost entirely from the literature of the West and in particular from North Africa and Spain. Consider, for example, the way in which Beatus's christology is formed by an apocalyptic ecclesiology which he inherited from Tyconius, and the way in which Elipandus's theology is entirely comprehensible as a development of certain themes in Augustine, as these themes themselves had been taken over and developed by Isidore and the Toledan councils, especially Toledo XI. There is no need to look outside these Western themes and strands of tradition to find the sources and contexts for the christologies of Elipandus, Felix, and Beatus. Accordingly, the exponents of the competing positions did not judge each other in the terms and polarities of the controversies of the East, but largely rather with reference to their own understanding of the body of Western literature which they accepted as authoritative.

But this means that the triumph of Alcuin and his colleagues over adoptionism is not necessarily what Alcuin thought it was, namely the victory of an ancient orthodoxy over a heretical novelty. Instead, particularly from a Western point of view, one could argue that the reverse happened, that in his triumph Alcuin ensured that a tradition of reflection with a lineage much more ancient than the Carolingian would lapse into oblivion.[8] It would be forgotten that one could ever do christology from Western contexts alone, that there could be a serious christology developed from issues and paradigms native to the West. One could argue that with the triumph of Alcuin any context for christological discussion apart from that governed by the parameters and paradigms of fifth-century Eastern controversies was lost, its very possibility forgotten.

Thus, from 799 until the present, it is the perspective of Alcuin that has dominated our reading of the Spanish adoptionists. It is *Alcuin* who has succeeded when *we* think of adoptionism as an insignificant moment in the history of doctrine, as a provincial, undisciplined construction which had actually made itself obsolescent. If the arguments presented here are found persuasive, then to accept uncritically the triumph of Alcuin as the triumph of orthodoxy over heresy is to accept uncritically the report of one of the interested parties, and to introduce distinctions that may finally be anachronistic and irrelevant.

This is not to say that Alcuin, and Hadrian before him, engage in deliberate distortion of the adoptionist position, or mean to decieve anyone. Rather, because they privilege not only particular christological formulae but a *way of looking at christology* derived from Eastern agendas and paradigms—namely, as a range of options between "Nestorianism" and monophysitism—the cultural context which gave the adoptionist christology its life and meaning is really invisible to them. Despite their reading of Elipandus, they perceive him as a Nestorian, because they engage in christological discussion only within the frame of reference that they privilege. This is a principled and creative stand, but it involves recontextualizing the adoptionist christology, linking it to controversies wholly foreign to its native genius and therefore missing the potentially significant contribution of theologians of the caliber of Elipandus, Beatus, and, especially Felix. It also means severing ties with the last christology developed wholly on Western turf and governed by concerns indigenous to Western texts, and the loss of the sense that such a thing is even possible. In this sense, and in this sense only, one can talk about adoptionism as the last christology truly belonging to the West.[9] If it could be said to have survived in any way, it survived only as a disfigurement survives, partly as a truncated precipitate in the texts of Alcuin and his Carolingian colleagues, partly as a few desultory letters, intact but ignored for centuries in the shadow of Carolingian arguments to the contrary. In this study, these texts and scraps of text have served as invitations to the rediscovery of a christological debate possessed of a degree of sophistication that belies all time-worn bromides about the lack of originality in the early Middle Ages. It may even be the case that these eighth-century Hispanic theologians have yet to make their most significant contributions to the Church's ongoing reflection upon the Christ of faith.

Appendix I: The Teaching of Felix

1. (a) Felix's teaching *developed*. This much is clear from evidence discussed above, in connection with his introduction of the new phrase "nuncupativus Deus." Reports of Felix's teaching prior to this time are vague and for the most part lacking. He is mentioned almost exclusively in conjunction with Elipandus and without any distinction between their positions. Thus it is easiest to assume that Felix's teaching on adoptionism began as an affirmation and continuation of Elipandus's position, with perhaps minor variations. We may take this point, without actually being able to date it, as the *terminus a quo* for Felix's own intellectual development.

(b) It is plausible that it was the controversy with the Carolingians, beginning at Regensburg in 792, that precipitated a course of development in Felix's thinking. Felix, it could be maintained, began a process of reflection and clarification which he hoped would produce a system more readily assimilable by his Carolingian opponents, one more easily recognizable to them as catholic, and one certainly quite in keeping with his own formal profession of orthodoxy.

(c) Oddly enough, the very word that so offended Alcuin and Leo may have been an attempt on Felix's part to reply to Alcuin's charge that the adoptionists taught that Jesus in his humanity was a "false god" (in *Alc.Ep.* 23, to Felix). Felix may have meant to explain that he did not mean, certainly, that Jesus was a "false" god, and quite to the contrary that he really did have a right to the title of "God," but to make clear as well that *as a truly human being* he was not *naturally* God.

(d) Thus, far from being in effect the positing of "two gods," as Alcuin charges (*passim*, see, e.g., *AFU* 1.11, 136C 2–3), the "Deus nuncupativus" seems actually to have been an attempt by Felix to explain the *communicatio idiomatum* between the two natures: for example, just as the divine nature does not strictly speaking suffer although we may legitimately say that "the Son of God suffers," so too the human nature is not strictly speaking divine, although we may legitimately *call* this man—and no other—"God."

(e) Further, it is probably his debate with Alcuin in 799 that committed Felix to further reflection on his position. In an attempt to revise it yet another time, he left out the offensive language (*adoptio* and its cognates, and *nuncupativus* and its cognates) altogether. In the question-and-answer pamphlet which Agobard found after his death, Felix teaches that the one Christ the Lord is Son of God in "two ways":[1] "affirmat [Felix], dicens quia 'sicut in se [sc., Christum Dominum] continet duas naturas, id est divinitatis suae et humanitatis nostrae, ita duobus modis unus creditur Dei Filius. . . . Prosequere, quibus subauditur modis. Secundum divinitatis essentiam, natura, veritate, proprietate, genere, nativitate atque substantia, iuxta humanitatem vero non natura,' ait, 'sed gratia, electione, voluntate, placito, praedestinatione, assumptione,' et cetera inquit his similia" (*ADF* 16.5–7, 17.2–6).

Agobard considered this tactic a wile (*ADF* 1.7–9), but it may admit of another explanation. Felix seems to have taken seriously the charge that he was verging on Nestorianism and attempted to explain that he did not mean that Mary was not "genetrix Dei," but, again, that she was "genetrix Dei" in a different "way" from the way she was "genetrix hominis": "'Licet eadem gloriosa Virgo Dei et hominis genitrix fideliter credatur, aliter tamen Dei genitrix et aliter hominis recte profitetur . . . ; natura quippe humanitatis adsumptae propriam eam esse genitricem, Dei vero matrem gratia et dignatione divinitatis factam'" (*ADF* 13.4–5, 14.23–25).

In comparison with the Carolingians, one can never entirely evade the feeling that Elipandus and Felix were more sophisticated thinkers. They seem to have found it almost impossible to communicate the subtlety of their thought to the junior theologians on the other side of the Pyrenees. Note that Elipandus, upon reading Alcuin's letter to him, described Alcuin to Felix as "confused" (*Alc.Ep.* 183). Despite the rich variety of insults that Elipandus reserved for Beatus, he never called him "confused," nor did he ever complain of any trouble communicating with Beatus, who argued with him from the same perspectives and with similar sophistication. At any rate, it is just as consistent with the evidence to suppose that Felix in his recantations was sincere, and that in each case the resumption of teaching represents a renewed effort at clarification, one of which he paid for, without having been forced to appear in debate, with loss of his see and perpetual imprisonment.

2. (a) It is important to try to gauge the *reliability of Alcuin* as a reporter of Felix's positions. This is conveniently done by comparing Al-

cuin's treatment of Elipandus with Elipandus's own writings. Alcuin's major work against Elipandus, the *AE*, was written in mid- to late 799, shortly after the *AFU*. It was written upon receipt of Elipandus's letter (*Alc.Ep.* 183). Alcuin received this letter just after the Council of Aachen. It was a reply to Alcuin's original letter to Elipandus of 798 (see Heil, *Alkuinstudien*, 71). Thus Alcuin is writing with a text of Elipandus in front of him, a text that we also possess.

(b) When Alcuin actually cites the text of Elipandus, he does it accurately, as even the most cursory comparison of the texts will show. Since he cites passages rather frequently, he never strays very far from issues which are real rather then imagined.

(c) This does not mean, however, that we necessarily receive an accurate picture of Elipandus from the set of citations that Alcuin gives us. Alcuin does not attempt to *reconstruct* Elipandus's position, or to recreate the framework or context from which Elipandus's individual points take their distinctive meaning, but instead replies to those points which he considers most saliently offensive, explaining them from a frame of reference which *he supplies*. Thus there is never any mention in Alcuin of the self-emptying of the Word as the context for Elipandus's teaching, even though at this point Alcuin has at hand almost all of the evidence that we now have for Elipandus's adoptionism. Even from a reading of the larger polemical work, the *AE*, one could never guess that Elipandus had had any use for Phil. 2:7 at all.

(d) Alcuin writes as though Elipandus had also incorporated the "new" teaching of Felix into his own teaching. He *assumes* that their teaching is continuous at all points. To his perception the two positions *amount to* the same thing and so become melded in his mind. Therefore, Alcuin writes as though *Elipandus* taught that Jesus was not only adoptive in his humanity, but also "Deus nuncupativus" as well (see, e.g., *AE* 1.18, 254A.5–7, "nuncupativum Deum et adoptivum filium . . . fingis"; also *AE* 1.12, 249A; 1.16, 252A 12–14, etc.). But Elipandus *never* used this word in any of the writings we possess.[2] Alcuin may have assimilated Felix's usage of it to Elipandus.

(e) Alcuin replies to Elipandus as though Elipandus had taught that some man named Jesus, in need of regeneration from sin, was *adopted* at a given point in his life, probably at his baptism, into the status of Son of God. Elipandus did not teach this doctrine, but Alcuin suspected him of believing it. Consequently anyone who had only the *AE* as evidence for Elipandus's position would imagine that he taught that Jesus was a *purus homo* who was adopted by God, very much as we ourselves are, except that in his case his adoption was also an assumption into personal unity with the Word. However, we have already argued from the texts of Elipandus themselves that this was not the case at all. Alcuin's presentation of Elipandus is thus an ultimately *inaccurate* reflection of Elipandus's position.

(f) Thus we have the strongest possible warning that we should not trust Alcuin's rendition of *Felix*'s teaching to be an accurate delineation of that teaching.

3. Is the assumption (see above, chapter 4) that Felix's teaching has substantial continuity with that of Elipandus correct? Is there any indication in the texts of Felix themselves, so far as they can be reconstructed, that Felix's teaching is susceptible to an interpretation similar to the one proposed above (chapter 2) for Elipandus?

(a) The first prerequisite for continuity with the teaching of Elipandus must be an emphasis on the *unity of subject* in Jesus, a unity which is continuous and unbroken from the time before the Incarnation to the time after it. Felix in fact took great care to emphasize just such a unity of subject in Christ, both explicitly and implicitly. Alcuin himself could not help but notice this:

> Dicis enim eumdem esse Filium Dei qui est et filius hominis, et filium hominis qui est Filius Dei, ut ex tuis verbis cognosci poterat: "Qui illum," inquis [Felix], "sibi ex utero matris, scilicet ab ipso conceptu in singularitate suae personae ita univit atque conseruit, ut Dei Filius esset hominis filius, non mutabilitate naturae, sed dignatione: similiter et hominis filius esset Dei Filius, non versibilitate substantiae, sed in Dei Filio esset verus Filius." (*AFU* 5.1, *PL* 101:188 D 3–D 11)

Alcuin even admired this way of putting it (he cites the last clause again at *PL* 101:189A 5–6). Felix presents the whole drama as an action of the "Son of God" who became a son of man not by any change in his own (divine) nature, but by a "condescension." The latter word cannot be taken in and of itself as an allusion to a process of self-emptying, but its use does become more significant once it is noticed that there is no balancing reference to the "exaltation" of a "human being" as there always is in the Carolingian parallels. The notion of any type of "elevation" of a human nature is absent here.

(b) Felix emphasizes the way in which the unity of subjectivity in Christ is conceived first and foremost as a *continuity* of subjectivity throughout a "process," if that word may be used without technical connotations. This is especially reminiscent of our conclusions about Elipandus. Alcuin cites Felix as follows:

> "Ipsum," inquis, "credimus verum et proprium Dei Filium, ac verum Deum, qui secundum formam Dei bis genitus est; primo videlicet de Patre sine carne absque matre: secundo vero ex matre cum carne sine Patre. Illum verum Deum ex utroque parente ineffabiliter genitum credimus, cui Pater per David loquitur: *Ex utero ante luciferum genui te.*" (*AFU* 5.2, *PL* 101:189 B2–B10)

Here there is a continuity of subject through "two births," one of the most characteristic traits of Elipandus's teaching (see above, chapter 2). The continuity of subject is emphasized by the initial *ipsum*, which is made to refer to the "true and proper Son of God, and true God," and which is then connected by the pronoun *qui* to the two births. This is made even more striking because Felix is willing to further specify that not only the first birth but also the second (the birth *from his mother*) involved the *forma Dei*, with the result that we can believe that "He was ineffably born true God of *both* parents." This does not mean that the divine nature was somehow in and of itself born of a human nature, but that the Son who was in the form of God was nevertheless also truly born *as* a human being *from* a human being. It is a singleness of person that permits this:

> "Et licet," ais, "ex Deo Deus, et homo ex homine in singularitate personae, unus atque idem sit Christus Dei; sicut quicunque homo ex anima de nihilo creata, et carne ex utroque parente formata unus est utrisque parentibus, patris sui videlicet et matris filius." (*AFU* 5.3, *PL* 101:189 D5–D13; note that *singularitas personae* is one of Felix's characteristic phrases: see the fragments at Agobard, *ADF* 33.1–9; Alcuin, *AFU* 3.17, *PL* 101:171D 4–172A 4)

(c) Note that in this passage Felix has taken care to remove all *personal* connotations from the word "God": he does not say "divinity from divinity," but (echoing the Creed) "God from God," making it clear that the Son's status as God is not a function of his *persona* but of the divine nature. The Word is not, *qua persona*, God.

Nevertheless this *persona* is *entitled* to the "form of God." He "does not deem it thievery" to have it. He is "in" the form of God, and is therefore properly called God. Thus, although the designation "God" refers to the nature and not the *persona*, the *persona* of the Word is not thereby trivialized or rendered equal to other, created *personae*. For it is only the *persona* for whom it is *not* "rapinam" to be in the form of God who can renounce this prerogative, who can "deign" to empty himself of it.

(d) This is the reason that one and the same *persona* can have "two births," being defined by them as different sorts of son with regard to the same Father, while yet remaining one and the same *persona*. It is this point which the "Deus nuncupativus" doctrine is meant to explain:

> "Deus est Christus secundum divinitatem, et Dei Filius verus: secundum humanitatem autem Deus est nuncupativus et adoptivus Filius." (*AFU* 7.11, *PL* 101:224 C11–C13)

The addition of the claim that the Christ is *Deus nuncupativus* according to his humanity is meant to clarify Felix's position—Felix is saying that Christ is God because of the *divinity* to which his *persona* is legitimately entitled, not, strictly speaking, simply because of his *persona*. Thus the very same *persona* can be "true" or "natural" Son, because of its legitimate claim to the "forma Dei" or divine nature, and can also be "adoptive" Son, because of its true humanity. Felix will not balk at saying that "the very same one"—"*idem . . . ipse*"—is both "true God" and "nuncupative God":

> " . . . idem qui essentialiter cum Patre et Spiritu sancto in unitate deitatis verus est Deus, ipse in forma humanitatis cum electis suis per adoptionis gratiam deificatus fieret, et nuncupativus Deus." (*AFU* 4.2, *PL* 101:173 C7–D10)

In another passage, Felix tries to explain this:

> "Certe enim idem redemptor noster in forma humanitatis, ut sacra eloquia testantur, filius David est et filius Dei. Quod utrumque verum est: quod tamen non absurde quaerendum est, quomodo in eum utrumque conveniat. Neque enim fieri potest, ut unus filius naturaliter duos patres habere possit: unum tamen per naturam, alium autem per adoptionem prorsus potest." (*AFU* 3.1, *PL* 101:161 D)

Striving to guard the unity of person in Christ, Felix explains that it is true that the same one ("idem") can be both an adoptive son and a natural son because these are two different *ways* of being a son which may belong to one and the same subject. Note how this passage is a *defense* of a one-subject christology—this is Felix's way of explaining the unity. Note that Felix's later theology of the two ways of being the one Son is simply a more explicit statement of what is given here, and is itself clearly an attempt to work within and intepret a one person christology. The same person is son in two different ways, depending upon the nature one is considering.

(e) In this connection it must be observed that Felix is not afraid to tackle some of the most classically difficult christological problems and press boldly to a conclusion:

> "Ipse est enim," inquis, "qui secundum praescientiam Deitatis diem judicii per Prophetam praedixit: *Dies enim ultionis in corde meo, annus redemptionis meae venit* (Is. 58:4). Ipse nihilominus est propter humanitatis naturam, qui in evangelio secundum Marcum protestatur: *De die autem illa et hora nemo scit, neque Filius, nisi Pater solus.*"(Mk. 13:32; *AFU* 5.9, *PL* 101:196 A7–15; cf. Paulinus, *CF* 3.3.7–11; 3.3.2)

As a human being, Jesus was in fact ignorant of the date of the Last Judgment, despite the fact that, speaking through the prophet Isaiah, *he himself* (note the emphatic repetition of the *ipse*, followed, in the second place, by an intensifier, *nihilominus*) foretold the day of judgment in the prescience which belongs to the divine nature. There is the sense here of a paradoxical, almost *active* ignorance, and ignorance which is an effort or an act or a creation or a gift, a willed ignorance that is part and parcel of the self-emptying of the Word who does not grasp even at the omniscience to which he is by nature entitled. Again (Alcuin speaking here):

> In sequentibus quoque ponens verba ipsius Veritatis, quibus cuidam diviti se bonum magistrum nominanti respondit: *Nemo bonus, nisi solus Deus* (Lk. 18:19), valde inconvenienter, quantum ad intelligentiae pertinet rationem, verba, O Felix, conjungis: "Ipse enim," ais, "qui essentialiter cum Patre et Spiritu sancto solus est bonus, est Deus, ipse in hominem licet sit bonus, non tamen naturaliter a semetipso fit bonus." (*AFU* 5.10, *PL* 101: 198 A6–A14; cf. Paulinus *CF* 3.10.22–25)

Again, the use of *ipse* emphasizes the personal unity of subject, while the passage explains that it is a difference in nature that is at stake: Felix is explaining that it is to the divine *nature* that one must attribute essential goodness, not to the *persona* of the Word *qua persona*, and that thus insofar as he is a human being, it is *given* to the Word to be good. The self-emptied Word is *given* goodness, he does not grasp at it even though he is entitled to it.

Along the same lines, Felix also taught that Jesus in Gethsemane truly felt fear on his own behalf (Paulinus, *CF* 3.4.5–10) and truly prayed for himself (see *CF* 1.24.11–12; 1.28.24–1.31.39). He cited Heb. 5:7 in support of his position (*CF* 1.31.12–17; cf. 1.37.1–64).[3]

4. (a) We can see another connection between Elipandus's teaching and Felix's teaching in Felix's insistence that Christ in his humanity is similar to us. If he is adoptive, he is adoptive with us:

> [Alcuin speaking:] . . . volentes [sc. Felix and followers] Christum Dominum nobiscum esse adoptivum. (*LAHF* 2, 88B)

Since this passage is from the *LAHF*, it probably reflects an early position of Felix, very likely continuous with Elipandus's use of this sort of language, especially his use of expressions involving *cum*: see above, chapter 2, n. 56 and chapter 4, n. 54.

Language reminiscent of Elipandus is also evident in the later work, where Alcuin tells Felix that "Hunc (Iesum) tu parvum et adoptivum, et servum conditionalem testari non times" (*AFU* 2.2, PL 101:148 A8–A10). This is not a direct citation of Felix's text, but it is sufficient for us to be able to glimpse the dependence it exhibits on Elipandus's favorite slogan in its use of the words *parvum, adoptivum,* and *servum* (see above, chapter 2, n. 56, for this slogan).

(b) Despite Alcuin's constant harangue that Felix has thus made Jesus simply one of us by insisting on this similarity, Felix is very careful to point out that this is a similarity in *nature* only, and that, if Jesus is similar to us, he is not for all that the *same* as we are:

> Non in gloria deitatis, in qua per omnia similis est Patri, dissimilis vero omni creaturae, sed in sola humanitate, in qua per omnia similis factus est nobis, excepta lege peccati: similis utique in natura, cui tamen nullus similis exstat, vel aequalis in gloria. In hoc autem illum adoptivum credimus apud Patrem, in quo secundum carnem filius est David; non tamen in hoc quod Dominus existit. (*AFU* 1.15, PL 101:139 D–140 A3)

The similarity extends to nature.

(c) In this passage there is the further and most significant qualification that Jesus is adoptive "apud Patrem," that is, with regard to *the Father*. Thus Jesus's relation to the Father is continuous with that in the pre-Incarnate state because, as the Word, his sonship is a relation *to the Father only*. The fact that this relation is realized in another mode or way because instantiated in a different nature, does not change the subjects that are related: the same *personae* exist as Father and Son that did before (see also *AFU* 2.12, PL 101:155C 5–13, for another use of the phrase "apud Patrem").

5. All three Carolingian commentators on Felix notice and pick out for criticism language which to them seems hopelessly divisive of the subject in Christ, and, if it is read from their perspective, some of this language certainly does appear divisive even to the modern reader. It is necessary to stop to look at some of this language, asking if it must be interpreted the way the Carolingians have insisted. Does it really betray a hidden Nestorianism?

(a) Felix will customarily use the language, familiar to anyone studying the Western christological tradition, of the *homo assumptus* theology (for example, "homo assumptus a Filio Dei," *AFU* 4.8, *PL* 101:182A 14–B 8; cf. the parallelisms at *AFU* 3.17, *PL* 101:171D–172A). But since this language is common currency shared by all parties to the dispute, no conclusions regarding the particular character of Felix's theology can be drawn from its use.

Thus, when Felix is cited as saying "Qui susceptus est, cum eo qui suscepit, connuncupatur Deus" (cited by Alcuin at *AFU* 7.3, *PL* 101: 213 B9–10), or even, more disturbingly, "non proprius Dei Filius, qui de substantia Patris genitus est, et per omnia Patri similis, pro nobis traditus sit, sed homo assumptus ab eo" (at Agobard, *ADF* 36.1–3), it cannot be seen or interpreted apart from the way even *Beatus* could with every approval cite passages which spoke of the "co-suffering of Him who assumed with him who was assumed," or the way Paulinus of Aquileia can say that the Lord of Glory never abandoned the man whom He assumed (see esp. *Sacrosyllabus* 137.19, 23, 40), or the way Alcuin himself can refer to the human nature with a personal pronoun (see also Benedict of Aniane's more divisive expressions, Appendix II, #4, below).

(b) It does not seem, however, that there was in Felix any expression coordinate to the language of *homo assumptus* but using the language of adoption: Felix seems never to have spoken of a *homo adoptatus*, nor does it seem that he ever used the verb "adoptare" in the active voice as though some entity, "homo" or otherwise, were adopted into sonship. It is almost always the adjective "adoptive," that is used. There are only two places which may seem to question the uniformity of this usage. The first passage is from Alcuin:

"Secundum," inquis, "Domini mandatum gestabat divinitatem, et habitator est templi sui." . . . Unicus igitur est Christus Filius Dominus noster, non velut conjunctione qualibet et unitate dignitatis et auctoritate hominis habentis ad Deum, quem tu soles conjunctum Deo, sive adoptatum vocitare, divinitate quoque gestare, et nescio quo insolito verbo usus, divinitatem "liniare" dicis. (*AFU*, 7.2, *PL* 101:214 B5–7, C14–D4; cf. 214D 8)

The language of conjunction is used by all or most of the parties in the dispute, on either side, and so in itself is not an indication of divisiveness beyond the custom of the age, and the "habitator" and "templum" language can be found also in Beatus (see above, in ch. 3; for Felix as well as for Beatus this language has implications beyond christology strictly speaking, since the *templum* = the church: see Alcuin's citation of Felix at *AFU* 2.4, *PL* 101:149B 15–C 4).

The usage "adoptatum" given here is highly suspicious: this is not a direct citation but a report by Alcuin of what Felix customarily "says," and it is in just such situations where report easily merges into analysis and is thus no longer simply a report but a claim. Here the scenario of a Christ who was "adopted or conjoined to God" fits all too well the analysis we have seen Alcuin making of Felix's position. We should be surprised not that Alcuin has reported his position thus, but that he has not found *other* occasions to slip into a usage which reflects so naturally the understanding or perception *he* has of Felix's system, but which Felix himself did not use. The most plausible explanation for this, in fact, is that Felix himself did *not* use the language here used to summarize his position. Otherwise Alcuin would have no reason in general to avoid such usage. Note that there are no direct citations which contain this usage.

Note too the interesting use of "liniare" which Alcuin points to— Felix seems to be developing a vocabulary with which to express as precisely as possible what he means. Alcuin is objecting to a technical use of this word by Felix. We might translate by talking about the humanity as "revealing" the divinity, "tracing it out" as it were. We may surmise that for Felix, as for Beatus, it is *as* a human being that the Word reveals the humility of God.

The second passage which may cause concern is from Paulinus:

> Et tu quid pejus ac scelestius, quam quod Verbum non in proprio, quod ex virgine assumendum essentialiter, proprium suumque fecit corpore, sed in adoptivo asseris habitasse? (cited by Paulinus, *CF* 3.24)

"Adoptivo" is here used as a substantive, and may seem to posit an adoptive subject in which the Word "dwells" (although more probably it qualifies "corpore" as its antecedent, in which case there is not another subject implied at all). We have already seen that the indwelling language is common parlance. Like the passage from Alcuin above, this is not a direct citation either. It is a report of Felix's position, one into which a charge or accusation can slip almost indistinguishably, and, even from the writer's point of view, imperceptibly. Paulinus believes that Felix is setting up two subjects or *personae*, and so he would be inclined without even noticing it to report Felix as saying something to that effect.

In fact, in what is clearly more likely a direct citation, Paulinus preserves the customary usage of Felix:

> Non, ut tibi videtur, hoc est 'adoptivus' quod et 'assumptus' seu 'applicatus,' vel caetera hujusmodi, quae tuo strematico digesta stylo leguntur. (Paulinus, *CF*, 1.22).

Here are two perfect passive participles which are equated with the adjective "adoptivus." There is pressure enough here from simply a rhetorical perspective for Paulinus to render the third member as a perfect passive participle "adoptatus" as well, especially when to render it that way would fit right in to the way Paulinus understands Felix (see, e.g., *Sacrosyllabus*, 155, a usage which is clearly an accusation, not a report, but which does reflect Paulinus's understanding of things). The fact that an adjectival form is retained here is most likely due to the precedent set by the consistency of Felix's own usage.[4]

(c) Paulinus and Alcuin (Alcuin at *AFU* 5.4, *PL* 101:191A 9–B 11, and Paulinus at *CF* 2.8; 2.3; 3.18) are both upset by another apparently divisive use of language by Felix, which occurs in his exegesis of Acts 10:38 (where Peter says of Christ "*Deus erat cum illo*") and of 2 Cor. 5:19 (where Paul says, "*Deus erat in Christo*"). Here are Felix's exegeses, as reported by Alcuin (substantially agreeing with the text attested by Paulinus):

> "Non [Petrus] dicit, 'Deus erat ipse,' sed 'Deus erat cum illo.' Nam si secundum veram professionem Deus verus esset homo ille susceptus a Verbo, nequaquam tantus apostolus auderet dicere, 'Deus erat cum illo,' sed potius, 'Deus erat ipse.'" Tertiam quoque sententiam beati Pauli praedicatoris egregii ponit [Felix], ubi ait, "'Quoniam Deus erat in Christo mundum reconcilians sibi.' Non ait, 'Deus erat Christus,' sed 'Deus erat in Christo,' non quod Christus, homo videlicet assumptus, Deus non sit, sed quia non natura, sed gratia atque nuncupatione sit Deus." (Alcuin, *AFU* 5.4, *PL* 101:190AB, 191B7–11)

Felix is saying that there are *not* two subjects in Christ: that Christ *is* God, but not in such a way that two subjects are implied, as would be the case if you read "Deus" as though it were a word referring to a *persona* separate from Christ. "God" is truly in Christ because Christ has a divine nature: but insofar as he is *human*—insofar as the Word is self-emptied—he is not *by nature* God. Felix is insisting that it is the *persona* of the Word which is the locus of unity quite prior to its association with either nature. He is *God* because he has a divine nature: he is *human* because he has a human nature, and insofar as he is human he cannot be properly, that is, naturally, said to be God. Felix is simply, from his point of view, trying to insist on the correct distinction of natures: "I," he says, "do not divide [Him into] persons, but rather distinguish the natures" (cited by Paulinus at *CFU* 1.9). He is saying that Christ's status as God is not a function of his *persona*, but of his divine nature, or, more exactly, of the entitlement of that *persona* to the divine nature. (Similar remarks could be made for Alcuin's report at *AFU* 7.11, *PL* 101:223 C14−226 A4.)

6. The pedigree of Felix's thought becomes clearer as we begin to examine his ecclesiology and his soteriology.

(a) There is a very close connection between his christology and his ecclesiology, very much like that found in the Spanish *anti-adoptionist* Beatus and unlike the very minimal connection observable in Alcuin. Some of the language is even the same. Both Paulinus (*CF* 3.27.8−9) and Agobard (*ADF* 37.14−15) attest Felix's teaching, based on an interpretation of Gregory the Great, that Christ and his Church were *una persona*, or that Head and Body were "unus homo unave caro." Paulinus is affronted at the teaching that Head and Body could actually be "one human being," and not "as though (*quasi*) one human being" (*CF* 3.27.15−16); Agobard is likewise willing to admit only a figurative sense in which Christ and the Church could be *una persona* (*ADF* 37.36−41).

(b) Felix insists that there is nothing which the members receive which they do not share with their Head and receive from or through him:

> Nihil enim habere potest Ecclesia quod ad vitam et pietatem pertineat, nisi quod a capite suo, id est Christo, acceperit . . . (cited by Agobard at *ADF* 37.23−25, who says this comes at the conclusion of Felix's work)

This means not only that we receive from him, but that in some sense he has preceded us in that which he confers. Paulinus notes,

> Addis [O Felix] adhuc et aliud, quia finem non habent verba ventosa (Job 16:3), non posse quidquam membra habere, nisi hoc quod praecesserit in capite. (cited by Paulinus at *CF* 1.28.1−3; *CF* 3.26.9; 3.27.90−92)

This cannot fail to remind us also of *Elipandus*'s corporate sense of christology, in which Jesus stands at the head of the redeemed as "primogenitus" (for Felix's use of this term in particular, see Paulinus, *CF* 1.33.14–16: "*Primogenitum* quidem tu ipse etiam adfirmas eum ex matre, et ideo non verum sed nuncupativum praedicas deum" (*CF* 3.19.20–30).

(c) For Felix, of course, one of the gifts which we receive through him and in which he precedes us is *adoption*:

> necesse est membra adoptiva adoptivum habere caput. (Alcuin citing, at *AFU* 2.14, 256D)

But this does not mean, as Alcuin, Paulinus, and Agobard think it means, that the Head was "adopted." The sentence just cited is careful to use the adjective "adoptive," and not the participle "adoptatum." Felix cites a passage from Augustine in which Augustine, commenting on "*Et dilexisti eos sicut et me dilexisti*" (Jn. 17:23), says, "Qui [Pater] enim diligit Unigenitum, profecto diligit et membra ejus, quae adoptavit in eum et per eum." (Alcuin, *AFU* 7.7, *PL* 101:218A 11–B 6.) Even though Alcuin scolds Felix for not going on to cite the rest of the passage where the difference between us and the Lord is made clear, Felix is guilty of no such guile. He has cited this passage because of the clarity of its language, a clarity which he considers to have sufficiently shown the uniqueness of Jesus already because it says that the Father adopts us "in Him and through Him"—but not *with* Him. Alcuin supposes that Felix has cunningly cited this passage as a way of deceitfully finding support in Augustine for the theory that Jesus was adopted as we have been adopted. But this is not Felix's intention, and for confirmation of this claim we can look more closely at a passage already partially cited above, from Agobard. It seems to be the closing passage from Felix's later question-and-answer text:

> Propter quod apparet in verba ejus [sc., Felicis], quod plus quodammodo conjungat corpus Salvatoris Ecclesiae, quam sanctae Trinitati. Unde et his verbis subjungit in conclusione operis sui dicens: "Nihil enim habere potest Ecclesia quod ad vitam et pietatem pertineat, nisi quod a capite suo, id est Christo, acceperit, Apostolo teste, qui in epistola ad Ephesios [cf. Eph. 1:3–5] scribens ait: *Benedictus Deus et Pater Domini nostri Hiesu Christi, qui benedixit nos in omni benedictione spiritali in caelestibus in Christo, qui elegit nos in ipso ante mundi constitutionem, qui praedestinavit nos in adoptionem filiorum per Jesum Christum in ipso.*" (Agobard, *ADF* 37.20–30)

Felix has once again selected his citation from Ephesians with care. The passage speaks of our adoption *through* Jesus Christ, *in* Him. This is spoken in the context of remarks about our union with Christ in the Church. The point is that in and because of our corporate, indeed *personal*, union with Christ, we have adoption, we are adopted, we become adoptive.

(d) This does not mean, as Agobard assumes it means, that "God elected us in Christ when he elected *him*, and predestined us unto the adoption of sonship in him and through him at the time when he predestined also ["et"] *him* . . ." (*ADF* 37.86–90). Agobard is picturing some sort of corporate predestination or adoption, whereby all who are to belong to Christ are adopted when the *homo* or human nature that is or will be Christ is "also" adopted.

But Felix does not add this "also." And if his pedigree in Hispanic christology is as genuine as it appears from the similarities we have been noticing, then he has in mind a different scenario, one which preserves the uniqueness of Jesus while yet permitting Him to mediate to us an adoption in which He shares.

By his act of self-emptying, the Word becomes *adoptive*, and by being joined to our adoptive Head, *we* are *adopted*: this is our salvation—our corporate, personal union with our Head, a union in which we too become "adoptive." This does not mean we have a parity with Jesus. As the self-emptied Word, he alone has a *persona* which is entitled to deity, which, indeed, possesses deity without grasping at it. As the *persona* of the Word, he alone can empty himself of the divine nature and the prerogatives of natural sonship that go with it, and become adoptive. He alone can mediate adoptive sonship to us in this way, by establishing a kind of relation to the Father, a sort of sonship or way of being a son, in which we too can participate.

Note that Jesus is not therefore simply the first in a line of adopted ones (Beatus's critique of Elipandus), but rather someone who is unique because he makes it possible for us to be adopted by mediating through his *persona* (but *as* a man) a share in divinity. As his Body, joined to his *persona*—the same *persona* which possesses divinity—we are exalted to the status which *for Him* was an emptying, that of nuncupative Gods.

7. (a) It is difficult, given the fragmentary nature of the evidence which remains, to be very precise about Felix's soteriological teaching, and what has just been advanced must be regarded as suggestive rather than definitive. However, what seems clear is that the proper intellectual con-

text for locating Felix's theology is the Hispanic christology whose contours we have already been able to describe by examining Elipandus and Beatus.

(b) Further, it seems clear that Felix represents a sort of median or mediating position between Elipandus and Beatus. He seems to have developed Elipandus's thought in such a way that some of the objections of Beatus are taken into account, and a system developed in which Beatus is refuted (from Felix's point of view) by incorporation of his critique.

Elipandus's weakest point, according to Beatus, was that there was no way in his system to speak effectively about the uniqueness of Christ (see above, in chapter 3). Elipandus had, Beatus was saying, forgotten about his mediatorial role. Felix will not abandon the adoptionist position because he believes that to do so would be to compromise the reality of the human nature in Jesus, just as he accuses Beatus and Alcuin of doing. True sonship is natural, that is, it involves a line of heredity, a continuity of substance. This is true of the Creedal statements about Father and Word ("God of God, Light of Light"), and it should be true as well in christology.

But this need not mean, however, that Christ becomes so like us that he cannot save us, as Beatus had objected he must if Elipandus's scheme were adopted. The key to the problem is to realize that the *persona* of the Word is the locus of the identity of Jesus, not either of his natures taken individually. If we insist on his being divine as the essential element in his identity, we are defining him in terms of one of his *natures*, not his *persona*, or else we are collapsing the identity of the *persona* into one of its natures. The *persona* of Jesus is just as much human as it is divine. The uniqueness of this *persona* consists in its entitlement to the divine nature (which he does not deem "thievery" to own), and of its consequent capacity therefore to empty itself of it. This is to produce an act so magnificent in its humility that it becomes our salvation. The Word becomes our brother, indeed, the "first-born," and *as such* the Mediator, the one who enables us to receive adoption by our union with Him, our brother.[5]

8. We may now move on to what may be the most difficult point to clarify. In the minds of Alcuin and Paulinus, Felix's worst error was that he called Jesus a "slave," teaching that, as such, he needed baptism. Felix is accused (Alcuin, *AFU* 1.18, *PL* 101:159C 11–D 8) of teaching that Jesus

was adopted to sonship from servantship at his baptism. The grounds for this accusation are difficult to clarify because we simply do not have enough of the text of Felix to do it properly. But what we do possess is intriguing:

(a) Felix clearly taught that Jesus had no sin. Even Alcuin and Paulinus testify to this, even though it is not to their advantage to point it out, except for the purposes of mocking Felix for teaching that Jesus was sinless and yet that he needed baptism (as, e.g., at Alcuin, *AFU* 1.18, *PL* 101:159C 11–13).

(b) Felix also taught that Jesus, insofar as he was human, needed a "second birth" or a "spiritual regeneration" or "rebirth." It should be noted, though, that there is no passage which is with certainty a direct citation of Felix claiming any need for *baptism* on Jesus's part. The passages in Paulinus and in Alcuin which mention such a need are clearly not citations of Felix but rather reports about his position (for example, compare what Alcuin says about Felix's position at *AFU* 2.16, *PL* 101:157C 13–14, to what Felix actually says, at *AFU* 2.16, *PL* 101:157D 3–158A 4, A 9–B 1). The report that Jesus needed *baptism* is probably a *charge*,[6] in effect, based on what is probably the genuine teaching of Felix that he did need a second or spiritual generation. This seems confirmed by the way Alcuin puts it in his letter to Elipandus, *Alc.Ep.* 166, p. 270.26–27: "Refert [Felix] quoque eum baptismo indiguisse; volens, ut videtur, eum in baptismo adoptari in filium, sicut et nos." The *ut videtur* makes it clear that what follows is an *inference* from what Felix says, *not* something actually claimed or argued by Felix.

(c) This spiritual generation cannot have been necessary because of sin, so we must ask what it might have entailed according to Felix. In the first place, it was because Jesus was a "servant" or "slave" that he needed a "second birth" (see Alcuin *AFU* 4.10, *PL* 101:184A 12–B4, which in this case can be trusted because there is an allusion to the servantship in the direct citation represented by *AFU* 4.2, *PL* 101:173C 7–D 10). Alcuin and Paulinus take Felix's teaching that Jesus was a servant to mean, as we have seen, that he was sinful, despite his disclaimers about the sinlessness of Jesus. They attribute to him the position that Jesus was a "debtor" to sin (implied at Alcuin, *AFU* 6.1–3, *PL* 101:199D–202A).

Felix, however, makes it clear that Jesus is a servant because of his *nature*, because of his *natural condition*. Insofar as he is born of a servile nature, he too is a servant (see Alcuin, *AFU* 3.3, *PL* 101:164A 13–14; *AFU* 6.4, *PL* 101:203C 8–14; etc.). This refers to the self-emptied state of the Word in which, just as he is not God by nature, so he is not good by nature ("essentialiter") and thus *even "goodness" must be given to him* (see Paulinus, *CF* 3.10). It is in this sense that he has another birth, a spiritual birth. It is a condition of his *nature*.

This is why Felix will insist that if he does not have this spiritual generation, then he does not share our nature at all, or, as he puts it, does not have a physical generation as the rest of us have (see, e.g., at Alcuin, *AFU* 2.16, *PL* 101:158A 9–B 1). It is not stated anywhere that this second generation is later than the first, that it is not coincident with it, as a condition of it. This would be consistent with Felix's insistence that from the moment of his conception and birth the *homo* Jesus is united to the *persona* of the Word. One could imagine that it is the spiritual birth of the Word— his emptying of himself of essential goodness and his consequent assumption of an accepted or received goodness (something, perhaps, like the goodness which Adam had, or which the saints in heaven have)—that is the Mediatorial act *par excellence*. When we are joined to his Body— that is, when we are baptized into the church—we become beneficiaries of his spiritual birth, and receive a standing as adoptive children and honorary Gods.

(d) Jesus' own baptism *typifies* our salvation, the mediation into a renewed humanity, a humanity like Adam's, upon our own baptism. Felix pictures Jesus gathering together the sins of humankind onto himself in the "likeness of sinful flesh," going into the water, and then on his ascent from the river presenting to God a renewed humanity with himself as its Head. Felix points out that in Matthew's Gospel the genealogy comes before the baptism and includes sinners. It is, furthermore, a genealogy which *descends* from Adam to Jesus, so that Jesus is depicted as descending into the water recapitulating and laden with the entirety of our sinfulness. Felix notes, on the other hand, that the Lukan genealogy *ascends*, includes no notorious sinners, and is almost a picture of the final moment of the saving mediation itself, when Jesus presents us all to God, washed clean of sin because of our incorporation into his renewed humanity. Jesus' baptism is a sacrament or mysterious demonstration of *our* salvation, but it is not necessary for himself, nor is it the moment of his own second birth, as discussed above. It is rather a demonstration of what *our* baptism—our incorporation into Jesus' body—makes available for *us*: our baptism unites us to a renewed Body eternally presented to God.

(e) Finally, it is not Jesus' baptism which initiates the sacrament of baptism, but rather his Resurrection from the dead.[7] We may in Felix's remarks here catch a brief glimpse of a theology of baptism inspired by the Pauline teaching that we are baptized into Jesus' death and resurrection. In this connection note Felix's designation of Jesus as the "second Adam," a Pauline teaching from the same section of Romans which teaches baptism into Jesus' death and consequently into his resurrection. It is Jesus' resurrection from the dead which makes a sacrament like baptism possible, which makes it possible for us to be joined to his Body in our own incorporation into his suffering and death.

(f) Here, however, I would like to consider another interpretation of the second, "spiritual" generation of Jesus, for it is at this point that arguments for the influence of Theodore of Mopsuestia on Felix seem to me to have the most force. After all, there is in Theodore a strong reliance on the understanding of Jesus as the second Adam. There is also in Theodore's theology a very close connection between the grace of *assumption*, by which the human being Jesus is taken (probably at his conception, not at his baptism) as the dwelling of the Logos, and the *Resurrection* of Jesus, which, in a way, completes what was begun in the assumption, as Greer explains:

> What exalts the *homo assumptus* to the level of Lordship (the name above every other name [Phil. 2:9]) is not grace alone, but God's gracious action in the resurrection. . . . The obvious implication . . . is that Christ as the *homo assumptus* had perfect freedom as appropriate to man, in such a way that at any time prior to his glorification at the resurrection, he could have repudiated the indwelling Word. Only when Jesus said 'it is finished' was the Incarnation completed." (*Theodore*, 51, 53)

In this context, Christ's Resurrection would itself be his "second" or "spiritual" birth (in Felix's language), and *his* second birth would also be our own (but "per adoptionem"): it is Christ's Resurrection or spiritual birth that *we* are born into at baptism. Christ's own baptism serves as a kind of figure or type of our baptism (on this point in Theodore see Greer, *Theodore*, 80) but it cannot serve this function apart from the Resurrection.

Ansprenger very usefully compares fragments from Felix with passages from Theodore's *Liber ad baptizandos* (from *Commentary of Theodore of Mopsuestia on the Lord's Prayer and on the Sacrament of Baptism and the Eucharist*). The passages do not in any way demonstrate a literary dependence, but they are suggestive. Ansprenger takes his cues from Neander, who argues "Probably, like Theodore, [Felix] supposed a revelation of the divine power manifesting itself in the form of Christ's humanity, and following, step by step, the course of the development of his human nature; and hence he probably supposed also that the resurrection of Christ was the completion of this revelation which began first, in the form of the supernatural, with the baptism" (Neander, *History*, vol. 3, 163; cf. Neander, *Lectures*, vol. 2, 446). Taking Theodore as his paradigm, Neander in a few pages writes what is probably the most perceptive analysis of Felix in all previous literature (if at times rather obscure; see Neander, *History*, vol. 3, 158–163, cf. Neander, *Lectures*, vol. 2, 442–447).

And yet the reader is never finally quite sure whether Neander is describing Theodore or Felix. One has the sense that Neander is in fact describing Theodore, and that this description then serves as a kind of formatting device for the citation of a small number of fragments from Felix.

What is most characteristic of *Felix*, namely his reliance on the vocabulary of adoption, is missing in Neander's description, as though it were simply a slightly more explicit way of talking about what is only implicit in Theodore. Thus the most distinctive characteristic of Felix's theology is overlooked, namely, the way he chooses to use the vocabulary of adoption *without* at the same time asserting that anyone was *adopted*. This would make no sense if Felix is in some fundamental way working off of a Theodorian model, for the adoption implied in Theodore's system is of a human being who remains a subject separate from the Word and is exalted (or adopted) to the status of Son and Lord (see Greer, *Theodore*, 63), even if that exaltation occurs at conception. If Felix had been using the adoptionistic language simply to draw out the adoptionism implicit in a Theodorian theology, surely he need have had no reluctance to speak about the human being who was assumed or *adopted*, for if he had had such a reluctance, it is difficult to see why he would have chosen the adoptionistic language at all, knowing that he would be continually sublating or subverting it.

In other words, like so many other analyses, Neander's description presumes that *assumption* and *adoption* are essentially the same for Felix.

He observes this connection in Theodore, and simply assumes it applies in Felix. He thereby fits Felix to a pre-existing template, but in so doing loses the distinctive character of Felix's theology. I argue instead that this distinctive character is preserved and indeed explained if the keystone in the structure is seen to be the same as that in Elipandus: the self-emptying of the Word to the point of himself becoming an adoptive Son, *not* the elevation or adoption of a subject separate from the Word to the status of Sonship.

This being granted, I am happy to think that Felix has enhanced his theology with some of the themes distinctive of Theodore of Mopsuestia. Some of Theodore's theology seems uncannily parallel not only to Felix, but to Beatus (for example, our corporate participation in the Lord's sonship and perfection, see Greer, *Theodore*, 70–71). My point is that Felix would *see* Theodore's theology from the perspective of, and as an elaboration of, the common Hispanic christological and soteriological scheme which he shares with Beatus and especially Elipandus, *not* the other way around.[8]

9. (a) Finally, the *Confessio*, Felix's retraction of 799, should be read very carefully. Felix does not anathematize anything that he actually taught, except for his agreement not to use the words "adoptive" and "nuncupative." Rather, he anathematizes the Carolingian caricature of his teaching, and agrees to refrain from using the words "adoptive" and "nuncupative," probably because these words by now were hopelessly implicated as tags of just this caricature. Felix anathematizes passages from Nestorius (actually from Theodore of Mopsuestia: see Werminghoff's note, p. 222, n.1), but we can expect this since they did not represent his own position but rather the Carolingian reduction of his position to heresy.

(b) One other thought: Felix confesses that he was vanquished by Alcuin without force and through reason, and that part of this process was Alcuin's presentation of arguments from the testimony of Fathers hitherto unknown to him (*Confessio*, p. 221.19–22, cf. *Alcuini Vita* 7). This cannot be taken literally, since he clearly knew the three Fathers he mentions, namely, Cyril, Gregory, and Leo, and in fact used all three himself, although Cyril only once or twice.

However, what Alcuin may have convinced him of was that the word "adoptive" was used by these authorities in such a way that it recalled all too clearly the sort of Nestorianism that Alcuin associates with it. Felix rejects *that* scenario of adoption, and becomes convinced that the tradition at large, outside of Spain, uses the word in such a way that the taint of Nestorianism is ineradicable, and that it would be better to start again without it. Perhaps he decided that the taint the word carries in the tradition had been the reason the Carolingians failed so miserably in understanding him. Felix's rejection, however, of these words and of Nestorianism which he had always rejected does not mean that he rejected his own christology, or that his subsequent efforts to make himself intelligible should be construed as relapses into heresy. It is simply to add insult to injury to talk about Felix's later activity as a lapse into heresy.

Appendix II: A Note on the Disputatio *of Benedict of Aniane*

Benedict of Aniane's little treatise against the adoptionists (the *Disputatio Benedicti levitae adversus Felicianam impietatem*, edited by Baluze and reprinted at *PL* 103:1399B–1411B) is perhaps one of the most idiosyncratic of all the non-Hispanic anti-adoptionist works. It deserves a study all its own. Perhaps the following remarks will serve to stimulate interest.

(1) Benedict never addresses Felix, nor are any of the positions or claims he reports identified as belonging to Felix or indeed to any individual, but rather to a group of people, the "infelices Felicianos" (*PL* 103:1399B; "haereticorum Felicianorum," 1400C; "haerectici Feliciani," 1410D; etc.), as though Felix himself were out of the picture and Benedict were dealing directly with whatever party or organization Felix had left behind. This may be one reason the treatise has such an oblique relation to Alcuin's work, even though Alcuin had intended his works to be the basis of Benedict's campaign of preaching. Perhaps Alcuin's and Paulinus's work are attestations to the more learned and complex debate with Felix himself, while Benedict's work is the only surviving direct witness to a more exoteric debate as it actually occurred on the frontlines, so to speak, in the West.

(2) For example, Benedict reports a slogan that neither Alcuin, Paulinus, or Agobard associate with Felix himself: "Inficiatores . . . veritati pellaces ac contra e contra aiunt: *Virtutem Dei et sapientiam* Apostolus Christum secundum assumentem, et non secundum assumptum, pronuntiat" (1399D, cf. 1400C). He decides to refute this not by showing, with Alcuin and Paulinus, that "adoption" and "assumption" are not the same thing, but by arguing that we should not talk about "assumption" at all:

> Prorsus nec adoptionem . . . neque assumptionem, quia dicit misisse Deum Filium suum *factum ex muliere*: quoniam *Verbum caro factum est* (Jn. 1:14), non assumpsit carnem. . . . Idem ipse, ipse Verbum, cum dives esset in forma Dei, aequalis Deo, pauper factus est, exinaniendo se, Verbum caro fiendo,

Filius Dei factus ex muliere, non assumptus, ut blasphemi aiunt, adoptione. Unus idem ipse qui descendit, non ut hominem assumeret, qui necdum erat formatus, sed ut homo fieret incarnatus. (1401AB)

This is an astonishing departure from Alcuin, Paulinus, and Agobard, not to mention Leo and Augustine. That Benedict would be willing to abandon such a long-standing fixture in Western christology as the *homo assumptus* may reflect the pressures of front line debate: perhaps it really *did* seem too adoptionist after all.

(3) Benedict's remarks also have links to the theology of *Beatus*, another indication that he is working in a milieu with a different mix of positions than the one to which the official theologians back East have been exposed. For example, Benedict's renunciation of the *homo assumptus* is argued on the basis of Phil. 2:6–7, and it is the self-emptying of verse 7 that is featured. Benedict explains that the Word's becoming flesh meant the Word's emptying of Himself, the Word's becoming "impoverished," not the Word's becoming "rich" because of the acquisition of another nature (1401B). This is an exegesis of Phil. 2:7 which runs directly opposite to Alcuin's interpretation of the passage. Alcuin virtually ignores the self-emptying, or (with Paulinus agreeing on this point) interprets it wholly in terms of the acquisition of another nature. For Benedict, a moment of true emptying is the focus.

Also, explaining that two natures does not mean two gods, Benedict echoes a phrase which was served Beatus almost as a slogan:

. . . vere Deus est ex duabus substantiis unigenitus Dei Jesus Christus Filius Dei, a quo non movebor dubietate, non emigrabo alterius ad culturam, quoniam *Deum* nescio *alium praeter eum.* (1403C)

Benedict also devotes considerable attention to a highly corporate ecclesiology, much like that of Beatus. Benedict will not speak of the *homo assumptus*, but will talk about Jesus as *our* "assumption" and "refuge," that is, by the Incarnation, *we* have been assumed into the Body of Christ by being taken into unity with its Head:

. . . fiendo Deus homo ex proprietatis essentia unigenitus Filius Dei nostra assumptio et refugium, ut ex hac plenitudine gratiae fierent homines Filii Dei adoptione. . . . Ille . . . assumptio et refugium nostrum est; . . . veram intelligamus substantiam carnis, ubi est plenitudo divinitatis, habitatio corporalis: qua utique etiam tota repletur Ecclesia, quae inhaerens capiti corpus est Christi; propter quod Domini assumptio nostra . . . (1405AB)

(4) In other ways, however, Benedict evinces a complete continuity with Alcuin's polemic. He likens the "Felicians'" doctrine to Nestorianism:

> Quis est autem *qui solvit Jesum* (1 John 4:3, cf. Beatus, *Adv.Elip.* 1.42, p. 29.1099–1110) nisi qui dicit proprium eum esse Filium Dei ex divinitate, adoptivum autem esse ex carne, dissolvens unam personam unius Jesu Christi Dei in duas filiorum personas Dei hominis cum Nestorio? (1404C)

Also, although the *homo assumptus* language is dropped, Benedict speaks in ways strongly reminiscent of just this christology: "Dei Filius in proprietate personae et Filii dignitate adunavit sibi hominem ut esset unus Christus et unus Deus et unus Dei Filius . . ." (1404D); "Deus homo factus, et homo in Deum clarificatus" (1403B); "et verbum in Christo homine et Christum hominem adoremus in verbo" (1407A). A priori, it would seem inconsistent to deny the *homo assumptus* but to continue to use phrases and expressions such as these. Further, Benedict has the lengthiest citation of Chalcedon of anyone involved in the adoptionism controversy in any way. At 1406AB he cites almost the whole Definition (as well as a short citation from Leo's Tome at 1404D).

Benedict's treatise is as a kind of melting pot of anti-adoptionist positions of various provenance. They are not always entirely worked out or rendered fully consistent with each other. They have been brought together by the pressures of front line debate, so to speak, in the March and vicinity. Benedict was in a position quite different from that of Alcuin and Paulinus, who were writing at one step removed from the sloganeering and political dynamics in the March. Alcuin and Paulinus also had the luxury of debating with only the most learned representatives of the adoptionist position. Benedict probably found their critiques of Felix helpful but at best only obliquely applicable in his situation. Working in the border areas, Benedict may also have had access to polemic of Beatus, which he could use as a resource in adapting the insights of Alcuin and Paulinus to a more Hispanic setting. And it is not out of place to remember that Benedict was, after all, a Visigoth.

Notes

Introduction

1. For a general introduction to Spain in the Middle Ages the reader is referred to Joseph F. O'Callaghan, *A History of Medieval Spain*. The classic reference work is R. Dozy, *Recherches sur l'histoire et la littérature de l'Espagne pendant le moyen âge*. Gabriel Jackson, *The Making of Medieval Spain* is a summary treatment of the period. In Spanish the most comprehensive treatment is the various volumes of R. Menéndez Pidal, ed., *Historia de España*, especially volumes 3, 6, and 7 part 1. E. Lévi-Provençal, *Histoire de l'Espagne musulmane*, must still be consulted, especially volume 1, *La Conquête et l'Émirat Hispano-Umaiyade (710–912)*. The best introduction to the early medieval period in English is Roger Collins, *Early Medieval Spain: Unity in Diversity, 400–1000*, with exhaustive bibliography on 269–283. Also very helpful are Thomas F. Glick, *Islamic and Christian Spain in the Early Middle Ages*; and S. M. Imamuddin, *Some Aspects of the Socio-Economic and Cultural History of Muslim Spain 711–1492 AD*. Most recently, see Roger Collins, *The Arab Conquest of Spain*.

2. As argued most recently by R. Gregg and D. Groh, *Early Arianism: A View of Salvation*, see especially 50–70.

3. For the Visigothic period in Spanish history, see the relevant sections in O'Callaghan, *History*, and Collins, *Early Medieval*. Works on the Visigothic period alone include E. A. Thompson, *The Goths in Spain* (this is the standard work, and quite excellent although challenged at some points by Collins); P. D. King, *Law and Society in the Visigothic Kingdom*; José Orlandis, *Historia de España: La España Visigótica*; Edward James, ed., *Visigothic Spain: New Approaches*. From the economic point of view Spain was hardly isolated; see Glick, *Islamic and Christian*, 31–32; Thompson, *Goths*, 23–25. For a less optimistic view, at least for the northeast frontier, see Edward James, "Septimania and its Frontier: An Archaeological Approach," in *Visigothic Spain*, 223–241. The judicious comments of Collins, *Conquest*, 11–22, seem conclusive.

4. Thompson provides a short synopsis of this period, *Goths*, 2–7.

5. The comments of Thompson are apropos here: "In Spain alone of the Western provinces did Roman life continue with the minimum of change and interference throughout the sixth century and half of the seventh." Thompson points out that on the local level throughout the kingdom it was the *Romans* who were responsible for collecting the taxes, even from the Goths. The separation of the two peoples was in no sense an "apartheid" of subjugation (Thompson, *Goths*, 311–312). For a more detailed description of the two co-existing social spheres, see

Thompson, chapters 5 and 6. Note the question that Thompson proposes as a kind of summary of the problematic of Visigothic history: "How, then, did these barbarians, who had so much to learn from the Romans, govern their civilized provinces, in each of which a Roman governor and his staff still survived, still administered Roman law, and still collected the Roman taxes?" (3)

6. See, e.g., Thompson, *Goths*, 36–37. On Hispanic Arianism, see Knut Schäferdiek, *Die Kirche in den Reichen der Westgoten und Sueven bis zur Errichtung der westgotischen katholischen Staatskirche.*

7. Even before Reccared's conversion, the Catholic Hispano-Roman population had conceived a loyalty to the Visigothic monarchy despite its Arian character, as shown by the disapproval which most of them evinced with regard to the *Catholic* rebel Hermenegild, son of Leovigild. See Thompson, *Goths*, 64–78; O'Callaghan, *History*, 44; Orlandis, *Historia*, 109–115. Collins argues, *Early Medieval*, 44–49, that Hermenegild was not a Catholic at the time of the rebellion, but converted partly out of a desire to make himself more acceptable to the Byzantines.

8. See Collins, *Conquest*, 9 and elsewhere.

9. See Collins, *Conquest*, 65–80.

10. From the time of Martin of Braga (ca. 520–580) to the time of Julian of Toledo (ca. 642–690) the Visigothic kingdom enjoyed the erudition of such leaders as Leander of Seville (ca. 540–600); his younger brother Isidore of Seville (ca. 560–636); Isidore's student Braulio of Saragossa (ca. 585–651); Fructuosus of Braga (died 665); Ildelfonsus of Toledo (ca. 610–667), and others, including at least one of the kings, Sisebut (612–621; on Sisebut's learning see Jacques Fontaine, "King Sisebut's *Vita Desiderii* and the Political Function of Visigothic Hagiography," 97–100).

11. Thompson's conclusions about Spain in the sixth century are also relevant: "Although Spain kept foreign political entanglements at a distance and indeed avoided them altogether when possible and resisted outsiders stubbornly when they forced themselves upon her, she was closely bound in the sixth century to France, Italy, Africa, and the Byzantine Empire by trade and the interchange of clergy and letters" (*Goths*, 24).

12. Collins, *Early Medieval*, 59–60, comments on the long-standing relation between North Africa and the Spanish church, a relation which was reinforced as waves of refugees fled successive invasions of Western N. Africa. He calls Augustine and Fulgentius the "established mentors" of the North African church (211), and refers the interested reader to J. M. Blasquez, "The Possible African Origin of Iberian Christianity," and, for a contrary point of view, to R. García Villoslada, ed., *La iglesia en la España Romana y Visigoda.* Also see Charles E. Dufourcq, *España y Africa durante la Edad Media,* and the comments of Jacques Fontaine, "Fins et moyens de l'enseignement ecclésiastique dans l'Espagne Wisigothique," 150.

13. See Collins, *Conquest*, 20: "Indeed it was upon these African foundations that much of the 'Isidoran Renaissance' may have rested." See also Fontaine, *Fins et moyens*, 165–166.

14. Toledo at the time of the controversy was under the Muslim control of the Umayyad dynasty, led until 796 by 'Abd ar-Rahman I, and by his son Al-Hakam I thereafter (d. 822). Urgel was part of the Spanish March and thus under

Carolingian control. The degree of cultural continuity in the church is emphasized by Collins (*Medieval Spain*, 212) when he calls the Mozarabic church a "fossil" of the Visigothic past; O'Callaghan, *History*, 88, too, is willing to remark on the continuity of learning and scholarship among the Mozarabs, although he is not impressed with the quality exhibited there. See Manuel C. Díaz y Díaz, *De Isidoro al siglo XI: Ocho estudios sobre la vida literaria peninsular*, 135–140, 163–174, 205–211 for some specifics. On the Mozarabs in general the reader may consult F. J. Simonet, *Historia de los Mozárabes de España*; I. de las Cagigas, *Los Mozárabes*; E. P. Colbert, *The Martyrs of Cordoba (850–859)*; Vicente Cantarino, *Entre monjes y musulmanes: El conflicto que fue España*, 96–147. See also Kenneth Baxter Wolf, "The Earliest Spanish Christian Views of Islam." He argues that Christians in the eighth century did not generally view Islam as a challenge or a threat to their religion.

15. "Mozarab" from the Arabic *must arib* ("like the Arabs"—was this originally an insult?—see O'Callaghan, *History*, 96; Collins, *Conquest*, 213, 219; Imamuddin, *Aspects*, 27, 37; etc.), referring to the fact that those Christians who did not convert to Islam nevertheless adopted Arabic dress and learned the language. On the topic of conversion, see Glick, *Islamic and Christian*, 33–35 and 283. Conversion accelerated rapidly in the middle of the ninth century. This did not mean, however, that the Christians who did not convert remained Christian in name alone, or that their religion was somehow compromised by their acceptance of Arabic custom—see Glick, chapter 5, especially 176–177.

16. Orthodox christology, as established by the Council of Chalcedon in 451, teaches that there are two *natures* (divine and human) but only one *person* in Christ. Nestorianism is the teaching, associated somewhat unfairly with Nestorius (patriarch of Constantinople from 428–431), that there are two persons in Christ (the human being and the divine Word who indwelt him). Along with Nestorius himself, this position was condemned in 431 at the Council of Ephesus, where Cyril of Alexandria presided. Monophysitism is a loose term associated with a variety of persons teaching (generally speaking) that after the Incarnation there was only one nature, and that divine, in Christ. The archimandrite Eutyches is often regarded as the founder of this position. His teaching was rejected by Pope Leo I, and he was condemned at the Council of Chalcedon. The best overview of the fifth-century controversies is in Alois Grillmeier, *From the Apostolic Age to Chelcedon*.

17. Jaroslav Pelikan, for example, describes the theology of Leo's Tome, which figured so prominently in the Chalcedonian settlement, as a "postion above the battle . . . achieved at the cost of ignoring many of the most serious issues" (*The Emergence of the Catholic Tradition, 100–600*, 259). Also note 264–266 for a similar evaluation of the Chalcedonian formula itself, where it is called an "agreement to disagree" which, "whether it was regarded as evasive or only naive . . . settled very little in the East." There is also the familiar position of J. N. D. Kelly, who says that the theses of Leo's Tome "left the issues which puzzled the Greek theologians largely untouched" (*Early Christian Doctrines*, 338).

18. One of the more successful attempts sees Hilary's theology of both "times" and "natures," "a theology of pre-existence, kenosis, and exaltation," as paradigmatic (Pelikan, *Emergence*, 256). This is a christology predicated upon a

particular interpretation of the early Christian hymn in Phil. 2:6–11, a passage which figures very prominently in the adoptionist controversy.

19. Note Harnack's description of the adoptionism controversy as a replay of the opposition between Nestorianism and Monophysitism, although in this instance on the sidelines: "It is the old antagonism of Monophysitism and Nestorianism, toned down, indeed, in phraseology, but not lessened in substance—how could it be lessened? . . . It is only surprising that it arose at the outskirts of Christendom . . ." (A. Harnack, *History of Dogma*, vol. 5, p. 280; hereafter, *History of Dogma*). This is Alcuin's analysis, almost to a tee. But even where the distinctively Western character of the controversy is noticed, it is devalued precisely as such. See, for example, the comments of Grillmeier: "Considerably more tenuous is the link to Chalcedon in the crisis in the West, precipitated by the Spanish Adoptionists. . . . The eighth century witnesses the so-called Adoptionist controversy. This was confined to the West and had nothing to do with the problem of the seventh century. Though it can point to a real connection with Ephesus and Chalcedon, it arose and died down under no special influence from the East. It can be reckoned as a side issue rather than a sequel. The iconoclastic struggle of the eighth century in the East is the true sequel" (A. Grillmeier, S. J., *From Chalcedon to Justinian I*, 13). To call the controversy a "side issue" because it is not directly related to Eastern agendas is still essentially to follow Alcuin's lead, since it judges not only the meaning but especially the *significance* of Western issues from the point of view of Eastern agendas.

Chapter One

1. In his Letter to Migetius Elipandus mentions at least one work which has not survived. See Elipandus, *Epistolae* 1.1 in J. P. Migne, *PL* 96:859 A3. Newly edited by J. Gil, *CSM*, I, p. 68, 1.1. Hereafter Letter to Migetius, *Ep.* 1.

2. Elipandus, Letter to Migetius, *Ep.* 1.1 (*PL* 96:859 A7–10; *CSM*, I, p. 68, 1.4–6).

3. The primacy of the See of Toledo over all the other sees in the Visigothic kingdom was permanently established in 681, at the Twelfth Council of Toledo. See O'Callaghan, *History*, 51, and Collins, *Early Medieval*, 71–80, who underscores the uniqueness of Toledo's position in the medieval West. Also see Horst Fuhrmann, "Studien zur Geschichte mittelalterlicher Patriarchate," *Zeitschrift der Savigny-Stiftung für Rechtsgeschichte* 70 (1953), 143–147. For the vicissitudes of the see of Toledo during the seventh century, see Collins, *Conquest*, 9, 65–80, 126–140, 217–230.

4. See Elipandus, Letter to Migetius, *Ep.* 1.2 (*PL* 96:859 B4–1.2; *CSM*, I, p. 69, 2.1–6).

5. See Elipandus, Letter to Migetius, *Ep.* 1.10 (*PL* 96:864 C2–865 D6; *CSM*, I, p. 75, 10.1–15). The exact claim of Migetius is difficult to define: "De sacerdotibus vero quod asseris, cur se pronuntient peccatores, si vere sancti sunt? aut

si certe se peccatores esse fatentur, quare ad ministerium accedere praesumunt?" (*PL* 96:865 C2–5; *CSM*, I, p. 75, 10.1–3) Elipandus taunts Migetius for speaking of himself as "holy" and "free from sin" (*PL* 96:864 D6–7, *CSM*, I, p. 75, 10.16–17; *PL* 96:865 C4–6, *CSM*, I, p. 76, 10.43–44). Was Migetius speaking of himself as a kind of prophetic figure or charismatic example of the holiness of priests? May we conclude that he was ordained? Behind what Elipandus construes as ridiculous fanaticism, is there some kind of charge being leveled by Migetius, a kind of prophetic, even apocalyptic, denunciation of Elipandus's clergy, who are not "holy" (i.e., unmixed with Muslims)?

6. First and most notably J. B. Enhueber, *Dissertatio dogmatica-historica qua contra Christianum Walchium adoptionis in Christo homine assertores Felicem et Elipandum merito ab Alcuino Nestorianismi fuisse petitos, ostenditur*; see *PL* 101:358.A.

7. Beatus of Liebana. See below, in ch. 3. There are two other possible links between Migetius and the Donatists (see below, n. 41).

8. "Tu . . . asseris quod cibus infidelium polluat mentes fidelium . . . et cum peccatoribus cibum sumere renuas . . . ," Elipandus, Letter to Migetius, *Ep.* 1.11 (*PL* 96:865 D11–866 A1,3–4; *CSM*, I, p. 76, 11.4–7). He cites Titus 1:15, "Omnia munda mundis; coinquinatis autem et infidelibus nihil est mundum."

9. Elipandus, Letter to Migetius, *Ep.* 1.11 (*PL* 96:866 A4–9; *CSM*, I, p. 76, 11.7–11).

10. See Imamuddin, *Aspects*, 36–41.

11. The question came from Egila, someone who was working in the south of Spain and who later belonged to the circle of Migetius. But it is not clear whether the dispute thus forwarded to Hadrian is the same one which divided Elipandus and Migetius. The issues appear to be somewhat different, and it is interesting to observe that Hadrian's solution seems to run against the reasoning of Elipandus. See Hadrian I, Letter to Egila (first letter) (*Codex Carolinus* #96; *MGH, Epistolae*, III, p. 646, 1–2, 3–6); repeated at [=] First Letter to the Bishops of Spain (*Codex Carolinus* #95, *MGH, Epistolae*, III, pp. 641–642. Hereafter *Codex Carolinus*).

12. "Asseris quia in sola Roma sit potestas Dei, in qua Christus habitat . . . et quia ipsa sit tantum Ecclesia catholica, ubi omnes sancti sint, 'absque macula et ruga'; et quia de ea sola dicatur, 'Tu es Petrus, et super hanc petram aedificabo Ecclesiam meam': Et quia non intrabit in ea aliquid coinquinatum, et faciens abominationem et mendacium: et quia ipsa est Jerusalem nova, quam [*quem*, Gil] vidit Joannes descendentem de coelo." Elipandus, Letter to Migetius, *Ep.* 1.12 (*PL* 96:866.C13–D10; *CSM*, I, p. 77, 12.5–8).

13. Elipandus, Letter to Migetius, *Ep.* 1.12 (*PL* 96:867 A11–13; *CSM*, I, p. 78, 12.15–18).

14. Elipandus, Letter to Migetius, *Ep.* 1.12 (*PL* 96:866 D12–867.A8; *CSM*, I, p. 78, 12.12–13).

15. Elipandus, Letter to Migetius, *Ep.* 1.12 (*PL* 96:866 A13–14; *CSM*, I, p. 78, 12.18–19).

16. Elipandus, Letter to Migetius, *Ep.* 1.12 (*PL* 96:867 A14–B11; *CSM*, I, p. 78, 12.19–27).

17. Elipandus, Letter to Migetius, *Ep.* 1.13 (*PL* 96:867 B12–C13; *CSM*, I, p. 78, 13.8–12). It is noteworthy that Elipandus's interpretation of the charge to Peter coincides almost exactly with that of Beatus, his enemy.

18. See Thompson, *Goths*, 184–185, 241; F. X. Murphy, "Julian of Toledo and the Condemnation of Monothelitism in Spain," 361–373; A. K. Ziegler, *Church and State in Visigothic Spain*, 50–53; E. Magnin, *L'Église Wisigothique au septième siècle*, 1–31, 200; P. B. Gams, *Die Kirchengeschichte von Spanien*, 224–227, 232–238. Note, however, the more moderate position of O'Callaghan, who says that contacts between Spain and the rest of Europe in the Visigothic kingdom were "not negligible," and notes that many exchanges between Spain and Rome are without doubt lost to us (*History*, 44). Thompson, however, observes that *none* of the exchanges of which we are now aware were originated by the Spaniards (*Goths*, 23–25). Collins (*Early Medieval*, 218) comments that the exchanges between Spain and Rome in the last quarter of the eighth century were the most active ever recorded, and we may add that these were none too cordial from Elipandus's point of view.

19. "Mingentius," attested at Hadrian I, First Letter to the Bishops of Spain, *Codex Carolinus* #95, p. 637.

20. Elipandus writing to a certain abbot Fidelis: " . . . tam in festis paschalium quam in caeteris erroribus Migetianorum haeresim emendavimus." Text preserved in Beatus of Liebana and Heterius of Osma, *Adversus Elipandum Libri II*. (Hereafter Letter to Fidelis.) See *PL* 96:918 D6–7; Löfstedt, p. 30.1149–1150. This would seem to be aimed at establishing a clear and visible separation of the Migetian church from the ecclesiastical structure of Toledo.

As in the case of the dietary dispute, Hadrian too had learned from Egila about a dispute over the calculation of the date of Easter, and it may well be that it is this same dispute (Letter to Egila [first letter], *Codex Carolinus* #96, pp. 644–645 = First Letter to the Bishops of Spain, #95, pp. 640–641). Hadrian has heard only that some unnamed parties in the (south of) Spain were failing to calculate Easter according to the Nicene method. From this scant information we cannot tell who it is who is calculating Easter incorrectly, nor can we tell from Elipandus's brief note what he feels the proper calculation of the date of Easter to be. Therefore we cannot match up the evidence with confidence. Isidore (*Etym.* 6.17, esp. 6.17.10), presumably reflecting practice in Seville, very carefully recommends the method which Hadrian champions. It would be difficult to imagine that Elipandus would have forsworn such a strong Hispanic mandate. Yet there are complaints of irregularities. See, e.g., those mentioned by Hadrian at *Codex Carolinus* #96, pp. 646.53–647.4 = #95, p. 643.1–9, discussed below at n. 33. Collins points out (*Conquest*, 71) that it would have been easier in many places for the Christians to celebrate Easter at the time the Jewish community was celebrating Passover. Note also the information given in the texts from 764 adduced by G. Morin, "Un Évêque de Cordoue inconnu et deux opuscules inédits de l'an 764." A. Hauck argues that it would hardly be Migetius who was deviating from Roman practice, given his admiration for that See, but this position assumes that he would have known what Roman practice was. A. Hauck, *Kirchengeschichte Deutschlands*, vol. 2, 300, n. 2. On the question in general see Joseph Schmid, *Die Osterberech-nung in der abendlandischen Kirche*, 95–98.

21. Elipandus, Letter to Fidelis, *Adv.Elip.* 1.44 (*PL* 96:919B3–4; Löfstedt, p. 31.1167).

22. "Ego [Elipandus] et caeteri fratres mei in Ispanlitanis tanto tempore di-judicavimus, et Deo auxiliante, tam in festis paschalium quam in caeteris erroribus Migetianorum haeresim emendavimus," Elipandus, Letter to Fidelis, *Adv.Elip.* 1.43–44 (*PL* 96:918 D4–7; Löfstedt, p. 30.1147–1150). See also J. Hefele and H. LeClercq, *Histoire des conciles d'après les documents originaux*, vol. 3, pt. 2, 985–992. Since the Letter to Fidelis, which contains this information, must be dated in October 785, as noted by Beatus at *PL* 96:894 D–895 A1, this is the *terminus ad quem* for the date of this Council. The *terminus a quo* is Elipandus's letter to Migetius, which speaks about condemnation in the future tense but which itself is not dated.

23. Note, too, that in the text given in n. 22 above the phrase "in Ispanlitanis" may be governed by "caeteri fratres mei," and not by the verb. See Wilhelm Heil, "Der Adoptianismus, Alkuin, und Spanien," 100. Compare Gams, *Kirchenge-schichte von Spanien*, 259.

24. Migetius did have followers. See Elipandus, Letter to Migetius, *Ep.* 1.2 (*PL* 96:859 C8; *CSM*, I, p. 69, 2.14), where he mentions Migetius's "socios," and also the Letter to Fidelis, *Adv.Elip.* 1.43 (*PL* 96:918 D7; Löfstedt, p. 30.1149), where he speaks of the Migetians, in the plural. Also see Elipandus's anecdotes about Migetius in his Letter of the Bishops of Spain to the Bishops of France (*Epistola Episcoporum Hispaniae ad Episcopos Franciae*, pp. 118–119; hereafter *Ep. ad Franc.*). Clearly this is a schismatic group. Saul of Cordova writes to the layman Paul Alvar in 862: "Sed plane nescio, quos salsuginosas asseritis, et prope Migeti-anos, Donatistas et Luciferianos notatis" (Letter to Paul Alvarus, p. 223.15–16). The essential characteristic, it would seem, of all three groups is their "salty" rigorism (Hefele-LeClercq, *Histoire*, 991; Heil, "Adoptianismus," 110).

25. F. Ansprenger, "Untersuchungen zum adoptianistischen Streit des 8' Jahrhundert," 21–23.

26. This position is well stated by Collins, *Conquest*, 221–223.

27. For example, "ignorante e idiota hasta el ultimo punto," the opinion of Marcelino Menéndez Pelayo, *Historia de los Heterodóxos Españoles*, 351.

28. See Collins, *Medieval Spain*, 208–211, on the Migetians.

29. The three letters are *Codex Carolinus* ##95, 96, and 97. The first letter written is #96 (Letter to Egila [first letter]). Abadal y de Vinyals dates it and the second letter (#97 [Letter to Egila (second letter)], which cannot have followed long after) to 782–784, and the third, #95 (First Letter to the Bishops of Spain), to early 786. D. Ramón Abadal y de Vinyals, *La batalla del adopcionismo y la desin-tegración de la iglesi visigoda*, 40, 46. Note that Hadrian makes no mention of Felix of Urgel (who was condemned for adoptionism at the Council of Regensburg in 792: see below, in chapter 4). This third letter must represent a very early stage of the controversy.

30. References to this earlier letter and to the questions it contained are abundant: Letter to Egila (first letter), *Codex Carolinus* #96, pp. 644.32; pp. 646.1;

pp. 647.4; Letter to Egila (second letter), #97, pp. 648.27; all scrupulously changed from second person singular to third impersonal singular at the corresponding points from First Letter to the Bishops of Spain, #95.

31. On Wilcharius see Abadal y de Vinyals, *La batalla*, 27–28, 38–43; Collins, *Early Medieval*, 208; and, in more detail, Collins, *Conquest*, 219–220, where among other things his curious designation "Archiepiscopus Galliarum" is discussed. This is probably the same Wilcharius who was Archbishop of Sens by 769.

32. Hadrian I, Letter to Egila (first letter), *Codex Carolinus* #96, p. 644.12–13; Letter to the Bishops of Spain, #95, p. 637.20–22. Collins, *Conquest*, 220–221, persuasively suggests that Egila's mission is evidence for a schism in the Spanish Church, since there is no precedent for sending a bishop to a community already possessed of one, and since the evidence that remains points to a continuity of episcopal succession in most of the sees in the peninsula. (On this point of continuity of church structures see also Abadal y de Vinyals, *La batalla*, 9–23, 44–45; and Zacarías García Villada, *Historia eclesiastica de España*, vol. 2, 47–53, concluding "En suma, la Iglesia mozárabe fue heredera en todo de la organizada por los Leandros, Isidoros, Ildefonsos y Julianes," 53.)

Egila has traditionally been located as bishop of Elvira (see Flórez, *España Sagrada*, V, p. 349). Hauck, *Kirchengeschichte*, 299, n. 7, doubts this because of Hadrian's stipulation that Egila usurp or seek to usurp the see of no one. This point is well taken, although in view of Collins's suggestion, he may have been asked in. And, at any rate, this stipulation is revealed to us only in the latest of the three letters, after Egila had turned heretic, as though this too were just one more good intention that went awry after all: "he was to solicit or to usurp the see of no one [but he did]," Letter to the Bishops of Spain, #95, p. 637.23.

33. Issues raised are (a) the date of Easter (Letter to Egila [second letter], *Codex Carolinus* #97, pp. 644.32–645.50); (b) dietary regulations regarding pork and meat suffocated in its own blood (#97, p. 646.1–6); (c) predestination and free will; (d) various practices including living in common with Jews and Muslims, marrying Muslims, the marriage of priests, etc. (#97, pp. 646.53–647.4). For other evidence regarding issues (a) and (b), see Collins, *Conquest*, 67–72, 221–223.

34. Letter to Egila (second letter), *Codex Carolinus* #97, p. 648.1–8.

35. About fasting on Friday and Saturday (Letter to Egila [second letter], *Codex Carolinus*, #97, p. 648.27–37), and how to correct heretics (#97, p. 648.9–26).

36. Letter to Egila (second letter), *Codex Carolinus*, #97, pp. 637.33–640.11.

37. Letter to Egila (second letter), *Codex Carolinus*, #97, p. 637.26. Lest it seem odd that an ordained bishop should become a follower or student of someone of lesser ecclesiastical rank, it should be noted, as Heil points out ("Adoptianismus," 101), that Beatus and the young bishop Heterius had a relation similar to that alleged of Migetius and Egila.

38. Letter to Egila (second letter), *Codex Carolinus*, #97, p. 637.21–22. The Pope seems horrified and truly surprised at the outcome of the project. The text makes it clear that this mission to Spain was undertaken as a result not of Hadrian's initiative but of someone else's scheming. Wilcharius may have been the major instrument in carrying out the arrangements and convincing the Pope, but it is not clear that he was the prime mover. Charlemagne's interest is apparent (see Abadal

y de Vinyals, *La batalla*, 38–50, and Hauck, *Kirchengeschichte*, 300). Migetius, too, could have sent to Wilcharius for someone, or even sent Egila (who has a Gothic name) to Wilcharius for ordination to the episcopacy (see Heil, "Adoptianismus," 101). Charlemagne could not have failed, then, to take an interest in such a project, which would have been almost like an invitation! For an opposing point of view see E. Amann, *L'Époque carolingienne*, 130. Amann highlights the Pope's role, likening the mission of Egila to that of Boniface. Others have followed him in this: see Collins, *Early Medieval*, 208–209, although in *Conquest*, 220, Collins seems to be thinking more of a tacit and implicit approval of the Pope for Egila's ordination and mission, which was actually set in motion by someone else.

39. As Hauck notes (*Kirchengeschichte*, 301, n. 3), Hadrian does not condemn Egila or formally dissociate himself from him, and the Pope is also careful to note that he is working from hearsay ("ut fertur," Letter to Egila [second letter], *Codex Carolinus* #97, p. 637.27; "Quod si ita est," #97, p. 637.28; "ut eius fama in auribus nostris sonuit," #97, p. 637.25). Heil, too ("Adoptianismus," 102), notes that the Pope is not entirely convinced of Egila's lapse. Ansprenger goes a little further ("Untersuchungen," 30), noting that Migetius did find support in Egila (who was sent to implement reforms similar to those Migetius was calling for), but implying that Elipandus overstated Egila's sympathy for Migetius and manipulated it against him: "Elipandus und seine Freunde versuchten, Egila wegen seiner Sympathie für Migetius beim Papst in Misskredit zu bringen" ("Untersuchungen," 197, n. 126).

40. The presiding bishop notes, "protulerunt nobis fratres et Coepiscopi nostres . . . de quosdam Acephalos nomine Casianorum in confinibus ejusdem Parochiis qui per tortuosum callem gradientes" (Council of Cordoba of 839, *Acta*, 23; hereafter Council of Cordoba, *Acta*). See also Gams, *Kirchengeschichte von Spanien*, 312–316.

41. *Ep. ad Franc.*, p. 118.35–36, where Elipandus calls Migetius "Casianorum et Salibaniorum magister"; see *apparatus criticus* for line 36 for this reading. The word "Salibaniorum" is problematic in itself and is treated below. Three possibilities have been suggested for the meaning of "Casianorum." (1) It is a reference to *Casis nigra* in Africa, where Donatus was bishop, and thus further evidence for a link between Migetius and the Donatists (see Enheuber, *Dissertatio*, PL 101:357D). (2) It is a reference to a place name, specifically, a local church dedicated to the martyr Casianus of Africa or the Casianus of Imola mentioned as a martyr by Prudentius. The text of the acts of the Council of Cordoba of 839 reads, "quod Casiani habientem ecclesiam supra arenam constructam; quae sita est in territorio Egabrense, villa quae vocatur Epagro, atque civitati Egabro vicina," all near Seville (Council of Cordoba, *Acta*, 24.48, and 23.2. See Gams, *Kirchengeschichte von Spanien*, 314–315). (3) Hefele-LeClercq, *Histoire*, 991, and, following them, Heil, "Adoptianismus," 110, see a reference to John Cassian, pointing especially to the report of Egila to Hadrian about disputes regarding predestination and freedom of the will.

42. The most provocative study of this question is that of Abadal y de Vinyals, *La batalla*, where he suggests that the mission of Egila was part of an attempt by Charlemagne to take over the hierarchy of the old Visigothic church in Spain and replace it by one more responsive to Frankish interests. This course of action recommended itself when it became clear that Charlemagne was not going to have,

apart from Narbonne and the Spanish March, any further success in "liberating" the territory from the Muslims, at least not without some internal preparation (see *La batalla*, 35–50). This thesis is generally rejected, but the observation that Egila was more of an intrigant than an apostle (42, 48) may be well taken. Collins brilliantly suggests (*Conquest*, 220–221) that it was a body of Christians in Spain who took the initiative to ask Wilcharius for a bishop—a body who had broken off from communion with the indigenous group: "In other words, there existed some form of schism in the Spanish Church." This would fit well with the depiction of Migetius as a charismatic, even apocalyptic preacher with prophetic claims, who wanted to have his authority underwritten by a more established, institutional claim—the farther away and the more anti-Muslim, the better.

43. See below, ch. 3, n. 9.

44. Ansprenger, "Untersuchungen," 21. Abadal y de Vinyals, *La batalla*, 51–54, leaves it out as not within his purview of study, except insofar as it provides an occasion for Elipandus to make a christological judgment of his own.

45. Heil, for example (see "Adoptianismus," 108–112).

46. The opinion of Menéndez Pelayo has already been noted above (n. 27). See García Villada, *Historia Eclesiastica*, 56; Ansprenger, "Untersuchungen," 21; Heil, "Adoptianismus," 112; and J. F. Rivera Recio, "Elipand," col. 207, all of whom reflect the standard view.

47. Elipandus, Letter to Migetius, *Ep.* 1.3 (*PL* 96:860 C12–13; *CSM*, I, p. 70, 3.1). "Schedulae fetidissimae" is probably another reference to the pamphlet of Migetius which Elipandus has received from him, and thus "in principio" probably indicates that Migetius himself discussed the doctrinal question first, perhaps as a way of buttressing the prophetic authority on the basis of which he denounced Elipandus.

48. Elipandus, Letter to Migetius, *Ep.* 1.2 (*PL* 96:859 D3; *CSM*, I, p. 69, 2.21).

49. Elipandus, Letter to Migetius, *Ep.* 1.2 (*PL* 96:860 A2–3; *CSM*, I, p. 69, 2.23–25).

50. Elipandus, Letter to Migetius, *Ep.* 1.3 (*PL* 96:860 C13; *CSM*, I, p. 70, 3.1–2).

51. See, for example, Enheuber, *Dissertatio, PL* 101:357.C–D; Hefele-Leclercq, *Histoire*, 991–992; Joseph von Bach, *Die Dogmengeschicte des Mittelalters*, 104.

52. Elipandus calls him "magister Salibaniorum" (*Ep. ad Franc.*, pp. 118.35–119.15). Not knowing what to make of this designation, scholars have found it very tempting to assimilate the word *Salibaniorum* to *Sabellianorum* (Enheuber, *Dissertatio, PL* 101:357C–D; Hefele-Leclercq, *Histoire*, 991; J. F. Rivera Recio, "Doctrina trinitaria en el ambiente heterodoxo del primer siglo mozárabe," 200). Werminghoff actually gives this as the reading of the text (118.36), and Heil, "Adoptianismus," 122, n. 166, cites the text without even noting that this is not the reading of the MSS. In fact, there is no MS which gives the reading *Sabellianorum* (see Werminghoff's apparatus for 118.35). And even if there were a choice, the normal procedure should be to accept the more difficult reading, especially since whoever copied the text was perfectly capable of rendering *Sabellium* correctly just below, at 119.17.

53. "Nullus in haereticis tibi aequalis, nullus tibi sodalis: quanto cunctis novissimus, tanto omnium haereticorum veneno refertus: omnium haereticorum coeno lethali inebriatus: aperte Antichristus dignosceris esse missus." Elipandus, Letter to Migetius, *Ep.* 1.5 (*PL* 96:863 A9–13; *CSM*, I, p. 73, 5.38–41). Migetius remained the Antichrist only until Beatus succeeded him in that title.

54. Rivera Recio, "Doctrina," 193–210, and now J. F. Rivera Recio, *El Adopcionismo en España (s. VIII): Historia y Doctrina*, 21–22.

55. See below, in ch. 2, although most of the evidence that can be adduced here comes from another part of the world.

56. See also Menéndez Pelayo, *Los Heterodóxos*, 351, and Rivera Recio, *Adopcionismo*, 33–37.

57. See, e.g., Braulio, *Ep.* 44 (*PL* 80:693D).

58. See Hefele-Leclercq, *Histoire*, 991–92; Enheuber, *Dissertatio, PL* 101: 356 D–357 B; Bach, *Dogmengeschichte*, 104; Heil, "Adoptianismus," 113; Hauck, *Kirchengeschichte*, 283, n.3 (against the theory of Priscillianist derivation).

59. Letter to Egila (first letter), *Codex Carolinus* #96, p. 647.5–6.

60. First Letter to the Bishops of Spain, *Codex Carolinus* #95, p. 643.9—the only letter, which, incidentally, contains Migetius's name.

61. See Amann, *L'Époque*, 131–132; "Migetius," 1722; and E. Amann, "L'adoptianisme Espagnol du VIIIè siècle," 285. There are other, stronger opinions along this line that suggest an actual monophysitism in Migetius: Bach, *Dogmengeschichte*, 104; Rivera Recio, "Doctrina," 203–204; Enheuber, *Dissertatio, PL* 101:359–360.

62. Amann, *L'Époque*, 131.

63. Harnack himself notes that "the doctrines ascribed to him [Migetius] do not seem to have been the reverse of Adoptianism, while the whole figure is obscure" (*History of Dogma*, vol. 5, 281). J. Pelikan, *The Growth of Medieval Theology, 600–1300*, 59, leaves the Trinitarian system of Migetius intact.

64. Elipandus, Letter to Migetius, *Ep.* 1.3 (*PL* 96:860 C13; *CSM*, I, p. 70, 3.1–2).

65. See also (d) "ipse David est persona Dei Patris." All from Elipandus, Letter to Migetius, *Ep.* 1, *PL* 96: (a) 860 C14–15; (b) 861 B9–10; (c) 861 C8–9; (d) 861 C12 (*CSM*, I, p. 70, 3.2–3; p. 71, 3.23–24; p. 71, 3.35; p. 71, 3.36–37). This position is based upon the passages "Eructavit cor meum verbum bonum" (Ps. 45:1) and "Non dabis Sanctum tuum videre corruptionem" (Ps. 16:10), where in both cases the speaker is imagined to be David, the psalmist. Elipandus reminds Migetius that David also said, "In iniquitatibus conceptus sum, et in peccatis peperit me mater mea" (Ps. 51:5), and, "Iniquitatem meam ego agnosco, peccatum meum ante faciem meam est semper" (Ps. 51:3), as well as, "Foderunt manus meas et pedes meos, et dinumeraverunt omnia ossa mea" and, "Diviserunt sibi vestimenta mea, et super vestem meam miserunt sortem" (Ps. 22:18, cf. Mt. 27:35; Lk. 23:24; Jn. 19:24), and, "Dederunt in esca mea fel, et in siti mea potaverunt me aceto" (Ps. 69:21). The use of the last three verses here is especially interesting, since they are almost never interpreted literally, i.e., as properly applied to the person of David or the psalmist himself, but rather are almost always applied figuratively, as pro-

phetic references to the Passion, following New Testament usage. These passages cited from *Ep.* 1.3 (*PL* 96:861B-D; *CSM*, I, p. 71, 3.22–42).

66. (a) *PL* 96:860.D4–861.A2; *CSM*, I, p. 70, 3.6–7; (b) *PL* 96:861 D6–9; *CSM*, I, p. 71, 4.1–3; (c) *PL* 96:863 C12–D2; *CSM* I, p. 74, 7.1–4; (d) Jn. 14:10; *PL* 96:863 D9–864 A2; *CSM*, I, p. 74, 7.9–11.

67. Texts from Letter to Migetius, *Ep.* 1, *PL* 96: (a) *PL* 96:862.A12–13; *CSM*, I, p. 72, 5.1–2; (b) *PL* 96:862.B7–8; *CSM* I, p. 72, 5.8–9; (c) *PL* 96:862 C11–D1; *CSM*, I, p. 72, 5.22–23; (d) *PL* 96:864 A3–6; *CSM*, I, p. 74, 8.1–3. These claims are said to have been warranted by the verses, "Spiritus oris ejus omnis virtus eorum" (Ps. 33:6), and "Non ab homine, neque per hominem sed per Deum Patrem et per Jesum Christum," (Gal. 1:1), which must have somehow been applied to Paul. Elipandus points out that if we agree to Migetius's position, then it must have been Paul, too, of whom it was said, "Spiritus Domini ferebatur super aquas" (Gen. 1:2), and "Cum abiero, Paracletus veniet ad vos" (cf. Jn. 16:7). He also reminds Migetius that "spiritus carnem et ossa non habet" (Lk. 24:39), and that at one time in his life it had been said to Paul, "Saule, Saule, quid me persequeris?" (Acts 9:4; 22:7; 26:14), and, by Paul himself with reference to himself, "Ego sum minimus (omnium) apostolorum, qui non sum dignus vocari apostolus, (quia) persecutus sum Ecclesiam Dei" (1 Cor. 15:9). From Acts Elipandus singles out Paul's words to the Lycaonians, "Viri, quid haec facitis? et nos mortales sumus similes vobis homines" (Acts 14:14; *PL* 96:862BD; *CSM*, I, pp. 72–72, 5.6–30). Note how none of these things, with the exception of the persecution of the Church, would be at all offensive had they been discussed in the context of the *second* person of the Trinity, inasmuch as in that context we are used to thinking about Incarnation, *communicatio idiomatum*, etc.

68. Note the use of the genitive, "Pauli," at citation "3d" above, and the clear focusing on the *persona* (not the name) of the earthly son, the son born of the seed of David according to the flesh. "David," in some of the citations under "1" above, could be genitive as well.

69. Not Sabellianism. There is no confusion of the three *personae*, or reduction of them to one *persona*, or any hint that the distinction among the Three is not eternal. This absence of a Sabellian or even quasi-Sabellian system works against the hypothesis of Priscillianist derivation.

70. Text is citation "2a" above.

71. As in citation "2b" above.

72. Citation "2c" above, and *PL* 96:862A 5–7 (*CSM*, I, p. 72, 4.7–8, cited in full below, n. 76) are annotated by Flórez, respectively, as follows: "Here Elipandus fails properly to distinguish the person of the Son" p. 549, note b = *PL* 96:863, note c; "Here Elipandus is speaking according to his error regarding the adoption of the Son," p. 546, note b = *PL* 96:861, note c. For similar views on these and other passages cited under "2" above, see Bach, *Dogmengeschichte*, 107; Gams, *Kirchengeschichte von Spanien*, 266; Rivera Recio, "Elipand," col. 208; Rivera Recio, "Doctrina," 208; J. Tixeront, *La fin de l'âge patristique (430–800)*, 528; M. Jugie, "Adoptiens," col. 586; Hefele-Leclercq, *Histoire*, 1003, n. 3, 1019; Hauck, *Kirchengeschichte*, 305; Heil, "Adoptianismus," 113; Abadal y de Vinyals, *La batalla*, 64, n.

2; Eleanor Shipley Duckett, *Alcuin, Friend of Charlemagne: His World and His Work*, 176.

73. Foremost among them Enheuber, *Dissertatio*, PL 101:361–393; Gams, *Kirchengeschichte von Spanien*, 266 (who summarizes, "Elipandum—782—reiner Nestorianer," and who finds even in the letter to Migetius a fully developed Nestorian system); and Tixeront, *Histoire des dogmes*, 528, 534–535 (who also claims that the letter to Migetius demonstrates Elipandus's incipient Nestorianism). Others may not use the word Nestorian but employ a fully suggestive circumlocution, speaking, for example, of Elipandus's doctrine of dual filiation, or of two persons in Christ, etc.: Hefele-Leclercq, *Histoire*, 1103, n. 3 (and note Harnack, *History of Dogma*, vol. 5, 238, against).

74. See below, in ch. 2.

75. For a similar position, although articulated somewhat differently, see Rivera Recio, *Adopcionismo*, 109–111.

76. Citation "2d" may seem more difficult. But even here the telltale "quam tu asseris" is present, something which is especially noteworthy in this case because of its omission in a very similar passage, at PL 96:862 A2–11; CSM, I, pp. 71–72, 4.5–9, "Cum in sancta Trinitate nihil credatur esse corporeum, nihil majus aut minus, quomodo formam illam servilem secundam in Trinitate asseris personam, cum ipse Filius Dei secundum eam formam qua [*quam*, Gil] minor est Patre [*Patri*, Gil], per semetipsum testatur, dicens: 'Pater major me est.'" Unlike passage 2d, Elipandus has done this exegesis himself, and, despite Flórez's annotation (see note 72 above), is impeccably orthodox. The interpretation of the verse "Pater major me est" by referring it to the servile "*forma*" of Phil. 2:7 hails from a very long tradition of anti-Arian polemic in the West going back at least to Augustine, who employs it frequently (e.g., at *De trinitate* 1.7). The *forma* to which the verse from John is made to refer is always the human *nature* of Christ. Elipandus is therefore reducing the contentions of Migetius to absurdity (as usual). How can that servile form, that created nature, admittedly "less than" the Father, be or be a reference to the second person in the Trinity? To claim this would be, in effect, Arian.

77. See Elipandus's taunt in the Letter to Migetius (PL 96:861 C8–11; CSM, I, p. 71, 3.34–36): "Certe si ipse est David persona Dei Patris, eo quod dixit, *Eructavit cor meum verbum bonum*, ergo ipse est Pater Filii Dei secundum divinitatem, qui dixit ad Filium, *Ego hodie genui te.*"

78. The text is one cited by Beatus, the *Symbolus fidei* of Elipandus, at *Adv.Elip.* 1.40–41 (PL 96:916 A13–917 C6; Löfstedt, pp. 27–29). If there was actually a Council of Seville (see above, n. 22), this could be a fragment of its *acta*. But Abadal y de Vinyals (*La batalla*, 51–53) and Amann (*L'Époque*, 132), are, I think, very likely correct when they claim that we still actually possess at least a part of the Creed issued in judgment against Migetius, whether it went with a council or not. It is clearly cited from a source separate from Elipandus's Letter to Fidelis, which is cited shortly thereafter (at 1.43–44; PL 96:918 B6–919.B11; Löfstedt, pp. 30–31). The styles of the two citations differ sharply. The letter is cast in a friendly, almost chatty, second person address; the first citation, on the other hand, is a very formally styled confession of faith, which seems to be a corporate product

("Ego Elipandus, Toletanae sedis archiepiscopus, *cum omnibus mihi consentientibus*" [*PL* 96:916 A13–B1; Löfstedt, p. 27.1025–1026], reminiscent of the phrase "et caeteri fratres mei in Ispanlitanis," which Elipandus uses to describe the group which condemned Migetius). In introducing the two citations Beatus is careful to distinguish the letter to Fidelis, which he intends to quote second, from the "faith of his [Elipandus's] church," which he intends to quote first: "*Tunc* [i.e., after the first citation] lecta est ipsa epistola" (C1). Note that Flórez, in his reconstruction of the letter of Elipandus to Fidelis, does not include the first of Beatus's citations (*España Sagrada*, V, pp. 554–556). If the first citation were in fact contained in the Letter to Fidelis, it would have been even there a citation of an earlier source, perhaps in amplification of the information that Elipandus gives in the letter about the judgment against Migetius.

79. Allowing for the fact that Beatus has cited *only* the creed, without any of the historical details, and that he has edited and abbreviated even this. See *Adv.Elip.* 1.38 (*PL* 96:915 C3–9; Löfstedt, p. 26.997–999).

80. Elipandus, "Symbolus fidei," in *Adv.Elip.* 1.40 (*PL* 96:916 A13–917 A2; Löfstedt, pp. 27.1025–28.1064).

81. Much as Augustine's christology is very often subservient to Trinitarian, i.e., anti-Arian, concerns, as at Augustine, *De trinitate*, 1.7 and the whole of *De trinitate*, 4.

82. See Gams, *Kirchengeschichte von Spanien*, 266–267.

83. See R. Dozy, *Supplément aux dictionnaires arabes*, 840. Thanks to John Boswell for assistance with the Arabic.

Chapter Two

1. See Flórez, *España Sagrada*, V, pp. 299–330; Gil, *CSM*, I, pp. xvii–xviii; J. F. Rivera Recio, *Los Arzobispos de Toledo*, xi–xii and 19–23; Collins, *Conquest*, 66–67.

2. 25 July, to be exact: see Elipandus, Letter to Felix, *PL* 96:88: A1, also at *Alcuini Epistolae* 183 in E. Dümmler, ed., *MGH Epistolae Karolini Aevi* IV, p. 308.29–30 (= "page 308, lines 28–30;" hereafter *Alc.Ep.*): "Me tamen cognoscite senectute iam decrepita octuagesimo secundo anno a die octavo Kalend. Aug. ingressus fuisse." The editor dates the letter at 799, giving 799 – 82 = 717 (followed, presumably, by Rivera Recio, *Adopcionismo*, 25) but the dating of W. Heil is preferable: see Wilhelm Heil, *Alkuinstudien I: Zur Chronologie und Bedeutung des Adoptianismusstreites*, 37, 71, where the letter is dated 798.

3. Alcuin says to Arno, "Elipandus . . . in damnata synodali auctoritate et apostolica censura herese permanens," *Alc.Ep.* 346, where Dümmler gives the date of the letter, generally accepted, as 800.

4. This is the dating given by J. F. Rivera Recio (*Elipando de Toledo*, 41–43; "Elipand," col. 207; *Los Arzobispos*, 172; *Adopcionismo*, 27–28). It is arrived at based on two data: (1) the episcopal list of 956 gives Cixila as the immediate predecessor of Elipandus, and (2) the anonymous *Chronicle of 754* (J. E. López Perreira, ed.,

Crónica muzárabe de 754) gives Cixila's dates as 744–753. Many have held that the entry for Cixila in the *Chronicle of 754* is an interpolation from the latter part of the eighth century, and, noticing that in 785 Elipandus is referred to as "novellum archiepiscopum" (Beatus, *Adv.Elip.* 1.132 at *PL* 96:977C–978C; Löfstedt, p. 102.3914–3942), date his episcopacy to 783 (see the literature cited in Rivera Recio, *Adopcionismo,* 27–28). Collins, relying in part on the work of López Pereira, argues convincingly that there are no good grounds for regarding the information on Cixila as an interpolation, arguing at the same time for a good fit between these dates and other information we have about Cixila (*Conquest,* 72–80). For a defense of the 783 date, see Heil, "Adoptianismus," 100, following A. Grössler, *Die Ausrottung des Adoptianismus in Reiche Karls des Grossen,* 4, n. 1, who points out that in a document of King Silo dated 777, Elipandus is still spoken of as an archdeacon of the bishop Cixila. But Rivera Recio (*Los Arzobispos,* 159–164) argues that this letter is a forgery.

5. Rivera Recio, *Elipando,* 18, 21–28, with reference especially to two passages in Beatus: (a) *Adv.Elip.* 1.63 (*PL* 96:931D 10–13; Löfstedt, p. 46.1766–1769), "Quid est catholicus? Qui nunquam fuit haereticus. Haereticus tamen a parva infantia nunquam fuit catholicus, quia nunquam fuit purus: sed sub nomine sanctitatis erat hypocrita religiosus." (b) *Adv.Elip.* 1.54 (*PL* 96:925 D2–5; Löfstedt, p. 39.1469–1471), " . . . illi quoque decepti sunt, qui se Deo servire promiserunt et post professionem monachi, nitore sermonis, et quibusdam sunt philosophorum dogmatibus illecti." Since, as Rivera Recio realizes, Elipandus is not mentioned by name, it must remain doubtful whether or not these passages really refer to him in any precise way—they may refer to Elipandus together with all his suffragan bishops, or even to heretics in general. The second passage is taken from John Cassian (*Conlationes* 1.20.2–3, M. Petschenig, ed., CSEL 13, 30:2–13 [see Löfstedt, p. 38, *apparatus criticus* for lines 1457–71]). Caution should be observed, therefore, in taking these passages as precise historical references to Elipandus. Especially questionable is the way Rivera Recio interprets every instance of Elipandus's use of the word *frater* as a reference to brother monks (see *Elipando,* 25–28), when it is more likely to mean brother *bishops,* as for example with reference to Heterius, youthful bishop of Osma (Letter to Fidelis, *Adv.Elip.* 1.44, *PL* 96:919A 3–4; Löfstedt, p. 31.1154–1155), or to those of his peers involved in conciliar decision making (Letter to Fidelis, *Adv.Elip.* 1.43, *PL* 96:918C 15, 919A 1; Löfstedt, pp. 30.1144–1145, 31.1152–1153), or, as Rivera Recio himself concedes, fellow *partisans* in the adoptionist cause (as in Elipandus, Letter to Felix, *Alc.Ep.* 183, p. 308.13). Since, except for the address of the abbot Fidelis as "fraternitati tuae" (Elipandus, Letter to Fidelis, *PL* 96:918B 11–12; Löfstedt, p. 30.1129) these two types cover all of the uses of *frater* by Elipandus, it is difficult to see how Rivera Recio's interpretation can be correct.

6. Rivera Recio, *Elipando,* 19, referring, with even less justification, to Beatus, *Adv.Elip.* 1.54 (*PL* 96:925D 5–7; Löfstedt, p. 39.1471–1473, "Ascendentes ad primas cathedras, ut publice ab hominibus ignaris viderentur esse magistri, sacerdotium sunt adepti"), and *Adv.Elip.* 1.63 (*PL* 96:932A 10–13; Löfstedt, p. 47.1777–1779, " . . . requirit laudatores suos, plus quam maxime saeculares, ut cum eis vindicet suam perversam doctrinam, et postquam maximam turbam imperitorum deceperit . . . "). There is very little in this passage which can be definitely identified with Elipandus. It sounds, once again, like a citation from somewhere else. There

is no indication that the word *magister* implies anything beyond the normal teaching function associated with the "prima cathedra," the episcopacy.

7. Rivera Recio, *Elipando*, 29–35, with reference to Beatus at *Adv.Elip.* 1.54 (*PL* 96:925C 4–926B 3; Löfstedt, pp. 38–39); 1.88 (*PL* 96:947C 2–D 13; Löfstedt, pp. 65–66); 1.93 (*PL* 96:952A 5–12; Löfstedt, pp. 70–71); 1.109 (*PL* 96:961C 15–962A 11; Löfstedt, pp. 82–83). Again, it cannot be clear that these are true historical references to Elipandus. Beatus is working from a tradition which understands most heresy as a function of too much worldly learning. The same bias against learning is apparent in his *Commentary on the Apocalypse*: see E. Romero-Prose, ed., *Sancti Beati Liebana Commentarius in Apocalypsin*, vol. 2, pp. 130–132, 135–137. None of these passages can have any reference to Elipandus, and may be further compared with other passages from the *Adv.Elip.* 1.14, 36, 37, 41, 132.

8. The question about whether Elipandus or Felix was the first to teach adoptionism must be resolved in favor of Elipandus. It is true that the *Annales* of Einhard (*Annales Einhardi, anno 792; Annales Mettenses Priores, anno 792,* B. de Simson, ed., in *MGH, Scriptores,* I) represent Elipandus as asking Felix's opinion on whether or not Jesus as a man should be called the adoptive son of God (cf. also the "Poeta Saxo," *Annalium de gestis B. Caroli magni imperatoris libri quinque,* book 3 *anno 792,* lines 1–10, in G. H. Pertz, ed., *MGH Scriptorum,* I; Jonas of Orleans, *De cultu imaginum* 1 [*PL* 106:308]; Dungal the Recluse, *Responsa contra perversas Claudii Taurinensis episcopi sententias* [*PL* 105:466]). This is, however, most likely a report of Elipandus seeking in Felix an ally or a learned apologist. Alcuin (in a letter to Leidrad, Nefridius, and Benedict of Aniane, *Alc.Ep.* 200) and Paulinus (*Libellus sacrosyllabus contra Elipandum* 1, = *Libellus sacrosyllabus Episcoporum Italiae* [*PL* 99:153]) both single out Elipandus as the originator of the heresy. Furthermore, Pope Hadrian's earliest letter against the adoptionists mentions only Elipandus and Ascaricus (*First Letter to the Bishops of Spain,* p. 637.34). Finally, Beatus appears completely ignorant of the existence of Felix; he makes no reference to him at all.

9. *PL* 96:916 A11–917 C6; *CSM,* I, pp. 78–80; Löfstedt, pp. 27–29. Date: 785 or earlier.

10. *PL* 96:918 B5–919.B11 (*CSM,* I, pp. 80–81; Löfstedt, pp. 30–31). Date: mid-October 785. The date of the letter is given by Beatus at *Adv.Elip.* 1.1 (*PL* 96:894C 20–895A 1; Löfstedt, p. 1.4). The date of the "Symbolus" cannot be later, of course, than that of the late 785 text.

11. This letter and the one to the Bishops of Frankland were written in response to the condemnation of Felix at Regensburg in 792, but they evince no knowledge of the Council of Frankfurt in June 794. Therefore the dating of Werminghoff (*MGH, Concilia,* II, pt. 1, pp. 120, 111), and Heil (*Alkuinstudien,* 66) is correct. Also, there is no reason to doubt the authorship of Elipandus, even though he does not write in his own name in these letters. The Letter to the Bishops of Frankland, *Ep. ad Franc.,* is ascribed to Elipandus by Pope Hadrian I (*Second Letter to the Bishops of Spain,* in *MGH, Concilia,* II, p. 122.42) and by the Italian Bishops at the Council of Frankfurt (*Libellus Sacrosyllabus Episcoporum Italiae,* in *MGH, Concilia,* II, p. 131.5–6). The authorship of Elipandus for either letter has never been contested.

12. Text in *Alc.Ep.* 182, p. 301 (*CSM*, I, pp. 96–109). Dated by Heil, *Alkuinstudien*, 37.

13. *Alc.Ep.* 183, pp. 307–308 (*CSM*, I, pp. 109–111), dated by Elipandus 23 October (307.28), omitting the year, which is supplied as 799 by the editor (307.20), and as 798 by Heil (*Alkuinstudien*, 37), whose dating I have followed. Elipandus mentions having responded to Alcuin's letter to him, so this letter must be later than the letter to Alcuin.

14. Although the sources agree that the unoccupied North was a stronghold of at least the visible opposition, it is not true that the only resistance to the adoptionist line came from the North. In the Letter to Fidelis, where Elipandus notes that just as he drove the Migetian heresy from Baetica, so he wants the heresy of Beatus driven from the confines of Asturia (*PL* 96:919B3–6; Löfstedt, p. 31.1163–1169), he seems to be contrasting the two geographical centers of the heresies, respectively. Heterius is bishop of Osma, and Beatus is at Liebana, both in the North. But Beatus himself notes, " . . . non solum per Asturiam, sed per totam Hispaniam, et usque ad Franciam divulgatum est, quod duae quaestiones in Asturiensi Ecclesia ortae sunt. Et sicut duae quaestiones, ita duo populi et duae Ecclesiae, una pars cum altera pro uno Christo contendunt . . . : et hoc non in minuta plebe, sed inter episcopos est." *Adv.Elip.* 1.13 (*PL* 96:901D 8–902A 2; Löfstedt, p. 9.334–340). Obviously the kingdom of the Asturias was divided on the question. But so to some extent was the southern part of the peninsula. There is evidence that Theudila, a bishop of Seville, was against Elipandus (*Albari Epistula* IV.27; *CSM*, I, pp. 114–16), and marginal annotations to Monte Cassino MSS 4 and 19 are further, if anonymous, evidence for Spanish anti-adoptionists (following Collins, *Conquest*, 228, who criticizes D. de Bruyne for taking the marginalia as adoptionist: see D. de Bruyne, "Un document de la controverse adoptioniste en Espagne vers l'an 800," *Revue d'histoire ecclésiastique* 27, pt 2: 307–312). On the question of the divided North, see also Díaz y Díaz, *Isidore*, 253, n. 34.

15. Letter to Fidelis, *Adv.Elip.* 1.43, *PL* 96:918B 10–12; Löfstedt, p. 30.29–30; *CSM*, I, p. 80, 3.4. Ascaricus is also mentioned in Hadrian's First Letter to the Bishops of Spain (*Codex Carolinus* #95, p. 637.34) where he is called a bishop, in agreement with this notice in the letter to Fidelis. Not very much else is known about Ascaricus. To Collins, the evidence suggests that Ascaricus's see was in the kingdom of the Asturias (*Conquest*, 228). If so, it is further evidence that there was important sympathy for the adoptionist position in the Asturias. See also the short notice by Antonio Ferrua, "Ascarico," *Enciclopedia Cattolica*, vol. 2, col. 82. The tradition that he was bishop of Braga has little foundation (see Hefele-LeClercq, *Histoire*, 3.2, 1002, n. 2, and 1021–1022). There is a short *Epistola* by Ascaricus preserved and edited along with its reply by the bishop Tusaredus at *CSM*, I, pp. 113–124. There is no mention of any adoptionistic theme.

16. Letter to Fidelis, *Adv.Elip.* 1.43 (*PL* 96:918B 15–C 2; Löfstedt, pp. 30–31).

17. Letter to Fidelis, *Adv.Elip.* 1.44 (*PL* 96:919A 3–5; Löfstedt, p. 31.1154–1156).

18. Letter to Fidelis, *Adv.Elip.* 1.43 (*PL* 96:918B 10,14; Löfstedt, p. 30.1131); cf. 1.44 (*PL* 96:919B 6–7; Löfstedt, p. 31.1170, 77).

19. Letter to Fidelis, *Adv.Elip.* 1.43 (*PL* 96:918 C2–5; Löfstedt, p. 30.1139–1142).

20. Letter to Fidelis, *Adv.Elip.* 1.43 (*PL* 96:918C 9–13; Löfstedt, pp. 30–31). Elipandus's jealous defense of the rights of his metropolitan see, even against Rome, added fuel to the fire in the adoptionist controversy. On this basis he resented the posture of both Beatus and Hadrian, whose rebukes he could only regard as meddling. See Heil, "Adoptianismus," 113–115. One can understand his resentment, especially since it was only during the tenure of his predecessor Cixila that the see of Toledo had begun to reconstruct its ascendancy and thus the unity of what was left of the Visigothic church after invasion and political upheaval. See Collins, *Conquest*, 65–80.

21. Letter to Fidelis, *Adv.Elip.* 1.43 (*PL* 96:918D 4–7; Löfstedt, p. 30.1147–1150).

22. Letter to Fidelis, *Adv.Elip.* 1.43–44 (*PL* 96:918D 9–919A 2,15–B 6; Löfstedt, pp. 30.1151–31.1153, 1165–69).

23. Letter to Fidelis, *Adv.Elip.* 1.44 (*PL* 96:919B 6–11; Löfstedt, p. 31.1169–1173).

24. See also Beatus, *Adv.Elip.* 1.13 (*PL* 96:901 C10–12; Löfstedt, p. 9.323–324), "Pastores Ecclesiarum auferre conantur [sc. lupi, i.e., haeretici], ut oves Domini facilius strangulent [*extrangulent*, Löfstedt]."

25. Not from Cordoba, despite what Alcuin says, "maxime origo hujus perfidiae de Corduba civitate processit" (*Alc.Ep.* 201). Most likely, this is simply an insult, saying, in effect, that the adoptionist doctrine hails from the capital of the Islamic regime in Spain. But even at best it is secondhand information reflecting Elipandus's report to Felix that he is sending on some help he received from certain "brothers" at Cordoba ("Ego vero direxi epistulam tuam ad Cordoba fratribus, qui de Deo recta sentiunt. Et mihi multa scripserunt, quae in tuo adiutorio debueram dirigere"), Elipandus, Letter to Felix, *Alc.Ep.* 183, p. 308.13–14. The relative clause "qui de Deo recta sentiunt" serves to identify the brothers in Cordoba, something unnecessary if Felix knew of them already.

26. "Qui non fuerit confessus Jesum Christum adoptivum humanitate, et nequaquam adoptivum divinitate, et haereticus est, et exterminetur," Elipandus, Letter to Fidelis (*PL* 96:918B 6–8; Löfstedt, p. 30.1125–1127). "Exterminetur" = "shall be banished," that is, from the territory in Elipandus's ecclesiastical jurisdiction: "proferat nunc dominus Elipandus fidem suam Ecclesiae suae, in qua fide nos redarguit, ut auditu [*aut ita*, Löfstedt] credamus, aut, si noluerimus, a diocesi sua [*dioecese suo*, Löfstedt] exsules habeamur" (Beatus speaking, at *Adv.Elip.* 1.38; *PL* 96:915B 13–C 1; Löfstedt, p. 26.992–995). Disdainfully emphasizing the possessives (Elipandus's "*own* faith of *his* church"), Beatus separates himself from the ecclesiastical structure of Elipandus. How far Elipandus's threats were carried out is uncertain, but it is clear that at least the threat of persecution did hang over Beatus and his associates: see also *Adv.Elip.* 1.2 (*PL* 96:895C 14; Löfstedt, p. 2.41); 1.13 (*PL* 96:901D 3–8; Löfstedt, p. 9.323–324); 1.14 (*PL* 96:902A 14–B5; Löfstedt, p. 10.351–357); 1.64 *passim*. It is true that Beatus is inclined to dramatize the theme of persecution, which he sees in an apocalyptic context and has inherited from the sources of his *Commentary on the Apocalypse*, but there are enough historical spe-

cifics in the passages cited here so that at least the very concrete threat of persecution may be established.

27. The earliest, *Codex Carolinus* #95, is from 785; the later one from ca. 793.

28. Beatus, *Adv.Elip.* 1.1 (*PL* 96:895A 6–7; Löfstedt, p. 1.3–10). The date of this public reading is given by Beatus as 26 November 785.

29. The demonstrative "ipsum" makes it likely that the pamphlet meant is the letter just mentioned in *Adv.Elip.* 1.1 (*PL* 96:894C 19; Löfstedt, p. 1.8–9): "*that* document was read aloud to all Asturia . . . " Note the description of this letter at 1.38 (*PL* 96:918C 1–4; Löfstedt, p. 30.1129–1130) and that Beatus never describes another such document—the "Symbolus," perhaps mentioned at 1.38, (*PL* 96:918B 12–C 1; Löfstedt, p. 30.1114), and the letter seem to be all he has.

30. See Rivera Recio, *Elipando,* 29–41, and *Adopcionismo,* 29–32 ("El tema de la diversidad religiosa debió de serlo de muchas conversaciones. Desde el lado católico se pudo apreciar las analogías que con el catolicismo profesaba el islamismo; el Alah de Mahoma era el Dios omnipotente cristiano; Jesús, reiteradamente citado en el Corán, hijo de la Virgen Maria, amado y protegido por Dios, era en ciertos aspectos el Mesías, Hijo de Dios, adorado por los cristianos. En el calor de la discusión los cristianos llegaron a conceder a los mahometanos, en un momento de generosidad apologética más de lo que podían: Jesús era realmente como ellos, los árabes le representaban, hijo adoptivo de Deos y siervo suyo, pero . . . sólo por razón de la naturaleza humana, vindicando al mismo tiempo para El la filiación divina propia y natural. Esta división de las dos filiaciones se la habían facilitado y descubierto las doctrinas nestorianizantes y les servía de maravilla en sus disputas religiosas con los invasores . . . "). This is a perfectly *plausible* scenario, but whether it occurred or not is another question. The literary parallels on 30–31 are not very convincing. At any rate the point must be decided by *fitting the adoptionist teaching convincingly into a context.* One can imagine contexts in Antiochene christology or Christian-Muslim apologetics, but I argue below that there is no need to look beyond literature of the patristic West, and of Hispania in particular, to find the context which makes the adoptionist christology come most compellingly to life.

31. The first line, "Ego Elipandus, Toletanae sedis archiepiscopus, cum omnibus mihi consentientibus . . ." Elipandus, Letter to Fidelis, *Adv.Elip.* 1.40 (*PL* 96:916A.13–14; Löfstedt, p. 27.1025–1026) indicates merely that Elipandus had support, not that a council had been held.

32. See *Adv.Elip.* 1.38 (*PL* 96:915 C3–9; Löfstedt, pp. 26.997–27.999).

33. Elipandus, Letter to Migetius, *Ep.* 1.9 (*PL* 96:864A 13–B 6; *CSM,* I, pp. 74–75).

34. See e.g. *De trinitate* 1.7–8, where the christological passage from Phil. 2:6–7 is given as a *regula* for determining the meaning of passages doubtful from a Trinitarian point of view (e.g., Jn. 14:28, "The Father is greater than I").

35. "Credo Trinitatem Patris, et Filii, et Spiritus sancti, in una Deitatis essentia atque natura, hoc est, Deum, et Principium, et Spiritum sanctum, in una natura Deitatis Trinitatem personarum," Elipandus, "Symbolus fidei," given at *Adv.Elip.* 1.40 (*PL* 96:916A 13–B 4; Löfstedt, p. 27.1026–1029). The use of the word *Deum* instead of *Patrem* gives the passage an archaic flavor noticeable throughout. It sounds decidedly non-Augustinian, since for Augustine *Deus* is never to be used

as a predicate for any of the *personae*, but rather for the substance. Still, Rivera Recio's comment that Elipandus's Trinitarian theology is a "manifest tritheism" seems extreme (*Adopcionismo*, 92).

36. Elipandus, "Symbolus fidei," *Adv.Elip.* 1.40 (*PL* 96:916C 3–D 3; Löfstedt, p. 28.1041–1051). This is an archaic analogy operating on the same principles as Tertullian's analogies in *Adv.Prax.* 8, for example, where the *personae* correspond to distinctions in the one substance. Note how impersonally the word *persona* is used at "Symbolus fidei," *Adv.Elip.* 1.40 (*PL* 96:916C 10–13; Löfstedt, p. 28.1046–1048): "Et sicut alia est *persona* frigoris manentis in lapide, atque alia ignis manentis in parente: et tamen procedens non desinit esse cum generante: ita Filii persona alia est. . . . "

37. "Symbolus fidei," *Adv.Elip.* 1.40 (*PL* 96:916B 7–8; Löfstedt, p. 27.1031–1035): the only analogy to which Augustine could agree (see *De trinitate* 6.3).

38. "Symbolus fidei," *Adv.Elip.* 1.40 (*PL* 96:916B 4–7; Löfstedt, p. 27.1029–1031): an antique analogy rejected by Augustine, *De trinitate* 12.5–6.

39. "Symbolus fidei," *Adv.Elip.* 1.40 (*PL* 96:916D 1–3; Löfstedt, p. 28.1049–1051).

40. " . . . uno Verbo Dei, id est unico Filio . . ." "Symbolus fidei," *Adv.Elip.* 1.40 (*PL* 96:916D 8–9; Löfstedt, p. 28.1056–1057).

41. "Symbolus fidei," *Adv.Elip.* 1.40 (*PL* 96:916D 2–3; Löfstedt, p. 28.1052). That is, there is *one* Word, *one* Son, although there is in the one Son (i.e., in and as His substance) fortitude, honor, and glory (*PL* 96:916D 9–10; Löfstedt, p. 28.1056–1067). These are different ways of looking at or of naming the same thing, just as light is simply the absence of darkness, and darkness the absence of light, without implying there is any multiplication of substances (*PL* 96:916D 6–10; Löfstedt, p. 28.1054–1046). And, "sicut spiritus pars animae est, per quam omnis ratio intelligentiaque percipitur: sicut memoria, quae meditari memoratur: sic in Verbo Dei pro suis officiis diversa meruerunt vocabula, quae nequaquam dividuntur in substantiam" (*PL* 96:916D 10–917A 2; Löfstedt, p. 28.1059–1064). How strange it is that the only thing even remotely resembling Augustine's psychological analogies are used for teaching not about the Trinity but about one of the *personae* of the Trinity. It would be interesting to study this Creed and locate its sources.

42. "Symbolus fidei," *Adv.Elip.* 1.40 (*PL* 96:917A2–10; Löfstedt, p. 28.1065–1071).

43. "Symbolus fidei," *Adv.Elip.* 1.40 (*PL* 96:917A 11–13; Löfstedt, p. 28.1071–1073).

44. The only exception to this is Rivera Recio (e.g., *Adopcionismo*, 115).

45. "Symbolus fidei," *Adv.Elip.* 1.40 (*PL* 96:917A13–B4). The editorial conjecture that the word *interior* represents a corruption comes from, respectively, Flórez (suggests "inter nos," see *PL* 96:917A 14) and Löfstedt (suggests "inferior," 28, line 1074, apparatus).

46. We recall that Beatus is editing this text. It is to his advantage both to leave out the context and to exaggerate the supposed dualism, as he clearly does when he repeats the phrase outside of direct citation (at *Adv.Elip.* 1.42 [*PL* 96:917D 6–918A 4; Löfstedt, p. 29.1104–1110] and elsewhere), embellishing it rhe-

torically so that it looks as though Elipandus is preaching two subjects in Christ. But there is no other clear instance of such preaching by Elipandus reported, not even by Beatus. If the argument that this "Symbolus" is a retort to Migetius seems unacceptable to some, then this passage, like that in the Letter to Alcuin (*Ep. ad Albinum*, PL 96:874A 9–14; Gil, p. 101, 7.67–71), must be interpreted as a reference to the same subject but pre- and post-Incarnation respectively. In the passage from the Letter to Alcuin, the distinction "ante saecula" and "in fine temporis" is clearly made, and the verse *Gloriam mei alteri non dabo* is cited (*PL* 96:874B 1; *CSM*, I, p. 101, 7.72–73) as in the "Symbolus." This is followed by a citation of Phil. 2:6 and 2:8, emphasizing the continuity of subject throughout the Incarnation (in the "Symbolus" these verses are recalled by the ablative absolute *deitate exinanita* [*Adv.Elip.* 1.40, PL 96:917A 4, Löfstedt, p. 28.1065–1066]). With regard to this passage, Rivera Recio agrees that it is not a statement of a doctrine of "two persons," and that Elipandus in general taught no such doctrine (*Adopcionismo*, 110–111).

47. Article 9 of the Symbol of Toledo XI: "Hic etiam Filius Dei natura est Filius, non adoptione, quem Deus Pater nec voluntate nec necessitate genuisse credendus est, quia nec ulla in Deo necessitas capit nec voluntas sapientiam praevenit" (in José Madóz, *Le Symbole du XIe concile de Tolède: ses sources, sa date, sa valeur*, 16–26; partial text also in J. de J. Perez, *La Christología en los Simbolos Toledanos IV, VI, y XI*, 26–51). Date: 675 (see Madóz, *XIe Tolède*, 4–8, 153). 7 November 675 is the date of the first day of Toledo XI. Despite its peninsular origin in latter seventh century Spain, this creed was widely recognized throughout the Middle Ages as possessed of singular clarity and perfection of doctrinal statement. It was cited by Alcuin (see *De fide sanctae et individuae Trinitatis* 1.14, PL 101:22B) and by Peter Lombard (*Sententiae in IV Libris Distinctae* III.V.1.4, 43, lines 4–10), to mention two of its prominent admirers (see Madóz, *XIe Tolède*, 144–162, for a more detailed discussion of its influence). Sources for the phrase in question here are: (1) the Pseudo-Augustinian *Dial.Quaest.* 1 and 7 (*PL* 40:734 and 736)—see Perez, *Christología*, 31 and 75; and (2) Gennadius, *Liber ecclesiasticorum dogmatum* 2 (text in C. H. Turner, ed., in *Journal of Theological Studies* 7: 89, also PL 58:981B)—see Madóz, *XIe Tolède*, 47.

48. On Bonosus and the Bonosians see Isidore, *De Viris Illustribus* 33, and *Etym.* 8.5.52 (cited by Madóz, *XIe Tolède*, 47–48). See also M. G. Mara, "Bonosus," in the *Encyclopedia of the Early Church*, Angelo Di Berardino, ed., Adrian Walford, tr., vol. 1, 125.

49. For Elipandus see *Ep. ad Franc.* 119.16–17, " . . . anathematizamus Bonosum, qui filium Dei sine tempore genitum, adobtivum fuisse blasfemat"; and the Letter to Fidelis at *Adv.Elip.* 1.43 (*PL* 96:919A 9–12; Löfstedt, p. 31.1159–1162): "Bonosus et Beatus pari errore condemnati sunt. Ille [= Bonosus] credidit de matre adoptivum et non de Patre ante saecula proprie genitum neque incarnatum. Iste credit de Patre genitum et non de matre temporaliter adoptivum." For Beatus, see *Adv.Elip.* 1.54 (*PL* 96:926A 12–14; Löfstedt, p. 39.1488–1489), and 2.94 (*PL* 96:1025B; Löfstedt, p. 162.2289–2290).

50. "Symbolus fidei," *Adv.Elip.* 1.41 (*PL* 96:917B 5–7; Löfstedt, p. 29.1078–1080): The point here is that it is the Word *after* the Incarnation who redeems the

world, i.e., "He who is Son at once of God and of Man," not He who is Son of God only.

51. As at *Adv.Elip.* 1.42 (*PL* 96:918D 6–919A 5; Löfstedt, p. 29.1104–1110), "Nunquid per illum qui natus est de Virgine, per ipsum visibilia et invisibilia condidit, an per illum qui non est adoptione sed genere, nec gratia sed natura, cuncta creavit? Et ideo absque dubio per illum quem sibi coaequalem et sine adoptione genuit, cuncta creavit. Et per ipsum Dei simul et hominis filium Verbum carnem factum, adoptivum humanitate, et nequaquam adoptivum divinitate, mundum redemit." This is a rhetorical elaboration of *PL* 96:917B 1–7 (Löfstedt, p. 29.1075–1080), cited above, itself an editorial product of Beatus, who is not always an accurate source for Elipandus's thought.

52. Article 42 (Madóz, *XIe Tolède*, 23). Perez, *Christología*, 46, points out the connection to Rom. 1:4 but mistakenly refers the reader to Fulgentius as the source.

53. Madóz, *XIe Tolède*, xx. There is, however, Augustinian precedent for this development; see, for example, *On the Predestination of the Saints* 15.30 (*PL* 44:981): "We have been taught that inasmuch as the Son of God became human, the Lord of Glory himself was the object of predestination."

54. Elipandus, "Symbolus fidei," *Adv.Elip.* 1.41 (*PL* 96:917B 7; Löfstedt, p. 29.1080). The phrase is meant at once to contrast him with the saints while at the same time affirming a point of similarity.

55. Elipandus, "Symbolus fidei," *Adv.Elip.* 1.41 (*PL* 96:917B 7–10; Löfstedt, p. 29.1080–1082).

56. Elipandus, "Symbolus fidei," *Adv.Elip.* 1.41 (*PL* 96:917B 10–14; Löfstedt, p. 29.1083–1085): " . . . et cum adoptivo adoptivi, et cum advocato advocati, et cum Christo christi, et cum parvulo parvuli, et cum servo servi." After the phrase "adoptivum humanitate, nequaquam adoptivum divinitate," this is probably the most famous adoptionist slogan. It is the passage from Elipandus most frequently cited by Beatus.

57. Elipandus, "Symbolus fidei," *Adv.Elip.* 1.41 (*PL* 96:917C 2–6; Löfstedt, p. 29.1088–1091), "Credimus enim quia in resurrectione *similes ei erimus*, non divinitate, sed carnis humanitate, videlicet carnis assumptione quam accepit de Virgine."

58. Collins points out that Elipandus's artistic insults are an Hispanic literary tradition. He points to such models as Julian of Toledo's *Insultatio in Tyrannidem Galliae* (*Conquest*, 229).

59. Confitemur et credimus Deum Dei filium ante omnia tempora sine initio ex patre genitum, quoeternum et consimilem et consubstantialem non adobtione, sed genere, neque gratia sed natura, id ipsut eodem filio adtestante: *Ego et pater unum sumus* et cetera, que de divinitate sua idem verus Deus et verus homo nobis loquutus est. Pro salute vero humani generis in fine temporis ex illa intima et ineffabili patris ad publicum humani generis apparens, invisibilis visibilis corpus adsumens de virgine ineffabiliter per integra virginalia matris enixus est. Secundum traditionem patrum confitemur et credimus eum factum ex muliere, factum sub lege, non genere esse filium Dei, set adobtione, neque natura, set gratia, id ipsut eodem Domino adtestante, qui ait: *Pater maior me est.* (Elipandus, *Ep. ad Franc.* III.34–112.7)

60. Elipandus, *Ep. ad Franc.* III.34–35.

61. That the "homo assumptus" christology is an ancient expression in the West is admitted by all (e.g., Amann, *L'Époque*, 139; Heil, "Adoptianismus," 118). Even Alcuin uses it. Note, too, the usage of the creeds of Toledo: "Hunc igitur Filium Dei, Deum, natum a Patre ante omne omnino principium, sanctificasse uterum Mariae Virginis, atque ex ea verum *hominem* . . . suscepisse" (Creed of Toledo I, art. 12 in both the longer and shorter recensions dated 447 and 400 respectively: text in J. A. De Aldama, ed., *El Simbolo Toledano I*, 29–37). This is repeated in the creed of Toledo IV (in 633, text in H. T. Bruns, ed., *Canones Apostolorum et Conciliorum Saeculorum IV, V, VI, VII*, vol. 1, 221; see also J. Madóz, "Le symbole du IVè Concile de Tolède"). In the Creed of Toledo VI, see articles 6–7: "Ex his igitur tribus divinitatis personis solum Filium fatemur . . . *hominem* sine peccato de Sancta semper Virgine Maria *assumpsisse*" (text in Perez, *Christologia*, 19). In Toledo XI see articles 36 (repeated from Toledo VI), 51 (" . . . Pater maior est *homine* quem sola Filii persona ssumpsit [sic]"), 53 (" . . . ab homine autem assumpto . . . "): text in Madóz, *XIe Tolède*, 22 and 24. See also J. Madóz, "El florilegio patristico del II Concilio de Sevilla," in *Miscellanea Isidoriana*, 177–220.

62. Scholars have universally defended at least the rough equivalence of these terms for the adoptionists, while conceding that differences in nuance lead to problems. See Heil, "Adoptianismus," 118–119; Ansprenger, "Untersuchungen," 40 (where "for Felix and Elipandus adoption and assumption were one and the same"); Amann, *L'Époque*, 137; Harnack, *History of Dogma*, 284; Hefele-LeClercq, *Histoire*, 1004–5; Hauck, *Kirchengeschichte*, implied, 304; Tixeront, *Histoire des dogmas*, 530; Bach, *Dogmengeschichte*, 105. In adopting this position, scholars have essentially appropriated *Alcuin's* critique that both Elipandus and Felix confuse adoption and assumption. This is also the position of Dominique Millet-Gérard, *Chrétiens mozarabes et culture islamique dans l'Espagne des VIIIe-IXe siècles*, 194.

63. Elipandus, *Ep. ad Franc.* 112.4,6.

64. Elipandus, *Ep. ad Franc.* 113.19–22; cf. 114.1,3 and 117.7.

65. Elipandus, *Ep. ad Franc.* 113.35–36. Cf. 114.809.

66. Elipandus, *Ep. ad Franc.* 116.18–20.

67. Elipandus, *Ep. ad Franc.*

68. E.g., *Ep. ad Franc.* 116.35–39, and 118.5 (" . . . quur filius Dei, secundum formam servi deitate exinanita corporeus et visibilis et palpabilis, *adoptivus* esse dicere dubitatur?").

69. Elipandus, *Ep. ad Franc.* 120.24. Cf. 116.31–32.

70. Elipandus, *Ep. ad Albinum* (*PL* 96:872B 15-C 1; *CSM*, I, p. 97, 4.15–16).

71. The frequent expression *adoptio carnis* (*Ep. ad Franc.* III.30; 112.10; 113.21,30; 117.9; 119.2; and elsewhere) is a subjective, not an objective, genitive construction, that is, "the adoption pertaining to, or having to do with, the flesh." It is not equivalent to the above cited uses of the active of *assumo* or *suscipio* with a direct object. See for example, the usage in the Letter to Alcuin (*Ep. ad Albinum*, *PL* 96:870B 10–12; *CSM*, I, p. 96, 3.1–3): " . . . asseris [tu Alcuinus] nullam carnis adoptionem in Filio Dei secundum formam servi de gloriosa Dei Virgine suscepisse . . . " This is not redundant, as it must be if *adoptionem = susceptionem*,

but is, rather, similar to the passage cited just above from the Letter to Charlemagne ("asseverat Dei Filium . . . adsumisse adobtionem," see also *Ep. ad Franc.* 113.21). Other types of usage of *adopto* or derivatives, if any, are confined only to passages which Elipandus cites, where his primary concern is not the precise sense in which the word is used but the actual attestation of precedent for its use at all. Thus "homo adoptatus" appears in a citation from Augustine (*Ep. ad Franc.* 113.3, citing from Aug., *In Iohannis* 28.2), and in the next line (*Ep. ad Franc.* 113.4) Elipandus identifies "adoptatus" specifically as Augustine's word (repeated in a review of citations at 117.28; 118.32; the citation from Augustine is also contained in the Letter to Alcuin [*Ep. ad Albinum, PL* 96:872D 8; *CSM* I, p. 99, 7.10–12]).

72. *Ep.* ad Franc. 113.19–22. See also 116.15–21.

73. Apart from Pelikan, *Emergence*, 256–259, who describes the christology of Hilary, Augustine, and Leo as "a theology of preexistence, kenosis, and exaltation" based on Phil. 2:6–11, see Albert Verwilghen, *Christologie et spiritualité selon saint Augustin: l'hymne aux Philippiens*, and Paul C. Burns, *The Christology in Hilary of Poitiers' Commentary on Matthew.*

74. This is a point, however, far short of sin. Elipandus is very clear regarding the sinlessness of Jesus. Jesus does not stand in need of salvation or baptism or any other kind of rebirth. See, e.g., in the Letter to Charlemagne, *Ep. ad Kar.*, p. 120.17–19: " . . . quod Deum Dei filium sine tempore unigenitum et sine adobtione nunc in fine temporis pro humani generis salvatione adque redemtione plenum et perfectum hominem praeter delicti contagium humano generi consimilem, consortem adque conformem [factum esse] . . . ." The subject of the sentence is the accusative *Deum Dei filium* and is continuous throughout. Again, at 121.10–12, "petimus ut fetidissimi Antifrasii Beati doctrinam, qui Dei filium veram de virgine *praeter peccatum* carnem nostre similem adsumsisse [NB not *adoptasse*] denegat. . . ." Compare also *Ep. ad Franc.* 117.22, and *Ep. ad Albinum, PL* 96:871D 3–5 (*CSM*, I, p. 98, 5.10–11) ("Quare non dicatur adoptivus qui ita totus est in nostris sicut totus est in suis, *preater delictum?*") and *Ep. ad Albinum PL* 96:872D 14 (*CSM*, I, p. 99, 7.17).

75. Letter to Charlemagne, *Ep. ad Kar.*, p. 120.23–24.

76. *deitate exinanita* (*PL* 96:917A 4; Löfstedt, p. 28.1065–1066).

77. *Ep. ad Franc.* 118.4–6.

78. *Ep. ad Franc.* 118.29–31.

79. *infima huius mundi, Ep. ad Franc.* 112.3.

80. Other citations or allusions to Phil. 2:6–11 include: in the "Symbolus," *Adv.Elip.* 1.40 (*PL* 96:916D 3–4; Löfstedt, p. 28.1052–1053); *Ep. ad Franc.* 114.40–115.3; 115.35; 116.32–36; *Ep. ad Albinum, PL* 96:874B 4–8 (*CSM*, I, p. 101, 7.75–78); etc. We are never very far from some allusion to or exegesis of Phil. 2:6–11, especially if one counts the ubiquity of the phrases *forma servi* and *forma Dei*. Rivera Revio is the only commentator who takes note of the kenotic motif in Elipandus's work (*Adopcionismo*, 89–91). He seems to see that it is the basis of the continuity of subject in Christ (90), but his position is finally difficult to assess. He says that the divine nature is the "victim" of the *exinanitio*, and that the expression *exinanitio deitatis* is the equivalent of the disconnection of the person of the Word from the divine nature. The person of the Word is left to monitor the relations

between the natures (see 90–91). Rivera Recio's position, despite its recognition of the personal unity in Elipandus's Christ, seems to present a Christ with a sort of split personality, if not a split *persona*, different according to which nature is active.

81. "Cum enim esset unicus Dei filius non gratia, sed natura, ut esset etiam plenus gratia, factus est hominis filius idem ipse utrumque ex utroque unus Christus, qui *cum in forma Dei esset, non rapinam arbitratus est*, quod natura est, id est *aequalis Deo*" (*Ench.* 10–11, best edition by E. Evans, *CCSL* vol. 46).

82. "Et tu negas Dei Filium de stirpe Abraham . . . carnem non suscepisse, *ut esset* adoptivus filius?" *Ep. ad Albinum, PL* 96:872B 13–C 2 (*CSM*, I, p. 99, 6.22–24).

83. *Ep. ad Franc.* 115.33–36: "Quum enim esset unicus Dei filius non [adoptione set genere, neque] gratia, set natura, ut esset etiam plenus [in formam servi adobtione et] gratia, factus est hominis filius . . . " Compare 113.2: "Filius Dei non est [adobtione, set genere, neque] gratia, set natura." (Bracketed material is Elipandus's gloss.) See also the *Ep. ad Albinum, PL* 96:872D 4–8 (*CSM*, I, p. 99, 7.10–12). In fact Elipandus's slogan "non adoptione, sed genere, neque gratia sed natura," and variations, may itself be viewed as a gloss of this passage from Augustine. Commentators less sympathetic to Elipandus refer to the bracketed phrases as interpolations, not glosses. Rivera Recio is a case in point (*Adopcionismo*, 137–138, and, for Elipandus's use of tradition in general, 127–142). But the premise of such a charge is that Elipandus's words *distort* the meaning of the text, that there is no sense in which he could have a legitimate claim to *developing* its thought. This view is also reflected in the passages which Rivera Recio cites. He limits himself only to passages containing the word "adoption" or its cognates. That, however, is to assume that we already know what this word means to the adoptionists, and that continuity with tradition depends on finding that word with that meaning in the traditional texts. The point is more to show that the adoptionists's use of the word is an *interpretation* of theological currents already in the tradition. Rivera Recio also assumes that every addition to any text is an interpolation by the adoptionists. But there are many additions (e.g., in #8 on 137–138, an extended version of the passage considered above) which are not as obviously self-interested—are these interpolations too? It is possible that some of the seemingly less disinterested additions to the text were already in the MSS which the adoptionists read.

84. Elipandus's text differs at more than 60 minor points from the *textus receptus* (C. Silva-Tarouca, ed., *Epistolae contra Eutychis haeresim*, 2 vols.), perhaps because he is following the text in the *Collectio Canonica Hispana* (see J. Solano, "El Concilio de Calcedonia y la controversia adopcionista del siglo VIII en España," in *Das Konzil von Chalkedon: Geschichte und Gegenwart*, vol. 2, A. Grillmeier and H. Bacht, eds., 866, n. 145). On the *Hispana* see G. Martínez-Díez, *La colección Canonica Hispana*, vols 1–4; he may also be glossing the text as he goes along.

85. "Propter quod sicut *Dominus majestatis* dicitur *crucifixus* (1 Cor. 2:8), ita qui ex sempiternitate aequalis est Deo, dicitur *exaltatus*." *Ep. ad Albinum, PL* 96:877D (*CSM*, I, p. 105, 9.104–105).

86. Elipandus renders Leo's text with "quia" instead of "qui." *Ep. ad Albinum, PL* 96:877D 4 (Gil gives *qui[a]*, *CSM*, I, p. 105, 9.104, but the meaning is

not affected). Rivera Recio devotes a chapter (*Adopcionismo*, 115–122) to the communication of idioms. Treating a passage from Felix, he comes to the conclusion that the "natural Son of God, the second person of the Trinity" was also the son of the Virgin and therefore the adoptive son of God. But Rivera Recio does not seem to see this as part of the *communicatio idiomata* proper. Rather, he seems more generally to distinguish between two "filiations" (for example, 100) and to note that the humiliations belonging to the "adoptive son" also belong (because of the *communicatio idiomata*) to the Son of God (121). Despite his recognition of the personal unity, the "filiations" almost become two subjects.

87. *Ep. ad Franc.* 113.19–20, citing the Nicene Creed.

88. *Ep. ad Franc.* 113.22.

89. For other uses of this term see *Ep. ad Franc.* 113.35; 114.8–9, 20–22; 116.18 where, as in 113.19–22, the context given by lines 15–22 shows again that the Unigenitus becomes the Primogenitus by assuming flesh from the Virgin *with no lapse in the continuity of the subject throughout*, "una eademque Dei et hominis persona"; 117.7–8, 10, 11, 13, 17, 20, 22; *Ep. ad Albinum, PL* 96:871C 15 (*CSM*, I, p. 98, 5.7–8).

90. The two-nature theory is a fundamental feature of the adoptionist christology which has often been described. See especially Solano, "La controversia," 842–846. Examples of Elipandus's usage: *Ep. ad Franc.* 114.36–39; 115.21; 116.19; *Ep. ad Albinum, PL* 96:873C 6–8 (*CSM*, I, p. 100, 7.43–45); see also the "Symbolus" (*PL* 96:917A 14–15; Löfstedt, p. 28.1074). I note that Harnack felt Elipandus's christology to be Augustinian (Harnack, *History of Dogma*, p. 283: "Elipandus was a loyal adherent to the Augustinian and Chalcedonian Christology"), although I point this out with some trepidation, since I do not wish to invoke Harnack's characterization of Augustine's christology or, *a fortiori*, of Elipandus as a function of it. Harnack essentially accuses *Felix* of Nestorianizing a Western christology (283), although Elipandus is not completely exonerated (283, n. 1). On Felix, see below, Appendix I, Section 8.

91. *Ep. ad Franc.* 113.22–23, also at 116.18; 117.16–17. I Jn 3:2 cited at 113.28–29; and "Symbolum" *PL* 96:917C 3; Löfstedt, p. 29.1087.

92. *Ep. ad Franc.* 113.29–30, 25.

93. See for example, *Ep. ad Franc.* 113.22, "primogenitum in adoptione et gratia."

94. "Unigenitus autem vocatur secundum divinitatis excellentiam, quia sine fratribus, primogenitus secundum susceptionem hominis, in qua per adobtionem gratiae fratres abere dignatus est, quibus esset primogenitus." This is from *Etym.* 7.2.13, cited here at *Ep. ad Franc.* 113.7–9 (and at 117.20–21), and again at *Ep. ad Albinum, PL* 96:873A 5–9 (*CSM*, I, p. 100, 7.21–24), where it is followed by other passages from *Etym.* 8. Elipandus has interpreted the "adoption" of which Isidore speaks to be that which the Word takes up, not that which we receive as sons of God. Isidore however probably had the latter meaning in mind. Beatus also cites this passage in his own defense. In the connection of "deigning" to have brothers, note Elipandus's use of Sirach 36:14, "Miserere, Domine, plebi tue, super quam invocatum est nomen tuum, et Israel, quem quoequasti primogenito tuo" (*Ep. ad Franc.* 114.24–25; *Ep. ad Albinum, PL* 96:873C 2–4 [*CSM*, I, p. 100, 7.40–42]). Elipandus comments, "Aequalitas ista non est in divinitate, sed in sola humanitate,

et in carnis adoptione, quam accepit de Virgine . . . " (*Ep. ad Albinum, PL* 96:873C 4–6 [*CSM*, I, p. 100, 7.42–43]). He has deemed, by receiving the adoption pertaining to the flesh, to make available an equality which was hitherto unthinkable.

95. *Ep. ad Franc.* 113.17–18, "Ecce, quos in adobtione participes esse non dubitat, consortes fieri in hereditate exobtat." This is a comment on a passage from the Mozarabic liturgy for the dead, cited at 113.17: "Quos fecisitis adobtioni participes iubeas hereditati tue esse consortes," also cited at *Ep. ad Albinum, PL* 96:875B 1–3 (*CSM*, I, p. 102, 8.25–26). As with the passage cited from Isidore (*Etym.* 7.2.13), Elipandus interprets this as a reference to the adoption which the Lord accepted, not to our adoption as sons (demonstrated also by the passages from the liturgy cited before this, at *Ep. ad Franc.* 113.11–14; *Ep. ad Albinum, PL* 96:874C 11–875A 11 [*CSM*, I, p. 102, 8.3–4]).

96. As, for example, at the *In Iohannis* 14.10.

97. *Ep. ad Franc.* 113.36, "in ceteris vero sanctis ad mesuram data est huius rei gratia unctionis."

98. *Ep. ad Franc.* 113.35–36, "Hanc plenitudinem unctionis (Ps. 14:8, "Unxit te Deus, Deus tuus, oleo letitie pre consortibus tuis," cited at lines 26–27) in solo filio Dei adobtivo et primogenito credimus esse . . . . " Note that "adoptivo et primogenito" represents a unique relation to the Father which is enjoyed *only* by Jesus.

99. *Ep. ad Franc.* 113.30–31, "Unctio vero illa Spiritus sancti, in qua maxime in filio Dei secundum humanitatem plus quam electis eius facta est . . . "

100. For example, in the long citation from Leo, *Ep. ad Albinum, PL* 96:875C 8 (*CSM*, I, p. 103, 9.10–12); *PL* 96:877A 13 (*CSM*, I, p. 105, 9.79).

101. "Hic enim qui ante saecula unigenitus est vocatus, temporaliter primogenitus factus est; unigenitus propter deitatis substantiam, primogenitus propter assumptae carnis naturam" (Madóz, *XIe Tolède*, 25).

102. *Etym.* 7.20.13 (see Perez, *Christología*, 50); *Differ.* 2.6.15 (see Madóz, *XIe Tolède*, 96–99).

103. See Augustine's discussion at *Contra Secundinum liber* 5 (Joseph Zycha, ed., *CSEL* vol. 25, pt. 2, 911–913).

104. Elipandus cites the liturgy at *Ep. ad Franc.* 113.10–17, and *Ep. ad Albinum* 11, *PL* 96:874C 11–875B 6 (*CSM*, I, p. 102, 8.1–29), with references to the sources. Critical edition of the Mozarabic liturgy in M. Ferotin, *Le Liber Ordinum en usage dans l'église wisigothique et mozarabe d'Espagne du Ve au XIe siècle*, vol. 5 of *Monumenta ecclesiae liturgica*; M. Ferotin, *Le Liber Mozarabicus sacramentorum et les manuscrits mozarabes*, vol. 6 of *Monumenta ecclesiae liturgica*; N. Prado, *Manual de liturgía hispanovisigótica o mozárabe*; José Vives, *Oracional visigótico*. Also see F. Cabrol, "Le 'Liber Ordinum' et la liturgie mozarabe," *Revue des Questions historiques* 77: 173–185; J. F. Rivera Recio, "La controversia adopcionista del Siglo VIII y la Ortodoxia de la Liturgia Mozárabe," *Ephemerides Liturgicae* 6: 506–536, esp. 525–526; Louis Brou, O.S.B., "Bulletin de Liturgie Mozarabe, 1936–1948," *Hispania Sacra: Revista de Historia Eclesiastica* 2: 459–484, esp. 3–8; D. de Bruyne, "De l'origine de quelques textes liturgiques mozarabes," *Revue Bénédictine* 30: 428–430; Rivera Recio, "La doctrina de la adopcion," Conclusion, 129–131. J. F.

Rivera Recio, *Estudios Sobre La Liturgía Mozárabe* contains a list of MSS of liturgical texts from the Mozarabic liturgy, as well as a number of essays. Rivera Recio, *Adopcionismo*, 143–146, sums up the arguments, defending the adoptionists's citation of the liturgy as accurate.

105. There is another, nonliturgical precedent for the use of the word *adoptio* or derivatives with regard to Christ in Western tradition. Hauck gives some of these, *Kirchengeschichte*, 302, n. 4. The adoptionists cite some themselves (apart from those which can easily be challenged as misinterpretations or interpolations or glosses), for example, the passage which Felix cites from Hilary, *De trinitate* 2.28 (see Alcuin, *Adversus Felicem Urgellitanum Episcopum Libri VII*, *PL* 101:68C; hereafter, *AFU*). Alcuin and Hincmar (*AFU* 6.6, *PL* 101:206C and *De praedesinatione* Preface, *PL* 125:55D respectively) charge Felix with erasing and altering the text and there is a pre-800 codex from Cordoba with an erasure at the word "adoptatur," but the reading is attested in other early MSS (see Rivera Recio, *Adopcionismo*, 130). Elipandus had cited the same passage (*Ep. ad Hisp.*, 112.21–23). Another passage, attributed by Elipandus to Jerome (*Ep. ad Franc.* 112) is actually from a text, recently attributed to the fourth century bishop Pacian of Barcelona (see D. G. Morin, "Un traité inédite du IVe siècle. Le 'De similitudine carnis peccati' de l'évêque S. Pacien de Barcelone," *Revue Bénédictine* 29: 1–28; text in *Études, textes et découvertes* I, 1–150).

106. See Elipandus's citations at *Ep. ad Franc.* 113.11–12, 13 and *Ep. ad Albinum*, *PL* 96:874C14,D10–11 (*CSM*, I, p. 102, 8.3, 11); *PL* 96:875A 7–8 (*CSM*, I, p. 102, 8.19).

107. See below, chapter 4.

108. For example Amann, *L'Époque*, 139–140, "Tout en se defendant, comme l'avaient fait les premiers Antiochiens, de parler de deux fils dans le concret, dans la réalité de l'histoire, ils disaient: autre est la relation entre Dieu le Père et Dieu le Verbe, qui est un rapport de filiation naturelle; autre la relation entre l'*homo assumptus* et le Père, qui est un rapport de filiation adoptive. . . . Poussé à bout . . . les Espagnols risquaient de compromettre l'une des données dogmatiques fermement acceptée par eux, à savoir l'unité de personne. Qu'ils le voulussent ou non, ce 'fils adoptif de Dieu' faisait figure de personne à côté du 'fils de Dieu par nature.' Comment ramener a l'unité cette dualité flagrante?" See also Hefele-Leclercq, *Histoire*, 1004–1005, "Dès le debut, les adoptianistes firent tous leurs efforts pour se placer sur le terrain du concile de Chalcedoine [which, incidentally, they never cite], et plus leurs adversaires leur reprochaient leur nestorianisme ou tout au moins leur penchant vers cette heresie, plus ils *pretendaient* professer et enseigner l'union hupostatique de les deux natures dans le Christ . . . dans la personne unique du *Logos*. Mais tandis qu'ils professaient ainsi de bouche la personnalité unique du Christ et condamnaient, par la même, le principe fondamental du nestorianisme, ils se laissaient glisser peu à peu . . . sur un chemin qui *logiquement* conduisait à l'ancien nestorianisme" (my emphasis). But the question is not what *logically* follows based upon premises we have ourselves erected, but what was *historically* the case. Amann must assume that the adoptionists were *pretending* to uphold a Chalcedonian position in order to satisfy his own analysis of the situation. H. Quilliet, "Adoptianisme au VIIIe siècle," *DTC* vol. 1, pt. 1: 409, 411, analyzes the heresy

logically as well, using a Thomistic rubric. The same is true in part of Solano (who treats the adoptionist teachings almost as though they were a logically faulty textbook of christology—see especially "La controversia," 845, 846–848), and Heil, "Adoptianismus," 117–125, esp. 117, n. 212.

109. The argument follows Augustine's analysis (as at *De trinitate* 5.5–6) of *persona* as a function of relation. "Son" is a predicate which pertains not to a substance (such as *deitas*) but which instead describes a relation, such as Father and Son. In the Trinity these relations, and hence the *personae* which they constitute, are eternal, and so do not imply subordination of one *persona* to another (against the Arians). Augustine, however, has a harder time explaining what these three eternally related things are. When he inquires about the status of these persons apart from these mutual relations, he finds that he cannot give an answer. He cannot answer the question, "Three what?" (see below, chapter 4, n. 144). Certainly Elipandus's brief discussion of the three *personae* in the Trinity is not much concerned with the Augustinian notion of eternal relation, and his analogies strike us as somewhat non-Augustinian and archaic. Perhaps he has abandoned, or is rethinking, what he perceives to be an Augustinian dead end, or, better, developing the implications of Augustine's use of *persona* in christology against his use of the term in Trinitarian discourse.

110. The evidence, however, all indirect, is for the *likelihood*, not for the fact, of the presence of Nestorians in eighth-century Spain. See Gams, *Kirchengeschichte von Spanien*, 261–267; see also the literature cited by Solano, "La controversia," 853, n. 58; also K. Werner, *Alcuin und sein Jahrhundert*, 54. More recently, see the analyses of K. Schäferdiek, "Der adoptianische Streit in Rahmen der spanischen Kirchengeschichte," 15–16, and especially Glick, *Islamic and Christian*, 288, and Collins, *Conquest*, 223, who cites (n. 70) the evidence of G. Levi della Vida ("I Mozarabi tra Occidente e Islam") that "Nestorian Christian texts were circulating and being translated into Latin in Spain or North Africa at this time" (Collins).

111. Especially true of the early Nestorian period up to 612, when there were varying reactions to the council of Chalcedon and to the vagaries of imperial theological favor. Note, for example, the variations in the texts presented in the anthology drawn up in the late eighth century and so roughly contemporaneous with the adoptionism controversy, text and translation in L. Abramowski and A. E. Goodman, eds. and trs., *A Nestorian Collection of Christological Texts*. For dating see vol. 2, p. xviii. Nor is the position of Nestorius himself clearly established. See R. Greer, "The Image of God and the Prosopic Union in Nestorius's *Bazaar of Heracleides.*"

112. Ansprenger, "Untersuchungen," 8–37, esp. 30.

113. This is the position especially of Rivera Recio (anticipated by others, e.g., A. Neander, *General History of the Christian Religion and Church*, vol. 3 [hereafter, *History*], translated from the German by J. Torrey, 159) expressed most forcefully in *Elipando* and "Elipand." He cites evidence ("Elipand," cols. 205–206) of a high degree of contact between Christians and Muslims, including evidence that Arabic was known by Christians as early as 754 (col. 206) in one case, and that study of the Latin classics had waned in favor of Arabic letters and sciences by the middle of the ninth century (*Elipando*, 29–36). More recent scholarship has con-

firmed that conversion from Christianity to Islam was not unknown in this period, although the greatest movement to Islam did not occur until the middle of the ninth century (Glick, *Islamic and Christian*, 33–35, 283). In such an environment it is easy to imagine an apologetic dialogue between Christianity and Islam. Felix himself was said to have written an *Apologia* against the Saracens (*Alc.Ep.* 284–285), and Beatus had accused Elipandus of overfamiliarity with secular philosophy. Rivera Recio imagines an overly generous apologetic moment which conceded so much that apology degenerated into heresy, i.e., adoptionism. Yet this scenario rests on two assumptions which need not be true at all. The primary one is that Elipandus's adoptionism is a heresy; the second one, that it offers any concession to Islam. One must find evidence of such a concession in the texts of Elipandus themselves in order for such a theory even to have any meaning. Pressure towards conformity does not always generate conformity. Even without a clear apologetic element in any of the surviving writings of Elipandus, one could well believe that Elipandus engaged in apologetic dialogue, and his adoptionism was perhaps affected in some way by this dialogue. Yet one seems bound to admit that it is a successful apologia, one which comes off without a single fundamental concession, and which develops the teaching of the West as it proceeds.

114. Text of *Apology of Timothy I* (in photographic facsimile of MS) and translation with notes and introduction in A. Mingana, *Woodbrooke Studies*, vol. 2, 15–90 (translation), 91–162 (text). (Hereafter *Apology*.)

115. *Apology*, 22.

116. *Apology*, 22–27.

117. *Apology*, 63.

118. *Apology*, 64.

119. *Apology*, 62–83.

120. *Apology*, 17.

121. *Apology*, 19. The King sounds uncannily orthodox in this critique.

122. *Apology*, 21.

123. Attributed by Timothy to the "Jacobites and Melchites," *Apology*, 87 (see 88 for the King's statement of agreement).

124. *Apology*, 87

125. *Apology*, 88.

126. The above study of the *Apology of Timothy* is corroborated by the observations of another contemporary, quoted by Schäferdiek, "Der adoptianische," 306, n. 64.

127. Ansprenger observes that the standard Nestorian formula became two-natures, two-hypostases, one-prosopon ("Untersuchungen," 40–41), perhaps implying that Elipandus has simply taken over the Nestorian "prosopon" and dropped it into the place of the "persona" in Latin christology. He observes that "prosopon" could only have been rendered "persona" in Latin (34). He claims that the issue on which the controversy between Nestorian and orthodox would turn, that is, the terminological issue of the difference between nature and hypostasis on the one hand, and "prosopon" and hypostasis on the other, was too subtle for the Latins to grasp, especially since the Mozarabs would have been unfamiliar with Greek or, even worse, Syriac (40). Therefore it was easy for the unwary Elipandus

to fall under the influence of a christology which sounded so much like the Western one but which accommodated collaborationist interests. But this argument cannot stand. In the first place, the Mozarabs would have to have understood some medium of communication between Nestorian and Catholic for there to have been any significant channel of influence at all. Perhaps this channel was Arabic. In the second place, the Latins may have known little Greek but they certainly knew enough to realize that what the Greeks expressed as "one ousia, three hypostases," the Latins knew as "one nature or essence, three *personae*"—if nowhere else, it is in Isidore (e.g., *Etym.* 7.4.11–12, where the terms are explained very precisely), in texts from which Elipandus cites. And the point is made at so many other places in Latin traditional literature that even apart from Isidore it is hard to imagine that Elipandus would have been ignorant on this one point of Greek vocabulary, namely, that "hypostasis" was the Greek word used to name the individuals of the Trinity, and that the Latin word to express the same thing was "persona." The place of the two "hypostases" in later (i.e., since AD 612; see Abramowski and Goodman, *Collection*, xxviii) Nestorian christology is not something which could easily be omitted. It is over and against the "hypostases" that the "prosopon" and the "natures" are constantly contradistinguished and defined. The terms mutually interdefine each other. To learn about the Nestorian prosopon is also, at the same time, to learn about the Nestorian *hypostasis*. See, for example, in Abramowski and Goodman, *Collection*: Babai the Great, 123–125; Isaac of Nineveh, 37–39 (with the explicit critique of Chalcedon for affirming not one "prosopon," but rather one "hypostasis"), 39–54; the Persian Bishops to Kosroes, "Controversial Chapters," 93–96; Henanisho the Monk, 101–106; Pseudo-Nestorius, 106–108 (a discussion of all three terms); 108–110 (*hypostasis* vs. *prosopon*); 110–111 (*hypostasis* and nature); and elsewhere in *Collection* (which reflects the tastes of an eighth-century compiler). Distinguishing the hypostases is also critical for Timothy I, as for example at *Epistola ad Nasr Fidelem*, where he attempts to explain how it is that Christ is not actually a slave (see O. Braun, ed. and tr., *Timothei Patriarchae I Epistolae*, CSCO 75, vol. 1, 140–164, esp. 160–162, 157–158, and, on the same subject, *Ep.* 34, pp. 123–125, 129). Elipandus's notion of the servantship of Jesus ("servus cum servis," Beatus, *Adv.Elip.* 1.41 [Löfstedt, p. 29.1084–1085 and *passim*], also *Ep. ad Franc.* 116.27–117.5), although it has served as additional reason for calling him Nestorian, comes from a completely different context than Timothy's.

128. See, for example, from Abramowski and Goodman, *Collection*, Pseudo-Nestorius, *Various Chapters and Diverse Questions* #3: "Hypostasis and prosopon are one and the same [when] applied successively to men. For the prosopon of Paul is the same as the hypostasis of Paul . . . . But when we apply prosopon to our Lord Christ, that is, to the two natures of the godhead and of the manhood, it is not one compounded hypostasis that is referred to in the ordinary way, but it [sc. the *prosopon*] signifies the honour and greatness and worship" (108.24–31). Also at #4: "When anyone says 'city,' he refers both to the inhabitants and to the habitation, and they are two hypostases, but one is the prosopon of the city. And also, in the same way, a house is named after him who dwells in it, and from [the fact that it is] his dwelling place; and the prosopon now is one, but the hypostases are two . . . ." (110.9–13). In these passages the *prosopon* appears as a function of

the union, something which is formed because of or after the union (as habitation and inhabitants are not, but by their union produce, the city), the locus for a united honor and worship. See also Eustathius of Tarihan, "Book on the Separation Between Orientals and Westerns" (Abramowski and Goodman, *Collection*, 31–32) for an even less unitary view of the prosopon.

129. "[Theodore] refuses to agree with the assertion of the Arians, the Apollinarians, and the Alexandrians that the Word is the subject of all Christ's activity. Unlike Athanasius and, later, Cyril, he is unable to accept a distinction in the times and manners of attribution as a safeguard against Arianism [a distinction which was completely acceptable in the West]. Whatever is predicated of a subject must be predicated by nature; therefore, the human attributes of Christ must be applied by nature to a human subject. The assumed Man . . . occupies this position." Note that for Theodore, as for the Nestorians, "the *prosopon* of union tends to be regarded as the *product* of the Christological union; and even though Theodore's language closely resembles the later Chalcedonian formula, his intention is really somewhat different. . . . [He] employs the term [prosopon] not as an equivalent of *hypostasis*, but as an expression of the union of honour and worship effected by the indwelling Word" (R. Greer, *The Captain of Our Salvation: A Study in the Patristic Exegesis of Hebrews* [hereafter, *Captain*], 211, 216). The two subjects in Christ are "autonomous and complete" (213). Theodore remarks: "Notandum est . . . quoniam grandem differentiam inter Deum Verbum et susceptum hominem prophetiae ipsius carmen ostendit, et tantam distinctionem inter susceptum et suscipientem faciat quanta descretio inter Deum et reliquos omnes invenitur" (Lucas De Coninck, ed. *Theodori Mopsuesteni expositionis in Psalmos Iuliano Aeclanensi interprete in Latinum versae quae supersunt*, 12). Elipandus never makes a distinction between the "one who takes up" and the "one who is taken up."

130. Creed of 612, Abramowski and Goodman, *Collection*, 91, lines 3–15.

131. See especially on this point Pseudo-Isaac, who interprets the exaltation as a reference to the clothing of Jesus with the *prosopon*, i.e., "the name and honour and authority" of the Son (Abramowski and Goodman, *Collection*, 47.34–39), or, alternatively, as the possession of him *as* his *prosopon* by God the Word (*Collection*, 47.14–19).

132. "Indeed, while He was in the *form of God*, He *took* the *form of a servant*. [Note omission of "emptied himself."] He did not *become* a servant. And being found *in fashion as a man* He was not a man, but *as* a man—He who was in the form of God, He who took the form of a servant. For a servant is certainly a human nature. Now the One who was hidden was as a man because of the one who was openly revealed" (Brière, frag. 14, at Greer, *Captain*, 161). Greer: "the form of God and the form of a servant are distinguished as two subjects"; also, "Diodore reads the passage by underlining 'the likeness of men' and 'in fashion as a man.'" (Timothy I is similar—see his *Ep.* 38, pp. 110, 123.)

133. See Greer, *Captain*, 250. The exegesis of Nestorius reflects the emphases of Diodore, too—see F. Loofs, *Nestoriana*, 253 (cited by Greer, *Captain*, 328).

134. Abramowski and Goodman, *Collection*, 90.9–27.

135. Ansprenger's citation of Theodore, and his claim that "in den Werken des Bischofs von Mopsuestia finden wir viele und recht genaue Anklänge an den

Adoptianismus" (42) is a case in point. Far from settling the issue, his citation of passages allegedly parallel to passages in Elipandus and Felix raises as many problems regarding the interpretation of Theodore as it does regarding the pedigree of Felix and Elipandus. The vocabulary of adoption is very rare in Theodore; it hardly suffices to cite Theodore to explain the reliance of Felix and Elipandus on this vocabulary, and Ansprenger does not advance any texts on this point. At one point he invokes the questionable cliché that the Western mentality was somehow more "juridical" than the East, alleging that Elipandus transposed philosophical categories such as *hypostasis* and *prosopon* into the legal categories of adoption (34; a similarly tortuous analysis is given by Neander, upon whom Ansprenger ultimately relies: "It is therefore evident that the doctrine of FELIX was altogether that of THEODORE, excepting that the latter could express himself more freely in an age when the doctrines of the Church were less rigorously defined, while FELIX was obliged to use a terminology which was opposed to his own system," A. Neander, *Lectures on the History of Christian Dogmas*, (hereafter, *Lectures*). Further, it is clear that where, if ever, such adoptionistic language is used or implied in Theodore, it presupposes the frankly "two subject" character of Theodore's theology, and operates as a predicate of only one of these subjects, the *homo assumptus*, as a description and interpretation of this subject's assumption (see, e.g., R. Greer, *Theodore of Mopsuestia: Exegete and Theologian* (hereafter, *Theodore*), 48–65, esp. p. 63). For further discussion of Felix in this connection, see below, Appendix I, section 8. See also Hefele-Leclercq, *Histoire*, 1018 and 1018, n. 1; and Rivera Recio, "Doctrina," 654.

136. Rivera Recio's position on this point is finally difficult to evaluate. He is willing to critique Alcuin on a specific point about using Nestorius and Pelagius as parallels to the adoptionists' teaching (*Adopcionismo*, 101), but can classify it as a teaching whose scheme is "almost Nestorian" (p. v), and can talk at length about its concessions to the Muslims based on Antiochene or Nestorian influence (e.g., 32). He can talk about the *communicatio idiomatum* and the continuity of the subject in Christ with the Word, but then speak of a double "filiation" almost as though, in effect, there were two sons (see, e.g., point 4f, 141–142: "Los adopcionistas . . . a pesar de que sostienen que es uno el Hijo de Dios cuando representa la persona, no es, sin embargo, *el mismo* el hijo del hombre que el Hijo de Dios. Lo cual estaría muy en consonancia con su ideología: las naturaleza determina la filiación"). This tension in Rivera Recio's treatment of the adoptionists reflects his position that they commit faults of logic (p. vi) and have fallen into heresy because they over-rationalize the faith (152–153). Ultimately, Rivera Recio accepts Alcuin's opinion that it is only in the one word *adoption* and its associated concepts (153) that the adoptionists are at variance with the church. But the assumption here is that "adoption" is a term from an alien context which has been inserted into an otherwise intact system: it is assumed that its proper context cannot be in any sense native or orthodox. That the adoptionist theology appears as a web of non sequiturs and lapses in logic mixed in with orthodox statements is simply a reflection of these assumptions.

137. It may be that there are elements which come from outside of a Western system (e.g., the expressions *homo deificus* and *humanatus Deus, Ep. ad Franc.*

114.39), but either they are taken from an earlier use in Western or Spanish tradition (Elipandus gets the two expressions cited above from Julian of Toledo—see *Ep. ad Albinum, PL* 96:880B 1–2; *CSM*, I, p. 108, 11.15–16), or they have been integrated by Elipandus into a context which is his own and draws mainly upon a Western tradition of reflection. Any foreign concepts derive their meaning for him from this context. In itself, finally, it is of little consequence whether or not Elipandus was influenced by Theodore or by Latin speaking Nestorians—the point is how he used what he may have taken from them. It *may* be true, especially of Felix, that *via* Latin translations of Theodore's commentaries on Paul, or the *acta* of the fifth ecumenical council, the adoptionists had access to Antiochene theology, but it cannot be assumed that their system is thereby fundamentally Antiochene. To say, as Harnack does, following Neander's lead, that "*Felix of Urgel gave a Nestorian (Theodorian) development to Augustine's Christology, and thus went beyond Augustine*" (*History of Dogma*, 283, and 283, n. 1; emphasis original), is to align oneself first with a particular understanding of Western and specifically Augustinian christology, and then to *assume* that the Antiochenes were not read and interpreted from a prior, non-Antiochene point of view, but themselves became the lens through which everything else was read. It is assumed that in the Antiochene school one has found the *key* for understanding the adoptionists. But it is impossible to agree to such an assumption a priori, and the textual evidence advanced for it by Neander (*History*, 159–163), and, following him, Ansprenger and Harnack, is slim enough. However, see Appendix I, section 8, below.

138. *Ep. ad Franc.* III.32–34. There are smaller lists at *Ep. ad Albinum, PL* 96:870A 6–7 (*CSM*, I, p. 96, 1.3–4): Ambrose, Augustine, Isidore, and Jerome; *PL* 96:872A 1 (*CSM*, I, p. 98, 6.2–3): Athanasius, Hilary, Ambrose, Augustine, and Isidore; *PL* 96:879A 14 (*CSM*, I, p. 107, 10.4): Ambrose, Augustine, and Jerome. On Elipandus's use of the Fathers see J. F. Rivera Recio, "Doctrina," 6–17, and *Adopcionismo*, 127–142. With regard to the continuity of adoptionist theology with Isidore, a major Hispanic figure, it is interesting to note that there has been a controversy over whether to attribute a treatise, *Liber de variis quaestionibus adversus iudeos ser ceteros infideles . . .* , to Isidore or to Felix of Urgel (see J. Madóz, "Una obra de Félix de Urgel, falsamente adjudicada a San Isidoro de Sevilla," *Estudios eclesiásticos* 23: 147–168; A. C. Vega, "El 'Liber de variis quaestionibus' no es de Félix de Urgel"; J. Madóz, "Contrastes y discrepancias entre el 'Liber de variis quaestionibus' y San Isidoro de Sevilla"; Rivera Recio, *Adopcionismo*, 140). This argument is implicit testimony to the credibility of the theory that adoptionist theology is in some sense a continuation or development of Isidore's.

139. Elipandus's list includes, in addition, the framers of those creeds (Isidore, Julian, etc.). Compare to Elipandus's list of sources the summary of sources for Toledo XI given by Madóz, *XIe Tolède*, 110–115. For Toledo IV and VI see Perez, *Christología*, 10–25. Note, however, the much wider scope of patristic authority drawn upon at the Second Council of Seville (AD 619, with Isidore presiding). See Jose Madóz, "El florilegio patristico del II Concilio de Sevilla," in *Miscellanea Isidoriana*, 177–220.

140. In his letters to the French bishops and to Charlemagne, Elipandus cites from Ambrose (in no. of lines), 11 (note that this data is only tentative, since some of Elipandus's sources have not been identified); Hilary, 3; Victorinus, 3; Jerome,

4; Augustine, 41; Isidore, 11; the Mozarabic liturgy, 10; 11 lines are from unidentified sources, mostly attributed to Augustine. In his letter to Alcuin Elipandus cites from Gregory the Great (2 *PL* lines); Isidore (30); Ambrose (1); Jerome (2); Victorinus (1); Augustine (29); Leo I (235); the Mozarabic liturgy (31). In his letter to Migetius Elipandus cites Gregory I (approximately 12 *PL* lines); "Efren" = (Pseudo-) Ephraem the Syrite (13); Isidore (7); and Fulgentius, John Chrysostom, Augustine, and Jerome (line nos. difficult to determine with accuracy for these writers). Note that there are only three Eastern figures mentioned at all, Chrysostom, Athanasius, and "Ephraem the Syrite," and of these only two are actually cited. None of them have any association with the fifth-century christological controversies, and only Athanasius and Ephraem had reputations as *anti-Arian* polemicists, not as christological writers.

    141. *Ep. ad Franc.*, 119.16–21. Noted, among others, by Rivera Recio, *Adopcionismo*, 154; Ansprenger, "Untersuchungen," 39, 41; and Harnack, *History of Dogma*, 283, n. 1.

    142. *Ep. ad Franc.* 119.21.

    143. Elipandus tells Charlemagne that Beatus denies that the Son of God assumed from the Virgin true flesh, similar to ours (*Ep. ad Kar.*, 121.11–12). There is no evidence that Beatus ever denied the true flesh of Christ, and Elipandus also makes the same charge against Alcuin (see below, c. 4), whom we know is beyond reproach in this matter. Elipandus's statements must be taken as analyses of anti-adoptionist positions: if one does not accept the adoptive status of Christ as a human, one is not taking seriously the reality of his humanity.

    144. Solano marshals the evidence against his ignorance very well—see "La controversia," 857–870. The argument, basically, is that Elipandus cites so many works in which there is explicit mention of Eutyches that we cannot responsibly conclude he was ignorant of him.

    145. Elipandus notes, " . . . beatus Augustinus [*Contra Faustum* 14.2] inquiens ait, 'Pius homo Faustus dolet Christum maledictum fuisse a Moisen, eo quod dicat': Beatus dolet Christum secundum formam servi quempiam dicere adobtibum" (*Ep. ad Franc.* 118.27–30). Elipandus analyses Beatus's position from a familiar description of an arch-heretic in the Western literature. Elipandus's name-calling tends to come not from the vocabulary of the fifth-century christological debates, but from the repertoire of the Arian controversy. He repeatedly compares Charlemagne to Constantine, citing Isidore's doleful interjection about good beginnings and bad ends. As Arius was Constantine's downfall, so Alcuin will be Charlemagne's. Both Alcuin and Beatus are likened to Arius (see *Ep. ad K*ar. 121.6–8; *Ep. ad Albinum PL* 96:870A 6; *PL* 96:872A 9–13; *PL* 96:880B 8, D 1–4; *Alc.Ep.* 183, Elipandus to Felix, p. 308.1; cf. *Ep. ad Franc.* 118.18 and 121.8). In addition to Arius, the heretics mentioned include Faustus the Manichaean (already noted), Migetius (*Ep. ad Franc.* 118.35), Bonosus (*Ep. ad Franc.* 119.16), Sabellius (*Ep. ad Franc.* 119.17), and the Manichaeans (*Ep. ad Franc.* 119.19). None of these have any decisive Eastern reference. Arius, of course, is an Eastern figure, but Arianism was established in many parts of the West, and in Hispania in particular under the Visigoths; the refutation of Arianism was a preoccupation of much later Western writing.

    146. See Solano, "La controversia," 857–870.

147. *Ep. ad Albinum, PL* 96:875B.7f (*CSM*, I, p. 102, 9.1). There is only one small citation from the Tome, at *Ep. ad Albinum, PL* 96:872D (*CSM*, I, p. 99, 7.14–16, one of its most cited lines), and one from Sermon 23 of Leo in the same paragraph of the Letter to Alcuin. Gil (102) points out that Elipandus follows the *Collectio Canonica Hispana*.

148. See the authorities Leo cites in his list of "Exemplaria Testimoniorum Diversorum Sanctorumque Patrum" (Silva-Tarouca, 34–43)—including Hilary, Ambrose, and Augustine from the West. (Note how many Eastern authorities Leo cites—Athanasius, Basil, John Chrysostom, Cyril of Alexandria, Gregory Nazianzus, Theophilus of Alexandria: more evidence that Elipandus was acquainted with these names.)

149. This would be especially where the liturgy has already suggested, but not explained, the propriety of this language.

Chapter Three

1. Beatus's dedication of his *Commentary on the Apocalypse* to the young bishop Heterius indicates a monastic context: "Haec ergo, sancte pater Etheri, te petente ob aedificationem studii fratrum tibi dicavi, ut quo consorte perfruor religionis coheredem faciem et me laboris." (Beatus, *Sancti Beati Liebana Commentarius in Apocalypsin*. Preface p. 5.1–3.) This passage is particularly significant because Beatus has departed at this point from an otherwise extremely slavish reproduction of a dedicatory letter of Isidore (*Contra Judeos, PL* 83:449). Note also the following: "Vere bonum, vere *iucundum habitare fratres in unum.* Unum fratrem dimisimus in saeculo; ecce quantos invenimus in monasterio. Frater meus saecularis non tantum me amabat, quantum substantiam meam" (*Adv.Elip.* 2.38; Löfstedt, 132.1113–1116). This is a citation from Jerome (*In psalm.* 122.1; see Löfstedt, 132, both apparatus at lines 1113–1116), *except for* the words "in monasterio." Beatus, almost as a reflex, specifies Jerome's remarks as a reference to the monastery. Further, it is probable that Beatus lived in the monastery of St. Martin in Liebana, later known as San Toribio. Alcuin, in a recently discovered letter to Beatus (text in J. F. Rivera Recio, "A Proposito du una Carta de Alcuino Recientemente Encontrada," *Revista Española de Teología*, 418–433, and W. Levison, *England and the Continent*, pp. 314ff.) refers to St. Martin as Beatus's "father and protector" (419). Furthermore, there exists a bill of sale from the time of Fruela, abbot at St. Martin's of Liebana, 757–767, which lists a certain Beatus as one of the monks living at St. Martin's at the time (there is a Vincentius mentioned too—maybe the one who had traveled to St. Martin's at Tours, and to whom Alcuin entrusted the delivery of his letter to Beatus—see Rivera Recio's text, 119). See also *España Sagrada* XXXIV, 380–381.

2. Alcuin remarks, "Quod vero quemdam Beatum *abbatem* et discipulum ejus Hitherium episcopum dicitis huic vestrae sectae primum contraire, laudamus eos in eo quod veritatem defendere conati sunt" (Alcuin, *AFU, PL* 101:133D 9–12). Elipandus, even while insulting him, presupposes the same (*Ep. ad Franc.*, 119.3–7).

3. Elipandus calls Beatus a "presbyter" twice: "iste nefandus presbyter et pseudopropheta" (*Ep. ad Karl.*, 120.22–33); "Ad notionem nostram pervenit lugubris et funesta opinio . . . Antifrasii Beati, nefandi Asturiensis presbyteri . . ." (*Ep. ad Franc.*, 111.27–28). Also, the bill of sale cited above, n. 1, calls "Beatus" a presbyter.

4. Elipandus calls him a priest of Asturia (see n. 3 above), and Beatus refers to himself and to Heterius as Liebanese (*Adv.Elip.* 2.2; Löfstedt, p. 104.19), as does Elipandus (in the Letter to Fidelis, at *Adv.Elip.* 1.43; Löfstedt, p. 30.1140).

5. *Vita Sancti Beati, PL* 96:887–894. The notes by Mabillon are still useful. It is not a contemporary work, having been drawn up from sources we already have at our disposal. One scholar (Mateo del Alamo, O.S.B., "Los Comentarios de Beato al Apocalipsis y Elipando," in *Miscellanea Giovanni Mercati*, vol. 2, 18) suspects the *Vita* was constructed by its first publisher, P. Tamayo.

6. *Vita Sancti Beati, PL* 96:893A.8–9. See also Beatus, *Adv.Elip.* 1.1; Löfstedt, p. 1.7–8. On Adosinda, see H. Flórez, *Memorias de las Reynas Catholicas*, vol. 1, 103–105; Díaz y Díaz, *Isidore*, 250–251; J. Orlandis, *Historia*, 121–123; Collins, *Conquest*, 231, 246.

7. Beatus, *Adv.Elip.* 1.1; Löfstedt, p. 1.8.

8. Heterius remains a very shadowy figure indeed. He is mentioned in the preface to the *Commentary on the Apocalypse* (see above, n. 1), and in the *Adv.Elip.* at:

(a) the salutation, " . . . Elipando, Toletanae sedis arciepiscopo, Eterius et Beatus in Domino salutem" (Löfstedt, p. 1.1–2);

(b) 1.13 (Beatus identifies Heterius and himself as members of the antiadoptionist party in Astruria, Löfstedt, p. 9.341–347);

(c) 1.39, " . . . ego Etherius Hoxomae sedis indignus nuncupatus episcopus, qui ab arciepiscopo Toletano nuncupor esse hereticus, profero fidem meam cunctis audientibus" (Löfstedt. p. 27.1001–1003, followed by a recitation of the Nicene Creed);

(d) 1.44 (by Elipandus, in the Letter to Fidelis), "Adolescentiam sane fratris nostri Heteri lacte adhuc alitam et nondum ad robur perfectae intelligentiae perductam vestra fraternitas erudiat . . ." (Löfstedt, p. 31.1154–1156).

We can conclude that Heterius was the titular bishop of Osma, young and still living under the rule of Beatus his abbot, but answerable to Elipandus as his metropolitain. There is said to be a cartulary, unexamined by me, dated 828 (see *Boletín de la Real Academia de la Historia* 46 [1905]: 73–74) listing a "Domno Eterio" as still living at St. Martin's. On Heterius, see Collins, *Conquest*, 227.

9. *Adv.Elip.* 1.39; Löfstedt, p. 27.1001–1023, a profession followed directly by Elipandus's "credo" and the direct invitation to compare them ("Ecce duos simbolos nimis inter se contrarios . . . , " 1.42; Löfstedt, p. 29.1093). Note that this is virtually the *only* use of "Ephesus"—more to establish a recognized pedigree, than to obtain a theological counter-position, as in Alcuin, who does both.

It is interesting that Beatus's initial salvo was a critique of language used in Elipandus's pronouncement against Migetius (see above, col. 2): Beatus thus in effect joined forces with an anti-Elipandine faction, and one with an extreme, if odd, affection for Rome, whose theology, like Beatus's, also had an apocalyptic

cast. It is probably no accident that Elipandus sees things this way too. He con-
nects Beatus to Migetius explicitly, likening their similarly charismatic or prophetic
(to Elipandus, outlandish) behaviors to each other. He says Beatus preached to
the people assembled at an Easter Vigil that the end of the world was immediately
at hand, and pretended to be sick and to arise on the third day (see *Ep. ad Franc.*,
118.35, 119.7–15). Beatus's consistent reference to Elipandus as the Antichrist is part
of his prophetic construal of the iniquity of Elipandus's stewardship (Elipandus
returns the compliment: Beatus is the "pre-cursor of the Antichrist," i.e., a false
prophet). This is not to say that Beatus was actually allied with Migetius, but it
certainly looks like he may have taken advantage of a schism in the Mozarabic
church to foster his own interests against Elipandus.

   10. Romero's edition (n. 1 above) supersedes that of Henry A. Sanders, *Beati
in Apocalipsin Libri Duodecim*. The *editio princeps* (H. Flórez, ed., *Sancti Beati, Presbyteri Hispani Liebanensis, in Apocalypsin . . . Commentaria . . . nunc primum edita*,
is rarer than the MSS themselves. Collins (*Conquest*, 224–226) reminds the reader
that the attribution of this Commentary to Beatus is not supported by any MS
evidence, and that the grounds for attributing it to Beatus are actually quite slim.
But he notes that there are no other equally likely candidates at present.

   11. See Sanders, *Commentary on the Apocalypse*, xi, and the literature he cites.
If there was any revision, however, it was not very thorough. Some of the most
characteristic themes and exegeses from the *Adv.Elip.* fail to surface in the *Commentary on the Apocalypse* at all, not even in places where we could most expect
them. *Commentary on the Apocalypse* 3.4.1, for example, begins the exegesis of the
"book written on the inside and outside" (Apoc. 5:1). The exegesis of this passage
is quite prominent in *Adv.Elip.* 1.111–118 (Löfstedt, pp. 84.3253–91.3517), where it is
interpreted as referring to Christ and is made to serve as the basis for a long
discussion of his two natures. In the *Commentary on the Apocalypse* there is no trace
of this interpretation. Instead, the "book" is intepreted as a reference to "praesentis
mundi omnis . . . creatura, cuius interiora praescit Dominus et exteriora cognos-
cit," or else to the two Testaments (cf. pp. 534–536). Note, too, that Apoc. 17:14,
"quoniam Dominus dominorum est et rex regum," is passed over in the *Commentary on the Apocalypse* without evincing the slightest awareness of the central role
that expressions such as "Lord of lords" play in the *Adv.Elip.*. See also *Commentary
on the Apocalypse* 11.1.10, a specifically christological context in which the word
"adoption" is used with reference to the faithful, and where the phrase "regem
regum et dominum dominatium" also appears. But there is no hint of anti-
adoptionist polemic, even at such a polemically propitious spot. Finally, at *Commentary on the Apocalypse* 12.2.54, 95–97, 103–107, there is a discussion of how none
of the saints can be said to be similar to Christ. This point preoccupies Beatus in
the *Adv.Elip.* But there is no reason to believe that this passage is the product of
a later revision, since there is no explicit mention of adoptionism or the proper or
adoptive sonship of Christ, etc. Rather, this passage represents the prior tradition
of thought out of which Beatus will react when he does come to respond to
Elipandus. Where there is evidence for a revision to fit an anti-adoptionistic perspective, it seems almost desultory, a kind of touch-up veneer, perhaps applied as
Beatus looked at the *Commentary on the Apocalypse* for passages to use in his anti-
adoptionist polemic.

12. Sander's edition is not very helpful in tracing sources. The extent to which this work is derivative is graphically illustrated by H. L. Ramsay, "Le Commentaire de L'Apocalypse par Beatus de Liebana," 424–425, where he shows that even the dedicatory letter to Heterius is a mosaic of texts, reproduced word for word, from various works of Isidore, with minor allowances for the circumstances of the present composition. Even the last sentence, personal as it seems, is copied from Isidore's dedication to his sister of the *Contra Judaeos* (cf. Romero, *Commentary on the Apocalypse*, 3–5). Romero's edition is much more helpful. It abounds in source tracing expertise. In view of his work it is possible to summarize Beatus's dependencies. His greatest debts are to Apringius, Gregory the Great, Isidore, Jerome, Tyconius, and Marius Victorinus. There is heavy and approximately equal reliance on these. Ambrose, Augustine, Fulgentius, and Gregory of Elvira are less well represented. In addition, twenty-seven other authors, all from the West with only two exceptions, are cited relatively infrequently (4 times or less each). Beatus gives his own list of authorities in the preface: "Jerome, Augustine, Ambrose, Fulgentius, Gregory, Tyconius, Irenaeus, Apringius, and Isidore "(4.3–5). Note how both Beatus's own conception of his indebtedness, and the actual character of his dependence as revealed by Romero, are *profoundly and almost exclusively Western*.

13. It is generally agreed that Beatus's *Commentary on the Apocalypse* represents the most heavily indebted medieval use of the Commentary of Tyconius, and the one which is the most reliable witness to the text. For a discussion of the issues, see Ramsay, "Le Commentaire," 430–449 (a very intelligent treatment); T. Hahn, *Tyconius-Studien*, 14–18. Paul Monceaux (*Histoire littéraire de l'Afrique Chrétienne depuis les origines jusqu'à l'invasion Arabe*, vol. 5, 200–201) stresses the accuracy of Beatus's transcriptions, although in terms which are not very complimentary to Beatus. The editor of the most recent edition of what are probably fragments of Tyconius's lost Commentary on the Apocalypse, agrees that Beatus is the most reliable attestation of the text of the Tyconian commentary (see Francesco LoBue, ed., with G. G. Willis, *The Turin Fragments of Tyconius' Commentary on Revelation*, 6, 24, and [especially] 32).

14. See Collins, *Conquest*, 219–220.

15. Information about MSS and previous editions may be found in Löfstedt, v–vii (see chapter 1, n. 20 for full reference for Löfstedt). Book 2 is incomplete in all attestations of the text.

16. There are two reasons for the supposition, otherwise without foundation, that Heterius played only a minor role in the composition of the *Adv.Elip.* First, both Beatus and Elipandus stress his youth, and he does generally appear more as a student than a teacher. Second, Beatus has a previous literary legacy, the *Commentary on the Apocalypse*, whereas Heterius has none surviving or even suspected. Note too that Alcuin mentions Heterius nowhere, not even in his letter to Beatus. Del Alamo ("Los Comentarios") argues that Book I of the *Adv.Elip.* was written by Heterius, while Book II is by Beatus. This on the basis, perhaps, that it is only in the first book that Heterius is mentioned by name, and that at 1.39 Heterius alone speaks, as given just above. But such a division of authorship seems artificial. There are no names at all mentioned in the second book, neither Beatus nor Heterius, and 1.39 is most probably the record of a public confession of faith reproduced from another context (it mentions "hearers," not readers), perhaps one

in which Heterius as bishop formally pronounced his split with Elipandus. Notice that the passage in which Heterius speaks as "ego" is introduced and surrounded by the first person *plural* editorial voice, which is that of the rest of the treatise and which, from the salutation on, refers consistently to Beatus and Heterius both.

17. Heaviest reliance on Ambrose, Augustine, Gregory of Elvira, Gregory the Great, Jerome, and Isidore. Less reliance on 16 others, including Apringius (cited once), Cassian (three times), Cyprian (once), Eucherius (once), and Filastrius (once). The only fifth century Eastern writer included is Cyril of Alexandria (cited once, 9 lines); the only other Eastern representation on the roster is Origen (11 lines from the *Commentary on the Songs*), Hegesippus (12 lines), and Constantinople I (2 lines).

18. *Adv.Elip.* 1.105; Löfstedt, p. 79.3041–3044.

19. *Adv.Elip.* 1.104 and 1.105–110; Löfstedt, pp. 78.3007–79.3040 and pp. 79.3044–84.3252.

20. But note *Adv.Elip.* 1.112: if Beatus has been in fact citing Tyconius or anyone else, it is clear that he has been able to appropriate and use the thought to which he is indebted, without becoming intellectually subservient to it.

21. See, for example, the section on the three parts of the Church at *Adv.Elip.* 2.16–17. It explains that despite the implication of Apoc. 13:11–17, there is really only one beast, and that the body of the devil, although part of this beast, is actually *within* the Church. There are within the Church three parties: those who are good Christians, those who are bad Christians (morally speaking), and those who are heretics. The heretics are false apostles; they seem to be holy and seem to preach Christ, but actually they are instruments of the devil, preaching deception.

22. *Adv.Elip.* 1.89–95. Löfstedt's edition does not identify the source. In general, Löfstedt's edition is very helpful as a beginning in tracing sources, and one is most grateful for the hard work he has done, but there is still more to do. There are, for example, words and phrases interior to the text which seem to mark passages taken over from earlier sources. The "Amen," e.g., at 2.92 (Löfstedt, p. 161.2259) may mark the ending of an earlier source. Also, the frequently encountered phrase "Hoc totum quare diximus?" (or variations) seems to serve at times as close quotation marks, as perhaps at 1.35 (Löfstedt, p. 23.884), where it comes after what looks like a citation of some commentary on the Lukan Infancy Narrative (1.29–1.35 = Löfstedt, pp. 20.744–23.884). The phrase definitely serves this purpose at 1.59 (Löfstedt, p. 43.1635) where it closes a long citation from the *Moralia in Iob* of Gregory (Löfstedt, pp. 40.1528–43.1618, with related material, probably also cited, from p. 43.1619–1634). See also the use of this phrase at 2.45 (Löfstedt, p. 136.1303) after a chain of glossed citations from Jerome's *In psalm.* 132; and at 1.102; 2.52; 2.77; etc. This phrase is also frequently found in the *Commentary on the Apocalypse* (540.2.20, etc.). There is also a citation of a text of Isidore (*Etym.* 7.2.13, cited at *Adv.Elip.* 2.38; Löfstedt, p. 131.1103–1107) which Elipandus also cites (*Ep.ad Albinum* 9, PL 96:873A; *Ep. ad Franc.* 113.7–9 [cf. line 25], 117.20–21); the ultimate source for this passage is, perhaps, Augustine's *Commentary on Galatians* 30.10, lines 19–22 (J. Divjak, ed., *CSEL* 84). Also, Isidore, *Etym.* 8.11.22, is cited at *Adv.Elip.* 8.11.22.

23. See Amann, *L'Époque*, 134–137. It is hard to credit such a damning judgment issued apart from any specific reference to the text. Ansprenger, citing

Amann, says that Beatus and Heterius border on docetism and monophysitism ("Untersuchungen," p. 2 and n. 14) although he cites only one passage in support of his claim. Heil, "Adoptianismus," 125–130, can talk about Beatus without calling him a monophysite, but does him no justice by virtually assimilating him into the anti-adoptionist party outside of Spain (127). He notices that the charge of Nestorianism is "barely" made against Elipandus—this "barely" with disapproval (128), as though it should have been made and would have been made more thoroughly had Beatus been more critically aware, like Alcuin. But because he holds such a presupposition, Heil is left to conclude that Beatus had no understanding of the actual concerns or intents of Elipandus's theology. Heil concludes that the "kernel" of the controversy is the understanding of the word "caro," where the adoptionists see a full humanity represented by that term, and Beatus evidently something less. But he cannot adduce any texts to support this assessment of the "kernel" of the issue. Hauck gives Beatus very little attention, and that not approvingly (*Kirchengeschichte*, 306), while Hefele-Leclercq (who, incidentally, give a bibliographical footnote on all the earlier scholarly literature on Beatus, *Histoire*, 1020, n. 1) are content to note that he was "orthodox" (1023). Menéndez Pelayo, although he locates the theological value of the *Adv.Elip.* in its supposed detection and refutation of the Nestorianism of Elipandus (*los Heterodóxos*, 363), has nevertheless an appreciation of the calibre of the work which is wonderful (see 365–366).

24. Apart from Beatus's authorship of the *Commentary on the Apocalypse* and the *Adv.Elip.*, it has been speculated that he was also the author of a famous Spanish hymn: see the discussion in Díaz y Díaz, *Isidoro*, who, however, rejects the authorship of Beatus, 250–261.

25. For example, both Elipandus and Beatus use the christological structure, distinctively Hispanic since at least Julian of Toledo, of "three substances in Christ " (see above, chapter 2, for Elipandus, and below, p. 173, n. 37, for Beatus); both talk about Bonosus (see above, chapter 2, n. 49) as though his heresy were part of a common but particularly Hispanic heretical tradition. Also, they are both especially fond of the phrase "perfectus Deus, perfectus et homo," from the Creed of Toledo XI (ultimately from the *Quicumque*: see Madoz, *XIe Tolède*, 23, 82).

26. Alcuin, by contrast, regularly appeals to the doctrinal authority of Rome (see below, chapter 4, n. 81). It is theorized that Beatus and Heterius first notified Rome of Elipandus's adoptionism (see, e.g., Amann, *L'Époque*, 134), but there is really no evidence.

27. *Adv.Elip.* 1.3; Löfstedt, pp. 2–3. Note especially, "Et quod Petro dixit, 'Super hanc petram aedificabo eclesiam meam,' *non soli Petro, sed nobis omnibus* dixit."

28. Although not for lack of knowledge of it: in both the *Commentary on the Apocalypse* and the *Adv.Elip.* Beatus cites copiously from the *Etymologia* of Isidore, which discusses Chalcedon (*Etym.* 5.39.39; 8.5.65; 8.5.66; 8.5.67; 6.6.9–10). In the *Commentary on the Apocalypse* (pp. 609, 619) he also cites Isidore's *Chronicon*, which contains many references to Chalcedon (*Chron.* 110–16). References in Isidore are collected by Solano, "La controversia," 857–865.

29. Nestorius is mentioned by name only in the following list: "Liquido enim patet, quod Arrius, Futinus, Bonosus, Macedonius, Nestorius, Euticius, Dioscorus, Severus, et huic nostris modo temporibus Elipandus multique horum

similes . . . " (*Adv.Elip.* 2.94; Löfstedt, p. 162.2289–2291. Plainly, he is listed as just another heretic. No special relation between Nestorius and Elipandus is implied. There is a passage at *Adv.Elip.* 2.59 (Löfstedt, pp. 142.1581–144.1585) which is striking because the reference here is *not* to Nestorius but is rather clearly tailored so that it refers to Elipandus in particular. What is striking is that Nestorius is not mentioned in such a context. Finally, the *Acta* of Ephesus (in this case Cyril's *Apologeticus contra Orientales* 62; 73) are cited at *Adv.Elip.* 1.21 (Löfstedt, pp. 14.542–15.551), but are never again, in the rest of the 170-page treatise, paid the slightest attention (although it may be noted that the Nicene Creed is cited but called the "simbolus fidei Efesenae" at Löfstedt, p. 27.1000, 1023). Nestorius is not mentioned. Beatus, further, never repeats the charge of dividing Jesus into two Christs in his own words, nor does he ever make the charge that Elipandus is preaching a doctrine of "two sons." At *Adv.Elip.* 1.12 (Löfstedt, p. 98.3770–3780) Beatus tells Elipandus that "one person and one Lamb cannot be partly proper Son, and partly adoptive; that is, part Son and part not-Son, part God and part not-God . . . . Try as you might, you cannot divide him. The unity is inseparable. The taking-up was accomplished in such a way that it made God man and man God and one Christ out of both." There is no "two-son" or "two-Christ" critique here, although it could easily have been raised. At *Adv.Elip.* 1.49 (Löfstedt, p. 34.1304–1307), Beatus once again raises the issue of the divisiveness of Elipandus's christology, but again, by not bringing up the charge of preaching two sons or two Christs or two persons, he does not imply any charge of Nestorianism. Rather, he chides Elipandus, ridiculing him because he can come up with no entity to correspond to the one name Jesus. At *Adv.Elip.* 1.42 (Löfstedt, p. 29.1102–1103) there is an echo of the Ephesus *Acta* when Beatus asks, " Quid est solvere Ihesum, nisi seorsum Deum et seorsum hominem praedicare?" (Cf. also *Adv.Elip.* 1.72; Löfstedt, p. 55.2094–2097, treated below at 157, 187.) All of this serves mainly to show that Beatus understood what Nestorianism was and that it could be, perhaps somewhat obliquely, applied to Elipandus's system or to an exaggeration of it, but that Beatus on the whole did not think in these terms, did not set himself up as a new Cyril against a new Nestorius, or try to reargue that controversy in a new context. He pays his respects to the East, but no more.

30. See Thompson, *Goths, passim,* on Visigothic legislation directed against the Jews. However, it is unclear what reality these laws reflect. Collins, *Conquest,* 70–71, suggests that more often than not there were cordial local relations.

31. *Adv.Elip.* 1.31; Löfstedt, p. 21.807–812. See also 2.60; 2.70 (Löfstedt, p. 149.1821–22).

32. *Adv.Elip.* 1.74–75; Löfstedt, pp. 150–151, lines 1866–1868 and 1902–06. Note the Trinitarian discussion at 1.74 (Löfstedt, p. 150.1850–1865). See also the discussions of the Trinity at 1.19; 1.69; 1.119; 2.55–56; 2.70; etc. It is hard to know what Amann has in mind when, without adducing any passages, he observes of Beatus and Heterius that "leur doctrine trinitaire ne vaut pas beaucoup mieux que leur christologie," *L'Époque,* 134). Perhaps it is Beatus's very occasional use of the expression "essentia de essentia," which is offensive; but he is hardly to be faulted for it, as Augustine says it too (*De trinitate* 7.2, W. J. Mountain, ed., CC 50, 50A, 250.23).

33. "In Domino igitur Ihesu Christo Deo et homine, auctore hac redemtore nostro, sicut unam absque dubitatione personam, ita duplicem constat esse substantiam " (*Adv.Elip.* 1.124; Löfstedt, p. 96.3696–3698, cited from the pseudo-Augustinian *Liber testimoniorum fidei* 2.12. See Löfstedt, p. 96.)

34. For similar "so that" language in Elipandus, see above, 94. For a similar usage in Beatus but in a contrasting sense, see at *Adv.Elip.* 1.12 (Löfstedt, p. 8.292–306), where Beatus says that *Jesus* received the Holy Spirit *so that* he might be *plenus gratiae*. This sounds almost "adoptionistic."

35. *Adv.Elip.* 2.57; Löfstedt, p. 143.1556–1567, 1562–1576. There could be no clearer statement of the dyophysite position, and there is special emphasis on the continuity of the *persona* in Christ with that of the Son, the second *persona* of the Trinity (as defined by Beatus in the previous sections, *Adv.Elip.* 2.54–56).

36. *Adv.Elip.* 2.55; Löfstedt, p. 142.1518–1520.

37. See, for example, Julian of Toledo's defense of this usage in his *Apologeticum de tribus capitulis* (in *Sancti Iuliani Toletanae Sedis Episcopi Opera*, part 1, J. N. Hillgarth, ed., *CCSL* 115, 127–139, esp. chapters 4–17, pp. 131–138). Note too the Creed of Toledo XI: "idem Christus in his duabus naturis tribus exstat substantiis: verbi, quod ad solius Dei essentiam referendum est; corporis et animae quod ad verum hominem pertinet" (Toledo XI, article 40, Perez, *Christología*, 45). Perez cites Isidore (*Diff.* 8.23–24, *PL* 83:74A) as the proximate source, and gives earlier warrants in n. 55, p. 45.

38. *Adv.Elip.* 2.70; Löfstedt, p. 149.1808–1811, 1817–1818, 1824. At 1.60 (Löfstedt, p. 44.1677–1687) there is an interesting passage where both the terms *substantia* and *natura* are used together: the full formula seems to be "one person, three substances [or] two natures."

39. *Adv.Elip.* 1.110; Löfstedt, pp. 83–84.3228–3229, 3245–3247.

40. E.g. at *Adv.Elip.* 2.77; Löfstedt, p. 152.1930.

41. E.g. at *Adv.Elip.* 2.74; Löfstedt, p. 150.1869.

42. E.g. *Adv.Elip.* 1.125; Löfstedt, p. 97.3714–3734.

43. On the history of *homo assumptus* theologies in both East and West, see A. Gaudel, "La théologie de l''Assumptus Homo': Histoire et valeur doctrinale": 64–90, 214–234.

44. "Nam quod homo dicitur Filius Dei verus et Deus verus, ipse Dominus de se dicit: *Nemo ascendit in caelum, nisi qui descendit de caelo, Filius hominis, qui est in caelo*. Et tamen illud hominem, quem Deus Verbum solus assumpserat, non eum adhuc in caelo imposuerat, sicut nec de caelo eum secum adduxerat, sicut et de illo legitur, 'Filius hominis descendit de caelo, et Filius Dei crucifixus est in terra.' Sed hoc totum verum est, quia ex utroque unus Christus Filius Dei est, quia ipse descendit de caelo et ipse est Filius Dei, qui sub Pontio Pilato crucifixus est in terra" (*Adv.Elip.* 1.83; Löfstedt, pp. 62–63, lines 2390–2399; see also 2.92; Löfstedt, pp. 160–162, lines 2238–2254).

45. "In illo enim patibulo nihil pertulit Deus patientis sensu, sed pertulit compatientis affectu. Nihil pertulit pro diversitate, sed pertulit pro unitate personae. Nihil Deus pro infirmitate passus est, sed pro dignatione *compassus* est" (*Adv.Elip.* 1.125; Löfstedt, p. 97.3723–3729).

46. *Adv.Elip.* 1.121; Löfstedt, p. 95.3646–3652. It could with justice be said

that this passage shows how little the patterns of thought represented by the *Acta* of Ephesus have ingrained themselves into Beatus. For even though he has quoted the prohibition of talking about worship of the *susceptum* because of the *susceptor*, he does almost exactly that here. On the general subject of the extreme independence which Beatus allows to the man Jesus, see the list at *Adv.Elip.* 50; Löfstedt, p. 36.1364, where "Jesus" is included almost as though he were just another name in the list, essentially on a par with the rest of those listed.

47. *Adv.Elip.* 1.41; Löfstedt, pp. 133–134, lines 1185–1194.

48. See Elipandus, *Ep. ad Franc.* 113.17–36. For both Elipandus and Beatus it is a *man* who is anointed, and the rest of us participate in that anointing, but not directly—only through Jesus. For Elipandus this means participating in his adoption. Jesus's becoming adoptive is the forging of a new possibility for relation to the Father, one in which we can participate with him. Both Elipandus and Beatus remark that only Jesus has this anointing fully; we have it only *ad mesuram*.

49. See Jerome, *In Psalm. 132*, D. G. Morin, ed., CCSL 78, 278.61–71, 73–75; cf. 277.51–55. For Jerome the unguent descends from "God the Word" to "the man whom He deigned to assume" (278.74–75). If anything, Beatus's language is slightly more divisive. His phrase "true God" (Jerome has "Word of God") highlights more starkly the distinction between creature and Creator. At *In Psalm. 132*, 277.53–54, Jerome is much less divisive—he speaks of the unguent descending from the "*divinity*" to the "*virum perfectum*" (Christ).

50. For example, at *Adv.Elip.* 1.113–116 where Christ is being compared to the book in the Apoc. 5:2 "written on on the inside and out," Beatus makes Ps. 2:7–8 ("Filius meus es tu; ego hodie genui te. Pete a me et dabo tibi gentes haereditatem tuam et possessionem tuam terminos terrae") applicable to the "outside" of the book, that is, to the humanity of Christ. This, unqualified, is prone to an adoptionistic interpretation; indeed, Elipandus does apply these verses to the humanity (*Ep. ad Franc.* 112.27; 114.15–16). Further, would it not be adoptionist to assign "Filius altissimi vocabitur," and "Quod nascetur ex te sanctum, vocabitur Filius Dei" (Lk. 1:32,35) to the inside of the book, that is, to the divinity? Wasn't this precisely the claim of the adoptionists, that the word Son applied most properly to the divinity? (*Adv.Elip.* 1.115; Löfstedt, p. 89.3416–3419, cf. p. 91.3486–3496.) The extremity to which Beatus is prepared to carry out this division along the lines of "intus" and "foris" serves to show how divisive a christological structure he is working with, one certainly just as divisive as that of Elipandus himself.

51. Note that no particular metaphor dominates for explaining the resultant structure. Beatus is just as completely at home using the body/soul metaphor as he is with the metaphor of indwelling (for example, *Adv.Elip.* 2.53; 2.75), images which in the East were associated with opposite christological schools. Augustine also uses both—the point is that in the West the controversy does not *hinge* around the use of any particular metaphor.

52. *Adv.Elip.* 1.60; Löfstedt, p. 44.1669–1676.

53. *Adv.Elip.* 1.60; Löfstedt, p. 45.1695. This is the basis for what is known classically as the *communicatio idiomatum*.

54. *Adv.Elip.* 1.112; Löfstedt, pp. 85–86, lines 3298–3299, 3300–3308. The source of this analogy, if it is necessary to suppose one, has not been determined.

55. This makes it more difficult to argue that Elipandus's christology is Nestorian or Antiochene in inspiration, inasmuch as no one would ever make this claim for Beatus.

56. This, of course, is very Augustinian, and could be viewed as a development of the way in which Augustine (and Gregory after him) spoke of the voice of the Psalm as that of Christ speaking *in the person of his members*, the Church. For example: "Loquitur . . . Christus. Sed multa dicta sunt ex persona corporis; audi et ex persona capitis: et non quasi distinguit, ut inducat ipsas personas, modo caput, modo corpus. Si enim distinguit, quasi dividit; non erunt duo in carne una. Si autem duo sunt in carne una; noli mirari si duo sunt in voce una" (*Enarrationes in Psalmos* 138.21.1–6); "Sive autem caput loquatur, sive membra loquantur, Christus loquitur: loquitur ex persona capitis, loquitur ex persona corporis. Sed quid dictum est? *Erunt duo in carne una. Sacramentum hoc magnum est; ego*, inquit, *dico, in Christo et in ecclesia* (Eph. 5:31–32) . . . Nam ut noveritis has duas quodammodo esse personas, et rursus unam copulatione coniugii, tamquam unus loquitur . . . " (*En. in Ps.* 74.4.16–23); "ille caput, nos corpus, unus homo loquitur. Et capitis est proprium loqui etiam in persona membrorum" (*En. in Ps.* 149.3.29–31; later on, Paulinus of Aquileia will scold Felix for using this *unus homo* language for Christ and the Church; Augustine uses the qualifier *"quasi* ex unius hominis ore" at *En. in Ps.* 40.1.11, as Paulinus recommends); "Si ergo ipse dixit: *Iam non duo, sed una est caro* (Mt. 19:6), quid mirum si una caro, una lingua, eadem verba, tamquam unius carnis, capitis et corporis? Sic audiamus tamquam unum, sed tamen caput tamquam caput, et corpus tamquam corpus. Non dividuntur personae, sed distinguitur dignitas; quia caput salvat, salvatur corpus" (*En. in Ps.* 37.6.43–48). On this topic see Hubertus R. Drobner, *Person-Exegese und Christologie bei Augustinus,* esp. 23–24, 73–74. Gregory's usage is even more dramatic: "Sicut autem isdem Redemptor noster una persona est cum congregatione bonorum, ipse namque caput est corporis et nos huius capitis corpus, ita antiquus hostis una persona est cum cuncta collectione reproborum quia ipse eis ad iniquitatem quasi caput praeeminet . . . " (*Moralia in Iob* 4.11.18.3–7); "Quia igitur Christus et Ecclesia, id est caput et corpus una persona est . . . " (*Moralia in Iob* 35.14.24.12–13).

57. *Commentary on the Apocalypse* 4.1.25 and elsewhere, frequently.

58. Note the following from the Turin fragments of Tyconius: "Duo enim populi sunt in ecclesia, id est pars Dei quae luci est comparata et pars diaboli tenebrarum obscuritatibus circumsepta . . . " (LoBue, *Turin Frag,* section 172; cf. section 413). The theme of an invisible division within the Church comes ultimately from Tyconius (see, e.g., William S. Babcock, "Christian Culture and Christian Tradition in Roman North Africa," 44–45). One cannot help but think in this context of the third of Tyconius's rules, as cited in Augustine's *De doctrina christiana,* 3.32, on the "bipartite" body of the Lord, as well as Rule 1, "On the Lord and His Body," and Rule 7, "On the Devil and His Body (*De doct.* 3.31; 3.37; compare to the subtitle of Book II of Beatus's *Adv.Elip.: De christo et eius corpore, quod est ecclesia, et de diabolus et eius corpore, quod est Antichristus*). On Tyconius's work see now Pamela Bright, *The Book of Rules of Tyconius: Its Inner Purpose and*

Logic, and also William S. Babcock, ed., *Tyconius: The Book of Rules*. Best edition of the *De doctrina* is by J. Martin, in *CCSL* vol. 32.

59. *Commentary on the Apocalypse* 7.1.4–5; 9.3.11–12; etc.

60. *Commentary on the Apocalypse* 9.3.16.

61. *Commentary on the Apocalypse* 2.2.80; see also Preface 4.115–117; etc. This theme is familiar to students of Carolingian theology as it is elaborated by Agobard, a figure of Hispanic provenance. See, e.g., *De fide veritate et totius boni institutione* 16, lines 1–3, 6; 17, line 1 (L. Van Acker, ed., *CCCM* vol. 52).

62. *Commentary on the Apocalypse*, Sanders, p. 491, 4.61–62; Romero, vol. 2, p. 151.6–7.

63. *Commentary on the Apocalypse* 5.8.14–16; 5.2.1; 6.2.23–24; and *passim*. This can be recognized as one Donatist concern which has in particular passed over into the *Adv.Elip.*

64. See *Commentary on the Apocalypse*, Sanders, p. 572 (9.3.1); Romero, vol. 2, p. 293.6–10: "*Hi decem reges cum agno pugnant* [Apoc. 17:14]. Et quia supra in decem regibus omnes omnino malos conprehendimus, hi cum agno pugnabunt, quod est Christus et ecclesia, unum corpus. Pugnabunt usque in finem . . . . "

65. *Commentary on the Apocalypse* 6.3.3–4.

66. *Commentary on the Apocalypse* 6.3.18.

67. *Commentary on the Apocalypse* 6.3.16.

68. *Commentary on the Apocalypse*. Steadfastness during persecution is a characteristic concern of the Donatists, and, indeed, of North African Christianity in general, since the time of our most ancient Latin records. Babcock is helpful here ("Christian Culture," 31ff.).

69. *Commentary on the Apocalypse* 6.8.23–26. Note the mention of Africa here, and just after this passage at 7.1.2. This passage is probably Tyconian in origin. Also see 3.4.105–106: "Sed quia patriarchas, prophetas, et apostolos ecclesiam diximus, et hanc ecclesiam corpus esse summi capitis Christi, haec membra cum capite aliquando in scripturis unus agnus nuncupatur; et quod olim caput passus est, nunc in ecclesiam patitur per membra, cotidie occiditur ecclesia pro Christo . . . " See, too, 3.4.25–26: " . . . peccatum non habuit et tamen eius corpus per passionis contumelias ad immortalitatem profecit. nam iuxta virtutes animae, quo percussionibus potuisset proficere, omnino non habuit. in membris autem suis, quae nos sumus, cotidie percussionibus proficit, quia dum nos tundimur et efficimur, ut eius esse mereamur, ipse proficit." Compare these passages to the the following, from the Turin fragments: "Semper enim cruciatibus parit ecclesia Christum, unde iuge Filii hominis adventum promisit in claritate similium passionum" (LoBue, *Turin Frag*, section 463).

70. See, for example, *Commentary on the Apocalypse* 12.2.1, Sanders, p. 619, Romero, vol. 2, p. 380.4–6: "Hanc Ierusalem ecclesaim dicit, quem recapitulat a Christi passione usque in diem, quo resurgat, et cum Christo invicta coronetur in gloria." From this sense of solidarity with Christ in persecution there arises a spirituality which is distinctly apocalyptic, exhorting the church to hold as naught the things of this world and to persevere in contemplation of the things above and beyond the hostile world. For example, on Apoc. 14:1, "stans super montem Sion: stare super montem, id est, ecclesia dicitur, quia surgere nos et excitare ad

penitentiam cohortatur stare enim pugnantis est, et bene stare dicitur, aui cum bestia in pugna certare perhibetur, pro peregrinatione autem praesentis saeculi ecclesia Sion dicitur, eo quod ab huius peregrinationis longitudine posita promissionem rerum caelestium speculetur. et propterea Sion speculatio nomen accepit, quia corporaliter terrena deserens, spiritu et mente in contemplatione perseverans, semper ad superiora tendit" (*Commentary on the Apocalypse* 6.8.18–20). The pilgrimage of persecution is understood as a penitential discipline, leading towards contemplation. See also at 3.3.52–57, 96–97. Beatus's work *Adv.Elip.* retains a contemplative tone from these sources, although it is no longer predicated upon a thoroughgoing apocalyptic world view.

71. *Commentary on the Apocalypse* 5.4.2–3. In the Turin fragments of Tyconius's commentary on the Apocalypse, it is noted that although the church is established in the four corners of the world, it still possesses one *persona*: "unius ecclesiae intelligimus esse personam quae in toto corpore *ara Dei* [Apoc. 9:13] est nuncupata" (LoBue, *Turin Frag*, section 236; cf. section 7, where reference is made to the "personam sanctorum").

72. *Adv.Elip.* 2.11; Löfstedt, p. 112, lines 330–331.

73. *Adv.Elip.* 2.13; Löfstedt, p. 113, lines 376–384.

74. *Adv.Elip.* 1.46; Löfstedt, p. 32.1208–1222. Cf. lines 1219–1222: " . . . Christus . . . patitur in singulis, non utique corporis dolore, sed animi compassione. Quae passio et compassio una est passio, quia unus [sic] est calix, qui bibitur, et una persona est caput et corpus, qui patitur."

75. *Adv.Elip.* 1.45; Löfstedt, p. 31.1180, 1182–1183. Beatus elaborates further on this unity in suffering. He observes that even though Saul was persecuting *the disciples*, Jesus called to him saying, "Saul, Saul, why are you persecuting *me*?" (*Adv.Elip.* 1.46; Löfstedt, p. 31.1185–1188). And Beatus further underscores the union between Christ and the church in suffering by citing the apocryphal story of Peter at the Gate, from Hegesippus. Peter, leaving Rome in fear of Nero's persecution, sees Christ appear to him at the Gate, heading in the other direction. Beatus points out that when Peter asks where he is going, Christ replies, "I am going to be crucified again," and Hegesippus notes, to the approval of Beatus, that he suffers in each of us, not only in the suffering of the body, but by a certain "co-suffering of mercy," or repetition of glory (*Adv.Elip.* 1.46; Löfstedt, p. 31.1188–1189; cf. *Adv.Elip.* 2.14; Löfstedt, p. 114.409–411). Paul, Beatus adds, that "vessel of election," says to his disciples, "Daily I am making up in my own flesh what is lacking in the sufferings of Christ" (*Adv.Elip.* 1.46; Löfstedt, p. 31.1188–1189, Colossians 1.24; see also *Adv.Elip.* 2.39; Löfstedt, p. 132.1140–1145). Beatus will later apply this passage to the Church as a whole, which (following Gregory of Elvira's use of Colossians 1:24, *In Cant.* 1.20) he can refer to as the "flesh" of Christ (*Adv.Elip.* 2.83; Löfstedt, p. 156.2058–2059). The section concludes observing that wherever the church is recognized, there too is Christ recognized, He who is the Head of the Church and who makes Himself and us *one* (*Adv.Elip.* 1.46; Löfstedt, p. 33.1240–1243).

76. "Our Lord and Redeemer is one substance with the holy Church, which he, according to the flesh, redeemed" (*Adv.Elip.* 2.40; Löfstedt, p. 132.1146–1147).

77. *Adv.Elip.* 2.51; Löfstedt, p. 139.1405–1412.

78. *Adv.Elip.* 1.72; Löfstedt, p. 55, lines 2095–2102. Note that Beatus has been very careful to identify the subject of the taking up as the Son; it is his *persona* which provides the reference here, as always.

79. "*Verbum carne* [sic] *factum est*, sed non est in carne conversum, sicut nec anima hominis convertitur in carne. Et qum in carne Christi habitat Verbum, in nostra natura habitat, quia ipsa caro nostra est. Illi carni adiungitur eclesia, et fit Christus totus una persona, caput et corpus" (*Adv.Elip.* 2.77; Löfstedt, p. 152.1929–1933).

80. See *Adv.Elip.* 1.81; Löfstedt, p. 60.2294–2297: " . . . omnes in uno sacrificio mediatoris reconciliamur, quia ipse est *mediator Dei et hominum homo Christus Ihesus* (1 Tim. 2:5), ipse est caput corporis eglesiae, una persona." See also at *Adv.Elip.* 2.14 and 2.68.

81. Parallel to a concern of Elipandus, where Elipandus comments that we cannot be "like" God if that means becoming like him in substance.

82. *Adv.Elip.* 2.70; Löfstedt, p. 149.1808–1819.

83. *Adv.Elip.* 2.70; Löfstedt, p. 149.1801–1807. Is there any echo or clue to the teaching of Migetius here? Is Beatus obliquely charging Elipandus of the heresy of his enemy? It is not clear.

84. *Adv.Elip.* 1.60; Löfstedt, p. 44.1669–1671.

85. *Adv.Elip.* 1.60; Löfstedt, p. 44.1671–1676.

86. *Adv.Elip.* 1.60; Löfstedt, p. 44.1677–1681.

87. *Adv.Elip.* 1.60; Löfstedt, p. 44.1682–1687.

88. *Adv.Elip.* 1.60; Löfstedt, p. 44.1688–1694.

89. *Adv.Elip.* 1.60; Löfstedt, p. 45.1695. It must be observed that this notion represents a step which Pope Leo does not seem himself to actually take. When Leo discusses the actions which are proper to the two natures respectively, he at times seems almost to make them into two agents, separate unto themselves. Note at the Tome 4, the famous passage where he talks about the "co-*operation*" of one nature or form with the other, the Word carrying out that which belongs properly to the Word, and the flesh carrying out or suffering that which properly appertains to the flesh. See also *Sermo* 54.2, and *Ep.* 124.5.

90. *Adv.Elip.* 1.60; Löfstedt, p. 45.1695–1701.

91. "Solum Filio dico mori, quia solus Filius se exinanivit. Exinanitio eius adventus est. Adventus eius humanitas eius est, quae humanitas anima et caro est, id est totus homo perfectus est." (*Adv.Elip.* 1.60; Löfstedt, p. 45.1703–1705).

92. In fact, the discussion of this emptying abruptly breaks off a long series of rhetorically parallel claims (*Adv.Elip.* 1.60; Löfstedt, p. 45.1695–1702), all beginning "*Naturale* est illi [Filio]" and ending with a verbal nominative like "esse aequalem cum Patre," or "esse localis," and, finally, "mori" (lines 1696, 1698, 1702). The reason that it is only the Son who can die is that it is only the Son who "emptied" himself. This act, however, is not said to be "naturale illi," but, rather, its mention breaks off the chain of natural attribution altogether because it does not belong to *either* of the natures in and of themselves.

93. See *Ep. ad Albinum* 14 (*PL* 877C 12–15, 878A 12–15), citing Leo's letter to the Emperor Leo I: "*Forma* autem *servi*, per quam impassibilis deitas sacramentum magnae pietatis implevit, humana humilitas est . . . "; "Quae autem est ejus exinan-

itio, quaeve paupertas nisi formae servilis acceptio . . . ?" Elipandus and Beatus are both reflecting and elaborating on the same theme.

94. *Adv.Elip.* 1.60; Löfstedt, p. 45.1705–1709.

95. Beatus's understanding of Christ's role as the Mediator is set into relief by his corresponding understanding of the devil, who plays *no* mediatorial role for his "body": "Diabolus vero non est mediator corpori suo, quia adhuc non ingressus est hominem illum damnatum, pro quo sit visibilis mediator ipse filius perditionis inter diabolum et genus humanum," (*Adv.Elip.* 2.14; Löfstedt, p. 114.414–416). In other words, the devil is the *terminus ad quem* so to speak in the relationship between himself and his body; he does not mediate to it a relation or posture to anything or anyone else beyond himself. Instead, the *heretics* are the *devil's* mediators, since by their deceitful use of Christ's name they facilitate the attachment of a great body of people to the person of the devil: "Sed habet [diabolus] falsos praedicatores suos hereticos, qui fingunt sub nomine Christi Christum, qualem sibi inspirante diabolo fingit, non qualem Veritas dicit. Est corpus diaboli, et tamen sub nomine falsitatis Christum praedicat et Christum se coli mentitur" (*Adv.Elip.* 2.14; Löfstedt, p. 114.417–420). Note how the *name* of the true mediator, when used falsely, effects a mediation which is perverse and false, but a mediation nonetheless. Cf. Augustine's comments on the devil as a false mediator in *De trinitate* 4 and *De civ.* 10.

96. See note 100 below. The idea of a "rule" is probably a reference not to a creed but, given Beatus's monastic background, to a monastic rule which serves as charter for a community of monks.

97. *Adv.Elip.* 2.37; Löfstedt, p. 131.1088–1092.

98. See *Adv.Elip.* 2.13; Löfstedt, p. 113.376–379: it is the observation of the rule of pride that joins the devil and his body into one *persona*; *Adv.Elip.* 2.9; Löfstedt, p. 110.257–264; cf. the "tumor cordis" of the Antichrist at *Adv.Elip.* 2.37; Löfstedt, p. 131.1082–1083. One is reminded of the way Augustine describes the pride of the devil as his failure to "stand fast in truth," that is, in the truth of his ontological stature, perversely attempting to imitate the stature of God instead (*De civ.* 11.13), and as a result constituting, with any who follow him, a city of pride, opposed to the city of God. For Beatus he is, similarly, the "head of all the proud," whom he has coupled into one body with himself. This body will sink with him into the lake of Gehenna (*Adv.Elip.* 2.9; Löfstedt, p. 110.268–270). I am not claiming direct dependence on Augustine here, but pointing to the background in North African theology which both Augustine and Beatus share.

99. The passage from "For, although . . . " to "First-born" is a citation from Isidore, ultimately from Augustine's *Commentary* on Galatians. In fact, this is one of Elipandus's favorite citations (see above, chapter 2, n. 101) from Isidore or from anyone else. It seems unlikely that Beatus has cited it knowing that he is returning Elipandus's use of the passage, since these are all later, or that Elipandus has cited it against Beatus's use, since he never alludes to this use or indeed to anything from the *Adv.Elip.* at all. These uses of it are therefore all the more interesting because they remind us of how much these two theologians are working out of a common tradition, and how much their respective christologies are an interpretation of a common heritage, since they each read this passage differently; Elipandus applies

"per adoptionem gratiae" to the Word, while Beatus applies it to us. For both Beatus and Elipandus, the *primogenitus* is the human being who exists because of and *as* the self-emptying of the Word. As a man he is perfectly self-standing and independent. As *primogenitus* he stands at the head of the redeemed, to whom his humility has granted the status of *brethren*. Beatus goes farther than Elipandus in his specification of the *primogenitus* of the Isidoran tradition as the Head of the Church, and in exploring the role of the *primogenitus* as Mediator, a term which Elipandus avoids.

100. *Adv.Elip.* 2.38, Löfstedt, p. 131.1098–1108; *Adv.Elip.* 2.39, Löfstedt, p. 132.1121–1122; *Adv.Elip.* 2.40, Löfstedt, p. 133.1157, 1160. Compare Beatus's interpretation of this oil or unguent as grace or the Holy Spirit (*Adv.Elip.* 2.40; Löfstedt, p. 133.1159, 1161) with Elipandus's idea that it is as participation in Jesus's adoption that *we* have the grace of adoption (*Ep. ad Franc.* 133.17–18; *Ep. ad Albinum* 875B 1–3). There is an interesting parallel in Beatus's *Commentary on the Apocalypse* to the language of descent in this passage, where it is not a rule which is said to descend, but the Church itself: "*et ostendit mihi civitatem sanctam Ierusalem, descendentem de caelo a Deo* (Apoc. 21:10) haec est ecclesia, civitas in monte constituta, sponsa agni, quia non est alia ecclesia et alia civitas, quia una est, quia semper in penitentia de caelo descendet a Deo, quia filium Dei imitando in penitentia de caelo descendere dicitur in humilitate. Sic enim filius Dei descendit de caelo, *quum in forma Dei esset, formam servi adsumens humiliavit se usque ad mortem* (Phil. 2:6). Descensio filii Dei incarnatio eius est. Haec civitas cotidie a Deo descendit imitando Deum, id est, sequendo vestigia Christi filii Dei" (*Commentary on the Apocalypse* 12.2.28–29, Sanders, p. 623, Romero, vol. 2, p. 387.5–15). The Church is formed by a descent, just like the Incarnation; it *is* a descent, just like the Incarnation. Note also *Commentary on the Apocalypse* 3.2.23, Sanders, p. 282, Romero, vol. 1, pp. 469.15–470.2: "humilitatem dixit ecclesiae, quae cum habeat adoptionem filiorum Dei, videtur ut homo nihil praeter humanitatem possidere, sicut de Domino dictum est: *quum esset in forma Dei, non rapinam arbitratus est, esse se aequalem Deo; sed semet ipsum exinanivit, formam servi accipiens, in similitudinem hominem factus, et habitu inventus ut homo; humiliavit se obediens factus usque ad mortem.*"

101. This is the best place to discuss the Eucharistic theology of Beatus, which is quite distinctive (by contrast, the Eucharist plays virtually no role in Alcuin's anti-adoptionist work, *pace* Harnack, *History of Dogma*, p. 291.). It is a kind of microcosm of his theology of the formation of the church. As the *sacrifice of the Mediator* (see *Adv.Elip.* 1.68, Löfstedt, p. 52.1986–2005, where Beatus quotes Augustine, commenting later at pp. 53.2006–2008, 2012–2016) the Eucharist recapitulates the self-emptying of Phil. 2:6–7 and provides for us a specific context and opportunity for affirming and participating in that self-emptying, and thus for being incorporated into the Body of Christ. We become the body and blood of Christ when we eat the body and blood of Christ (*Adv.Elip.* 1.71, Löfstedt, p. 54.2058–2059; *Adv.Elip.* 1.75, Löfstedt, p. 58.2213–2219; *passim*). By our participation with the sacrifice of Christ on the altar, we become formed as his body. This sacrifice is of one piece with the Incarnation; it is one continuum of self-emptying, of the humility of God. The point is that *because* this humility is ex-

tended even to the daily sacrifice of the altar, we may find our participation in it there, as "food for the small" (see *Adv.Elip.* 1.71, Löfstedt, p. 54.2059–2071). This is the mystery of the sacrifice of the Mediator: that by his giving himself up to us and our receiving him, we are transformed into him, into one body and one *persona*: " . . . omnes in uno sacrificio mediatoris reconciliamur, quia ipse est *mediator Dei et hominum homo Christus Ihesus* (1 Tim. 2:5), ipse est caput corporis eglesiae, una persona. Obinde manducamus corpus eius et sanguinem eius bibimus, ut, sicut illud in nos invisceratur et traicitur visibiliter, sic nos in illo transformamur et invisceremur, quia sacramentum est, misterium est" (*Adv.Elip.* 1.81, Löfstedt, p. 60.2294–2301). For other discussions of the Eucharist see *Adv.Elip.* 1.66, Löfstedt, p. 51. 1953–1958 (where an explicit connection to Phil. 2:7 is made); *Adv.Elip.* 1.126–127, Löfstedt, pp. 97.3735–99.3801 (which cite an unkown "blessed Andreas"); *Adv.Elip.* 1.86, Löfstedt, pp. 58.220–59.2242 (citing Cyprian, *Ep.* 63.13); *Adv.Elip.* 1.97, Löfstedt, pp. 73.2804–74.2865; *Adv.Elip.* 1.110ff., Löfstedt, pp. 83.3227; *Adv.Elip.* 2.57, Löfstedt, p. 143.1556–1561 (more on sacrifice); etc.

102. *Adv.Elip.* 1.121, Löfstedt, p. 94.3611–3612.

103. John Cassian, *Conlationes* 1.20.4, cited at *Adv.Elip.* 1.55; Löfstedt p. 40.1505–1517.

104. *Adv.Elip.* 1.83–84; Löfstedt p. 63.2399–2411, 2412–2413, 2416–2417. The passage cited from Cassian is probably the source for this idea.

105. Note that the phrase "deitate exinanita" is an ablative absolute peculiar to Elipandus; Beatus never uses it unless he is referring to Elipandus's usage.

106. *Adv.Elip.* 1.49, Löfstedt p. 35.1310–1314. The phrase "servum cum servis" is bracketed by the editor as a gloss, but the reason is unclear, since it is in the text of Elipandus as quoted by Beatus any number of times.

107. *Adv.Elip.* 1.2; Löfstedt p. 2.45–54, citing Ambrose, *In Luc.* 10.74–82, and Matt. 26:72.

108. *Adv.Elip.* 1.2; Löfstedt, p. 2.99.

109. *Adv.Elip.* 1.3; Löfstedt, p. 3.93–94; see also lines 85–84.

110. *Adv.Elip.* 1.7; Löfstedt, pp. 4–5, lines 147–153, 156–159.

111. *Adv.Elip.* 1.7, p. 5.160–168. (For the text see p. 69, above.)

112. *Adv.Elip.* 1.13; Löfstedt, p. 9.316–317: " . . . Jesum Christum, qui de virgine natus est, verum Deum et verum Filium Dei esse proprium firmaremus."

113. "Una pars episcoporum dicit, quod Iesus Christus adobtibus est humanitate et nequaquam adobtibus divinitate. Altera pars dicit: Nisi ex utraque natura unicus est Dei Patris Filius proprius, non adobtibus; in tantum proprius, ut ipse sit Dei Filius Deus verus; et ipse adoretur et colatur, qui sub Pontio Pilato est crucifixus. Haec pars nos sumus, id est Eterius et Beatus cum ceteris ita credentibus" (*Adv.Elip.* 1.13; Löfstedt, p. 9.341–347).

114. *Adv.Elip.* 1.13, Löfstedt, p. 9.318; *Adv.Elip.* 1.8, Löfstedt, p. 5.178–185. Are these phrases citations or paraphrases from some work or speech of Elipandus?

115. *Adv.Elip.* 1.8; Löfstedt, pp. 5–6, lines 185–193. For Elipandus's use of the phrase "Deus inter Deos," see *Adv.Elip.* 1.41, Löfstedt, p. 29.1080.

116. *Adv.Elip.* 1.9; Löfstedt, p. 6.196–198.

117. *Adv.Elip.* 1.9; Löfstedt, p. 6.198–199.

118. *Adv.Elip.* 1.9; Löfstedt, p. 6.199–206.

119. *Adv.Elip.* 1.9; Löfstedt, p.6.207–210. In Beatus's view, omnipotence is an identifying characteristic of the "form of God" of Phil. 2:6.

120. *Adv.Elip.* 1.13, Löfstedt, p. 9.319; *Adv.Elip.* 1.41, Löfstedt, p. 29.1084–1085: "servus cum servis."

121. *Adv.Elip.* 1.9; Löfstedt, p. 6.215–218.

122. *Adv.Elip.* 1.9; Löfstedt, p. 6.220–222.

123. "Non hoc loco dixit volumtatem [sic] Dei facere, sed Patris" (*Adv.Elip.* 1.9; Löfstedt, p. 6.222–223).

124. *Adv.Elip.* 1.9; Löfstedt, p.6.219–220.

125. *Adv.Elip.* 1.9; Löfstedt, p. 6.223–228.

126. *Adv.Elip.* 1.9; Löfstedt, p.6.228–231. The language about "greater than" or "less than" himself has roots in the anti-Arian polemic of the West, and specifically in the rebuttal of the Arian exegesis of Jn. 14:28: "The Father is greater than I." For Augustine, the verse refers to the inequality between the human nature of Jesus and the divine nature of the Father. From this perspective, it could just as easily be said that Jesus is greater than himself; that is, his divine nature is greater than his human nature (*De trinitate* 1.7, p. 45.23–25). Even this usage is somewhat imprecise, but to say further that Jesus in his human nature is a servant to himself in his divine nature is to begin to sound too much as though the natures represented *personae* that are truly relatable as lord and servant, parallel to the creature/Creator relation of a human being to God. The christology begins to get too divisive, like a screen that is holding together two subjects but hiding the ultimate reluctance, the reluctance of God to really become one of us. Ernst Kantorowicz (*The King's Two Bodies: A Study in Mediaeval Political Theology*, 49–52) calls attention to the "singular" language of the Creed of Toledo XI ("Item et major et minor se ipse esse credendus est"). He discusses this within the context of a emphasis on the language of "twinning" in christology, language which he believes is especially *Hispanic* in tradition and provenance.

127. See below, p. 66.

128. *Adv.Elip.* 1.9; Löfstedt, p. 7.234–239, citing Phil. 2:8–11.

129. *Adv.Elip.* 2.50; Löfstedt, p. 138.1376–1384.

130. Just as Elipandus does, Beatus points out that as a human being, Jesus receives the Holy Spirit and is called "full of grace" (*Adv.Elip.* 1.11; Löfstedt, p. 8.293–294), but that his anointing with the Holy Spirit is from his conception (*Adv.Elip.* 1.12; Löfstedt, p. 8.298–315). Beatus, however, sees in this teaching a guarantee of Jesus's distinction from the rest of us, noting that he received the Holy Spirit in such a way that he can *give* it.

131. *Adv.Elip.* 2.50; Löfstedt, p. 139.1385–86. See also 2.83, where there is a citation from Gregory of Elvira (Löfstedt, p. 155.2037–2046) that plays upon the word "exinanitum" as found at Song of Songs 4:10. Gregory remarks that all who before Christ were called "lords" or "anointeds" have had these titles "emptied" of meaning in the comparison to Christ. Beatus hears the irony: Christ, in emptying Himself, empties the pretensions of others as well, most notably, those of Elipandus and his christology.

132. *Adv.Elip.* 2.50; Löfstedt, p. 139.1388–1402.

133. *Adv.Elip.* 2.53, Löfstedt, p. 140.1450–1454; *Adv.Elip.* 2.50, Löfstedt, p. 138.1376–1377. On Col. 2:9, a favorite passage of Beatus, see e.g., its use at *Adv.Elip.* 2.69. In connection with the exegesis of Ps. 67:17, see also *Adv.Elip.* 2.53, Löfstedt, p. 141.1469–1472 for the very orthodox christology underlying the exegesis. Lines 1473–1484 recapitulate and develop the passage quoted in the text.

134. *Adv.Elip.* 2.52; Löfstedt, p. 140.1433–1435.

135. *Adv.Elip.* 2.33; Löfstedt, p. 128.954–971.

136. Evidence for this already discussed above. Note Beatus's remark that Christ as Sun will dawn only on those Christians who fear Him, that is, who believe in Christ and *imitate him* (*Adv.Elip.* 2.33; Löfstedt, p. 128.957–960). The language of imitation is part of the vocabulary of the rule which forms the church.

137. *Adv.Elip.* 1.72; Löfstedt, p. 55.2094–2102.

138. *Adv.Elip.* 2.70; Löfstedt, p. 149.

139. *Adv.Elip.* 1.12; Löfstedt, p. 8.307–309.

140. *Adv.Elip.* 2.99–100, Löfstedt, p. 164.2374–2375, 78–81; *Adv.Elip.* 1.118, Löfstedt, p. 92.3527–3532; *Adv.Elip.* 1.121, Löfstedt, p. 94.3620–3624 (these passages include the ones actually cited together with their contexts). See also *Adv.Elip.* 1.112, Löfstedt, p. 85.3287–3293; *Adv.Elip.* 1.59, Löfstedt, p. 43.1635–1637.

141. *Adv.Elip.* 2.14, Löfstedt, p. 114.417–420; *Adv.Elip.* 1.84, Löfstedt, p. 63.2419–2428; *Adv.Elip.* 2.17, Löfstedt, p. 116.492–499; *Adv.Elip.* 1.112, Löfstedt, p. 85.3291.

142. *Adv.Elip.* 2.42; Löfstedt, p. 135.1252–1254.

143. George E. McCracken, ed. and trans., with Allen Cabaniss, *Early Medieval Theology*, 211.

144. "The Adoptionist controversy was, all in all, . . . a very profitable exercise in theological method" (André Wilmart, quoted by G. Ellard in *Master Alcuin, Liturgist: A Partner of Our Piety*, 179). Note, too, David Knowles and D. Obolensky, *The Middle Ages*, vol. 2. of *The Christian Centuries: A New History of the Catholic Church*, L. J. Rogier, general ed., 51, 159.

Chapter Four

1. Alcuin's comment to Arno (ca. 798) that "adhuc se tota Spania errat in adoptione" (*Alc.Ep.* 146, p. 236.11) is exaggerated. Yet there is Beatus's comment that the Asturian church was divided "in duas partes," over the question, and there is Elipandus's threat of disciplinary action against his own clergy. There are also reports of supporters of Elipandus in Cordoba, and of his friends Fidelis and Ascaricus who had become involved in one way or another. Collins (*Conquest*, 229–230) believes that the divisions in the church over adoptionism were large enough to be a critical factor contributing to the eclipse of the primatial authority of Toledo during the ninth to eleventh centuries.

2. *Alc.Ep.* 183-I, p. 307, lines 29–31. This evidence indicates a literary dimension for the controversy wider than the exchange between Elipandus and Beatus.

3. *Alc.Ep.* 183-II, p. 308, lines 13–15.

4. *Einhardi Annales, anno* 792: "Orgellis est civitas in Pyrine; montis iugo sita, cuius episcopus nomine Felix, natione Hispanus, ab Elipando Toleti episcopo, per litteras consultas, quid de humanitate salvatoris dei et domini nostri Jesum Christi sentire debet, utrum secundum id quod homo est, proprius an adoptivus Dei filius credendus esset ac dicendus . . ." (p. 179.1–4; cf. "Poeta Saxo," *anno* 792).

5. Alcuin mentions a treatise of Felix "Against the Saracen," presumably non-adoptionist and early. He tells Leidrad, Archbishop of Lyon, that he has not seen it personally, but has reason to think there might be a copy in Leidrad's possession. He asks Leidrad to send a copy if in fact he has one (*Alc.Ep.* 172, pp. 284.30–285.2).

6. There is some evidence that the Mozarabs themselves preferred Muslim rule to that of either the Visigoths or the Franks. See, for example, Imamuddin, *Aspects*, 36.

7. Here is Alcuin's report regarding the progress of the mission to reconvert people from adoptionism: "Sciat tamen dilectio vestra, quod filius noster Laidradus episcopus, frater vester, magnum profectum in illis partibus Deo donante egit cotidieque agit. Ut mihi vere dixerunt ex illis partibus viri religiosi et veraces, usque viginti milia conversi sunt inter episcopos sacerdotes monachos populum viros et feminas plangentes pristinum errorem, gaudentesque cotidie Deo agentes gratias in agnitione veritatis et in catholicae fidei firmitate" (*Ep.Alc.* 208, p. 346.13–18; cf. *Ep.* 200, p. 332.20). More interesting than the actual number given (20,000 could be a guess or exaggeration) is the indication of the various types of people involved. Acceptance of adoptionism seems not to have been confined to clerics, or indeed to any particular social class. See also on this question, L. Halphen, *Charlemagne et l'empire carolingien*, 87–91. Ardo's comments, in his life of Benedict of Aniane, are also worth noting: "cum pene provintiam illam eodem tempore perversum Feliciani invaserit dogma, ic ab omni pestifero perfidiae errore in laesus ope divina intus evasit multosque, *non solum infimos, verum etiam presules aecclesiae,* suo eripuit [Benedictus] studio et adversus nefandum dogma veris disputationum iaculis armatus sepe congressus est (my emphasis; *Vita Benedicti abbatis Anianensis et indensis autore Ardone* 8.17.34–38, edited by G. Waitz, in *MGH Scriptores* 15, 204).

8. The Council of Narbonne. See Hefele-Leclercq, *Histoire*, 1024–1027 for a review and good analysis of the data. It is there argued, no doubt correctly, that the condemnation of Felix which is attached to the *acta* of this council is an interpolation, probably attracted by the presence of Felix's signature. Note also that Felix was not even mentioned at the Synod of Aix of 789, despite Charlemagne's explicit concern there for religious unity.

9. The *acta* have been lost. For accounts of the council see Alcuin, *AE* 1.16 (*PL* 101:251D-252A); the *acta* of the 798 Council of Rome (*MGH, Concilia*, II, p. 203.32—204.9); *Einhardi Annales, anno* 792; also see the "Poeta Saxo," *anno* 792; see also J. Böhmer and Mühlbacher, *Die Regesten des Kaiserreichs unter den Karolingern, 751–918, Regesta Imperii* I, 2nd ed. For the theory that Elipandus and Felix were in fact acting with explicit political motivation, see Abadal y de Vinyals, *La batalla*, 76–77. Against the view that adoptionism was a fundamentally political movement see Schäferdiek ("Streit," 8).

10. Leidrad (archbishop of Lyons), Nefridius (archbishop of Narbonne), and Benedict of Aniane were the three entrusted with this campaign. Alcuin's anti-adoptionist works from the *AFU* on were written primarily for the use of these and associated preachers. On this campaign see esp. *Alc.Ep.* 200 (to Leidrad, Nefridius, and Benedict, presenting them with the *AE*); 201 (to the same persons); 208 (to Arno, describing the effects of the campaign); 205 (to the abbots and monks of the area); 206 (to Nefridius); 202 (to Charlemagne, asking whether he can publish the *AFU*). Charlemagne's commissioning is evident from *Alc.Ep.* 200, p. 331.7–13; see also *Alc.Ep.* 207. *Alc.Ep.* 204 serves as a kind of anti-adoptionist primer, pre-prepared with the questions pro-adoptionists might ask followed by made to order answers.

11. For example, Amann (*L'Époque*), who not only accepts Alcuin's critique wholecloth, he *interprets* that critique using Augustinian and/or scholastic terminology which Alcuin himself does not actually use. On 147 he reproduces Alcuin's distinction between "assumption" and "adoption." On 139 he systematizes these observations beyond Alcuin's actual words: "Tout en se defendant, comme l'avaient fait les premiers Antiochiens, de parler de deux fils dans le concret, dans la realité de l'histoire, ils disaient: autre est la relation entre Dieu le Verbe, qui est un rapport de filiation naturelle; autre la relation entre *l'homo assumptus* et le Père, qui est un rapport de filiation adoptive. . . . Qu'ils le voulussent ou non, ce 'fils adoptif de Dieu' faisait figure de personne à coté du 'fils de Dieu par nature.' Comment ramener à l'unité cette dualité flagrante?" Amann has reproduced Alcuin's position by insisting that there is a difference between what the adoptionists *said*, and what was actually or necessarily *implied* ("dans la realité de l'histoire") by their position in spite of what they said.

12. See below, Appendix I: The Teaching of Felix, 2.

13. On the first of these, see above, ch. 1, n. 11. The second must be dated before the Council of Frankfurt—see the arguments of the Werminghoff, *MGH, Concilia aevi Karolini*, p. 122. Hadrian does not mention Felix in either letter, something especially significant in the case of the second, since he seems to know of no "relapse" of Felix.

14. Hadrian, First Letter to the Bishops of Spain, *Codex Carolinus* #95, p. 637, lines 34–35.

15. Hadrian, First Letter to the Bishops of Spain, *Codex Carolinus* #95, p. 636, line 33.

16. Hadrian, First Letter to the Bishops of Spain, *Codex Carolinus* #95, p. 637, lines 35–37. Note that this can be *only* a perception of the teaching. Hadrian has no documentation or any first-hand evidence whatsoever to analyze. This comparison of adoptionism to Nestorianism is simply the way Hadrian *perceives* a teaching about which he has been given only the sketchiest of reports.

17. Hadrian, First Letter to the Bishops of Spain, *Codex Carolinus* #95, p. 638, lines 10–12, 15–16. From "Athanasius," or so Hadrian thinks. Really from Apollinaris of Laodicea, *De incarnatione Dei verbi*, 2.2 (see *PG* 28:28–29).

18. Hadrian, First Letter to the Bishops of Spain, *Codex Carolinus* #95, p. 638, lines 18–21. From Gregory of Nazianzus, *Ep.* 101.

19. Including passages from Nyssa, Chrysostom, Augustine, Hilary, Leo, and Amphilochius. Hadrian, First Letter to the Bishops of Spain, *Codex Carolinus* #95, pp. 638.27–640.5.

20. Hadrian, Second Letter to the Bishops of Spain, *MGH, Concilium*, II, p. 122.41–123, line 1.

21. Hadrian, Second Letter to the Bishops of Spain, *MGH, Concilium*, II, p. 123, lines 5–6, 21–23. Cf. p. 124, lines 16–17, 21–22, and also p. 126 lines 7–9, where Hadrian may be reflecting Elipandus's claims about the "similarity" of Jesus to us. Cf. also p. 128, lines 33–35, where Hadrian poses the alternatives as though Elipandus taught a separation of persons.

22. Hadrian, Second Letter to the Bishops of Spain, *MGH, Concilium*, II, p. 124, lines 33–35; p. 125, lines 5–6.

23. This sentence from Hadrian's letter is not only evidence for Hadrian's understanding of Elipandus's position, but also corroborates the reading of Elipandus presented in chapter 2.

25. "Nam etsi in umbra prophetiae dictus est servus propter servilis formae conditionem, quam sumpsit ex virgine, sicut scribtum est: *Considerasti servum meum Iob, quod non sit ei similis in terra* [Job 1:8], hoc nos una cum beato Gregorio [*Moralia in Iob* 27.2.3] intellegimus et secundum historiam de sancto Iob et allegoricae de Christo dictum. Numquid propterea servi ei nomen inponere debemus, quia sub persona Iob scriptura eum typice designabat? Hinc etiam alius propheta, membrum scilicet sacri corporis, ex persona summi capitis tropica clamat involvente vaticinia nube: *O Domine, ego servus tuus et filius ancillae tuae* [Ps. 115:16], et rursus: *Da imperium puero tuo et salvum fac filium ancillae tuae* [Ps. 85:16], et illud: *Noli timere, serve meus Iacob et rectissime, quem elegi* [Is. 44:2], et cetera" (Hadrian, Second Letter to the Bishops of Spain, *MGH, Concilium*, II, p. 126.21–30).

26. Hadrian, Second Letter to the Bishops of Spain, *MGH, Concilium*, II, p. 126, lines 15–17. The French bishops think exactly the same way—see their letter, Alcuin, *Ep. ad Hisp., MGH, Concilia*, II, p. 152.14–34 (note too how they chide Elipandus later in the text, "Considerate, quale est hoc scandalum inter paganas gentes ut dicatur Deum Christianorum servum esse vel adoptivum!", p. 157.2–5). But Elipandus explicitly excludes sin from Christ in his letter to Charlemagne (also part of the conciliar documents from Frankfurt, Elipandus, *Ep. ad Karl., MGH, Concilia*, II, p. 120.19).

27. "Postquam autem cessavit umbra veritatis et ipsa in prompto manifesta est veritas, quae sub allegoriae silva latebat, nusquam eum a patre servum vocatum legimus, sed filium et dilectum suum, nec filium eum dominum suum appellasse, sed patrem. . . . Nullus umquam evangelistarum, nemo apostolourm servum eum commemorat, sed Dominum et salvatorem" (Hadrian, Second Letter to the Bishops of Spain, *MGH, Concilium*, II, pp. 126.38–41, 127.6–8).

28. Hadrian, Second Letter to the Bishops of Spain, *MGH, Concilium*, II, p. 127.10–11, 32–37, 39–43: "Paulus, clarissima mundi tuba, semper eum Dominum et ipse confitetur et omnem linguam confiteri perdocet. . . . Paulus namque, mundi lilium et ecclesiae pulcherrima rosa, templum scilicet Spiritus sancti et praedicabilis doctor, in universo ore suo Dominum eum et non servum appellat. Ait namque: *In Iesu nomine omne genu flectatur caelestium, terrestrium et infernorum; et omnis*

lingua confiteatur, quia Iesus Christus in gloria est Dei patris. [Phil. 2:10–11] . . . Paulus, electionis vas, docet, ut omnis lingua confiteatur, quia dominus Iesus in gloria est Dei patris: cur surda aure et errorum obvoluto tenebris corde hunc locum scripturae legendo transilitis? Paulus omnem linguam dominum Iesum eum confiteri hortatur et docet: et verstra lingua non confunditur servum eum et adoptivum latrare?" Cf. citation of Phil. 2:11 in Hadrian's First Letter to the Bishops of Spain, *Codex Carolinus* #95, p. 640, lines 3–5.

29. This is not to say that Hadrian does not *notice* verse 6, but that he interprets the phrase "forma servi" with emphasis on the word *forma*—see Second Letter to the Bishops of Spain, *MGH, Concilium*, II, p. 126.22, where he freely paraphrases "forma servi" as "servilis formae conditionem, quam sumpsit ex virgine." Also note the passage which the French bishops cite from "Augustine": "'Dominus noster etiam in forma servi non servus, sed in forma etiam servi dominus fuit'" (Alcuin, *Epistola episcoporum Franciae* [hereafter, Alcuin, *Ep. ad Hisp.*], *MGH, Concilia*, II, p. 152.9–10). Clearly the emphasis here is on the *forma*. Hadrian is thinking out of a similar tradition. But the only actual reference to Phil. 2:6 in the whole text of Hadrian's Second Letter to the Bishops of Spain is at p. 127.26, where only the allusive phrase *forma servi* is used—but note that it is immediately referred not to the self-emptying of Phil. 2:7 which is its natural context, but rather to the more triumphalistic context at Heb. 2:7–9.

30. We may suppose such influence especially because Hadrian had read Elipandus's letter, although it was addressed not to him but to the bishops of Frankland and probably referred to him for comment by the addressees.

31. Stylistic considerations in support of this attribution: 1. the letter's insistent claim that Elipandus cites the doctors of the church against himself (characteristic of Alcuin but not of Paulinus); 2. the way the letter *cites* Elipandus's letter, which is very reminiscent of his method of citation in later works, that is, fair-sized snippets, in order, but with gaps of varying sizes in between. See Luitpold Wallach, *Alcuin and Charlemagne: Studies in Carolingian History and Literature*, 147–177.

32. Paulinus, *Libellus Sacrosyllabus Episcoporum Italiae*, pp. 130–142. Paulinus identifies himself as the author at p. 131.20.

33. Charlemagne, *Epistola Karoli Magni ad Elipandum et episcopos Hispaniae*, in *MGH, Concilium*, II, pp. 157–164. (Hereafter, *Ep. Karoli ad Elipandum.*)

34. In particular the role which he believed himself obligated to play in the resolution of such doctrinal matters. Note, e.g., *Ep. Karoli ad Elipandum*, p. 159.33, where he says he "ordered" the Council (of Frankfurt). On the question in general one may consult Thomas F. X. Noble, *The Republic of St. Peter: The Birth of the Papal State, 680–825*, esp. 277–299.

35. Alcuin, *Ep. ad Hisp.*, p. 154.20–22.

36. Alcuin, *Ep. ad Hisp.*, p. 154.19–20, 24–31.

37. Alcuin, *Ep. ad Hisp.*, p. 154.5–7.

38. For example: "Nos per illum adoptivi sumus, non ille nobiscum adoptivus, nos per illum a servitute liberati, non ille nobiscum servus. . . . Non simus ingrati tantorum beneficiorum domini nostri Iesu Christi, per quem conditi sumus et a quo iterum redempti sumus et in gloriam filiorum Dei adoptati." (Alcuin, *Ep. ad Hisp.*, p. 157.4–5, 23–25.)

39. Alcuin, *Ep. ad Hisp.*, p. 152.4–6. (Alcuin returns to the theme of the prophetic use of *servus* at *AFU* 168B [cf. 182D].)

40. For example, at Alcuin, *Ep. ad Hisp., MGH, Concilia*, II, p. 151, the French bishops have taken up a citation the Hispanic bishops took from Augustine's *Enchiridion* (c. 11) which contained an allusion to Phil. 2:6 (at Elipandus, *Ep. ad Franc., MGH, Concilia*, II, p. 115.29–116.2). They not only cited it, but extended it to *Ench.* 10, containing an explicit reference to the self-emptying of Phil. 2:7 (Alcuin, *Ep. ad Hisp., MGH, Concilia*, II, p. 151.19–21). But, although it is mentioned in this citation, the French bishops make no use whatsoever of the self-emptying in their reply to Elipandus. (There is also an allusion to Phil. 2:8 at Alcuin, *Ep. ad Hisp., MGH, Concilia*, II, p. 152.5–6.)

41. Alcuin, *Ep. ad Hisp., MGH, Concilia*, II, p. 152.2–3.

42. Alcuin, *Ep. ad Hisp., MGH, Concilia*, II, p. 155.1–3.

43. For them, adoptionism is a resuscitation of an older heresy (Paulinus, *Libellus Sacrosyllabus, MGH, Concilia*, II, p. 132.33–34, no doubt a reference to Nestorianism), and amounts to the theory that a "purus homo sine Deo natus" (*Libellus Sacrosyllabus*, p. 133.3) was adopted into sonship by the Father, or, if not born "sine Deo," then adopted into sonship while still in the womb of Mary (*Libellus Sacrosyllabus*, p. 133.1–6, cf. p. 137.14–15). In either case it is a "purus homo" that is elevated to sonship. The bishops make such an analysis because of their a priori premise about the meaning of "adoptive": "Porro adoptivus dici non potest nisi is, qui alienus est ab eo, a quo dicitur adoptatus" (*Libellus Sacrosyllabus*, p. 134.3–4). But this a priori understanding of the implications of "adoptive" is not Elipandus's understanding. They remark, "Adoptivus vero dicitur, cum nihil a patre adoptante debetur, sed gratis indulgendo conceditur" (*Libellus Sacrosyllabus*, p. 135.32–33). Such a remark presumes that there would be no *self*-renunciation of rights due to equality of nature. Indeed, the Italian bishops place no special importance on Phil. 2:7. They never cite it, even though they use other verses from Phil. 2, at *Libellus Sacrosyllabus*, p. 134.27–33.

44. For example, Alcuin, *Ep. ad Hisp., MGH, Concilia*, II, p. 155.2–3: "Si mox a tempore conceptionis verus Deus Dei filius conceptus est [here recognizing Elipandus's position], quando fuit, ut homo esset sine Deo, unde adoptaretur in filium?" Also, Alcuin, *Ep. ad Hisp.*, p. 152.2–4: "Si ergo Deus verus est, qui de virgine natus est [again, pressing Elipandus with his own position], quomodo tunc potest adoptivus esse vel servus? Deus enim nequaquam audetis confiteri servum vel adoptivum . . ."—which, in a way, is precisely what Elipandus *does* confess.

45. See *Alc.Ep.* 5, p. 30, Alcuin's very first, admiring, letter to Felix, dating from a time before the controversy began; *Alc.Ep.* 23, which speaks of Felix's "widely celebrated fame for holiness;" *Alc.Ep.* 166 to Elipandus, where Alcuin describes Felix as "vir venerabilis" and compliments his piety, etc. See also *Alc.Ep.* 201.

46. In *Alc. Ep.* 207 (to Arno), pp. 344.23–345.8, Alcuin tells Arno about the debate with Felix at Aachen, and then (p. 346.19–22) tells him that Felix parted from Alcuin with affection for him.

47. Including, it is reported, nearly all of the bishops at the 799 Council of Aix, as well as a devoted circle of conversation centered around him in his imprisonment: See *Alcuini Vita* 7 (*PL* 100:98B–D; also, *MGH, SS*, XV, Arndt, editor) for Felix's effect on the bishops at the Council. Cf. *Alc.Ep.* 192 and 207; Paulinus's

account given at *Contra Felicem Libri III* (*Paulini Aquileienses Opera Omnia Pars I: Contra Felicem Libri Tres*, Dag Norberg, editor *CCCM*, 95, 1.5, 7; hereafter, *CF*). Agobard refers to a circle of persons who listened to Felix's teaching, and states explicitly that it was Felix's good character which attracted them (*Adversum Dogma Felicis*, L. Van Acker, editor, in *Agobardi Lugdunensis Opera Omnia, CCCM* 52, 5.6– 7, 15–16 [hereafter, *ADF*], ("Coepit aliquando quosdam docere . . ."; ". . . accessi ad eum coram ipsis, quibus ista suadebat . . ."; and 2.5–10, "Qui incaute admirantes vitam praedicti Felicis, probanda putant cuncta, quae dixit, necscientes quia non ex vita hominis metienda est fides, sed ex fide probanda est vita. . . .").

48. *Einhardi Annales, anno* 792, p. 179. See also *Annales Mettenses Priores, anno* 792, p. 79.

49. Alcuin says he "fled back" to Elipandus (*AE* 1.16, *PL* 101:252A.6). Pope Leo says "Et postmodum transgressus legem Dei excelsi fugiens apud paganos consentaneos periuratus effectus est" (*Concilium Romanum, MGH, Concilia,* II, pp. 204.7–9).

50. In *Alc.Ep.* 23 (798) Alcuin addresses him as follows: "viro venerando et in Christi charitate desiderando Felici *episcopo*." He also sends a letter to Leidrad telling him to fetch Felix, presumably from Urgel, for the 799 council: *Alc.Ep.* 194, p. 322.9. In his *Confessio*, Felix reports that Laidrad had indeed fetched him from Urgel (*Confessio fidei Felicis*, in *MGH, Concilia,* II, p. 221.13; also at *Alc.Ep.* 199). The "Poeta Saxo" reports that Felix did return to his see (". . . meruitque reverti / Ad propriae rursus retinendum sedis honorem" [*anno* 792, p. 249.21–22]). Elipandus's letter to Charlemagne, however, seems to presuppose at least some time when he was not reinstated (see *Ep. ad Kar., MGH, Concilia,* II, p. 121.3–5).

51. Text in the *Capitulare Francofurtense*, in *MGH, Concilia,* II, p. 165.18–25. Apart from this, Elipandus is mentioned by name in the conciliar literature five times (see *MGH, Concilia,* II: Hadrian, Second Letter to the Bishops of Spain, p. 122; Paulinus, *Libellus Sacrosyllabus*, p. 131 and p. 140; Alcuin, *Ep. ad Hisp.*, p. 155; and Charlemagne, *Ep. ad Hisp.*, p. 158), i.e., at least once in every document. Felix is mentioned only at p. 140 (by Paulinus of Aquileia, *Libellus Sacrosyllabus*). Charlemagne's letter singles out Elipandus in the salutation (p. 158), even though the letter to which he is replying was from the bishops of Spain collectively. This cannot be due simply to protocol, since he did not do it in his First Letter to the Bishops of Spain.

52. This is *Alc.Ep.* 23; date in Heil, *Alkuinstudien*, 14–17, 67. See also Donald A. Bullough, "Alcuin and the Kingdom of Heaven: Liturgy, Theology, and the Carolingian Age," 49, n. 113. Alcuin's letter to Elipandus (*Alc.Ep.* 166) is slightly later (again, see Bullough, "Kingdom," 50).

53. Alcuin, *CFU*, charges Felix as follows: "fingentes [vos] . . . illius novum adoptionis nomen, quod in tota Veteris Novique Testamenti serie non invenitur" (*PL* 101:121C); "quid vultis ei [Jesu] nomen adoptiri imponere?" (122A). In fact, this seems to be the *only* charge Alcuin sees grounds for pressing: "Cave ne *in hoc solo adoptionis nomine* a sensibus sanctorum Patrum dissentias" (122B); "In uno tantummodo adoptionis verbo a sancta et apostolica Ecclesia discordamini" (125B).

54. Good critical edition by Gary B. Blumenshine, *Liber Alcuini Contra Hae-resim Felicis: Edition with an Introduction* in *Studi e testi* 285. Hereafter, *LAHF*. Blumenshine dates the treatise to the winter of 797–798 (see 32), following Heil.

In this work Alcuin charges the adoptionists as follows: "They prattle on about the Lord Christ, that he is according to the flesh an adoptive son" (*LAHF* 13, *PL* 101:92A 6–8; Blumenshine, pp. 61–62); They affirm that in his divinity he is the proper Son of God the Father, but, in his humanity, an adoptive son" (*LAHF* 35, *PL* 101:101B 15–C3; Blumenshine, pp. 73–74). This is exactly the platform of Elipandus, but other statements suggest a position advancing beyond it. Alcuin notes that "they are not afraid to publicly deny that he is the true Son of God, but instead a participant in the same adoption that is ours" (*LAHF* 37, *PL* 101:102D 8–11; Blumenshine, pp. 75–76). Also, "They assert that Christ Jesus is not the true Son of God the Father, nor his proper Son, but is rather adoptive. . . . They deny that [the most blessed Virgin Mary] is truly the genetrix of the Son of God, but rather of his adoptive son, desiring that Christ—God—be adoptive just as we are" (*LAHF* 2, *PL* 101:88A 4–6, B 14–C 2; Blumenshine, pp. 55–56). Finally, "You, as is your custom, . . . say that the phrase 'Christ the Son of God' is said *usurpative* or adoptively." It is not clear how much of this reflects the actual teaching of Felix, and how much is analysis of that teaching presented as though Felix were actually teaching it. The statements about Christ "participating in our adoption" and being "adoptive as we are" echo Elipandus's statements that Christ is "adoptivus cum adoptivis." These statements are therefore probably accurate reflections of Felix's teaching. Elipandus, however, seemed never to have made any assertions about Mary, nor did he ever actually say that Christ, even as a human being, was not the *true* son of God (although see the implied disjunction at one place in the Letter to the Bishops of Frankland, *Ep. ad Franc.*, p. 112.12–13 [in a citation; but contrast Elipandus's own way of speaking at p. 115.20–22]). Note that the argument at *LAHF* 37 (Blumenshine, p. 75) shows that Alcuin was not yet aware of any teaching about Jesus as "nuncupative" God, since the argument does not work if the addressee does not grant that he is true God: "Quomodo noluit eum verum filium esse quem verum voluit esse deum? Aut illud potuit et hoc non potuit? Ubi est tunc omnipotentia dei cuius voluntati nullus resistit (cf. Rom. 9:19)? Si potuit et noluit cur invidit ei veritatem filii et cui non invidit veritatem deitatis?" (Blumenshine, p. 75.15–18; cf. lines 2–3). On the *LAHF* see Bullough, "Kingdom," 50–54.

55. See Heil, *Alkuinstudien*, 27–28, 36, 67, for this date. See Bullough, "Kingdom," 53.

56. See *Alc.Ep.* 148 (to Charlemagne), p. 241.11–19: "Nuper mihi venit libellus a Felice infelice directus. Cuius propter curiositatem cum paucas paginolas legendo percucurri, inveni peiores hereses vel magis blasphemias, quam ante in eius scriptis legerem. Adserens Christum Iesum nec filium Dei esse verum nec etiam verum Deum esse, sed nuncupativum . . ." Note also *AFU* 1.1 (*PL* 101:127D.10–129A.7), especially: ". . . nomine nuncupativum Deum nominare illum non timet, dividens Christum in duos filios, unum vocens proprium, alterum adoptivum [Felix's original position]: et in duos deos, unum verum Deum, alterum nuncupativum Deum [the new position]" (A4–7). *Alc.Ep.* 241 is, according to Bullough, a postscript to *Ep.* 148: see "Kingdom," 54.

57. Pope Leo reports the innovation thus: "Et ut nobis visum est, peiores hereses vel maiores blasfemias, quam ante in eius scriptis vel dictis umquam audissemus, ibidem cognovimus. Asserens autem Christum Iesum dominum nostrum

nec filium Dei verum nec etiam verum Deum, sed nuncupativum" (*Concilium Romanum, anno* 798, *MGH, Concilia*, II, p. 203.24–27. On this Council in general see Heil, *Alcuinstudien*, 17–20).

58. *Alc.Ep.* 194.

59. Bullough, "Kingdom," 54–55, reviews the chronology of the correspondence associated with the *Seven Books [AFU]*.

60. Paulinus's work was written in response to the same treatise of Felix which prompted Alcuin's *Seven Books Against Felix [AFU]*. But Paulinus cites it far less frequently than Alcuin does, and where he does cite the text it is usually a much shorter citation. Further, it is more difficult to tell whether Paulinus is directly quoting the text as opposed to paraphrasing than it is for Alcuin. For these reasons I have chosen to use Alcuin's work as the primary attestation of the work of Felix and as the primary example of non-Hispanic anti-adoptionism. I will make reference to Paulinus's text as appropriate, both to show argumentation parallel to Alcuin's, and to supplement the attestation to Felix's text that Alcuin gives. For the argument that Alcuin owes a debt of dependence to certain passages in Paulinus, see Norberg, *Paulini Opera*, vii–viii.

61. *Alc.Ep.* 193 and 207. Of course this may be just a rhetorical flourish of the writer, who wanted to emphasize the triumph of Alcuin. Note the comments of Paulinus, *CF* 1.5; 1.7.

62. This is the so-called *Confessio Felicis* (*MGH, Concilia*, II, pp. 220–225). Note Felix's report of the debate at Aachen: ". . . sententias nostras, quas ex libris sanctorum habere nos de adoptione carnis in filio Dei seu nuncupatione in humanitate eius habere credebamus, presentaremus, qualiter non in violentia, sed ratione veritatis nostra adsertio rata iudicaretur, si ab illis per auctoritatem sanctorum patrum minime repudiaretur. Quod ita factum est" (p. 221.14–18). Alcuin gives a brief report of the debate in a letter to his friend Arno, archbishop of Salzburg: "cum Felice heretico magnam contentionem . . ." (*Alc.Ep.* pp. 344ff.) See also *AE* 1.16.

63. In the *Confessio* he calls himself "*olim* episcopus" (p. 221.1).

64. Alcuin tells Arno that Felix was remanded into Leidrad's custody (*Alc.Ep.* 207, p. 345.1–2). Benedict of Aniane's short anti-adoptionist treatise (*Disputatio Benedicti levitae adversus Felicianam impietatem, PL* 103:1399–1411) is probably to be dated to this time just after the Council of Aix or even later. It is a fascinating work which deserves a study all its own. Some suggestions in that direction are given in a second Appendix, below.

65. Agobard, *ADF* 5.

66. Agobard, *ADF* 1.

67. Tixeront is representative. He observes that for Elipandus *adoptio* was a synonym for *assumptio*. As such it had a more or less innocuous physical connotation, while for Felix the word had a more juridical meaning which to Tixeront was something inexcusably heretical (see *Histoire*, vol. 3, 530).

68. The severest judgment, although not unrepresentative, is passed by Allen Cabaniss: "Was there any flaw to be discovered in his character? . . . It may be phrased thus: no matter how admirable Felix's manner of life appeared, it was in fact a lie. It was a life of chronic, habitual deceit. . . . He may have thought each time [he recanted] he was sincere, but we will recall that no delusion is quite so

vicious as self-deceit. We detect in Felix also a fundamental instability in seeking outwardly to change his expressions in conformity with requirements of official opinion and popular applause. We note further the touch of vainglory implicit in his life in the desire for approbation. And, finally, we see a trace of cowardice in a preference for peace at the price of truth. Many heretics have dared to die for their beliefs, but not Felix of Urgel" ("The Heresiarch Felix," 141).

69. It is interesting to note that the *Confessio* repudiates teachings which he clearly never held. It seems most important simply as a promise not to use certain terminology (see the *Confessio*, pp. 222.1–2, 16–18, 34–35; 224.5–7).

70. A more complete, if also more hypothetical, attempt to reconstruct the teaching of Felix is presented in the Appendix, below.

71. Cf. *Alc.Ep.* 101, p. 148.2–3. Heil notes (*Alcuinstudien*, 11) that Alcuin had planned to visit England until the death of Northumbrian king Aethelred (18 April 798) made him change his mind. This is significant because it indicates that Charlemagne, who had presumably agreed to Alcuin's visit, felt confident about the prospects for a settlement of the adoptionist controversy after Frankfurt. And Alcuin's letters of this period (*Alc.Ep.* 23 to Felix, and 166 to Elipandus) were part of a campaign to bring the whole controversy to a friendly close by writing the chiefs of the position.

72. Heil believes that this study resulted in a work predating the *Libellus Sacrosyllabus* which has not survived (*Alkuinstudien*, 11–13).

73. "In uno tantummodo adoptionis verbo a sancta et apostolica ecclesia discordamini. Facile est hoc verbum, divina vos auxiliante gratia, inmutare, et evangelicis et apostolicis uti verbis" (*Alc.Ep.* 23 to Felix, p. 65.3–5). Also, "Plurima in scriptis tuis iusta et vera inveniuntur. Cave, ne in hoc solo adoptionis nomini a sensibus sanctorum patrum dissentias . . ." (p. 62.23–24).

74. "Plurima in scriptis tuis iusta et vera inveniuntur" (Alcuin, *AFU, PL* 101:122B 7–8; cf. also, perhaps, *AFU* 2.11, *PL* 101:154C 7–10). The question is, what writings? None have survived, but there is a reference in the *Einhardi Annales* (*anno* 792) to an early writing of Felix, possibly the writing against the Saracen, which some believe to have been an early adoptionist treatise. If so, it is hard to believe Alcuin has actually read it, since he cites no passages either in this letter or in any other treatise against Felix, and Alcuin is always careful to cite his opponent copiously in cases where we know he is responding to a written document. It is difficult to believe that this earlier writing could have been an adoptionist writing at all, since not even the Council of Frankfurt seems to know of it. (See Heil, *Alkuinstudien*, 12, and Blumenshine, *LAHF*, 32, n.4.) But again, if there was such an early work, it has left no trace in any of the anti-adoptionist literature, either in Spain or in Gaul (especially true of the *LAHF*: on this point see Heil, *Alkuinstudien*, 26–29). This early work, if it did exist, was probably not distinguishable in position from the work of Elipandus, and may even have been a brief apology for the position of Elipandus, which could explain why in the early stages of the controversy it is mainly Elipandus who is cited.

75. Alcuin, *AFU, PL* 101:122A 5.

76. Alcuin, *AFU, PL* 101:123B.10–11.

77. For example, Augustine (at Alcuin, *AFU, PL* 101:123CD, 124A);

Gregory the Great, (at 124A); Chromatius (at 124CD, 125A); Hilary (at 122D).

78. "Tota evangelica clamat auctoritas omnia apostolorum protestantur dicta, mundi latitudo credit, Romana praedicat Ecclesia, Christum Jesum verum esse Dei Filium et proprium: quid vultis ei nomen adoptivi imponere? Quid est adoptivus filius, nisi falsus filius? Etsi Christus Jesus falsus est Deo Patri Filius, et (quod impium est dicere) falsus est et Deus, falsa est et tota nostrae salutis dispensatio" (Alcuin, *AFU, PL* 101:122A 1–9). This is not yet a polemic against a doctrine of *nuncupation*; merely a more general polemic against what seems to the authors to be in effect idolatry.

79. *LAHF* 2 (*PL* 101:87A 3–B.1; Blumenshine, p. 55).

80. The passage illustrates well how a perception or analysis of the adoptionist position tends to blur into or even replace actual reporting of the position. Alcuin states that the adoptionists teach that Mary was not the Mother of the Son of God, as though they taught that Mary was the mother of someone who was merely human and at some later point adopted into sonship. But as far as we know Elipandus, and at this point Alcuin is still basing his observations on Elipandus's letter, never raises the issue, and Felix seems to touch on it only late in his career, after 799, perhaps in response to just such an accusation as this. J. Rivera Recio ("La Maternidad divina de Maria, en un controversia cristologica española de fines del siglo VII," in *Publicaciones de la Academia P. Bibliografica-Mariana*, 5–37) argues Felix's dependence on Theodore of Mopsuestia and Diodore of Tarsus, but the literary parallels are not as convincing as one might wish. Also, Felix's remarks on the subject permit an interpretation other than Alcuin's, namely, that Mary is the mother of the eternal Son of God insofar as he was a man, that is, at his "second," physical birth, although she is not his mother insofar as he is God, since she does not participate in his eternal generation from the Father. This is not a Nestorian position, because, as Felix repeatedly states, Jesus is from conception united to the Word.

81. For Alcuin it is not a new heresy from an analytic point of view. But from a linguistic point of view Alcuin derides it as "new" and "unheard of," something never taught by Apostle or doctor. For example, at *Alc.Ep.* 23 Alcuin admonishes Felix "ut tota animi intentione apostolicam et evangelicam omni fidei firmitate et veritate sequamur doctrinam, non nova fingentes nomina: non inconsuetum quid proferentes, non nomini nostro per novitatem cujuslibet doctrinae vanam cantantes laudem. . . ." Note, too, Alcuin, *AFU* 1.1 (*PL* 101:129A 3–5): ". . . novo et inaudito sanctae Dei Ecclesiae nomine nuncupativum Deum nominare illum non timet." Also, at *AFU* 1.2 (*PL* 101:129C 1–4): ". . . toto Ecclesia Christi ab initio predicationis apostolicae hoc nomen adoptionis in Christo, vel nuncupatviae divinitatis nunquam habuerit, nunquam praedicavit." Not only was it new, but it had the additional stigma of being *parochial*: "Probate, si potestis, verum esse quod dicitis, ostendite nobis vel unam gentem vel unam urbem, vel sanctam Romanam Ecclesiam, quae est caput Ecclesiarum, vel Constantinopolitanam vel Hierosolymitanam ipsius Domini praesentia dedicatam; aut Antiochenam, in qua primum sanctum Christianitatis nomen esse legitur; aut Alexandrinam, vel ullam Ecclesiam in tota Italia, vel Germania, vel etiam Gallia, aut Aquitania, imo aut Britannia, quae vobis consentiat in hac vestra assertione, ut verum probetis, aliquos vos ha-

bere socios sententiae vestrae . . ." (*AFU* 1.6, *PL* 101:132D 13–133A 10). Note in particular Alcuin's pride in his unity with Rome: "nos enim Romana plus auctoritate quam Hispana, veritate assertionis et fidei nostrae fulciri desideramus; licet nec illa reprobemus, in his tamen quae catholice dicuntur. Unusquisque in hoc se refutandum sciat, in quo ab universali dissentit Ecclesia. Romana igitur Ecclesia, quae a catholicis et recte credentibus sequenda esse probatur, se per verum Filium Dei et in missarum solemniis, et in caeteris quoque omnibus scriptis suis . . ." (*AFU* 7.13, *PL* 101:226C 12–227A 6). See also *AFU* 1.4, *PL* 101:131A 6–B.2; *Ep. ad Hisp.*, p. 145.37–40; *Alc.Ep.* 166, p. 269.5–10; 272.1–5; etc.

82. Here Alcuin himself gives warrant for thinking of this first treatise as a dossier of precedent: "Hanc ego pestilentiae luem abhorrens, antiquorum patrum pigmentarias perscrutare curavi cellas, vel posterioris temporis venerabilium doctorum florentia percurrere prata festinavi ut aliquod medicamenti genus civibus meis, filiis scilicet sanctae ecclesiae conficerem, quo se ab hac pestilentiae contagione praemunire, divina auxiliante gratia, potuissent. Ex paternis videlicet thesauris species colligens pigmentorum vel florum, et singulorum adnectens nomina auctorum ut salubrior esset et firmior confectio quo ex clarissimorum virorum sapientiae et sanctitatis erueretur gazis" (*LAHF* 2, Blumenshine, pp. 55.24–56.6).

83. *LAHF* 20 (Blumenshine, p. 64.4–28) and 62 (Blumenshine, p. 90.19–20) amplify Hadrian's citation of Nazianzus *Ep.* 101 (cited by Hadrian in the First Letter to the Bishops of Spain at *Codex Carolinus* #95, p. 638.19–26 and in his Second Letter to the Bishops of Spain, at *MGH, Concilia*, II, p. 125.1–6). Also, compare *LAHF* 58 (Blumenshine, p. 89.11–19 = Pseudo-Athanasius [Apollinaris of Loadocia, *PG* 28:28–29]) to Hadrian's First Letter to the Bishops of Spain, *Codex Carolinus* #95, p. 639.19–26 and in the Second Letter to the Bishops of Spain at *MGH, Concilia*, II, p. 124.33–39. Perhaps Alcuin gives the citations in translations different from Hadrian's because he himself had first hand access to a Latin translation of the *acta* of Ephesus.

84. Alcuin cites Augustine, *In Iohannis* 14.11 at *LAHF* 27 (Blumenshine, p. 69.17–24). The last three lines are a constant in the literature since Hadrian's First Letter to the Bishops of Spain (see *Codex Carolinus* #95, p. 639.26–30, and in the Second Letter to the Bishops of Spain, *MGH, Concilia*, II, p. 125.25–26).

85. Alcuin cites Gregory's *Moralia in Iob* 1.18 at *LAHF* 23 (Blumenshine, pp. 65.24–66.4), only a slight variation of Hadrian's citation of the same passage in his Second Letter to the Bishops of Spain at *MGH, Concilia*, II, p. 125.30–34. Alcuin also used this passage at *Alc.Ep.* 23 (p. 64.6–7), and uses it again at *AFU* 7.4, *PL* 101:215C 15–D 2. *Moralia in Iob* 18.52 is cited at *LAHF* 24 (especially note Blumenshine, p. 67.18, "'Non purus homo conceptus atque editus, post per meritum ut deus esset accepit . . .'").

86. Including, above all, Augustine, and then Leo, Hilary, Ambrose, and Cassian (Blumenshine gives a complete list of sources, 105–109). Alcuin retains his citation of Gennadius of Marseilles, *Liber de eccles. dogmat.* 2.27 (*LAHF* 30, Blumenshine, p. 71.1–8, cited in part in his *Ep. ad Hisp., MGH, Concilia*, II, p. 153.19–22), and of Hilary *De trin.* 6.22–24 (*LAHF* 4, Blumenshine, pp. 56.25–58.10; it had been partially cited in the *Ep. ad Hisp., MGH, Concilia*, II, pp. 152.38–

153.5). See Bernard Bischoff, "Aus Alkuins Erdentagen," *Mittelalterliche Studien* 2, 12–19, notes 33–34, for citations retained from the *Ep. ad Hisp.* As Amann points out (*L'Époque*, 146), Alcuin's use of citations in this work is not always as apt as it could be, and certainly not as skilled as in the *AFU*.

87. The Latin translation of the Greek *acta* of Ephesus which Alcuin used is presently the Bibliothèque Nationale latinus 1572 (text of this MS given by E. Schwartz, *Acta conciliorum oecumenicorum*, Tome 1, vol. 3). Alcuin found it at Tours when he arrived there in 796/7 (see Bullough, "Kingdom," 49–50, 51–52). Alcuin's use of this MS of the Ephesus *acta* has been studied by Bischoff, "Aus Alkuins Erdentagen," *Mittelalterliche Studien* 2, 12–19; L. Ott, "Das Konzil von Ephesus (431) in der Theologie der Frühscholastik," in *Theologie in Geschichte und Gegenwart*, edited by J. Auer and H. Volk, 279–308; and Amann, "l'Adoptianisme," 307, n.3. See also Heil, *Alkuinstudien*, 55–63, and the other literature cited by Blumenshine, 18, n.17 and 33, n. 5. Alcuin's knowledge of the fifth century controversies extended well beyond what the Ephesus *acta* could have told him, however. He knows and cites the Council of Chalcedon (*AFU* 4.13), and is aware that ultimately the polarity in christology is between Nestorianism and Eutychianism. He characterizes Eutyches's position as a confusion of natures: "Nos non sequimur nec Nestorianam divisionem, qui propter duas naturas duas personas in Christo inserere voluit; nec Eutychetis confusionem, qui propter unam personam unam naturam in Christo inserere voluit" (*AFU* 1.11, *PL* 101:136A 3–7, cf. C 6–10, and 1.7, *PL* 101:133B 7–9). Alcuin obtained his knowledge, most likely, from the letters and sermons of Leo, and from Isidore, both of whom he cites frequently.

88. *LAHF* 69 (*PL* 101:116C; Blumenshine, p. 95.7–10). Amann takes this critique over as the definitive solution to the question of adoptionism. He is so impressed by the brilliance and clarity of Alcuin's analysis that he forgets that it may not in fact be a correct analysis, i.e., one corresponding to what the adoptionists in fact taught. Blumenshine also accepts Alcuin's position: "[Alcuin's] statement that adoptionism and Nestorianism are similar doctrines, the latter having been rejected as heretical by an ecumenical council, is historically accurate" (35).

89. Alcuin, *LAHF* 71 (*PL* 101:119A, Blumenshine, p. 98). This line of argument reappears in Alcuin's letter to Elipandus, *Alc.Ep.* 166.

90. Alcuin, *LAHF* 71 (*PL* 101:118C, Blumenshine, p. 97).

91. Alcuin, *LAHF* 71 (*PL* 101:118CD, Blumenshine, pp. 97–98).

92. Alcuin, *LAHF* 71 (*PL* 101:119A, Blumenshine, p. 98) and 70 (*PL* 101:117D, Blumenshine, p. 96; citing Augustine's *Enchiridion*).

93. *LAHF* 70 (*PL* 101:117B, Blumenshine, p. 96).

94. ". . . improba caecitate illum [Christum] in divinitate proprium Dei Patris esse Filium, adoptivum vero ejusdem Dei Patris in humanitate affirmant. Et si ita esset, omnino duo Filii essent; quia nequaquam, ut praefati sumus, una esse potest persona in proprio Filio et in adoptivo; quia unus ex illis verus est Filius: alter itaque non verus" (*LAHF* 35 [*PL* 101:101C, Blumenshine, pp. 73–74]).

95. *LAHF* 36 (*PL* 101:102B, Blumenshine, p. 75).

96. Note usages at *LAHF* 21 (*PL* 101:95A, Blumenshine, pp. 64–65); 51 (108D–109A, Blumenshine, p. 84); 28 (*PL* 101:98C, Blumenshine, p. 69).

97. For example, as at *LAHF* 42 (*PL* 101:105–106, Blumenshine, pp. 78–80) and 51 (*PL* 101:109A, Blumenshine, p. 84 [especially note the *aliud/aliud* language]).

98. Elipandus enjoys rehearsing for Felix his latest strategic maneuvers. He mentions writing to the new Arius (Alcuin); reading the "epistolam foetidissimam" which he had earlier received from him (see *Alc.Ep.* 183, p. 307.25–27, "denuo adsumpsi laborem et scripsi ad ipso heretico piceo Albino, quantum potui pro sua confusione scribere," and, p. 308.1–6); forwarding a letter from Felix to Cordoba (p. 308.13); receiving a reply with material Elipandus felt could be helpful to Felix (p. 308.14). Elipandus tells Felix wistfully of the passing of his own 82nd birthday, and remarks that he is asking "all the brothers" to say Mass for Felix's benefit (p. 308.31–32).

99. Further discussion on the continuity of Felix's thought with that of Elipandus is given in Appendix I, below.

100. Alcuin refers to this work on a number of occasions; Paulinus is citing from the same text. Alcuin says the *AFU* was written after the debate, apologizing because its structure reflects more the give and take of discussion than the ordered formality of a treatise (see *Ep.Alc.* 202, to Charlemagne).

101. Alcuin describes the intense campaign of reading which culminated in the *AFU*. He gives a partial listing of his authorities in the preface: "ex sanctorum Patrum certissimis . . . testimoniis . . . , id est, beati Hieronymi, atque sancti Augustini, Gregorii papae Romani, Hilarii Pictaviensis episcopi, Leonis quoque papae, et Fulgentii epsicopi, Ambrosii quoque Mediolanensis episcopi; sed et fortissimi contra Nestorium militis beati Cyrilli; Petri etiam Ravennensis episcopi, et beati Bedae presbyteri, Gregoriique Nazianzeni; nec non et Isidori Hispaniensis et Juvenci ejusdem provinciae scholastici . . . Origenis quoque quaedam vel Cassiani exempla posui . . ." (*Alc.Ep.* 203). Alcuin also describes his intensive inquiry into the conciliar literature, both Eastern and Western: "Legimus namque Orientales synodos, quae a sanctis Patribus congregatae sunt, temporibus diversis contra varios haeresiarchas; et nullam invenimus usquam dicere vel affirmare, adoptivum filium, vel nuncupativum Deum Christum esse. Simul et Occidentales synodos perspeximus, nec in illis tale aliquid invenimus: sed nec in aliqua earum quae in Hispania, vel Gallia, vel istis partibus promulgatae sunt, haec nomina, quae nuper nova temeritas protulit, comperimus. Sed ubique per omnes synodos et libellos sanctorum doctorum semper unum Filium Dei proprium legimus . . ." (*AFU* I.4, *PL* 101:131B 2–13).

102. See, e.g., *AFU* I.11 (*PL* 101:136B 2–4, B 9–C 3): "Igitur sicut Nestoriana impietas in duas Christum dividit personas, propter duas naturas . . . ita et vestra indocta temeritas in duos eum dividit filios, unum proprium, alterum adoptivum. Si vero Christus est proprius Filius Dei Patris et adoptivus, ergo est alter et alter. Similiter, si in divinitate Deus verus est et in humanitate Deus nuncupativus, alter [et alter] est, et nullatenus sic sentientes potestis vobis evitare impietatem Nestorianae doctrinae: quia quem ille in duas personas dividit propter duas naturas, hunc vos dividitis in duos filios et in duos deos per adoptionis nomen et nuncupationis." Also see 1.11, 136C 5–11; 1.13, 138C 2–8; 2.20, 162B 14–C 2; 3.3, 164A 14–B 3; 4.11, 186A 13–B 5, B 13–C 2; 5.2, 189D 1–4; 5.4, 191B 13–C 5; 5.5

192A 7 (introducing a passage from Cassian's *Seven Books Against Nestorius*); 7.2, 213C 10–D 3 (introducing a passage from Cyril); 7.9, 222A 12–14; 7.11, 223C 2–11; 7.12, 226A 4–14; 7.15, 228C 7 (introducing a passage from Cyril); etc., not to mention all the places where Alcuin uses explicitly anti-Nestorian citations in direct reply to a passage or position of Felix.

Alcuin's second major anti-adoptionist treatise, the *Adversus Elipandum* (*AE*) (*PL* 101:231–300; see also Paul V. Gonzalez, *Alcuin's "Adversus Elipantum Libri IV," Books I–II Edited with an Introduction*, 177) repeats even more insistently his analysis of adoptionism as a form of Nestorianism, highlighting in particular the heresy of adducing two persons in Christ. See, for example, (from the *PL*) 1.2; 1.22; 2.1; 2.13; 4.6–9; etc. Alcuin also argues that while Nestorius concentrated on denying the *Theotokos*, Elipandus concentrates on denying the true divine Sonship of Jesus, which amounts to the same thing, i.e., that Mary was not after all the Mother of God: see *AE* 4.5; 1.13. Also, see Alcuin's letter to Elipandus, *Alc. Ep.* 166. In general the *AE* contains argumentation that is less varied and complex than that in the *AFU*. There is very little new argumentation. The last two books are occupied largely with refuting Elipandus's citation of authorities.

103. E.g., at *AFU* 5.1, *PL* 101:187D.

104. Alcuin cites Felix as follows: "Dicis enim eumdem esse Filium Dei qui est et filius hominis, et filium hominis qui est Filius Dei, ut ex tuis verbis cognosci poterat: 'Qui illum,' inquis, 'sibi ex utero matris, scilicet ab ipso conceptu in singularitate suae personae ita univit atque conseruit, ut Dei Filius esset hominis filius, non mutabilitate naturae, sed dignatione: similiter et hominis filius esset Dei Filius, non versilitate substantiae, sed in Dei Filio esset verus Filius'" (*AFU* 5.1, *PL* 101:188D 3–11). Paulinus also praises Felix's orthodoxy on this point, although in the passage in which he discusses this, the reader can see the difference between his report *about* what Felix confesses, and Alcuin's solicitude to cite Felix's own words ("inquis"): "Confitetur enim se dominum Iesum Christum verum deum verumque credere hominem, ab ipso scilicet conceptu virginalis uteri a verbo dei in singularitate adsumptum personae inseparabiliter absque ulla confusionis mutabilitate utriusque naturae. Unum eundemque dei hominisque filium, nec alterum dei, alterum hominis sed unum eundemque dei et hominis filium, non duos filios nec duos deos et his similia iuxta regulam catholicae satis perspicuae prolixae disputationis effusum praetendit sermonem" (*CF* 1.9.7–15). Later (1.9.42–43) Paulinus actually cites Felix: "*Personas* ait *non divido, naturas prorsus distinguo.*"

105. Alcuin cites Felix: "'Ipsum,' inquis, 'credimus verum et proprium Dei Filium ac verum Deum, qui secundum formam Dei bis genitus est; primo videlicet de Patre sine carne absque matre: secundo vero ex matre cum carne sine Patre. Illum verum Deum ex utroque parente ineffabiliter genitum credimus, cui Pater per David loquitur: *Ex utero ante luciferum genui te*'" (*AFU* 5.2, *PL* 101:189B 3–10).

106. *AFU* 5.1, *PL* 101:187D. Paulinus muses along the same lines: "Et ubi est illud aut quis putas spiritus nequam rapuit tam subito de corde tuo, quod paulo ante professus labiis, non corde agebas? *Non*, inquis, *duo dii vel duo filii. Absit, sed unus dei homenisque filius* [sic]. Age ergo quo pacto tunc unum, quomodo nunc duos filios confteris?" (*CF* 2.27.9–13); cf. 1.9.15–18: "Quo igitur pacto cuiusque

suasibilis inspirationis instinctu statimque obliviscitur, quis paulo ante fuerat, in-memor subito quasi in alienatione insani capitis quid dixerit?"

107. "Verum et non verum nullatenus unum esse potest; sic etiam verus filius, et non verus filius nullatenus unus esse poterit filius: nec Deus verus et Deus nun-cupativus unus esse poterit: quia aliud est omnimodis veritas divinitatis, et aliud nuncupatio nuda deitatis, ut supra ostendimus in Moyse et caeteris sanctis; sed utrumque in una persona nullatenus esse poterit, quia alia est veritatis dignitas, alia nuncupationis largitas" (*AFU* 5.2, *PL* 101:189C 7–15).

108. Paulinus makes a similar argument: "Nam verus et nuncupativus duo sunt, proprius et adoptivus similiter duo sonant duarumque personarum, non per-functoriae tantummodo sono sed rei substantialis efficit veritatem" (*CF* 2.22.34–37; see also 3.27.47). Paulinus's accusation is a little more forthright than Alcuin's, if somewhat less sophisticated. He seems to know less about Nestorianism than Alcuin does, although see *CF* 1.8.13.

109. "Nec iterum Christum dividimus in duos filios, vel duos deos, vel duas cum Nestorio personas. Qui licet duas palam non dixisset personas, tamen omnia quae duabus inesse necesse est personis, in sua professione fatetur. Simili modo et tu, licet fugias verba duarum personarum, tamen omnia quae necesse est duabus inesse personis, te in tuis litteris invenimus profiteri. Quis enim nesciat, apud unum Patrem alteram esse personam adoptivi filii, alteram proprii Filii?" (*AFU* 7.11, *PL* 101:223C 2–11.) For Alcuin, given Felix's premises, Nestorianism is ineluctable: "Quicunque vero hanc simulationem nuncupativae vel appellativae di-vinitatis, scilicet in humanitate Christi affirmare nititur, nullatenus Nestorianae im-pietatis foveam evadere poterit" (*AFU* 5.2, *PL* 101:189D 1–4).

110. *AFU* 7.12, *PL* 101:223B 9-C 5 (Augustine, at *Contra Maximinum* 2.2, *PL* 42:759–760). Note Alcuin's relatively extensive use of Phil. 2:8–11 at *AFU* 6.4, *PL* 101:203D 1–204A 9, where he uses these verses to explain why Jesus cannot be called a "servus conditionalis." Because of the obedience of Christ, he has been given the name above all other names, that is, Lord. Alcuin's refutation of the adoptionist characterization of Jesus as a servant is thus different from Beatus's refutation, which presupposed that the self-emptying of the pre-existent Word per-mits us to understand the servantship of Jesus properly. Alcuin does not seem to allow *any* proper way to speak of the servantship of Christ; he prefers to concen-trate on the exaltation of Christ to Lordship as his refutation of the adoptionists's claims about the servantship of Jesus. Alcuin will also argue from Phil. 2:9–11 that Jesus cannot be adoptive because *adoptivus* is not a "name above all other names." Beatus argues that to call Christ adoptive is to misunderstand the *exinanitio* of 2:7, but Alcuin simply does not notice Elipandus's central reliance on this verse. He reads Phil. 2:6–10 from the point of view of the exaltation at the end. Note too Alcuin's use of Phil. 2:9 at *AFU* 3.2, *PL* 101:163C 5–D 11. The verse is contained within a citation of Pope Leo I's letter to the Emperor Leo I (*Ep.* 165.8), and is significant because Elipandus had also cited this passage from Leo in his letter to Alcuin but much more fully. Alcuin *removes* all reference to Phil. 2:7 and retains only the citation of 2:9. Alcuin also chooses to cite from Peter Chrysologus a passage containing a reference only to Phil. 2:10 (*AFU* 4.4, *PL* 101:177B 9–10). In Alcuin's *AE* note the exclusive focus on Phil. 2:10 at 1.1 and 3.17 (in a citation of

Augustine); the discussion of the elevation of Christ's human nature at 3.6; and the similar treatment of the human nature and even the divine nature, the *divinitas*, as a virtual subject at the end of 3.4: "Without doubt it is the human nature that receives the honor and glory which the divinity of the Son of God had eternally with God the Father and the Holy Spirit." Phil. 2:6–7 is cited at *AE* 4.8, but only as a source for the "form" language (*forma servi, forma Dei*)—the self-emptying is not mentioned.

111. *AFU* 7.11, *PL* 101:223C 9–15: "Quis enim nesciat, apud unum Patrem alteram esse personam adoptivi filii, alteram proprii Filii? Nec enim ullus pater, juxta humanae consuetudinis rationem poterat proprium filium sibi adoptare, quasi alienum: aut quem adoptat sibi in filium, poterit sibi proprium facere, quem paternitas alterius sibi fecit alienum" (cf. *AFU* 3.2, *PL* 101:163AB). Paulinus argues similarly that the status of sonship as a relation precludes the same individual from have two sorts of sonship relative to the same parent: "Animadverte quid dixerim: non poteris filium et filium et filium quod est relativum ad aliquid, hoc est proprium et adoptativum, uni adscribere genitori" *CF* (1.34.40–42; a similar argument at 2.23.1–3).

112. As Alcuin notes at *AFU* 1.11, *PL* 101:223.C3. Paulinus aligns himself squarely with the position that Felix teaches Jesus was "purus homo": See *CF* 1.27.5–6; 1.9.32–33 (an interesting variation, "purum communemque hominem"); 1.30.17; 2.11.5, 24; 2.18.10; 2.25.50; 3.10.25; etc.

113. Paulinus adheres to the same exaltation model of christology when he interprets Phil. 2:5–9. For example, alluding to Phil. 2:6–7, Paulinus omits all mention of the self-emptying: "Qui cum in forma dei esset, formam servi suscepit" (*CF* 1.36.16–17). Paulinus explains, "sed per divinitatis plenitudinem in Christo corporaliter inhabitantem exaltatus est homo Christus Iesus in deum, ita ut unus idemque sit deus homo die hominisque filius" (24–28); cf. *CF* 2.24.50–51, "quia numquam fuit purus primum conditus homo, ut postmodum transiret in deum. . . ."

114. *AFU* 1.10, *PL* 101:135B9–C2, C14–D8, D11–136A 2. The last sentence of the text runs thus: "Ergo quia *forma Dei* accepit *formam servi*, utrumque Deus, utrumque homo; sed utrumque Deus propter accipientem Deum, utrumque autem homo, propter acceptum hominem." Alcuin later cites another instance of Augustine's use of Phil. 2:7 where Augustine's language is similarly divisive, despite Alcuin's antecedent explanation to the contrary: "Filius Dei [which here seems to refer strictly speaking to the Word] . . . *habitu inventus ut homo* [Phil. 2:8], sed divinitate ut Deus. Nec in illa assumptione alius est Deus, alius homo, vel alius Filius Dei, et alius filius Virginis: et idem filius Virginis, qui et Filius Dei: ut sit unus Filius etiam proprius et perfectus in duabus naturis Dei et hominis. De quo etiam Christi *habitu* beatus Augustinus ait [*De div. quaest.* 73.2], 'Sic assumptus est homo, ut proficeret ["commutaretur," Aug.] in melius, et ab eo formaretur ineffabiliter excellentius atque conjunctius, quam vestis, cum ab homine induitur. Hoc ergo nomine habitus satis significat Apostolus, quemadmodum dixerit: *In similitudine hominum factus* [Phil. 2:7]: quia non transfiguratione in hominem, sed *habitu* factus est, cum indutus est homine, quem sibi coaptans ["uniens," Aug.] quodammodo atque conformans immortalitati aeternitatique sociaret [*AFU* 2.12,

PL 101:156A 8–B 10].'" Note that the operative metaphor here is that of the Word being "clothed" by a man, a much less unitive metaphor than the one of "body and soul" to which Alcuin sometimes has recourse as well.

115. Cf. *AFU* 4.3–4, *PL* 101:176B 6–C 10. Here Alcuin chooses passages from Augustine's *De trinitate* which employ the *forma Dei/forma servi* language liberally, but with all the emphasis on the *susceptio* and no mention at all of the *exinanitio*. Also, at *AFU* 4.9, *PL* 101:183A 8–10, Alcuin picks a citation from Jerome (*In Isaiah* 49) which paraphrases Phil. 2:6–7, but which omits any reference to the self-emptying in these verses, and not only retains the language of acquiring, but strengthens it from "accipiens" to "assumere": "*Servus meus es tu Israel, quia in te glorificabor* (Is. 49:3). *Servus,* quia *cum in forma Dei esset, formam servi* est dignatus assumere." As with Hadrian, the emphasis in the phrase *formam servi* is on the word *formam,* as can be seen from Alcuin's explanation a few lines following this: "Dominus autem, ut ait sanctus Augustinus, in forma servi, non servus: sed in forma servi Dominus fuit" (*AFU* 4, *PL* 101:183C 3–5). That is, the human nature which was assumed is not actually a servant, but rather was the *form* of a servant. Because attention is focused exlcusively on the status of the "homo" which is taken up, Alcuin does not admit any proper use of the word "servant" with regard to Christ. The idea of the Hispanic school that the Word *empties himself* into servantship, and that thus servantship might be a freely willed characteristic of the *Word* strictly speaking, never occurs to Alcuin in these texts. Cf. Alcuin's comments at *AFU* 2.12, *PL* 101:156A 8–9 (cited in previous note).

116. Unique among the non-Hispanic anti-adoptionists, Paulinus has a lengthy explanation of the "emptying" imagery from Phil. 2:6–7. Generally, Paulinus treats the phrases *forma Dei* and *forma servi* rather mechanically, as simple equivalents for divinity and "humanity" respectively, much as Alcuin does, and at *CF* 2.12, Paulinus argues that *forma servi* means nothing more or less than *forma hominis.* The emptying is not even mentioned in this context, and at *CF* 1.14.18–23 the *exanitio* is abruptly passed over, in favor of the *susceptio.* Clearly the emptying is hardly an emptying at all; it is not a process which has a terminus (servantship) of its own. This is illustrated graphically at *CF* 2.3–5, the most extended discussion of Phil. 2:6–7 in the whole controversy. Paulinus vigorously defends the continuity of the pedigree or identity of the Unigenitus throughout the self-emptied state. He uses an extended analogy, where the Only-begotten is compared to a king who dresses as a servant, but who does not lose his kingly title. The most telling section is this: "nunquid pro his dominum indulgentiae exhibitis rebus dominantis amisisse privilegium estimatur, vel pristinae potestatis perdedit vel minuit vel inmutavit dignitatem, aut propter inlato servilis famulatus beneficio dominatui suo contulit deformitatis iniuriam, aut propter vestem servi quam induerat, desiit eius esse cuius verus erat filius regis? Non utique. Sed permansit ipse qui fuerat verus filius regis. His ita peractis non amisit veri filii nomen nec duplicavit in adoptivum nec inmutavit in nuncupativum. Si ergo hominem hoc posse absque sui dominatus detrimento perficere possibilitatis ratio non contradicit, cui non cuncta possibilia constant, quanto magis deus, *qui omnia quaecumque voluit fecit*" (Ps. 134:6; *CF* 2.4.33–44). On its own terms this analogy is rather moving, but Felix would probably object because this way of putting it still makes the

humanity simply a covering or dress (cf. Paulinus's reference, lines 59–60, to the *incarnationis velamen*). Ultimately, the analogy shows how little Paulinus's notion of "emptying" actually includes any emptying. By comparing the earthly ministry of Jesus to a king's son who has gone among his people disguised in rags, he makes it clear that Jesus was not really a servant, but only wore the "clothes" of one. Paulinus avoids at all cost any implication that Jesus was really, in any sense, a slave. On the *exinanitio*, see also *CF* 3.9.8–11. Paulinus comments that the humility of God (line 18) is the opposite of the pride of Lucifer.

117. Compare this language ("accipientem Deum/acceptum hominem") in the Augustine passage with the language Alcuin condemns at *AFU* 7.12, *PL* 101: 226A 3–4.

118. There are several other examples of divisive usage in Alcuin's text. Note the use of the relative pronouns (especially the "qui") in the following passage, where Alcuin pictures the natures in Christ as the addressees of discourse: "Cui autem naturae dictum est, *sede a dextris meis* (Ps. 110:1), divinae an humanae? Humanae, scilicet, ut in symbolo cantatur: *qui ascendit in coelos, et sedet a dextris Dei. . . .* Naturae cui dictum est, *terra es et in terram ibis* (Gen. 3:19), huic dictum est, *sede a dextris meis.*" (*AFU* 1.16, *PL* 101:141C 10–14, D 2–4.) Also, "Apostol[us] . . . ait, *Cum introducit primogenitum in orbem terrae, dicit: Et adorent eum omnes angeli Dei* [Heb. 1:6]. Hoc vero de suscepto homine dictum esse, Joannes . . . affirmat " (*AFU* 3.14, *PL* 101:170B 14–C 2). Alcuin also quotes with approval the following passage from Augustine, which seems to imply a division between "susceptor" and "susceptus": "'Respondendum est, Deum oblivionem non pati, ut pro illis commoneatur semper, quos ipse elegit: sed in hoc interpellat eum, dum semper Patri hominem quem suscepit, quasi nostrum pignus ostendit, et offert ut verus pontifex et aeternus." (*AFU* 5.7, *PL* 101:194B 10–15; Alcuin gives his own toned-down version at 7.15, *PL* 101:228B 7–C 6.) Note, finally, at 2.12, *PL* 101:156A 2–3: "In assumptione namque carnis a Deo, persona perit hominis, non natura"—implying a virtual subject "before" the assumption. Also of interest here is some of Paulinus of Aquileia's language in the *Libellus Sacrosyllabus* against the adoptionists. See, for example, p. 137.19–23 (the "Lord of Glory" never deserted the man whom he assumed), and p. 137.39–40 ("redemptor noster perfectum hominem adsumpsit in Deum"). In the *CF*: ". . . quatenus et deus propter susceptum hominem et homo propter suscipientem deum ex utroque et in utroque verus deus verusque homo unus idemque Christus" (1.12.37–40; cf. 2.3.17–18).

119. Note the following: "Christus namque nunquam vetus homo fuit, nunquam corpus peccati habuit, sed ab initio conceptionis Deus verus, et verus Filius Dei, absque omni peccato conceptus est et natus. Nos vero omnes veteres homines fuimus in peccatis Adam: sed in novos gratia baptismi per Christum Jesum conversi et adoptati et praedestinati in filios adoptionis. . . . Nos vero praedestinatos esse per illum in adoptionem filiorum. . . . Nos per illum, non ille per nos, praedestinationem habemus." (*AFU* 2.13, *PL* 101:156CD). Also, at 5.4 (*PL* 101:191CD), "Quod si verum est ut simulatio tantum sit nuncupativa nominis in Christo, non veritas divinitatis, quomodo est verus Redemptor humani generis? Si est imaginatio potestas in capite, unde est veritas salutis in corpore?" At 2.11 (*PL* 101:155B 12–

14, C 2–4), Alcuin reminds Felix that "redempti siquidem magno pretio Filii Dei, non cujuslibet adoptivi. . . . Ideo factus est ille verus Filius Dei, cujus sanguis pro nobis effusus est, ut nos possimus esse adoptivi per illum." At 7.10 (*PL* 101: 198D 8–10), Alcuin asks, "Quomodo ergo Christus naturaliter non est bonus, per quem omnes, quicunque boni sunt, efficiuntur boni?" Cf. 6.9 (*PL* 101:211C 5–8); 6.10 (*PL* 101:212D 6–8); 7.17 (*PL* 101:230C 3–7, citing Aug., *In Psalm.* 56); 2.11 (*PL* 101:154C 1–4).

120. See especially *AFU* 4.10 (*PL* 101:184A 5–7): "Hinc enim totius erroris sui videtur origo processisse, ut esx servo quodam adoptivum Filium facere potuisset [Editor's emendation of "facere *non* potuisset"], vel Deum nuncupativum" (cf. the *Ep. ad Hisp.* of Alcuin, *MGH*, *Concilia*, II, p. 154.5–7). Paulinus exhibits perfect continuity with Hadrian and Alcuin on this score: "Liberator etenim ille, non liberatus, quia numquam fuit servus peccati. *Omnis* refert *qui facit peccatum, servus est peccati*. Nos namque liberati qui sub iugo peccati depressi, servi facti demoniacae dominationis" (*CF* 1.25.20–23).

121. At *AFU* 4.10 (*PL* 101:184A 5–7) Alcuin insists that the heretics misunderstand the prophetic usage.

122. See at *AFU* 4.9 (*PL* 101:182C 7–D 2): "Iste etiam Felix hunc conditionalem servum saepius solet affirmare, non intelligens quod divinae dispensationis sacramento servus nominaretur: scilicet non conditione, ut superius diximus, debitae servitutis, sed implendae paternae voluntatis in salute humana voluntaria obedientia. Nam in Christo quidquid gestum est, totum voluntatis fuit, non necessitatis, qui Apostolo testante, *humiliavit semetipsum factus obediens Patri usque ad mortem, mortem autem crucis* [Phil. 2:8]. Alia est namque voluntaria humilitas, alia servilis necessitas." Even in this passage, with its insistent distinction between voluntary humility and servile necessity, there is no hint of reference to the pre-existent Word. The passage is thought of as having reference to the human being Christ, who has (who *is*) the *form* of a servant, but is not a servant. See also *AFU* 6.6, *PL* 101:207C 1–14.

123. *AFU* 6.3, *PL* 101:202B 8.

124. *AFU* 6.3, *PL* 101:202B8–15.

125. *AFU* 6.3 (202.C3–5). This argument from the omnipotence of God is odd. Presumably there can be no question of "creating" a "son" for God. The argument here seems a little desperate; see also 1.9 (*PL* 101:134C 3–D 5), and 7.10 (*PL* 101:222C 1–D 9). This argument reappears in the *AE*: "Quomodo de herbis virentibus flores diversi coloris nascuntur; sicut de spinis rosae, et de calamo viridi candidissimi lilii flos: sic fructus omnium arborum aliud proferunt in fructu, aliud in radice ostendunt. Totus mundus miraculis est plenus ejus *qui facit mirabilia magna solus* (Ps. 135:4), et adhuc incredula mens dubitat, si proprium sibi Filium procreare potuisset ex virginali utero, cujus virtus omnipotens, cujus voluntas omnis bonitas" (*AE* 2.6; cf. 4.3). There are similar arguments in Cassian, *De incarnatione Domini* 7.4–5.

126. *AFU* 6.3, *PL* 101:202A. For Alcuin's understanding of this phrase, see his *Interrogationes et responsiones in Genesin* 78 (*PL* 100:524D, citing, without acknowledgment, Augustine, *De Genesi ad litteram* 11.34, J. Zycha, ed., *CSEL* 28.1).

127. *AFU* 6.3, *PL* 101:202D-203A, cited from Gregory's *Moralia in Iob* 24.3. "By assuming a free nature belonging to a human being" = "naturam hominis

assumendo liberam," virtually as though there were a human being with a free human nature ready to be assumed.

128. See *AFU* 6.4 at *PL* 101:203D 1–8, cited above. It is in this context that we should read such christological statements as 4.17, *PL* 101:172A 11-B3, and also *AFU* 2.4, *PL* 101:149D 9–11: "Non enim minoratio fuit divinitatis in assumptione humanitatis: sed humanitatis exaltatio in participatione divinitatis."

129. In some places, where one might even have expected a reference to the self-emptying of verse 7, none is given. For example, at *AFU* 7.9 (*PL* 101:221C13–D1): "Nam altitudo divinitatis ad humilitatem descendit humanitatis, et humilitas humanitatis ad altitudinem ascendit divinitatis, non versibilitate naturae, sed dignatione honoris."

130. For example, at *AFU* 2.12, *PL* 101:155D 7–156A 2: "Assumpsit namque sibi Dei Filius carnem ex Virgine, et non amisit proprietatem, quam habuit in Filii nomine. Sed quanquam duas habuisset post nativitatem ex Virgine naturas, tamen unum proprietatem in Filii persona firmiter tenuit. Accessit humanitas in unitatem personae Filii Dei; et mansit eadem proprietas in duabus naturis in Filii nomine, quae ante fuit in una substantia." See also *AFU* 3.2 (*PL* 101:163B 11–C 5); 3.8 (*PL* 101:167D 1–9); 4.17 (*PL* 101:172A 7–B.7); 4.13 (*PL* 101:188B 13–C 4); 6.2 (*PL* 101:201B 8–14); 7.14 (*PL* 101:227D 10–228A 4); 7.6 (*PL* 101:223D 11–224A 7), etc.

131. "Accessit humanitas in unitatem personae Filii Dei; et mansit eadem proprietas in duabis naturis in Filii nomine, quae ante fuit in una substantia. In assumptione namque carnis a Deo persona perit hominis, non natura" (*AFU* 2.12, *PL* 101:155D-156A). Bullough remarks that this is one of the few places where Alcuin "transcends the limits of inherited thought and learning" ("Kingdom," 55). Compare the following passage from *AE* 1.22 (*PL* 101:258A), where Alcuin seems to have modified this teaching somewhat: "Naturae nostrae assumpsit veritatem, non adoptionis nostrae personam: non mutans naturam humanitatis nostrae in naturam divinitatis suae, sed mutavit personam adoptionis nostrae in personam proprietatis suae, sua non minuens, sed nostra augens." But changing of the "*persona* of our adoption" into something else still implies at least the virtual existence of the human *persona*.

132. *AFU* 4.5, *PL* 101:177C 9–11. Note the terms here: "Dicit ipsa veritas: *Quod Deus conjunxit homo non separet. Deus* conjunxit seipsum humanae naturae, ut esset unus Deus in duabus naturis." *God* conjoins a *human nature* to himself. Compare this to Cassian's use of this verse at *De incarnatione Domini* 5.11. Alcuin's debt in the *AFU* to this anti-Nestorian work of Cassian is very high, and it includes not only lengthy acknowledged citations but also lengthy unacknowledged citations. Perhaps, indeed, Alcuin has modeled the *AFU* on Cassian's work. Like the *De incarnatione Domini*, it has seven books, and Alcuin also begins his treatise with clear echoes of Cassian's opening discussion comparing heresy to a hydra (*AFU* 1.1; *De incarnatione Domini* 1.1).

133. Is it Felix who has brought up Eutyches's name? If so, it is the only time any of the adoptionists refer to any of the Eastern figures involved in the fifth century controversies. It seems more likely that it was Alcuin who has supplied the clarification, since neither Paulinus, who was working from the same text of Felix, or Agobard cite a similar usage.

134. *AFU* 3.17, *PL* 101:172A 7–B 6. Cf. 7.11, *PL* 101:223D–224A.

135. *AFU* 7.10, *PL* 101:222C 5–9.

136. *AFU* 7.10, *PL* 101:222C 9–14.

137. For example, *AFU* 7.2, *PL* 101:215A.

138. As well as in other important statements of the unity in Christ, e.g., *AFU* 4.17 (*PL*101:172A 7–B 7); 7.14 (*PL* 101:227D 10–228A 4); 7.6 (*PL* 101:223D 11–224A 7); 2.3 (*PL* 101:148A 11–149B 14); 1.8 (*PL* 101:133D 9–134C 2, a major introductory statement); 2.10 (*PL* 101:154A 8–B 10).

139. See for example *AFU* 7.9, *PL* 101:222A 12–B 15.

140. For example, *AFU* 2.4 (*PL* 101:149D 12–150A 12, citing from Augustine, *De pecc. mer. et remmiss.* 1.31, with significant differences from the text); *AFU* 3.19 (*PL* 101:161B 5–11, from Bede, *In Acta Apost.* 10); *AFU* 7.9 (*PL* 101:221D 8–13, from Aug. *Ench.* 40); *AFU* 7.11 (*PL* 101:224 D, from Augustine, *Contra Maximinum* 2.10.2).

141. *AFU* 3.2 (*PL* 101:163B 11–C 5).

142. *AFU* 3.2, *PL* 101:163C 6–D 11.

143. This is one reason Alcuin finds it necessary to appeal to the divine omnipotence and its presumed ability to do anything it wishes, including the ability to *create* a Son natural to the Father. Alcuin must resort to question-begging precisely because he has no way of explaining how it is that the unity between God and a human being can occur. His understanding of *persona* is so limited that he is not able to give such an explanation.

144. See Augustine, *De trinitate* 7.6, p. 262.28–33; 7.4, p. 259.118–120. Augustine explains that the word *persona* in Trinitarian usage is almost a kind of theological placeholder, a word used only so that one does not have to remain silent when asked "Three *what*?" What precisely a divine *persona* might be in and of itself cannot be specified further. The *personae* of the Trinity are defined by mutual and eternal relations but what a *persona, qua persona*, is in itself cannot be specified. Alcuin was completely committed to this conception of *persona*, as is well-known and amply documented in his *De fide sanctae et individuae Trinitatis* (*PL* 101:15–52, see J. Cavadini, "The Sources and Theology of Alcuin's Treatise *de fide*"). The implied adoptionist critique of this notion of *persona* is that it cannot account for the reflexive construction (an emphatic construction, "semetipsum" in the Vulgate) of Phil. 2:7. Augustine's notion of *persona* cannot account for the "self" of *he emptied himself.*

145. Augustine, *De trinitate* 5. See also Alcuin's use of these passages in his *De fide sanctae et individuae trinitatis* 1.3–7 (*PL* 101:16A–18C).

146. *AFU* 5.3, *PL* 101:190A 3–6.

147. *AFU* 7.10, *PL* 101:222C 15–D 3.

148. See *Ep. ad Franc.* p. 113.19–20. Note too that Elipandus's Trinitarian analogies are for the most part analogies of substantial distinction, like Tertullian's (that is, the *personae* are likened to distinctions in substance such as that between light and its radiance). See Elipandus's Symbolum in Beatus, *Adv.Elip.* 1.40, p. 28.1041–1058. The effect of analogies like this is to emphasize the continuity of substance. This is why Elipandus's Trinitarian theology seemed archaizing above: it insists on emphasizing the continuity of substance which is the absolute prerequisite for any discussion of relations among the three *personae* (see above, chapter 2).

149. See above, p. 95. But note how such an idea, that of "making" a son, echoes the interpretation of Phil. 2:6–11 which emphasizes the exaltation of a human being.

150. It may be worthwhile to inquire into the suggestion that adoptionism is a remnant not of Visigothic Arianism (an old and long discredited theory, taking its cue from Alcuin, who reminds Elipandus, for example, at *AE* 1.22, that if he is preaching that the *Word* is adoptive, he is an Arian) but of an *anti*-Arian polemic in which older Western understandings of the Trinity (such as Tertullian's), in themselves unable to withstand the logic of Arianism because inherently subordinationistic, have been adapted so that they can confront Arianism successfully. The point would be that the self-emptying of the Word implies an equality of agency despite the subordination implied by the Son's being a part or derivation from God's substance, just the sort of analogies that Elipandus uses. If Robert Gregg and Dennis Groh (*Early Arianism: A View of Salvation*) are correct in describing early Arianism as a soteriology in which the hope of salvation comes from the belief that the Logos, as "one of many brothers" (43), was himself adopted to the stature of divine Sonship for his obedience and faithfulness (see especially 50–70), then the christology of the Spanish adoptionists is perfectly suited as an *anti*-Arian polemic, explaining that the salvific adoptive status of Jesus does not imply that the Word was "adopted" or "less than the Father," but that the Word became "adopt*ive*." The possibility of our salvation comes about precisely because God's co-eternal Word became adoptive. Beatus's scheme may be understood as another version of this anti-Arian christology, although dropping the emphasis on the adoptive status.

Conclusion

1. On Alcuin's attitude toward *novitas*, novelty or newness, see above, chapter 4, n. 81; see also Bullough, "Kingdom," 51.

2. Felix is addressed as "O novae sectae inductor" (*AFU*, 2.10, *PL* 101:154A, cf. *AFU* 6.1, 199A).

3. For example, in the extended metaphor at *Adv. Elip.* 3.1 and 3.3 (*PL* 101:271A, 271D–272A), it is the flowers collected from "the fields of the Fathers" that permit us to put together a crown of "ecclesiastical truth" for Jesus Christ. Only after walking through these Patristic lands (*possessiones*) can we come to the place where we can follow the footsteps of Jesus to the banks of the River Jordan, or to the mountain whose peak he climbed with two of the Apostles, etc. We cannot find the footsteps of the Lord unless we start in the lands owned by the Fathers.

4. "*My heart is ready, O God, my heart is ready!* (Ps. 56:8) *Ready*, if divine grace will inspire it, to adduce the teaching of truth! *Ready*, to reply to the errors of falsehood! *Ready*, Lord Jesus, to love, to praise, and to preach you! *Ready* to understand you as true God and the true Son of God, with the blessed Evangelist who . . . says, *These things have been recorded to help you believe that Jesus is the Christ, the Son of God* (Jn. 20:31). . . . With God's mercy, Father Elipandus, the reason I

am writing against you is the same one as John's for writing his Gospel, namely, that I may show by the authority of the Scriptures and by the truth of the Catholic faith that Jesus Christ is the true Son of God, not only in the nature in which he is eternally born of God the Father, but also in the one which was made in the course of time from his Virgin Mother . . ." (*AE* 1.1,2, *PL* 101:243B–D).

5. Explicitly voiced, in a way, at *AE* 4.14 (*PL* 101:298B): "sufficiat nobis . . . catholicorum Patrum longo tempore explorata fides."

6. *LAHF* 2 (Blumenshine, 55–56): "Hanc ego pestilentiae luem abhorrens antiquorum Patrum pigmentarias perscrutari curavi cellas; vel posterioris temporis venerabilium doctorum florentia percurrere prata festinavi, ut aliquod medicamenti genus civibus meis, filiis scilicet sanctae Ecclesiae conficerem . . . ex paternis videlicet thesauris species coilligens pigmentorum, vel florum. . . ."

7. This is Hauck's term. Hauck's remarks seem completely apropos: "Die dortige [sc., in dem benachbarten Spanien] Theologie trug nicht den Stempel der Renaissance; sie war vielmehr der letzte Auslaufer der altkirchlichen Wissenshcaft. Manche alte Idee lebte noch fort, besonders waren die alten Probleme nicht ganz vergessen; aber der Anschluss an die alten Formeln war bei weitem nicht so enge und ängstlich wie dei der fränkischen theologie: man hatte sie nicht wie jene aus Buchern gelernt, man hatte *sie ererbt*" (my emphasis; Albert Hauck, *Kirchengeschichte Deutschlands*, vol. 2, p. 297). Harnack (*History of Dogma*, p. 289) accuses Alcuin of abandoning the Augustinian tradition, and comments on the "Greek" character of Alcuin's christology as a function of an Anglo-Saxon predilection.

8. Memories of the adoptionism controversy persist into the eighth century, but references to it then sputter out. Jonas of Orléans accused Claudius of Turin (who was from Spain) of being a disciple of Felix (*De cultu imaginorum* 1, *PL* 106:307D–310C), and Hincmar argues against adoptionism (*De deitate* 9, *PL* 125:553). There is also an interesting discussion of adoptionism by Paschasius Radbertus in his *Expositio in Psalmum XLIV* (*PL* 120:993–1060). See the recent article by Alf Härdelin, "An Epithalamium for Nuns: Imagery and Spirituality in Paschasius Radbertus's Exposition of Psalm 44(45)," in *In Quest of the Kingdom*, A. Härdelin, ed., *Bibliotheca Theologiae Practicae* 48, 1–32, esp. 24–25 (my thanks to David Ganz for this reference).

9. On this point Harnack notes, "The decisive result of the whole controversy was that the West set aside its own earlier Christological system, and—for the sake of the Lord's Supper and the imposing tradition of the Greeks—thought like the latter *within the sphere of dogma*" (original emphasis; *History of Dogma*, 292). I endorse the first part of this statement but perhaps not in the way in which it was intended. As the full sentence indicates, all the terms in the sentence take their value and meaning from their context in the brilliantly idiosyncratic interpretation of the history of dogma for which Harnack is so well known. The context for my own conclusions is quite different. In the first place, for Harnack "the controversy" itself is "the old antagonism of Monophysitism and Nestorianism" (*History of Dogma*, 280) and I have tried to show that this is only one particular view of the controversy, that of the Carolingians, and that, further, it is necessary to consider the earlier phase of the controversy in Spain on its own terms. Also, I do not attempt to isolate a "Christological system" which is the christology of the West

par excellance, nor do I attempt to evaluate such a system vis à vis "the tradition of the Greeks" or any other tradition. I attempt a more descriptive endeavor, which shows that for the most part the evidence remaining for the adoptionist positions can be explained without looking beyond the literature of the Latin West. In other words—Harnack does not agree with this either—these positions can be adequately accounted for as developments of themes rooted in literature predating the major controversies of the East, literature which itself then becomes the source for the reflection of such later figures as Leo, Julian, and Isidore. It is this process of development and reflection within a primarily Western circle of concerns, contexts, and meanings, which, in my opinion, is lost in the controversy over adoptionism, along with a sense of how to interpret the fruits of this reflection. Nevertheless, it is gratifying to learn, at the end of a long course of research, that one's conclusions have at least in some way touched on those of someone as eminent as Harnack.

Appendices

1. On this point see Solano, "El Concilio," 847–848.

2. Although it must be noted that Beatus seems to accuse him of teaching that Christ was "one god among gods," e.g., *Adv.Elip.* 1.13, p. 9.318; cf. *Symbolum Elipandi*, "Qui est Deus inter deos," *Adv.Elip.* 1.41, p. 29.1080, but note that the formula "cum deo dei" does not appear in the string of phrases "cum adobtibo adobtivi et cum advocato advocati et cum Christo christi et cum parvulo parvuli et cum servo servi," *Symbolum Elipandi*, *Adv.Elip.* 1.41, p. 29.1084–1085, frequently repeated, 1.49, p. 35.1311–1312; 1.61, p. 45.1710; 1.112, p. 3291–3293; 1.121, p. 94.3618–3619. At *Adv.Elip.* 1.59, p. 43.1640–1642 Beatus accuses Elipandus of collapsing the difference between "qui est Deus essentialis super omnia, et deos nuncupatibos," but he never accuses Elipandus of using this word.

3. Paulinus's reply is one of his most quotable quotes: "Posso si sibi vel pro se oravit, sibi et pro se est natus et passus ac mortuus et sepultus, pro se etiam proprium sanguinem fudit. Nihil ergo habuit amplius quam purus homo, si pro se necessitate cogente oravit" (*CF* 1.30.15–18). Paulinus claims Felix argued that Jesus must be God *nuncupative*, since *Deus verus* would not have to pray for anything, much less for himself (*CF* 1.30.3–4, cf. 1.36.36–37).

4. Other, less troubling uses of the verb "adopto" and derivatives which may seem disturbing are also easily explained. In the passage preserved by Alcuin at *AFU* 2.16, *PL* 101:158A, the *per* in the phrase *per adoptionem* has the sense of "pertaining to"; at *AFU* 1.18, *PL* 101:159C, the word "adoptari" is contained in a sentence which is clearly not a citation. Paulinus's usage is generally much looser than Alcuin's. For example, *CF* 1.22 starts off discussing whether *adoptivus* is the same as *adsumptus* or *adplicatus* vel cetera huiusmodi quae tuo stromatico digesta stilo leguntur (1–3, already pairing an adjective with two perfect participles). The verb forms are fluid here because Paulinus is showing that the words are not used in the same way in the Bible: the devil, in "assuming" Jesus to a high place, did not "adopt" him as his son (1.22.4–10; cf. *Alc.Ep.* 166, p. 269.13–19), nor can *adplicavit*

at Job 40:14 be replaced with *adoptavit* (11–21). But whenever Paulinus cites Felix's formula, it is always *adoptivus*: Quisnam sit ille Christus quem tu, heretice, *nuncupativum deum et adoptivum filium adfirmare conaris* (1.34.20–21). A few lines down in a sentence clearly of his own making, Paulinus says *adoptativum* (33; *passim*), as though this were his analysis of or even a kind of insult to Felix's position. At 1.26.1–24, Paulinus explains that the Savior is not *adoptatus* but rather, although not a common Latin word, *adoptator*: "Adoptator quapropter ille, sicut salvator, liberator et redemptor, non adoptatus, quia nec salvatus nec liberatus nec redemptus" (17–19). But as soon as Paulinus *quotes* Felix, the *adoptatus* disappears: "Tu causaris: 'qui negat' inquis 'eum adoptivum secundum hominem filium dei, neget necesse est eum verum fuisse hominem'" (1.27.1–3).

5. Felix does employ the word "mediator," which Elipandus avoided but which Beatus used so lavishly. For Felix's usage see Paulinus, *CF* 1.23.5–6, where Felix has adjusted Elipandus's phrasing to include the word "mediator" (for Elipandus's phrasing see *Ad Episc.Franc.* pp. 113.4, 118.32; see also Alcuin, *AFU* 5.7, *PL* 101:194A5–13, which may be Alcuin's citation of the passage from Paulinus).

6. Ansprenger, "Untersuchungen," 142, n. 301, agrees on this point, following Neander. It is worth noting that even in the lengthy passages that Alcuin has preserved for us on the subject (the longest of all the fragments, see n. 7 below), Felix *never* identifies the baptism of Jesus with an adoption of him into sonship, nor is that claim made anywhere else.

7. Alcuin cites Felix as follows: "Quoniam sicut in prima generatione, ex qua secundum carnem nascimur, nullus homo esse potest ["homo" = predicate nominative], qui aliunde originem trahat, nisi de primo illo Adam, qui ex terra virgine creatus est; ita in hac secunda generatione spirituali, in qua renascimur ex aqua et Spiritu sancto, nemo gratiam adoptionis consequi valet, praeter illum, qui eam ["locus corruptus," notes Froben] in eam in Christo ex carne virginis creatum et natum, qui est secundus Adam, accepit has geminas generationes: primam videlicet, quae secundum carnem est; secundam vero spiritalem, quae per adoptionem fit; idem Redemptor noster secundum hominem complexus in semetipso continet: primam videlicet, quam suscepit ex Virgine nascendo; secundam vero, quam initiavit in lavacro a mortuis resurgendo" (*AFU* 2.16, *PL* 101:157D 3–158A 4). Also note the following citation of Felix: "'Matthaeus,' inquit [Felix], 'in exordio Evangelii seriem generationis, quae secundum carnem ad Christum descendit, a David seu Abraham incipiens, usque Joseph sponsum Mariae, per reges et caeteros de tribu Juda sibimet succedentes, dinumerando perducit: in qua generatione carnis quatuor feminae introducuntur. Tres videlicet ex gentibus; quarta vero illa, in qua David peccavit: ut liquide patesceret, quod idem Redemptor noster non solum ex Judaeis, sed et de gentibus; neque de justis, sed etiam et de peccatoribus veram carnem ex Virgine suscepit. Lucas vero seriem generationis, quae per adoptionem est, non per genealogiam carnis, quemadmodum Matthaeus, sed a baptismo, in quo baptizatus est Christus in Jordane, ab ipso Christo incipiens non per tribum Juda, ut prior, sed per tribum sacerdotalem texens: neque deorsum descendendo, sicut ille, sed sursum versus: non per Salomonem ex Bersabee genitum, sed per Nathan in David recopulans usque in Adam perduxit ad Deum, caput videlicet replicans ad caput'" (*AFU* 2.18, *PL* 101:160 A5–B10).

8. In order to obtain a Theodoran reading of the crucial passage from the fragments of Felix cited in the previous note, Neander must amend Felix's words as follows: "'secundam vero, quam initiavit in lavacro [et consummavit] a mortuis resurgendo.' Without the parenthetic clause, the words give no sense" (*History*, p. 163). They do in fact "give sense" without the addition if one does not assume, in order to fit Felix's remarks into Theodore's scheme, that it refers to *Jesus'* baptism, but rather to the sacrament of baptism, thus: "The same Redeemer, Our Savior, insofar as he is a human being, contains both generations, conjoined in himself: the first, clearly, which he took up from the Virgin by being born, and the second, which he initiated in the [sacrament of] washing, by rising from the dead." This could mean, although does not necessarily mean, that the second birth of Jesus is his rising from the dead, but it does mean that whatever *his* second or spiritual birth is, for *us* it is the birth which occurs through adoption and is appropriated at baptism.

Bibliography

PRIMARY SOURCES

Acta conciliorum oecumenicorum, Tome 1, vol. 3. Edited by E. Schwartz. Berlin-Leipzig: W. de Gruyter, 1929.

Agobard of Lyons. *Adversum Dogma Felicis*. Edited by L. Van Acker. In *Agobardi Lugdunensis Opera Omnia, CCCM* 52, pp. 71–111. Turnhout: Brepols, 1981. Abbreviated *ADF*.

———. *De fide veritate et totius boni institutione*. Edited by L. Van Acker. In *CCCM* 52. Turnhout: Brepols, 1981.

Albari Epistula. In *CSM*, I, pp. 144–270.

Alcuini Vita. In *PL* 100:89–106. Critical edition in *MGH, Scriptores*, XV, edited by W. Arndt, pp. 182–197. Hanover: *Impensis*, Bibliopolii Hahniani, 1887.

Alcuin. *Adversus Elipandum Libri IV*. In *PL* 101:243–300. Books I and II edited by Paul V. Gonzalez, *Alcuin's 'Adversus Elipantum Libri IV,' Books I–II. Edited with an Introduction*. Ph.D. dissertation, University of Illinois at Urbana-Champaign, 1971. Abbreviated *Adv. Elip.*

———. *Adversus Felicem Urgellitanum Episcopum Libri VII*. In *PL* 101:119–230. Abbreviated *AFU*; English title, *Seven Books Against Felix of Urgel*.

———. *Carmina*. In *MGH, Poetae Latini Aevi Carolini*, I, edited by E. Duemmler, pp. 160–351. Berlin: 1881.

———. *Epistola episcoporum Franciae*. In *MGH, Concilia*, II, edited by A. Werminghoff, pp. 142–157. Berlin and Leipzig: 1906. Abbreviated *Ep. ad Hisp.*

———. *Epistolae*. In *MGH, Epistolae*, IV, edited by E. Duemmler, pp. 1–481. Berlin: 1895.

———. *De fide sanctae et individuae Trinitatis*. In *PL* 101:13–58.

———. *Interrogationes et responsiones in Genesin*. In *PL* 100:516–568.

———. *Liber Adversus Haeresin Felicis*. In *PL* 101:87–120. Also in *Liber Alcuini Contra Haeresim Felicis: Edition with an Introduction*, edited by Gary B. Blumenshine. In *Studi e testi* 285. Vatican City: Biblioteca Apostolica Vaticana, 1980. Abbreviated *LAHF* and *Libellus*.

———. *Letter to Beatus*. In J. F. Rivera Recio, "A propósito de una carta de Alcuino recientemente encontrada." *Revista Española de Teología* 1 (1941): 418–433. Text also in W. Levison, *England and the Continent in the Eighth Century*, pp. 314–322. Oxford: Clarendon Press, 1943.

Annales Mettenses Priores. In *Scriptores rerum Germanicarum in usum scholarum ex monumentis Germaniae Historicis separatim editi*, vol. 10. Edited by B. de Simson. Hanover: 1905.

Apollinaris of Laodicea. *De incarnatione Dei verbi*. *PG* 28:23–30.

Ardo. *Vita Benedicti abbatis Anianensis et Indensis autore Ardone.* Edited by G. Waitz. In *MGH, Scriptores,* vol. 15, pp. 198–220. Hanover: 1887.

Ascaricus. *Epistola.* In *CSM,* vol. 1, pp. 113–124.

Augustine of Hippo. *Contra Maximinum libri duo.* In *PL* 42:743–814. *Contra Secundinum.* Edited by J. Zycha. In *CSEL* 25, pp. 905–947. Prague: 1892.

———. *De civitate Dei.* Edited by B. Dombart and A. Kalb. In *CCSL* 47–48. Turnhout: Brepols, 1955. Abbreviated *De civ.*; English title, *City of God.*

———. *De doctrina christiana.* Edited by J. Martin. In *CCSL* 32. Turnhout: Brepols, 1962. Abbreviated *De doct.*

———. *Enchiridion de fide, spe, et caritate.* Edited by E. Evans. In *CCSL* 46. Turnhout: Brepols, 1969.

———. *Enarrationes in Psalmos.* Edited by E. Dekkers and I. Fraipont. In *CCSL* 38–40. Turnhout: Brepols, 1956.

———. *Epistolae ad Galatas expositio.* Edited by J. Divjak. In *CSEL* 84, pp. 55–141. Vienna: 1971.

———. *De Genesi ad litteram.* Edited by J. Zycha. In *CSEL* 28.1. Vienna: 1894.

———. *In Iohannis Evangelium tractatus CXXIV.* Edited by R. Willems. In *CCSL* 36. Turnhout: Brepols, 1954.

———. *De peccatorum meritis et remissione et de baptismo parvulorum ad Marcellium.* Edited by C. F. Urba and J. Zycha. In *CSEL* 60, pp. 3–151. Leipzig: 1913.

———. *De praedestinatione sanctorum.* In *PL* 44:959–992. English title, *On the Predestination of the Saints.*

———. *De trinitate.* Edited by W. J. Mountain and Fr. Glorie. In *CCSL* 50–50A. Turnhout: Brepols, 1968.

Beatus of Liebana. *Beati in Apocalipsin Libri Duodecim.* Edited by H. A. Sanders. Rome: American Academy in Rome, 1930. Also, *Sancti Beati Liebana Commentarius in Apocalypsin,* 2 vols. Edited by E. Romero-Prose. Rome: Typis Officinae Polygraphicae, 1985. Referred to in text as *Commentary on the Apocalypse.*

Beatus of Liebana and Heterius of Osma. *Adversus Elipandum Libri II.* In *PL* 96:893–1030. Also in Löfstedt, pp. 30–31. Abbreviated *Adv.Elip.*

Benedict of Aniane. *Disputatio Benedictae levitae adversus Felicianum impietatem.* In *PL* 103:1399–1411.

Braulio of Sargossa. *Ep. PL* 80:639–714.

Cassian, John. *Conlationes XXIIII.* Edited by Michael Petschenig. In *CSEL* 13. Vienna: F. Tempsky, 1886.

———. *De incarnatione Domini contra Nestorium libri VII.* Edited by Michael Petschenig. In *CSEL* 17. Vienna: F. Tempsky, 1888.

Charlemagne. *Epistola Karoli Magni ad Elipandum et episcopos Hispaniae.* In *MGH, Concilia aevi Karolini,* II, edited by A. Werminghoff, pp. 157–164. Hanover and Leipzig: 1906.

Chronicle of 754 or *Crónica muzárabe de 754.* Edited by J. E. López Perreira. Zaragoza: 1980.

Council of Cordoba of 839. *Acta.* In *Coleccion de Canones y de todos los concilios de la Iglesia de Espana y de America (en latin y castellano),* part 2, vol. 3, edited by D. Juan Tejada y Ramiro. Madrid: 1861. Also in *CSM* I, pp. 135–141.

Council of Frankfurt. *Capitulare Francofurtense*. In *MGH,Concilia aevi Karolini*, II. Edited by A. Werminghoff, pp. 165–171. Hanover and Leipzig: 1906.

Creed of Toledo I. In *El Simbolo Toledano I*. Edited by J. A. Del Aldama. Rome: Pontificiae Universitatis Gregorianae, 1934.

Creed of Toledo IV. In *Canones Apostolorum et Conciliorum Saeculorum IV, V, VI, VII*, vol. 1. Edited by H. T. Bruns. Berlin: G. Reimeri, 1839.

Dungal the Recluse. *Responsa contra perversas Claudii Taurinensis episcopi sententias*. In *PL* 105:465–530.

Einhard. *Einhardi Annales*; *Annales Mettenses Priores, anno 792*, edited by B. de Simson. In *MGH, Scriptores*, I. Edited by G. H. Pertz, pp. 135–218. Hanover: 1826.

Elipandus of Toledo. *Epistola Episcoporum Hispaniae ad Episcopos Franciae*. In *MGH, Concilia aevi Karolini*, II. Edited by A. Werminghoff, pp. 111–119. Hanover and Leipzig: 1906. Also in *CSM*, I, pp. 82–93. Abbreviated *Ep. ad Franc.*

———. *Epistola Episcoporum Hispaniae ad Karolum Magnum*. In *MHG, Concilia aevi Karolini*, II. Edited by A. Werminghoff, pp. 120–21. Hanover and Leipzig: 1906. Also in *CSM* I, pp. 93–95. Abbreviated *Ep. ad Kar.*

———. *Epistola ad Albinum*. At *Alcuini Epistolae* 166 in *MGH, Epistolae*, IV, edited by E. Duemmler, pp. 268–274. Berlin: 1895. Abbreviated *Alc.Ep.*

———. *Letter to Felix*. In *PL* 96:880–882. Also at *Alcuini Epistolae* 183, in *MGH, Epistolae*, IV, edited by E. Duemmler, pp. 307 ff. Berlin: 1895.

———. *Letter to Fidelis*. Contained in Beatus of Liebana and Heterius of Osma, *Adversus Elipandum Libri II* 1.43–44. In *PL* 96:918–919. Also in Löfstedt, I, pp. 30–31. Also in *CSM*, I, pp. 80–81.

———. *Letter to Migetius, Epistolae* 1. In H. Flórez, *España Sagrada*, vol. V. Madrid: 1750. Reprinted at *PL* 96:859–867. Also in *CSM* I, pp. 68–78.

———. *Symbolus fidei*. Contained in Beatus of Liebana and Heterius of Osma, *Adversus Elipandum Libri II* 1.40–41. In *PL* 96:916–17. Also in Löfstedt, I, pp. 27–29. Also in *CSM*, I, pp. 78–80.

Felix of Urgel. *Confessio Felicis*. In *PL* 96:881–88. Also in *MGH, Concilia aevi Karolini*, II, edited by A. Werminghoff, pp. 221–25. Hanover and Leipzig: 1906.

Gennadius. *Liber ecclesiasticorum dogmatum*. Text in *Journal of Theological Studies* 7 (1906): 89, edited by C. H. Turner. Also in *PL* 58:981.

Gregory I, Pope. *Moralia in Iob*. Edited by M. Adriaen. In *CCSL* 143, 143A, 143B.

Gregory of Elvira. *In Canticum canticorum Libri V*. Edited by J. Fraipont. In *CSEL* 69, pp. 165–210.

Gregory of Nazianzus. *Ep.* 101. In *Lettres Théologique*, edited by P. Gallay and M. Jourjon, pp. 36–69. Paris: Éditions du Cerf, 1974.

Hadrian I, Pope. First Letter to the Bishops of Spain. At *Codex Carolinus* #95, in *MGH, Epistolae*, III, edited by W. Gundlach, pp. 636–643. Berlin: 1892.

———. Second Letter to the Bishops of Spain. In *MGH, Concilia*, II, edited by A. Werminghoff, pp. 122–129. Hanover and Leipzig: 1906.

———. *Letters to Egila*. At *Codex Carolinus* #96 (first letter) and #97 (second letter). In *MGH, Epistolae*, III, edited by W. Gundlach, pp. 643–647, 648–650. Berlin: 1892.

Hincmar of Reims. *De praedestinatione dei et libero arbitrio*. In *PL* 125:65–474.

———. *De una et non trina deitate*. *PL* 125:473–618. Abbreviated *De deitate*.

Isidore of Seville. *De fide catholica contra Judaeos. PL* 83:449–538. Abbreviated *Contra Judeos.*

———. *Differentiarum Libri II. PL* 83:9–98. Abbreviated *Diff.*

———. *Etymologiae.* Edited by W. M. Lindsay. Oxford: Clarendon Press, 1911. Abbreviated *Etym.*

———. *De Viris Illustribus. PL* 83:1081–1106.

Jerome. *Tractatus in Psalmos.* Edited by D. G. Morin. In *CCSL* 78. Turnhout: Brepols, 1958. Abbreviated *In psalm.*

Jonas of Orléans. *De cultu imaginum.* In *PL* 106:306–388.

Julian of Toledo. *Apologeticum de tribus capitulis.* In *Sancti Iuliani Toletanae Sedis Episcopi Opera*, part 1, edited by J. N. Hillgarth. In *CCSL* 115, pp. 127–139. Turnhout: Brepols, 1976.

Leo I, Pope. *Epistolae contra Eutychis haeresim.* Edited by C. Silva-Tarouca. Rome: Pontificia Universitas Gregoriana, 1934.

Leo III, Pope. *Concilium Romanum.* In *MGH, Concilia aevi Karolini*, II, edited by A. Werminghoff, pp. 202–204. Hanover and Leipzig: 1906.

Lombard, Peter. *Sententiae in IV Libris Distinctae*, third edition, 2 volumes. Grottaferrata: Editiones Collegii S. Bonaventurae ad Claras Aquas, 1971 (vol. 1, pts. 1 and 2) and 1981 (vol. 2).

Mozarabic Liturgical Texts. In *Le Liber Ordinum en usage dans l'église wisigothique et mozarabe d'Espagne du Ve au XIe siècle*, edited by M. Ferotin. Vol. 5 of the *Monumenta ecclesia liturgica*. Paris: Firmin-Didot, 1904. Also in *Le Liber Mozarabicus Sacramentorum et les manuscrits mozarabes*, edited by M. Ferotin. Vol. 6 of the *Monumenta ecclesia liturgica*. Paris: Firmin-Didot, 1912. Also in N. Prado. *Manual de liturgía hispanovisigótica o mozárabe.* Madrid: Editorial Voluntad S.A., 1927. Also in José Vives, *Oracional Visigótico.* Barcelona: Biblioteca Balmos, 1946.

A Nestorian Collection of Christological Texts, 2 vols. Edited and translated by L. Abramowski and A. E. Goodman. Cambridge: Cambridge University Press, 1972.

Paulinus of Aquileia. *Paulini Aquileiensis Opera Omnia Pars I: Contra Felicem Libri Tres*, edited by Dag Norberg. In *CCCM* vol. 95. Turnhout: Brepols, 1990. Abbreviated *CF* and *Three Books Against Felix.*

———. *Libellus sacrosyllabus Episcoporum Italiae.* In *PL* 99:151–182. Also in *MGH, Concilia aevi Karolini*, II, edited by A. Werminghoff, pp. 130–142. Hanover and Leipzig: 1906.

Poeta Saxonis. *Annalium de gestis B. Caroli magni imperatoris libri quinque.* In *MGH, Scriptores*, I, edited by G. H. Pertz, pp. 227–279. Hanover: 1826.

Radbertus, Paschasius. *Expositio in Psalmum XLIV. PL* 120:993–1060.

Saul of Cordova. *Letter to Paul Alvarus.* In *España Sagrada*, XI, edited by H. Flórez. Madrid: 1750. Also in *CSM*, I, pp. 222–224.

Tertullian. *Adversus Praxean liber.* Edited and translated by Ernest Evans. London: Society for the Preservation of Christian Knowledge, 1948.

Theodore of Mopsuestia. *Theodori Mopsuesteni expositionis in Psalmos Iuliano Aeclanensi interprete in Latinum versae quae supersunt.* Edited by Lucas De Coninck. In *CCSL* 88A. Turnhout: Brepols, 1977.

———. *Commentary of Theodore of Mopsuestia on the Lord's Prayer and on the Sacrament of Baptism and the Eucharist*. Edited and translated by A. Mingana. In *Woodbrooke Studies*, vol. 6. Cambridge: Heffer and Sons, 1933.

Timothy I, Nestorian Patriarch. *Apology of Timothy I*. Edited and translated by A. Mingana. In *Woodbrooke Studies*, vol. 2. Cambridge: Heffer and Sons, 1928.

———. *Timothei Patriarchae I Epistolae*. In *CSCO* 75, vol. 1. Edited and translated by O. Braun. Louvain: 1953.

Tyconius. *Tyconii Afri in Apocalypsin*. In *The Turin Fragments of Tyconius' Commentary on Revelation*, edited by Francesco LoBue, prepared for press after his decease by G. G. Willis. Cambridge: Cambridge University Press, 1963. Reprinted Liechtenstein: Kraus, 1978.

———. *Tyconius: The Book of Rules*. Edited by William Babcock. Ithaca, N.Y.: Scholars Press, 1989.

Vita Beati. In *PL* 96:887–894.

STUDIES

Abadal y de Vinyals, D. Ramón d'. *La batalla del adopcionismo en la desintegración de la iglesia visigoda*. Barcelona: 1949.

Amann, Emille. "L'adoptianisme Espagnol du VIIIè siècle." *Revue des Sciences Religieuses* 16 (1936): 285–302.

———. *L'Époque carolingienne*. Vol. 6 of *Histoire de l'Église depuis les origines jusqu'à nos jours*. Edited by Augustin Fliche and Victor Martin. Paris: Bloud & Gay, 1937.

Ansprenger, F. "Untersuchungen zum adoptianistischen Streit des 8' Jahrhundert." Ph.D. dissertation. Frei Universität Berlin, 1952.

Babcock, William S. "Christian Culture and Christian Tradition in Roman North Africa." In *Schools of Thought in the Christian Tradition*, edited by Patrick Henry, 31–48. Philadelphia: Fortress Press, 1984.

Bach, Joseph von. *Die Dogmengeschichte des Mittelalters*. W. Braumuller, 1873.

Beumann, Helmut, ed. *Lebenswerk und Nachleben*, vol. 1 of *Karl der Grosse*. Düsseldorf: L. Schwann, 1965.

Bischoff, Bernard. "Aus Alkuins Erdentagen." *Medievalia et Humanistica* 14 (1962): 31–37. Reprinted in *Mittelälterliche Studien* 2. Stuttgart: Hiersemann, 1967.

Blasquez, J. M. "The Possible African Origin of Iberian Christianity." *Classical Folia* 23 (1969): 3–31.

Böhmer, J. and Mühlbacher. *Die Regesten des Kaiserreichs unter den Karolingern, 751–918, Regesta Imperii* I, 2nd ed. Innsbruck: Wagner, 1908. Reprinted Hildesheim: G. Olms, 1966.

Bright, P. *The Book of Rules of Tyconius: Its Inner Purpose and Logic*. Notre Dame, Ind.: Notre Dame Press, 1989.

Brou, Louis, O.S.B. "Bulletin de Liturgie Mozarabe, 1936–1948." *Hispania Sacra Revista de Historia Eclesiastica* 2 (1949): 459–484.

de Bruyne, D. "Integrité et orthodoxie des messes mozarabe." *Revue Bénédictine* 30 (1913): 428–430.

————. "Un document de la controverse adoptianiste en Espagne vers l'an 800," *Revue d'histoire ecclésiastique* 27, pt. 2 (1931): 307–312.

Bullough, Donald A. "Alcuin and the Kingdom of Heaven: Liturgy, Theology, and the Carolingian Age." In *Carolingian Essays: Andrew W. Mellon Lectures in Early Christian Studies*, edited by Uta-Renate Blumenthal, 1–69. Washington, D.C.: Catholic University of America Press, 1983.

Burns, Paul C. *The Christology in Hilary of Poitiers' Commentary on Matthew*. Rome: Institutum Patristicum Augustinianum, 1981.

Cabaniss, Allen. "The Heresiarch Felix." *Catholic Historical Review* 39 (1953): 129–141.

Cabrol, F. "Le 'Liber Ordinum' et la liturgie mozarabe," *Revue des Questions Historiques* 77 (1905): 173–185.

Cantarino, Vincente. *Entre monjes y musulmanes: El conflicto que fue España*. Madrid: Alhambra, 1978.

Cavadini, John C. "The Sources and Theology of Alcuin's Treatise *De fide*." *Traditio* 46 (1991): 123–146.

Colbert, E. P. *The Martyrs of Cordoba (850–859)*. Washington, D.C.: Catholic University of America Press, 1962.

Collins, Roger. *The Arab Conquest of Spain*. Oxford and Cambridge, Mass.: Basil Blackwell, 1989.

————. *Early Medieval Spain: Unity in Diversity, 400–1000*. New York: St. Martin's Press, 1983.

de las Cagigas, I. *Los Mozárabes*, 2 vols. Madrid: Consejo Superior de Investigaciones Escelier, 1948.

Del Alamo, O.S.B., Mateo. "Los Commentarios de Beato al Apocalipsis y Elipando." In *Miscellanea Giovanni Mercati*, vol. 2, pp. 16–33. *Studi e testi* 122. Vatican City: Biblioteca Apostolica Vaticana, 1946.

Di Berardino, Angelo, ed. *Encyclopedia of the Early Church*. Translated by Adrian Walford. New York: Oxford University Press, 1992.

Díaz y Díaz, Manuel C. *De Isidoro al siglo XI: Ocho estudios sobre la vida literaria peninsular*. Barcelona: Ediciones El Albir, 1976.

Dozy, Reinhart P. Anne. *Recherches sur l'histoire et la Littérature en Espagne pendant le moyen âge*, 3rd edition, 2 vols. Paris/Leiden: 1881. Reprinted Amsterdam: Oriental Press, 1965.

————. *Supplément aux dictionnaires arabes*, 2 vols. Leiden: 1881.

Drobner, Hubertus, R. *Person-Exegese und Christologie bei Augustinus: zur Herkunft der Formel "Una Persona"*. Vol. 8 of *Philosophia Patrum: Interpretations of Patristic Texts*, edited by J. H. Waszink and J. C. M. van Winden. Leiden: E. J. Brill, 1986.

Duckett, Eleanor Shipley. *Alcuin, Friend of Charlemagne: His World and His Work*. Hamden, Conn.: Shoestring Press, 1965.

Dufourcq, Charles E. *España y Africa durante la Edad Media*. Barcelona: 1976.

Ellard, Gerald. *Master Alcuin, Liturgist: A Partner of our Piety*. Chicago: Loyola University Press, 1956.

Enhueber, J. B. *Dissertatio dogmatica-historica qua contra Christianum Walchium adoptionis in Christo homine assertores Felicem et Elipandum merito ab Alcuino Nestorianismi fuisse petitos, ostenditur*. In *PL* 101: 337–438.

Favier, H. *Essai historique sur Laidrad*. Lyon: 1898.

Ferrua, Antonio. "Ascarico." In *Enciclopedia Cattolica*, vol. 2, col. 82. Vatican City: Ente per l'Enciclopedia cattolica e per il Libro cattolico, 1949.

Flórez, H. *Memorias de las Reynas Catholicas*, 2 vols. Madrid: 1761. Reprinted Madrid: Aguilar, 1964.

Fontaine, Jacques. "Fins et moyens de l'enseignement ecclésiastique dans l'Espagne Wisigothique." In *La scuola nell'Occidente latino dell'alto medioevo*. Acts of the *Settimane di studio del Centro italiano di studi sull'alto medioevo XIX*, 1971. Spoleto: 1972. Reprinted in J. Fontaine. *Culture et spiritualité en Espagne du IVe au VIIe siècle*. London: Variorum Reprints, 1986.

———. "King Sisebut's *Vita Desiderii* and the Political Function of Visigothic Hagiography." In Edward James, ed., *Visigothic Spain: New Approaches*, pp. 93–129. Oxford: Clarendon Press, 1980.

Fuhrmann, Horst. "Studien zur Geschichte mittelalterlicher Patriarchate." *Zeitschrift der Savigny-Stiftung für Rechtsgeschichte* 70 (1953): 112–176.

Gams, P. B. *Die Kirchengeschichte von Spanien*. Regensburg: Joseph Manz, 1874.

García Moreno, L. A. *Prosopografia del Reino Visogodo de Toledo*. Salamanca: Universidad de Salamanca, 1974.

García Villada, Zacarías. *Historia eclesiástica de España*, 5 vols. Madrid: Razon y Fe, 1929–1936.

García Villoslada, R., editor. *La iglesia en la España Romana y Visigoda*. Vol. 1 of *Historia de la iglesia de España*. Madrid: Razon y Fe, 1979.

Gaudel, A. "La théologie de l'‘Assumptus Homo’: Histoire et valeur doctrinale." *Revue des Sciences Religieuses* 17 (1937): 64–90, 214–234.

Glick, Thomas F. *Islamic and Christian Spain in the Early Middle Ages*. Princeton, N.J.: Princeton University Press, 1979.

Greer, Rowan A., III. *The Captain of Our Salvation: A Study in the Patristic Exegesis of Hebrews*. Tubingen: Mohr, 1973.

———. "The Image of God and the Prosopic Union in Nestorius' *Bazaar of Heracleides*." In *Lux in Lumine*, edited by R. A. Norris, Jr., 46–61. New York: Seabury Press, 1966.

———. *Theodore of Mopsuestia: Exegete and Theologian*. Westminster: Faith Press, 1961.

Gregg, R., and D. Groh. *Early Arianism: A View of Salvation*. Philadelphia: Fortress Press, 1981.

Grillmeier, Alois, S.J. *Christ in Christian Tradition*. Vol. 1, *From the Apostolic Age to Chalcedon*, translated by John Bowden, 2nd revised edition. Atlanta: John Knox Press, 1975. Vol. 2, *From Chalcedon (451) to Gregory the Great (590–604)*, part 1, *From Chalcedon to Justinian I*, translated by P. Allen and J. Cawte, vol. 1 and vol. 2, pt. 1, 2nd revised ed. Atlanta: John Knox Press, 1987.

Grössler, A. *Die Ausrottung des Adoptianismus in Reiche Karls des Grossen*. Eisleben: 1879.

Hahn, T. *Tyconius-Studien*. Leipzig: Dieterich, 1918.

Halphen, L. *Charlemagne et l'empire carolingien*. Paris: A. Michel, 1947.

Härdelin, A. "An Epithalamium for Nuns: Imagery and Spirituality in Paschasius Radbertus' Exposition of Psalm 44(45)." In *In Quest of the Kingdom*, edited by A. Härdelin. *Bibliotheca Theologiae Practicae* 48. Stockholm: 1991.

Harnack, A. *History of Dogma*, 7 vols. Translated from the 3rd German edition by Neil Buchanan. New York: Dover, 1961.

Hauck, Albert. *Kirchengeschichte Deutschlands*, vol. 2. Berlin: Akademie-Verlag, 1954.

Hefele, K., and H. LeClercq. *Histoire des Conciles d'après les documents originaux*, 8 vols. Paris: Letouzey et Ané, 1910.

Heil, Wilhelm. *Alkuinstudien I: Zur Chronologie und Bedeutung des Adoptianismusstreites*. Düsseldorf: L. Schwann, 1970.

———. "Der Adoptianismus, Alcuin, und Spanien." In *Das Geistige Leben*, edited by B. Bischoff. Vol. 2 of *Karl der Grosse: Lebenswerke und Nachleben*, 5 vols. Edited by H. Beumann and B. Bischoff. Düsseldorf: L. Schwann, 1965. Abbreviated as "Adoptianismus."

Iguanez, D. M. "Un frammento visigotica del secolo VIII del "De Trinitate" di S. Agostino." *Miscellanea Cassinese* 9 (1931): 1–4.

Imamuddin, S. M. *Some Aspects of the Socio-Economic and Cultural History of Muslim Spain, 711–1492 AD*. Leiden: Brill, 1965.

Jackson, Gabriel. *The Making of Medieval Spain*. New York: Harcourt, Brace, Jovanovich, 1972.

James, Edward, ed. *Visigothic Spain: New Approaches*. Oxford: Clarendon Press, 1980.

Jugie, M. "Adoptiens." *DHGE*, vol. 1, col. 586–590. Paris: 1912.

Kantorowicz, Ernst H. *The King's Two Bodies: A Study in Medieval Political Theology*. Princeton, N.J.: Princeton University Press, 1957.

Kelly, J. N. D. *Early Christian Doctrines*, 2nd ed. New York: Harper and Row, 1960.

King, P. D. *Law and Society in the Visigothic Kingdom*. Cambridge: Cambridge University Press, 1972.

Kleinclauz, Arthur. *Alcuin*. Paris: Société d'Édition Les Belles Lettres, 1948.

Knowles, David, and D. Obolensky. *The Middle Ages*, vol. 2 of *The Christian Centuries: A New History of the Catholic Church*, edited by L. J. Rogier. New York: McGraw-Hill, 1968.

Levi della Vida, G. "I Mozarabi tra Occidente e Islam." *Settimane di studi dell Centro italiano sulla'alto medioevo* 12 (1965): 667–695.

Lévi-Provençal, Evariste. *Histoire de l'Espagne musulmane: 711–1031*, 3 vols. Vol. 1: *La Conquête et l'Émirat Hispano-Umaiyade (710–912)*. Paris and Leiden: G.-P. Maisonneuve, 1950–53.

Levison, W. *England and the Continent in the Eighth Century*. Oxford, Clarendon Press, 1946.

McCracken, George E., editor and translator, with the assistance of Allen Cabaniss. *Early Medieval Theology*, vol. 9 of the Library of Christian Classics. Philadelphia: Westminster Press, 1957.

MacDonald, J. A. *Authority and Reason in the Early Middle Ages*. London: Oxford University Press, 1933.

Madóz, José, S. J. "Contrastes y discrepancias entre el 'Liber de variis quaestionibus' y San Isidoro de Sevilla." *Estudios eclesiásticos* 24 (1950): 435–458.

———. "Los 'Excerpta Vincentii Lirinensis' en las controversia adopcionista." *Revista Española de Teología* 3 (1943): 475–483.

————. "El Florilegio Patristico del II Concilio de Sevilla." In *Miscellanea Isidoriana*, pp. 177–220. Rome: 1936.

————. "Le symbole du IVe Concile de Tolède." *Revue d'Histoire Ecclésiastique* 34 (1938): 5–20.

————. *Le symbole du XIe Concile de Tolède: ses sources, sa date, sa valeur*. Louvain: Spicilegium sacrum Lovaniense, 1938.

————. "La teología de la Trinidad en los símbolos Toledanos." *Revista Española de Teología* 4 (1944): 457–477.

————. "Una obra de Félix de Urgel, falsamente adjudicada a San Isidoro de Sevilla." *Estudios eclesiásticos* 23 (1949): 147–168.

Magnin, E. *L'Église Wisigothique au septième siècle*. Paris: Librairie Alphonse Picard et Fils, 1912.

Martínez-Díez, Gonzalo. *La colección Canonica Hispana*, 4 vols. to date. Madrid: Consejo Superio de Investigaciones Cientificas, Instituto Enrique Florez, 1966–1984.

Menéndez Pelayo, Marcelino. *Historia de los Heterodóxos Españoles*, vol. 1 of *España romana y visigoda. Periodo de la Reconquista. Erasmistas y protestantes*. Madrid: La Editorial Católica, 1956. Reprint of 1880 edition.

Menéndez Pidal, Ramón, editor. *Historia de España*, 13 vols. to date. Madrid: Espasa Calpe, 1940–1980.

Millet-Gérard, Dominique. *Chrétiens mozarabes et culture islamique dans L'Espagne des VIIIe–IXe siècles*. Paris: Études Augustiniennes, 1984.

Monceaux, Paul. *Histoire littéraire de L'Afrique Chrétienne depuis les origines jusqu'à l'invasion Arabe*, 7 vols. Paris: E. Leroux, 1901. Reprinted by *Culture et Civilization*. Brussels, 1963.

Monnier, F. *Alcuin et Charlemagne: avec des fragments d'un commentaire inédit d'Alcuin sur Saint Matthieu, et d'autres pieces publiées pour la première fois*, 2nd. ed. Paris: Henri Plon, 1863.

Morin, D. G. "Un évêque de Cordoue inconnu et deux opuscules inédits de l'an 764." *Revue Bénédictine* 15 (1898): 289–295.

————. "Un traité inédite du IV siècle. Le 'De similitudine carnis peccati' de l'évêque S. Pacien de Barcelone." *Revue Bénédictine* 29 (1912): 1–28. Text in *Études, textes et découvertes* I, pp. 1–150. Paris: 1913.

Murphy, F. X. "Julian of Toledo and the Condemnation of Monothelitism in Spain." In *Mélanges Joseph de Ghellinck, S.J.*, vol. 1, pp. 361–373. Gembloux: Éditions J. Duculot, S.A., 1951.

Neander, A. *General History of the Christian Religion and Church*, 3 vols. Translated from the German by J. Torrey. Boston: Crocker and Brewster, 1872.

————. *Lectures on the History of Christian Dogmas*, 2 vols. Edited by J. L. Jacobi. Translated from the German by J. E. Ryland. London: Bell and Daldy, 1866.

Noble, Thomas F. X. *The Republic of St. Peter: The Birth of the Papal State, 680–825*. Philadelphia: University of Pennsylvania Press, 1984.

O'Callaghan, Joseph F. *A History of Medieval Spain*. Ithaca, N.Y.: Cornell University Press, 1975.

Orlandis, José. *Historia de España: La España Visigótica*. Madrid: Gredos, 1977.

Ott, L. "Das Konzil von Ephesus (431) in der Theologie der Frühscholastik."

In *Theologie in Geschichte und Gegenwart*, edited by J. Auer and H. Volk, pp. 279–308. Munich: K. Zink, 1957.

Pelikan, Jaroslav J. *The Emergence of the Catholic Tradition, 100–600* and *The Growth of Medieval Theology, 600–1300*, vol. 1 and vol. 3 of *The Christian Tradition: A History of the Development of Doctrine*. Chicago: University of Chicago Press, 1971, 1978.

Perez, J. de J. *La Christología en los Símbolos Toledanos IV, VI, y XI*. Rome: Typis Pont, Universitatis Gregorianae, 1939.

Quilliet, H. "Adoptianisme au VIIIe siècle." *DTC*, vol. 1, pt. 1, pp. 403–413. Paris: 1930.

Ramsay, H. L. "Le commentaire de l'Apocalypse par Beatus de Liebana." *Revue d'Histoire et de Littérature Religieuses* 7 (1902): 419–447.

Rivera Recio, Juan Francisco. *El Adopcionismo en España (s. VIII): Historia y Doctrina*. Toledo: Seminario Conciliar de San Ildefonso, 1980.

———. *Los Arzobispos de Toledo*. Toledo: Diputación Provincial, 1973.

———. "La controversia adopcionista del Siglo VIII y la Ortodoxia de la Liturgia Mozárabe." *Ephemerides Liturgicae* 6 (1933): 506–536.

———. "La doctrina de la adopción de Cristo-hombre y sus argumentos en los escritos adopcionistas españoles del siglo VIII." *Revista Ecclesiastica* 8 (1934): 643–657 (part one); 9 (1935): 3–17 (part two), 129–139 (part three).

———. "Doctrina trinitaria en el ambiente heterodoxo del primer siglo mozárabe." *Revista Española de Teologia* 4 (1944): 193–210.

———. "Elipand." *DHGE* 15, cols. 204–214. Paris: 1963.

———. *Elipando de Toledo*. Toledo: Editorial Católica Toledana, 1940.

———. *Estudios Sobre La Liturgía Mozárabe*. Toledo: Diputación Provincial, 1965.

———. "La maternidad divina de María en una controversia cristológica española de fines del siglo VIII." *Academia P. Bibliográfica-Mariana*, tercera parte, pp. 5–37. Lerida: 1933.

———. "La theologia de la Trinidad en los Simbolos Toledanos." *Revista Española de Teologia* 4 (1944): 457–477.

Schäferdiek, Knut. *Die Kirche in den Reichen der Westgoten und Sueven bis zur Errichtung der westgotischen katholischen Staatskirche*. Berlin: de Gruyter, 1967.

———. "Der adoptianische Streit in Rahmen der spanischen Kirchengeschichte." *Zeitschrift fur Kirchengeschichte* 80 (1969): 291–311, and 81 (1970): 1–16.

Schmid, Joseph. *Die Osterberechnung in der abendlandischen Kirche*. Vol. 9, pt. 1 of *Strassburger Theologishen Studien*. 1907.

Simonet, F. J. *Historia de los Mozárabes de España*, 4 vols. Madrid: Ediciones Turner, 1903. Reprinted 1983.

Solano, Jesùs, S. J. "El Concilio de Calcedonia y la controversia adoptionista del siglo VIII en España." In *Das Konzil von Chalkedon: Geschichte und Gegenwart*, edited by A. Grillmeier and H. Bacht, 841–879. Wurzburg: Echter-Verlag, 1952.

Thompson, E. A. *The Goths in Spain*. Oxford: Oxford University Press, 1969.

Tixeront, J. *La fin de l'âage patristique (430–800)*. Vol. 1 of *Histoire des dogmes dans l'antiquité chrétienne*, 3 vols. 6th ed. Paris: J. Gabalda, 1922.

Vega, A. C. "El 'Liber de variis quaestionibus' no es de Félix de Urgel." *Ciudad de Dios* 161 (1949): 217–228.

Verwilghen, Albert. *Christologie et spiritualité selon Saint Augustine: l'hymne aux Philippiens.* Paris: Beauchesne, 1985.

Wallach, Luitpold. *Alcuin and Charlemagne: Studies in Carolingian History and Literature,* 2nd ed. Ithaca, N.Y.: Cornell University Press, 1968.

Werner, Karl. *Alcuin und sein Jahrhundert.* Paderborn: F. Schoningh, 1881.

Wolf, Kenneth Baxter. "The Earliest Spanish Christian Views of Islam." *Church History* 55 (1986): 281–293.

Wolff, Philippe. "L'Aquitaine et ses marges." In *Personlichkeit und Geschichte,* Vol. 1 of *Karl der Grosse: Lebenswerke und Nachleben,* 5 vols. Edited by H. Beumann and B. Bischoff. Düsseldorf: L. Schwann, 1966–68.

Ziegler, Aloysius K. *Church, and State in Visigothic Spain.* Washington, D.C.: Catholic University of America Press, 1930.

Index

Abelard, Peter (1079–1142), 1
Agobard, archbishop of Lyons (ca.769–840, archbishop from 816), 82, 83, 108; *Adversum Dogma Felicis*, 188 n.47; *De fide veritate et totius boni institutione*, 176 n.61
adoption, relation to assumption, 32–33, 86–87, 125–26, 153 n.62, 153 n.71, 191 n.67
Adoptionism: and Cordoba, 148 n.25, 183 n.1; and Nestorianism, 5–6, 8–9, 68–69, 74, 90, 100, 127, 134 n.19, 158 n.108, 163 n.136, 195 n.88, 206 n.9; as a concession to Islam, 27, 39–41, 149 n.30; eastward spread, 71–72, 184 n.7; relation to Trinitarian teaching, 101–2; types of, 1
Aix, Council of (799), 1, 82, 89–90, 188 n.47
Alaric II (King 484–507), 2
Alcuin of York (ca.734–804): accuracy of his report of Felix's positions, 108–10; *Adversus Elipandum Libri IV*, 196 n.102; *Adversus Felicem Urgellitanum Episcopum Libri VII*, 82, 88–102; *De fide sanctae et individuae Trinitatis*, 204 nn.144, 145; *Interrogationes et responsiones in Genesin*, 202 n.126; Letter to the Bishops of Spain, 77–79, 91; Letter 23, to Felix, 81, 83, 89; *Liber Contra Haeresim Felicis* (*Libellus*), 81, 85–88
Ambrose, bishop of Milan (ca.339–97, bishop from 374): *Commentary on Luke*, 61
anti-adoptionist party, 25, 45, 147 n.14, 15, 148 n.26, 167 n.9
Apollinaris of Laodicea (ca.310–ca.390), 185 n.17
Arians, Arianism, 1, 2, 132 nn.6, 7, 165 n.145, 205 n.150
Arius (ca.250–ca.336), 165 n.145, 196 n.98
Ascaricus, 25, 147 n.15
Asturia, 45, 46, 147 n.14, 149 n.29, 183 n.1

Augustine, bishop of Hippo (354–430, bishop from 395): *De civitate Dei*, 68, 179 n.95; *Contra Maximinum*, 92, 198 n.110, 204 n.140; *Contra Secundinum*, 157 n.103; *Enarrationes in Psalmos*, 175 n.56; *Enchiridion*, 34, 155 n.81, 188 n.40, 204 n.140; *Epistolae ad Galatas expositio*, 170 n.22, 179 n.99; *De Genesi ad litteram*, 202 n.126; *In Johannis Evangelium tractatus CXXIV*, 30, 153 n.71, 194 n.84; *De peccatorum meritis et remissione*, 204 n.140; *De praedestinatione sanctorum*, 152 n.53; *De trinitate*, 99, 143 n.76, 144 n.81, 149 n.34, 159 n.109, 172 n.32, 204 nn.144, 145

Beatus of Liebana, 7–8, 24–25; and monophysitism, 47, 48, 51, 170 n.23; christology, 47–52; ecclesiology, 52–59; Eucharistic theology, 180 n.101; *Adversus Elipandum Libri II*, 46–47, 53–54, 73; *Commentary on the Apocalypse*, 46, 52–53, 166 n.1, 168 nn.10, 11, 169 nn.12, 13; life, 45–46; soteriology, 64–67
Benedict of Aniane (ca.750–821), 82, 115, 184 n.7, 185 n.10; *Disputatio*, 128–30, 191 n.64
Bonosus, 29, 151 nn.48, 49, 165 n.45, 171 n.29

Casiani, 13
Cassian, John (ca.360–435), 60; *De incarnatione Domini*, 80, 202 n.125; 203 n.132
Cassiodorus (ca.485–ca.580), 95
Chalcedon, Council of (451), 5, 6, 44, 47, 133 nn.16, 17, 158 n.108, 171 n.28
Charlemagne (ca.742–814), 1, 187 n.34; Letter to Elipandus, 77
Christology: Christ as Mediator, 37, 55–56, 58–59, 65–66, 121, 208 n.5; self-emptying of the Word, 28, 33–36, 41–43, 57–60,

University of Pennsylvania Press
MIDDLE AGES SERIES
Edward Peters, General Editor

F. R. P. Akehurst, trans. *The* Coutumes de Beauvaisis *of Philippe de Beaumanoir.* 1992

Peter Allen. *The Art of Love: Amatory Fiction from Ovid to the* Romance of the Rose. 1992

David Anderson. *Before the Knight's Tale: Imitation of Classical Epic in Boccaccio's* Teseida. 1988

Benjamin Arnold. *Count and Biship in Medieval Germany: A Study of Regional Power, 1100–1350.* 1991.

Mark C. Bartusis. *The Late Byzantine Army: Arms and Society, 1204–1453.* 1992

J. M. W. Bean. *From Lord to Patron: Lordship in Late Medieval England.* 1990

Uta-Renate Blumenthal. *The Investiture Controversy: Church and Monarchy from the Ninth to the Twelfth Centuyry.* 1988

Daniel Bornstein, trans. *Dino Compagni's* Chronicle *of Florence.* 1986

Maureen Barry McCann Boulton. *The Song in the Story: Lyric Insertions in French Narrative Fiction, 1200–1400.* 1993

Betsy Bowden. *Chaucer Aloud: The Varieties of Textual Interpretation.* 1987

James William Brodman. *Ransoming Captives in Crusader Spain: The Order of Merced on the Christian-Islamic Frontier.* 1986

Kevin Brownlee and Sylvia Huot, eds. *Rethinking the* Romance of the Rose*: Text, Image, Reception.* 1992

Matilda Tomaryn Bruckner. *Shaping Romance: Truth and Closure in Twelfth-Century French Fictions.* 1993.

Otto Brunner (Howard Kaminsky and James Van Horn Melton, eds. and trans.). Land *and Lordship: Structures of Governance in Medieval Austria.* 1992

Robert I. Burns, S.J., ed. *Emperor of Culture: Alfonso X the Learned of Castile and His Thirteenth-Century Renaissance.* 1990

David Burr. *Olivi and Franciscan Poverty: The Origins of the* Usus Pauper *Controversy.* 1989

Thomas Cable. *The English Alliterative Tradition.* 1991

Anthony K. Cassell and Victoria Kirkham, eds. and trans. *Diana's Hunt/Caccia di Diana: Boccaccio's First Fiction.* 1991

Brigitte Cazelles. *The Lady as Saint: A Collection of French Hagiographic Romances of the Thirteenth Century.* 1991

John C. Cavadini. *The Last Christology of the West: Adoptionism in Spain and Gaul, 785–820.* 1993

Karen Cherewatuk and Ulrike Wiethaus, eds. *Dear Sister: Medieval Women and the Epistolary Genre.* 1993

Anne L. Clark. *Elisabeth of Schönau: A Twelfth-Century Visionary.* 1992

Willene B. Clark and Meradith T. McMunn, eds. *Beasts and Birds of the Middle Ages: The Bestiary and Its Legacy.* 1989

Richard C. Dales. *The Scientific Achievement of the Middle Ages.* 1973

Charles T. Davis. *Dante's Italy and Other Essays.* 1984

Katherine Fischer Drew, trans. *The Burgundian Code.* 1972

Katherine Fischer Drew, trans. *The Laws of the Salien Franks.* 1991

Katherine Fischer Drew, trans. *The Lombard Laws.* 1973

Nancy Edwards. *The Archaeology of Early Medieval Ireland.* 1990

Margaret J. Ehrhart. *The Judgment of the Trojan Prince Paris in Medieval Literature.* 1987

Richard K. Emmerson and Ronald B. Herzman. *The Apocalyptic Imagination in Medieval Literature.* 1992

Theodore Evergates. *Medieval Society: Documents from the County of Champagne.* 1993

Felipe Fernández-Armesto. *Before Columbus: Exploration and Colonization from the Mediterranean to the Atlantic, 1229–1492.* 1987

Robert D. Fulk. *A History of Old English Meter.* 1992

Patrick J. Geary. *Aristocracy in Provence: The Rhône Basin at the Dawn of the Carolingian Age.* 1985

Peter Heath. *Allegory and Philosophy in Avicenna (Ibn Sînâ), with a Translation of the Book of the Prophet Muḥammad's Ascent to Heaven.* 1992

J. N. Hillgarth, ed. *Christianity and Paganism, 350–750: The Conversion of Western Europe.* 1986

Richard C. Hoffmann. *Land, Liberties, and Lordship in a Late Medieval Countryside: Agrarian Structures and Change in the Duchy of Wrocław.* 1990

Robert Hollander. *Boccaccio's Last Fiction: Il Corbaccio.* 1988

Edward B. Irving, Jr. *Rereading* Beowulf. 1989

C. Stephen Jaeger. *The Origins of Courtliness: Civilizing Trends and the Formation of Courtly Ideals, 939–1210.* 1985

William Chester Jordan. *The French Monarchy and the Jews: From Philip Augustus to the Last Capetians.* 1989

William Chester Jordan. *From Servitude to Freedom: Manumission in the Sénonais in the Thirteenth Century.* 1986

Ellen E. Kittell. *From* Ad Hoc *to Routine: A Case Study in Medieval Bureaucracy.* 1991

Alan C. Kors and Edward Peters, eds. *Witchcraft in Europe, 1100–1700: A Documentary History.* 1972

Barbara M. Kreutz. *Before the Normans: Southern Italy in the Ninth and Tenth Centuries.* 1992

E. Ann Matter. *The Voice of My Beloved: The Song of Songs in Western Medieval Christianity.* 1990

María Rosa Menocal. *The Arabic Role in Medieval Literary History: A Forgotten Heritage.* 1987

Alastair J. Minnis. *Medieval Theory of Authorship: Scholastic Literary Attitudes in the Later Middle Ages.* 1988

Lawrence Nees. *A Tainted Mantle: Hercules and the Classical Tradition at the Carolingian Court.* 1991

Lynn H. Nelson, trans. *The Chronicle of San Juan de la Peña: A Fourteenth-Century Official History of the Crown of Aragon.* 1991

Charlotte A. Newman. *The Anglo-Norman Nobility in the Reign of Henry I: The Second Generation.* 1988

Joseph F. O'Callaghan. *The Cortes of Castile-León, 1188–1350.* 1989

Joseph F. O'Callaghan. *The Learned King: The Reign of Alfonso X of Castile.* 1993

William D. Paden, ed. *The Voice of the Trobairitz: Perspectives on the Women Troubadours.* 1989

Edward Peters. *The Magician, the Witch, and the Law.* 1982

Edward Peters, ed. *Christian Society and the Crusades, 1198–1229: Sources in Translation, including The* Capture of Damietta *by Oliver of Paderborn.* 1971

Edward Peters, ed. *The First Crusade: The* Chronicle of Fulcher of Chartres *and Other Source Materials.* 1971

Edward Peters, ed. *Heresy and Authority in Medieval Europe.* 1980

James M. Powell. *Albertanus of Brescia: The Pursuit of Happiness in the Early Thirteenth Century.* 1992

James M. Powell. *Anatomy of a Crusade, 1213–1221.* 1986

Jean Renart (Patricia Terry and Nancy Vine Durling, trans.). *The Romance of the Rose or Guillaume de Dole.* 1993

Michael Resler, trans. Erec *by Hartmann von Aue.* 1987

Pierre Riché (Michael Idomir Allen, trans.). *The Carolingians: A Family Who Forged Europe.* 1993

Pierre Riché (Jo Ann McNamara, trans.). *Daily Life in the World of Charlemagne.* 1978

Jonathan Riley-Smith. *The First Crusade and the Idea of Crusading.* 1986

Joel T. Rosenthal. *Patriarchy and Families of Privilege in Fifteenth-Century England.* 1991

Steven D. Sargent, ed. and trans. *On the Threshold of Exact Science: Selected Writings of Anneliese Maier on Late Medieval Natural Philosophy.* 1982

Sarah Stanbury. *Seeing the* Gawain-*Poet: Description and the Act of Perception.* 1992

Thomas C. Stillinger. *The Song of Troilus: Lyric Authority in the Medieval Book.* 1992

Susan Mosher Stuard. *A State of Deference: Ragusa/Dubrovnik in the Medieval Centuries.* 1992

Susan Mosher Stuard, ed. *Women in Medieval History and Historiography.* 1987

Susan Mosher Stuard, ed. *Women in Medieval Society.* 1976

Jonathan Sumption. *The Hundred Years War: Trial by Battle.* 1992

Ronald E. Surtz. *The Guitar of God: Gender, Power, and Authority in the Visionary World of Mother Juana de la Cruz (1481–1534).* 1990

William H. TeBrake, *A Plague of Insurrection: Popular Politics and Peasant Revolt in Flanders, 1323–1328.* 1993

Patricia Terry, trans. *Poems of the Elder Edda.* 1990

Hugh M. Thomas. *Vassals, Heiresses, Crusaders, and Thugs: The Century of Angevin Yorkshire, 1154–1216.* 1993

Frank Tobin. *Meister Eckhart: Thought and Language.* 1986

Ralph V. Turner. *Men Raised from the Dust: Administrative Service and Upward Mobility in Angevin England.* 1988

Harry Turtledove, trans. *The* Chronicle *of Theophanes: An English Translation of* Anni Mundi *6095–6305 (A.D. 602–813).* 1982

Mary F. Wack. *Lovesickness in the Middle Ages: The* Viaticum *and Its Commentaries.* 1990

Benedicta Ward. *Miracles and the Medieval Mind: Theory, Record, and Event, 1000–1215.* 1982

Suzanne Fonay Wemple. *Women in Frankish Society: Marriage and the Cloister, 500–900.* 1981

Jan M. Ziolkowski. *Talking Animals: Medieval Latin Beast Poetry, A.D. 750–1150.* 1993

This book has been set in Linotron Galliard. Galliard was designed for Mergenthaler in 1978 by Matthew Carter. Galliard retains many of the features of a sixteenth-century typeface cut by Robert Granjon but has some modifications that give it a more contemporary look.

Printed on acid-free paper.